Encyclopedia of
School Crime and Violence

Encyclopedia of School Crime and Violence

O–Z
VOLUME 2

Laura L. Finley, Editor

Foreword by Evelyn Ang

Santa Barbara, California • Denver, Colorado • Oxford, England

Copyright 2011 by Laura L. Finley

All rights reserved. No part of this publication may be reproduced, stored in a retrieval system, or transmitted, in any form or by any means, electronic, mechanical, photocopying, recording, or otherwise, except for the inclusion of brief quotations in a review, without prior permission in writing from the publisher.

Library of Congress Cataloging-in-Publication Data

Encyclopedia of school crime and violence / Laura L. Finley, editor ; foreword by Evelyn Ang.
   v. ; cm.
Includes bibliographical references and index.
   ISBN 978–0–313–36238–5 (hard copy : alk. paper) — ISBN 978–0–313–36239–2 (ebook)
   1. Students–Crimes against–United States–Encyclopedias. 2. School violence–United States–Encyclopedias. I. Finley, Laura L.
HV6250.4.S78E53   2011
371.7′8097303—dc22   2011009812

ISBN: 978–0–313–36238–5
EISBN: 978–0–313–36239–2

15 14 13 12 11   1 2 3 4 5

This book is also available on the World Wide Web as an eBook.
Visit www.abc-clio.com for details.

ABC-CLIO, LLC
130 Cremona Drive, P.O. Box 1911
Santa Barbara, California 93116-1911

This book is printed on acid-free paper ∞

Manufactured in the United States of America

Contents

Alphabetical List of Entries, vii

Topical List of Entries, xiii

Foreword by Evelyn Ang, xvii

Preface, xxiii

Acknowledgments, xxv

Timeline of Significant Events Related to School Crime and Violence, xxvii

The Encyclopedia, 1

Discussion Questions, 547

Extension Activities Related to School and Campus Crime and Violence, 549

Appendix 1: Important Federal Legislation Related to School and Campus Crime and Violence, 551

Appendix 2: Primary Source Documents: Sample Legislation: K–12 Public Schools, 553

Appendix 3: Primary Source Documents: Sample Legislation: Colleges and Universities, 633

Appendix 4: U.S. Supreme Court Cases Related to School and Campus Crime and Violence, 643

Appendix 5: U.S. Supreme Court Decisions Relevant to School Crime and Violence, 647

Recommended Films About School and Campus Crime and Violence, 659

Recommended Resources, 665

Index, *677*

About the Editor and Contributors, 687

Alphabetical List of Entries

A

Abuse and Crime and Violence
ADD/ADHD
Adult Trials for Juveniles
Africa and School Crime and Violence
Alcohol and School Crime and Violence
American Civil Liberties Union (ACLU)
Amnesty International
Anger Management
Anonymous Tip Lines
Arts-Based Programs
Asia and School Crime and Violence
Athletes and Crime and Violence, College
Athletes and Crime and Violence, High School
Athletes and Violence Prevention
Auvinen, Pekka-Eric

B

Bath, Michigan, School Bombing
Baylor College Basketball Murder Case
Beslan School Hostage Crisis
Bias, Len
Big Brothers Big Sisters
Biological Theories
Bishop, Amy
Board of Ed. of Independent School District No. 92 of Pottawatomie County v. Earls
Bosse, Sebastian
Bowling for Columbine
Brazill, Nathaniel
Brewer, Michael
Bullycide
Bullying, College
Bullying, High School
Bullying Laws

C

Canada and School Crime and Violence
Carneal, Michael
Centers for Disease Control and Prevention (CDC)
Central Asia Institute (CAI)
Choice Theories
Clery Act
Columbine High School Massacre
Comprehensive Crime Control Act
Conflict Resolution/Peer Mediation
Conflict Theories
Control Theories

Coon, Asa
Corporal Punishment
Crime and Violence in Private Secondary Schools
Crime Stoppers
Cyber-offenses, College
Cyber-offenses, High School

D

Dann, Laurie
Dating Violence, College
Dating Violence, High School
Davis v. Monroe County Board of Education
Democratic Front for the Liberation of Palestine Attack on Ma'alot School
Dhein, Alaa Abu
Domestic Violence Prevention Enhancements and Leadership Through Alliances (DELTA) Program
Do Something
Dress Codes
Drug Abuse Resistance Education (D.A.R.E.)
Drug Offenses, College
Drug Offenses, High School
Drug Testing
Duke University Lacrosse Team Sexual Assault Case

E

Educational Programs and Training, College
Educational Programs and Training, High School
Elementary Schools and Crime and Violence
Elephant
Emergency Response Plans

European Union and School Crime and Violence
Expect Respect

F

Fear of School Crime and Violence
Federal Bureau of Investigation (FBI)
Fiction and School Crime and Violence
Flores, Robert
Free Speech

G

Gambling
Gang Resistance Education and Training (G.R.E.A.T.)
Gangs and School Crime and Violence
Gender and School Crime and Violence, College
Gender and School Crime and Violence, High School
Gender-Related Theories
Gill, Kimveer
Glen Ridge, New Jersey, Rape Incident
Goss v. Lopez
Gun Control Legislation

H

Hamilton, Thomas
Hamilton Fish Institute
Hate Crimes, College
Hazing, College
Hazing, High School
Hazing Laws
Honor Codes
Houston, Eric
Human Rights Education
Human Rights Watch

I

In loco parentis
Integrated Theories

J

Jeremy
Journals Devoted to School Crime and Violence

K

Kent State National Guard Shootings
King, Lawrence
Kinkel, Kip
Krestchmer, Tim

L

Labeling Theories
La Salle University Sex Scandal and Cover-up
Latin America and School Crime and Violence
Lépine, Marc
Lo, Wayne
Loukaitis, Barry
Lu, Gang

M

Manson, Marilyn
Mental Illness and School Crime and Violence
Mentoring
Metal Detectors
Middle East and School Crime and Violence
Middle Schools and Crime and Violence
Monitoring the Future Survey
Moral Panics and Campus Crime and Violence
Moral Panics and High School Crime and Violence
Movies and School Crime and Violence
Music and School Crime and Violence
Muslims and School Crime and Violence

N

National School Safety Center
National Threat Assessment Center
National Youth Survey
National Youth Violence Prevention Resource Center
Natural Born Killers
New Jersey v. T.L.O.
No Child Left Behind Act
Northern Illinois University Shooting
Northwestern High School Sex Scandal

O

Odighizuwa, Peter
Office of Juvenile Justice and Delinquency Prevention (OJJDP)
Ophelia Project
Owens, Dedrick

P

Parens patriae
Parents and School Crime and Violence
Peace and Justice Studies Association
Peace Education, College
Peace Education, High School
Pennington, Douglas
Police and Surveillance, College
Police and Surveillance, High School
Policies and Campus Violence Laws

Poulin, Robert
Prescription Drugs and School Crime and Violence
Prince, Phoebe
Professor-Perpetrated Crime and Violence
Property Crimes, College
Property Crimes, High School
Public Health Approach
Punitive Responses, College
Purdy, Patrick

R

Race and School Crime and Violence
Ramsey, Evan
Religion and High School Crime and Violence
Resolving Conflict Creatively Program (RCCP)
Restorative Justice
Roberts, Charles
Rural School Violence

S

Saari, Matti
Safe and Drug-Free Schools and Communities Act
Safe Schools/GLSEN
Safford Unified School District #1 v. Redding
Save the Children
School Crime and School Climate, College
School Crime and School Climate, High School
School Crime Victimization Survey
School-to-Prison Pipeline
Search and Seizure, High School
Security on Campus, Inc.
Sexual Assault Crimes, College
Sexual Assault Crimes, High School
Sexual Harassment
Sexual Orientation and School Crime and Violence, College
Sexual Orientation and School Crime and Violence, High School
Social Learning Theories
Social Networking
Social Structure Theories
Solomon, T. J.
South America and School Crime and Violence
Southern Poverty Law Center
Spencer, Brenda
Spur Posse
Steinhäuser, Robert
Stop Bullying Now
Suburban School Violence
Suicide, College
Suicide, High School
Systemic/Structural Violence, College
Systemic/Structural Violence, High School

T

Teacher-Perpetrated Crime and Violence, High School
Technological Responses, High School
Technology and Campus Crime and Violence
Teen Courts
Tinker v. Des Moines School District
Treacy, Wayne

U

United Nations Children's Fund (UNICEF)
U.S. Department of Education
U.S. Department of Justice

V

Vernonia School District 47J v. Acton
Victimless Offenses, College
Victimless Offenses, High School
Video Games
Violent Nonsexual Crimes, College
Violent Nonsexual Crimes, High School
Virginia Tech Massacre

W

Weise, Jeff

Whitman, Charles
Wimberley, Teah
Woodham, Luke
Wurst, Andrew

Y

Youth Activism
Youth Crime Watch of America

Z

Zero-Tolerance Laws

Topical List of Entries

Case Studies

Auvinen, Pekka-Eric
Bath, Michigan, School Bombing
Baylor College Basketball Murder Case
Beslan School Hostage Crisis
Bias, Len
Bishop, Amy
Bosse, Sebastian
Brazill, Nathaniel
Brewer, Michael
Carneal, Michael
Columbine High School Massacre
Coon, Asa
Dann, Laurie
Democratic Front for the Liberation of Palestine Attack on Ma'alot School
Dhein, Alaa Abu
Duke University Lacrosse Team Sexual Assault Case
Flores, Robert
Gill, Kimveer
Glen Ridge, New Jersey, Rape Incident
Hamilton, Thomas
Houston, Eric
Kent State National Guard Shootings
King, Lawrence
Kinkel, Kip
Kretschmer, Tim
La Salle University Sex Scandal and Cover-up
Lépine, Marc
Lo, Wayne
Loukaitis, Barry
Lu, Gang
Northern Illinois University Shooting
Northwestern High School Sex Scandal
Odighizuwa, Peter
Owens, Dedrick
Pennington, Douglas
Poulin, Robert
Prince, Phoebe
Purdy, Patrick
Ramsey, Evan
Roberts, Charles
Saari, Matti
Solomon, T. J.
Spencer, Brenda
Spur Posse
Steinhäuser, Robert
Treacy, Wayne
Virginia Tech Massacre
Weise, Jeff
Whitman, Charles
Wimberley, Teah

Woodham, Luke
Wurst, Andrew

Correlates

Abuse and Crime and Violence
ADD/ADHD
Alcohol and School Crime and Violence
Fear of School Crime and Violence
Free Speech
Mental Illness and School Crime and Violence
Muslims and School Crime and Violence
Parents and School Crime and Violence
Prescription Drugs and School Crime and Violence
School Crime and School Climate, College
School Crime and School Climate, High School
Social Networking
Technology and Campus Crime and Violence
Video Games

Court Cases

Board of Ed. of Independent School District No. 92 of Pottawatomie County v. Earls
Davis v. Monroe County Board of Education
Goss v. Lopez
New Jersey v. T.L.O.
Safford Unified School District #1 v. Redding
Tinker v. Des Moines School District
Vernonia School District 47J v. Acton

Global Comparison

Africa and School Crime and Violence
Asia and School Crime and Violence
Canada and School Crime and Violence
European Union and School Crime and Violence
Latin America and School Crime and Violence
Middle East and School Crime and Violence
South America and School Crime and Violence

Measuring

Monitoring the Future Survey
National Youth Survey
School Crime Victimization Survey

Media

Bowling for Columbine
Elephant
Fiction and School Crime and Violence
Jeremy
Journals Devoted to School Crime and Violence
Manson, Marilyn
Moral Panics and Campus Crime and Violence
Moral Panics and High School Crime and Violence
Movies and School Crime and Violence
Music and School Crime and Violence
Natural Born Killers

Organizations

American Civil Liberties Union (ACLU)
Amnesty International
Big Brothers Big Sisters
Centers for Disease Control and Prevention (CDC)
Central Asia Institute (CAI)
Crime Stoppers
Do Something
Federal Bureau of Investigation (FBI)
Hamilton Fish Institute
Human Rights Watch
National School Safety Center
National Threat Assessment Center
National Youth Violence Prevention Resource Center
Office of Juvenile Justice and Delinquency Prevention (OJJDP)
Ophelia Project
Peace and Justice Studies Association
Safe Schools/GLSEN
Save the Children
Security on Campus, Inc.
Southern Poverty Law Center
Stop Bullying Now
United Nations Children's Fund (UNICEF)
U.S. Department of Education
U.S. Department of Justice
Youth Crime Watch of America

Prevention

Athletes and Violence Prevention
Domestic Violence Prevention Enhancements and Leadership Through Alliances (DELTA) Program
Drug Abuse Resistance Education (D.A.R.E.)
Educational Programs and Training, College
Educational Programs and Training, High School
Expect Respect
Gang Resistance Education and Training (G.R.E.A.T.)
Honor Codes
Human Rights Education
Mentoring
Peace Education, College
Peace Education, High School

Responses

Adult Trials for Juveniles
Anger Management
Anonymous Tip Lines
Arts-Based Programs
Bullying Laws
Clery Act
Comprehensive Crime Control Act
Conflict Resolution/Peer Mediation
Corporal Punishment
Dress Codes
Drug Testing
Emergency Response Plans
Gun Control Legislation
Hazing Laws
In loco parentis
Metal Detectors
No Child Left Behind Act
Parens patriae
Police and Surveillance, College
Police and Surveillance, High School
Policies and Campus Violence Laws
Public Health Approach
Punitive Responses, College
Resolving Conflict Creatively Program (RCCP)

Restorative Justice
Safe and Drug-Free Schools and Communities Act
School-to-Prison Pipeline
Search and Seizure, High School
Technological Responses, High School
Technology and Campus Crime and Violence
Teen Courts
Youth Activism
Zero-Tolerance Laws

Theory

Biological Theories
Choice Theories
Conflict Theories
Control Theories
Gender-Related Theories
Integrated Theories
Labeling Theories
Social Learning Theories
Social Structure Theories

Types of Crime/Violence

Athletes and Crime and Violence, College
Athletes and Crime and Violence, High School
Bullycide
Bullying, College
Bullying, High School
Crime and Violence in Private Secondary Schools
Cyber-offenses, College
Cyber-offenses, High School
Dating Violence, College
Dating Violence, High School
Drug Offenses, College
Drug Offenses, High School
Elementary Schools and Crime and Violence
Gambling
Gangs and School Crime and Violence
Gender and School Crime and Violence, College
Gender and School Crime and Violence, High School
Hate Crimes, College
Hazing, College
Hazing, High School
Middle Schools and Crime and Violence
Professor-Perpetrated Crime and Violence
Property Crimes, College
Property Crimes, High School
Race and School Crime and Violence
Religion and High School Crime and Violence
Rural School Violence
Sexual Assault Crimes, College
Sexual Assault Crimes, High School
Sexual Harassment
Sexual Orientation and School Crime and Violence, College
Sexual Orientation and School Crime and Violence, High School
Suburban School Violence
Suicide, College
Suicide, High School
Systemic/Structural Violence, College
Systemic/Structural Violence, High School
Teacher-Perpetrated Crime and Violence, High School
Victimless Offenses, College
Victimless Offenses, High School
Violent Nonsexual Crimes, College
Violent Nonsexual Crimes, High School

O

Odighizuwa, Peter

On January 16, 2002, Peter Odighizuwa, a 43-year-old immigrant from Nigeria who had flunked out of law school, killed three and wounded three others at Appalachian School of Law. Odighizuwa had actually flunked out of the school once before, and just before the shooting he had been notified that he had flunked out again. After discussing his academic problems with professor Dale Rubin in the morning, Odighizuwa went home, but he returned to the school at approximately 1:00 P.M. with a .380 ACP semi-automatic handgun. He proceeded to the offices of Dean Anthony Sutin, a former acting Assistant Attorney General, and Professor Thomas Blackwell, shooting both at point-blank range. He also killed student Angela Dales and wounded three other students. Odighizuwa then fled the building, whereupon several students tackled and disarmed him.

Odighizuwa came to the United States in 1980. He worked for several years as a bus driver and a factory clerk in Portland, Oregon, then moved to Ohio. He enrolled briefly at Ohio State University, then transferred to Central State University, where he studied math. Odighizuwa had developed an interest in law, however, and says he wanted to practice public interest law so that he could help persons with disabilities and immigrants like him. He began applying to law schools and was accepted at Appalachian School of Law in Grundy, Virginia. Despite never having heard of the school before, Odighizuwa enrolled and moved there with his wife and four children. He found law school to be difficult academically and had a hard time fitting in. Odighizuwa claims that other students made fun of him and would leave the room when he entered.

Odighizuwa had purchased a pistol several months before the shooting after finding an unfired bullet outside his door. He claims he was targeting individuals who were particularly mean to him.

Odighizuwa has been diagnosed as a paranoid schizophrenic, but he was found incompetent to stand trial for murder in January 2002. He faced a death sentence. In the end, he pleaded guilty to avoid being executed and is serving three life sentences and an additional 28 years without the chance of parole. In an interview with the Associated Press, Odighizuwa claimed that he thinks of the incident often, but the details are murky. He cannot explain why he committed his crime, although he said he sometimes feels as though he is God exorcising demons. He also claims he got C grades and did not flunk out.

Several lawsuits have been filed against the law school in the wake of the shootings. The family of victim Angela Dales and three students who survived claim that school officials knew that Odighizuwa had a history of spousal abuse and should have known he posed a threat. Further, their suit contends that Odighizuwa was allowed to re-enroll in the law school after flunking out because the administration desperately needed to show some diversity and he was one of only a few black students. A diverse campus was part of the criteria for the accreditation the school was seeking. The law school's administration has denied these claims. In his interview with the Associated Press, Odighizuwa scoffed at the lawsuits, arguing there was no way the school could have known what he would do, and stating that he was not a violent person. His paranoia was evident, though, as he spoke of involvement with the FBI, CIA, and KGB.

After the shooting, school administrators issued a statement saying they were shocked and saddened by the crime. Classes were canceled for the rest of the week. Gun enthusiasts used the opportunity to note that it was an armed student who was able to intervene before the shooting got even worse.

Laura L. Finley

Further Reading

Associated Press. (2002, January 17). Law students tackled gunman, held him down until police arrived. *Fox News*. Retrieved May 3, 2010, from http://www.foxnews.com/story/0,2933,43254,00.html

Grundy, V. (2002, January 17). Suspect in law school slaying arraigned. *CNN*. Retrieved May 3, 2010, from http://archives.cnn.com/2002/US/01/16/law.school.shooting/

Grundy, V. (2003, September 27). Students recount law school shooting. Retrieved May 3, 2010, from http://www.legaled.com/shooting.htm

Kahn, C. (2004, June 11). Appalachian School of Law killer still haunted by paranoia, delusions. Retrieved May 4, 2010, from http://www.healthyplace.com/thought-disorders/articles/appalachian-school-of-law-killer-still-haunted-by-paranoia-delusions/menu-id-64/

Office of Juvenile Justice and Delinquency Prevention (OJJDP)

In 1974, Congress established the Office of Juvenile Justice and Delinquency Prevention (OJJDP) as part of the Juvenile Justice and Delinquency Prevention Act. It is considered part of the U.S. Department of Justice, Office of Justice Programs. Its mission is as follows:

> The Office of Juvenile Justice and Delinquency Prevention (OJJDP) provides national leadership, coordination, and resources to prevent and respond to juvenile delinquency and victimization. OJJDP supports states and communities in their efforts to develop and implement effective and coordinated prevention and intervention programs and to improve the juvenile justice system so that it protects public safety, holds offenders accountable, and provides treatment and rehabilitative services tailored to the needs of juveniles and their families.

OJJDP is charged with improving juvenile justice policies and practices, conducting research, and providing funding for research and programs addressing topics relevant to juvenile crime and violence, responses to them, and prevention programs. Specific areas of focus include, but are not limited to, gang reduction and prevention, Internet crimes, girls' delinquency, child abduction, commercial sexual exploitation of children, and underage drinking.

The OJJDP website includes annual reports from each fiscal year, which detail the office's activities and expenditures. Currently available are reports for the years 1996–2008. Additionally, the website offers a wealth of information through a topically organized list and its searchable database. Information available includes reports, programs, funding, events, and other resources. Current publications include the following:

- *Causes and Correlates of Girls' Delinquency*
- *Highlights of the 2008 National Youth Gang Survey*
- *Youth's Needs and Services: Findings from the Survey of Youth in Residential Placement*
- *Introduction to the Survey of Youth in Residential Placement*
- *Girls' Delinquency in Focus Fact Sheet*
- *Juveniles in Residential Placement: 1997–2008*

The statistics link provides links to bulletins on juvenile arrests, juvenile sex crimes against minors, and a comprehensive survey of children's exposure to violence. Interested persons can review demographic data about juvenile offenders and victims, the juvenile justice system (at all phases), and juveniles in corrections. The events link provides information about training and conferences occurring throughout the United States.

OJJDP also offers training and technical assistance for those involved in responding to juvenile violence or in prevention programs. Training and technical assistance might include conducting needs assessments, strategic planning, team building and collaboration, staff development, and program evaluation. The site also features a model program guide.

Under the subtopic of schools, the OJJDP site provides information about bullying, dropout and expulsion, school involvement, school safety, and truancy.

OJJDP is a clearinghouse of information for anyone interested in or involved in juvenile justice. The agency lists the following milestones in its history:

1974
- Act signed into law
- Created the Formula Grants program
- Established the separation requirement
- Established the deinstitutionalization of status offenders (DSO) requirement

1977
- Increased and expanded DSO and separation requirements
- Emphasized prevention and treatment

1980
- Established jail removal requirements

1984
- Enhanced and amended jail removal requirements

1988
- Addressed disproportionate minority confinement (DMC) as a requirement

1992
- Amended the DSO, jail removal, and separation requirements
- Elevated DMC to a core requirement
- Established the Title V Incentive Grants for Local Delinquency Prevention Grants Program (Title V)

- Established new programs to address gender bias
- Emphasized prevention and treatment, family strengthening, graduated sanctions, and risk-need assessments

2002
- Broadened the scope of the DMC core requirement from "disproportionate minority confinement" to "disproportionate minority contact"
- Consolidated seven previously independent programs into a single Part C prevention block grant
- Created a new Part D, authorizing research, training and technical assistance, and information dissemination
- Added Part E, authorizing grants for new initiatives and programs
- Reauthorized Title V
- Required states to give funding priorities of their formula and block grant allocations to evidence-based programs
- Reauthorized the Title II Formula Grants Program
- Revised the Juvenile Accountability Incentive Block Grants program, which is now called the Juvenile Accountability Block Grants program (as part of the Omnibus Crime Control and Safe Streets Act)

Laura L. Finley

Further Reading

Office of Juvenile Justice and Delinquency Prevention: http://www.ojjdp.ncjrs.gov/

Ophelia Project

In recent years, experts in school crime and violence have begun to pay more attention to bullying and have focused on the unique forms it may take. In addition to cyberbullying, focus has been directed toward girl-on-girl bullying. In contrast to the traditional forms of bullying more often perpetrated by boys against boys, girls may use more subtle forms, including gossip, spreading of rumors, and exclusion. Experts call this approach "relational aggression." The Ophelia Project, based in Erie, Pennsylvania, is an organization that serves youth and adults who have been affected by relational aggression. Using the latest and best research on the topic, and headed by Dr. Charisse Nixon, author of *Girl Wars: 12 Strategies That Will End Female Bullying,* group members devise tools and strategies to assist those

Two girls exclude and gossip about a third girl. Girls often practice relational aggression when bullying other girls. Bully tactics include gossiping, exclusion, and spreading rumors. (Monkey Business Images/Dreamstime.com)

who have been victimized. They also help prevent relational aggression through training, conferences, consultation, and curricula. Most of these materials are available on Ophelia Project's website (www.opheliaproject.org).

The Ophelia Project's curriculum for girls, "It Has a Name: Relational Aggression," is available for five age levels, from kindergarten through high school. It describes what relational aggression is, addresses cyberbullying, and seeks to help girls develop prosocial norms. Curricula are also available for parents, for mentors, and for college students, and specific prevention curricula have been developed for young girls. Parents can download basic communication tips, as well as access links to additional information on bullying, empowering girls, and much more.

For teachers, the Ophelia Project offers articles and activities that can be downloaded for free as well as additional web links. A number of downloadable items for teens and links for more information are available as well. Finally, the website provides links and downloadable resources related to community action. Multimedia packages are available for purchase, too. School districts can purchase assessment tools designed to assist them in creating a safe school climate

(CASS: Creating a Safe School). One evaluation of the CASS program found it to have reduced relational aggression by 23% in girls and 10% in boys.

The Ophelia Project has also partnered with Penn State—Erie to create the Ophelia Institute, which is still in development. When complete, it will conduct research, develop and disseminate educational materials (including web-based instructional tools), and provide workshops and training for educators and parents.

Testimonials credit the Ophelia Project with providing the appropriate language with which to discuss relational aggression with youth, and with identifying the importance of bystanders. Commenters have also highlighted the assistance available through the informative and interactive workshops. Many educators indicate that training from the Ophelia Project has helped them transform their classrooms and even their schools into safer places for students.

Laura L. Finley

Further Reading

Ophelia Project: http://www.opheliaproject.org/main/index.htm
Simmons, R. (2002). *Odd girl out: The hidden culture of aggression in girls.* New York: Houghton Mifflin.

Owens, Dedrick

On February 29, 2000, Kayla Rolland was in her first-grade classroom at Theo J. Buell Elementary School in Mount Morris Township, Michigan, clearing her desk before going to computer class. Most of her classmates were already lined up in the hallway, along with their teacher, Alicia Judd. Kayla and classmate six-year-old Dedrick Owens were exchanging words. Some reports state that Kayla yelled at Dedrick for spitting and standing by her desk. All reports agree on what happened next: Dedrick pulled a .32-caliber pistol and pointed it at two other girls in the room. Then he turned to Kayla and said, "I don't like you!" Some say Kayla responded, "So?" Owens then pulled the trigger, fatally shooting six-year-old Rolland in the chest. When Judd heard the shot, she returned to the classroom and called 911 from her cell phone. Owens put the gun back in his desk and ran into the hall, where he was stopped by school officials. Paramedics arrived on the scene to find Rolland bleeding profusely from her wound. She was transported to Hurley Medical Center, where she was pronounced dead.

When Owens left for school that morning, he carried both the Davis .32-caliber semi-automatic handgun and a knife. He had stolen both items from Jamelle James, a 19-year-old tenant in his uncle's house, where he (Dedrick) lived with his eight-year old brother. Dedrick's father was in jail for parole violation following a conviction for "intent to distribute" illegal drugs. His mother was also a known drug user and had been evicted from her home. James would ultimately be charged in the Kayla Rolland murder case with involuntary manslaughter, contributing to the delinquency of a minor, and gross neglect. Because he was only six years of age, Owens could not be charged with any crime.

Nevertheless, many knew that Owens was a troubled child. School officials acknowledge that Owens was previously suspended from school and was regularly held after school for "saying the F word, flipping people off, pinching, and hitting." Earlier in the school year, he had stabbed a classmate with a pencil. Rolland had also been previously targeted by Owens. It has been reported that the day before her murder, Owens attempted to kiss Rolland, but was rebuffed. Schools officials said in interviews following the shooting that Owens was scheduled to attend anger management classes. Many of these reports are difficult to verify due to Owens's young age and the laws designed to protect a child's privacy. The Genesee County prosecutor noted that laws in most states contend that children younger than the age of seven are not capable of understanding the consequences of their actions. Additionally, many news reports failed to name six-year-old Owens as the shooter in Rolland's case.

The fact remains there were many red flags concerning Owens—even on the day of the shooting. On that morning, a student reported that Owens was in possession of the knife. Although the teacher took the knife away from Owens, she failed to send him to the office or report the incident to school administration. A classmate of Rolland and Owens, Chris Boaz, reported to his grandmother that Owens also threatened Boaz's uncle earlier that morning and said, "Do you want me to take my gun out and shoot you?" Boaz was seven years old when he witnessed the shooting of Rolland; after the event, his mother reported, he did not want to return to school and suffered from fear and anxiety.

In an interview with County Sheriff Bill Pickell, Dedric Darnell Owens, the father of Dedrick Owens, stated he knew instantly his son was involved in the Buell Elementary School shooting. "A cold, sickening feeling came over me . . . I knew it was my son that did the shooting," he said. Pickell asked how Owens could be so sure and Owens stated, "Because of his past violent acts." Owens went on to say that his son "watched violent movies and TV." Once Owens asked his son why he fought other children, and his son replied, "Because I hate them."

Rolland's murder sent shockwaves throughout the United States. How and why could a first-grade squabble end with one six-year-old killing another? This question raised public consciousness and ultimately helped form public policy regarding school violence and gun control in the United States. At the national level, President Bill Clinton, along with gun control proponents, publicly asked questions that were echoed around the country: "How did that child get that gun?" and "Why could the child fire the gun? If we have the technology to put in these child safety locks, why don't we do it?" Immediately, new calls were made for additional gun control legislation at the national level. President Clinton urged Congress to pass legislation before April 20, 2000, the first anniversary of the shooting at Columbine High School. Sociocultural interest in the subjects of violence in schools, the effects of domestic violence and child abuse on children, and the larger political debate concerning Second Amendment rights and gun control also swelled.

On April 20, 2000, an article appeared in *The New York Times* with follow-up on the Rolland case. A spokesman for Tamarla Owens, Dedrick's mother, had issued a statement on April 19: Owens was enrolled in an unspecified private school in the Flint, Michigan, area. State officials had placed the boy in the school, and the state of Michigan was paying his expenses.

Filmmaker Michael Moore brought additional attention to the case in 2000 with his award-winning documentary *Bowling for Columbine.* In the film, he suggests that Tamarla Owens was a hard-working mother caught up in welfare reform laws that required her to work two jobs.

Karen Lindsey

Further Reading

Cannon, A. (2000a). The youngest shooter. *U.S. News & World Report, 128*(10), 27.

Cannon, A. (2000b). Kayla's law: Gun control. *U.S. News & World Report, 128*(11), 39.

First grade killing: Who shares the blame? (2000, April 17). *Current Events, 99*(23), 3.

Lebeskind, K. (2000). Tragedy in Michigan. *Editor & Publisher, 133*(10), 6

National news briefs: Killer, 6, back in school. (2000, April 20). *New York Times.* Retrieved from http://www.nytimes.com/2000/04/20/us/national-news-briefs-killer-6-back-in-school.html

Naughton, K., Thomas, E., & Raymond, J. (2000). Did Kayla have to die? *Newsweek. 135*(11), 24.

Rosenblatt, R. (2000). The killing of Kayla. *Time, 155*(10), 26.

U.S. press outraged. *BBC News.* Retrieved from http://news.bbc.co.uk/2/hi/americas/662749.stm

P

Parens patriae

Parens patriae is a Latin term meaning the "parent of the country"; it traditionally refers to the role of the state as sovereign and guardian of persons under legal disability. *Parens patriae* is the authority of the state to act in the best interest of a child and provide care and protection equivalent to that of a parent. This term is rooted in English common law and dates back to the chancery courts of England during the Middle Ages. The chancery court's jurisdiction included the welfare of children in cases involving the guardianship of orphans and gradually expanded to justify the court's intervention in the lives of family and children. The premises of the chancery courts were that children were under the protective custody of the king, and that the king's authority extended to children in his role as the father of the country.

The evolution of *parens patriae* in the United States had its beginnings when early juvenile courts began to recognize as important the role of the parent in meeting the physical, emotional, and educational needs to the child. The court, it was thought, had the right to intervene in cases where the parents were unable or unwilling to provide for the child. This doctrine was expanded to address circumstances where the child was at risk for criminal behavior. As a result, a system of rehabilitative treatment programs was developed for youth deemed at risk, with the goal being that they grow up and become productive adults. In this way, the *parens patriae* model allowed the court to serve as surrogate parents for wayward children.

The first juvenile court was established in Chicago in 1899. The goal of this juvenile court was to protect neglected children and rehabilitate delinquent children. Its charge was to use the *parens patriae* concept to protect the state's right to officially intervene in the juvenile's life, especially if the youth was neglected. Under this principle, the state has the power to intervene in cases if the child has not reached full legal capacity. Moreover, the state has the inherent power and the responsibility to provide these protections to children whose natural parents were not providing appropriate care or supervision. This power, which the court recognizes as inherent, has since been strengthened by legislation that defines the scope of child protection within each state. The original juvenile court's focus was on the child's welfare, which included dependent, neglected, abused, and delinquent children.

In subsequent years, the states have expanded the doctrine of *parens patriae* to include protections for other members of their citizenry. In *Louisiana v. Texas* (1900), the U.S. Supreme Court recognized the propriety of allowing the state to sue on behalf of its citizenry. In *Georgia v. Tennessee Copper Co.* (1907), Justice Oliver Wendell Holmes wrote that individual states have recourse to the judicial power of the United States to resolve disputes between the states.

This evolution of an increasingly broad application of the *parens patriae* doctrine permits the state to bring an action on behalf of its citizens to protect its sovereign or quasi-sovereign interests. This sovereign interest is the guarantee of the well-being of the state's citizenry. The U.S. Supreme Court has recognized two general categories of quasi-sovereign interests. The first is the protection of the health and well-being, both physically and economically, of the state's residents in general. The second is the protection of the state's interest in not being discriminatorily denied its rightful status within the federal system. In deciding whether a state can use the *parens patriae* doctrine in a specific claim, the Court may look to whether the injury is one that the state might address through its sovereign law-making powers and whether the conduct infringes, either directly or indirectly, on a significant portion of the population, per the ruling in *Snapp and Son, Inc. v. Puerto Rico* (1982).

The doctrine of *parens patriae* was established as a mechanism for the states to act in the best interest of children. When children are considered at risk, the state can step in and act as the parent. Over time, however, this doctrine has been expanded so that the state can act in the best interest of all citizens where the well-being of the state's citizenry is at stake.

Dennis Bulen

Further Reading

Benekos, P., & Merlo, A. (2004). *Controversies in juvenile justice and delinquency.* Newark, NJ: LexisNexis.

Elsea, K. (1995). The juvenile crime debate: Rehabilitation, punishment, or prevention. *Kansas Journal of Law and Public Policy,* 5(1), 135–146.

Georgia v. Tennessee Copper Co. 206 U.S. 230 (1907).

Greenberg, D. (1985). Age, crime, and social explanation. *American Journal of Sociology,* 9(1), 1–21.

Nolan, J., & Connolly, M. (1983). *Black's law dictionary* (5th ed.). St. Paul, MN: West.
Siegel, L., & Welsh, B. (2005). *Juvenile delinquency: The core* (2nd ed.). Belmont, CA: Thomson.
Snapp & Son, Inc. v. Puerto Rico, 458 U.S. 592 (1982).

Parents and School Crime and Violence

When a major incident of school violence occurs, often the first response is to blame the parents. Parents can, however, be tremendous allies and advocates for their children. If parents are open and available to communicate with young people, many times serious violence can be averted. In some cases, it has been parents who have led the way to important school and community reforms.

One of the major challenges for parents is knowing what is happening at school when they are not around. It is imperative that parents communicate with their

Open communication is essential to reduce violence. (Keith Spaulding/Dreamstime.com)

children about what is happening at school—not just about academics, but also about social issues. Additionally, parents should maintain regular communication with school districts, checking web-based updates, calling the school and teachers when necessary, and attending school functions.

Fortunately, many wonderful resources are available for parents to help them identify warning signs of bullying and other problem behaviors. The U.S. Department of Health and Human Services' Substance Abuse and Mental Health Services Administration (SAMHSA) has a link on its website that provides information about the frequency, types, warning signs, and effects of bullying. The same site also has tips for what parents can do if their child is being bullied. Specifically, parents are advised not to give up, even if their child begs them not to contact adults, as research suggests the most effective way to stop bullying is adult intervention. Parents should allow the school to set up a meeting involving the parents of the bully, rather than seeking to make those arrangements themselves. It is important that parents keep pressure on schools to ensure victims are being adequately protected.

In addition, for parents whose child has endured bullying, the advice is to help the child build his or her self-esteem by joining positive clubs, sports, or other activities. Parents must support those efforts and, in some cases, may need to reach out to help establish them if the victim is particularly socially awkward. If a child appears especially distraught, parents are advised to seek the help of a mental health professional.

SAMHSA also offers advice to parents of bullies. First, it is imperative that parents inform their children that they take bullying seriously and that such behavior will not be allowed. Providing positive reinforcement for prosocial behavior in the home and in the community can encourage bullies to make better choices. Above all, parents are discouraged from excusing or justifying bullying.

The website operated by Stop Bullying Now (www.stopbullyingnow.hrsa.gov) also has recommendations about what adults can do in situations where children are being bullied. It includes a wealth of information about bullying, warning signs, laws, and interventions across the United States. Additional information is available at the Center for the Study and Prevention of Violence (http://www.colorado.edu/cspv/publications/factsheets/safeschools/FS-SC09.pdf).

Parents can learn about other issues related to school crime and violence, including child abuse, sexual violence, dating violence, and suicide, at the Centers for Disease Control and Prevention (CDC) website (http://www.cdc.gov/ViolencePrevention/index.html).

Adults and Children Together Against Violence (http://actagainstviolence.apa.org/) is a resource that features a database of more than 250 journal articles, book chapters, and other publications related to youth violence. Topics for parents include anger management, conflict resolution, discipline, media violence, and parenting skills.

Laura L. Finley

Further Reading

Adults and Children Together Against Violence: http://actagainstviolence.apa.org/
Center for the Study and Prevention of Violence Bullying Fact Sheet: http://www.colorado.edu/cspv/publications/factsheets/safeschools/FS-SC09.pdf
Parents, grandparents and caregivers. (n.d.). SAMHSA's National Mental Health and Information Center. Retrieved from http://mentalhealth.samhsa.gov/15plus/parent/
Stop Bullying Now: http://www.stopbullingnow.hrsa.gov.
Violence Prevention: http://www.cdc.gov/ViolencePrevention/index.html

Peace and Justice Studies Association

The Peace and Justice Studies Association (PJSA), a nonprofit organization, was formed in 2001 when the Consortium on Peace Research, Education and Development (COPRED) merged with the Peace Studies Association (PSA). It is devoted to bringing together academics, K–12 educators, and activities to envision a more peaceful world, to share ideas and strategies for peace building, and to work toward social change for social justice. PJSA is the professional organization for scholars in the field of peace and conflict resolution and is the North American affiliate of the International Peace Research Association.

Specifically, PJSA's mission is to create a just and peaceful world through the following activities:

- The promotion of peace studies within universities, colleges, and K–12 grade levels
- The forging of alliances among educators, students, activists, and other peace practitioners so as to enhance one another's work on peace, conflict, and nonviolence
- The creation and nurturing of alternatives to structures of inequality and injustice, war, and violence through education, research, and action

Members share several values and beliefs, including the belief that nonviolent strategies are the most effective way to make social change. Additional shared values and beliefs include, but are not limited to, critical analysis of social structures and institutions, equitable sharing of world resources, lifelong education and community service, innovative and effective pedagogy, and building of collaborations and alliances.

PJSA hosts an annual conference in which it educates and honors activists and members; it also hosts a blog on peace-related topics. In 2010, the organization hosted its first Youth Summit. Additionally, PJSA compiles and disseminates the Global Directory of Peace Studies and Conflict Resolution Programs.

Members of PJSA receive two publications: *The Peace Chronicle* and *Peace & Change: A Journal of Peace Research.* Members can also participate in a listserv to keep up-to-date on the group's events. In addition, the PJSA website features a job board and links to other peace and justice resources.

PJSA partners with a variety of other groups and organizations. In 2005, for example, it entered into a partnership with Bridge Connect Act (BCA) designed to "promote peace and justice through education, research and action and to engage students, faculty, and college and university staff members in international programs focused on peace, justice and other issues of mutual concern." Members of PJSA institutions receive special consideration for BCA's programs throughout the world, and BCA will waive the application fee from students involved in PJSA who would like to study abroad in one of BCA's peace and justice studies programs.

Another partnership is with the Higher Education Consortium for Urban Affairs (HECUA). HECUA is a group of 18 colleges, universities, and associated organizations that promote interdisciplinary, community-based learning related to civic engagement and social justice. HECUA has program sites in the United States as well as in Bangladesh, Ecuador, Northern Ireland, Norway, Sweden, Denmark, and Poland. Established in spring 2005, this collaboration allows students the opportunity to participate in experiential learning programs that focus on social change and social justice. Undergraduate students enrolled at PJSA member institutions receive special benefits when they enroll in HECUA study-away programs, including discounted fees.

In November 2008, PJSA announced a partnership with the Center for Global eEducation (CGE). CGE is based at Augsburg College (Minneapolis) and offers discounts to individual members and member institutions who want to travel to the Center's Mexican or Central American locations to study. The Canadian School of Peacebuilding (CSOP) also partners with the PJSA to provide intensive one-week courses on peace building. PeaceVoice is an organization devoted to changing media by offering articles and commentary by peace and justice professionals to newspapers and online news sources; it solicits brief articles from PJSA members and then distributes them to appropriate news sources.

Laura L. Finley

Further Reading

Peace and Justice Studies Association: www.peacejusticestudies.org

Peace Education, College

Peace education "involves students and educators in a commitment to create a more just and peaceful world order" (Harris & Morrison, 2003, p. 4). It has 10 main goals:

1. To appreciate the richness of the concept of peace
2. To address fears
3. To provide information about security
4. To understand war behavior
5. To develop intercultural understanding
6. To provide a "futures" orientation
7. To teach peace as a process
8. To promote positive peace, or peace accompanied by social justice
9. To stimulate a respect for all life
10. To manage conflicts nonviolently

Peace education takes many forms—some more focused on negative peace (the reduction of violent conflict) and others more inclusive. Peace making, or conflict resolution education, involves the learning and utilization of conflict resolution strategies. The narrowest programs focus on student-to-student conflicts, often utilizing peer mediation. In peer mediation, trained students help their peers resolve conflicts.

Human rights education is one form of peace education that is intended to address injustices related to political oppression, prejudice, and abuses of civil, political, social, and economic rights. Most human rights education programs take as their basis the Universal Declaration of Human Rights. This type of education encourages the eradication of social ills well beyond violent conflict.

International education aims to help students better understand the ways states provide for their citizens, in terms of both security and other essential needs. Teachers try to elicit among their students the feeling that we are all global citizens. International education often focuses on globalization and its impact on humanity. At the college level, it might include study-abroad programs.

Many peace education programs draw on the work of women's studies scholars. Such programs emphasize what has been called the three C's: care, compassion, and connectedness. Environmental education, although traditionally not a main emphasis of peace educators, has received far more attention in recent years. It stresses the need for ecological security and encourages students to reduce waste and limit their consumption. Community-based environmental education is a form of peace education that enables students to participate in the planning, implementation, and evaluation of educational activities aimed at resolving local environmental concerns that the students themselves have identified. Community-based service, also known as service learning, can be a useful peace education strategy.

In higher education, many schools offer peace studies courses, although most often they are embedded in social sciences curricula. The Peace and Justice Studies Association compiles the Global Directory of Peace Studies and Conflict Resolution Programs (available for order from http://www.peacejusticestudies.org/resources/publications.php). This guide is currently in its seventh edition and features 450 undergraduate, master's degree, and doctoral programs in more than 40 countries and 38 U.S. states. An online edition is available with up-to-date information.

Some universities have established innovative peace education programs on their own. James Madison University, for example, has incorporated peace education into its elementary education program. An innovative approach is to create an entire program based on peace, or what historian Riane Eisler has called "partnership education." The Peace Education Center at Teacher's College, Columbia University, trains educators in what it calls a "pedagogy of engagement." The pedagogy draws from a variety of disciplines and approaches that emphasize inquiry, reflection, and transformation. In 1993, the Human Rights School began at McMaster University. This undergraduate interdisciplinary program offers a 24-credit minor. In contrast, the Lindeman Center for Community Empowerment Through Education at Northern Illinois University is an adult education program through which the university partners with the community to provide a variety of educational sessions.

Some programs focus on international human rights law. The International Human Rights Law Clinic (IHRLC) is one of seven clinical programs at Washington College of Law at American University. It provides students with full case responsibility for human rights litigation. Participants work with two types of clients: those seeking asylum and victims of human rights abuses. St. Thomas University in Miami, Florida, has also established an international human rights law program.

In the past, human rights or peace education have rarely been part of health or medical training programs. The Harvard School of Public Health has developed a program that includes a course on human rights for public health practitioners. It also offers a health and human rights seminar series, in collaboration with the International Federation of the Red Cross; the Danish Center for Human Rights; the McGill Center on Ethics, Law, and Medicine; the International Commission of Jurists; and the Society of Women Against AIDS in Africa.

One concern about peace education courses is that they may focus exclusively on content, or the material that is taught, and pay little attention to the teaching and learning methods used. The use of passive, competitive instructional methods is common in higher education. College classrooms tend to be what Riane Eisler called "dominator structured." The large lecture hall creates a structure in which the professor or instructor is the "sage on the stage" and the students are sitting in nice, even rows, facing forward. This structure is not ideal for student collaboration. Moreover, students have very little voice in the authority structure of a typical college classroom, as professors generally select the material to be included, the methods of delivery, and the assignments to be used.

Given that positive peace addresses the synthesis of many different content areas—history, women's studies, race and ethnic understanding, environmental awareness, and much more—-their highly specialized training may not adequately equip professors to teach about and work for peace in the most impactful way. As noted previously, another barrier to implementing education about and for peace in higher education is related to the lack of training many professors have in teaching methods. Thus, while those charged with teaching peace education courses specifically or integrating peace education content into their existing courses are likely very capable of teaching about peace, they may not be well trained to use peaceful teaching methods. Because they are under such tremendous pressure to become professionalized, young graduate students also tend to focus most of their time on research and publication, not on learning to teach. Faculty wishing to integrate education about and for peace must overcome these difficult, but not insurmountable barriers.

Laura L. Finley

Further Reading

Eisler, R. (2000). *Tomorrow's children.* Boulder, CO: Westview.

Finley, L. (2004). Teaching peace in higher education: Overcoming the challenges to addressing structure and methods. *Online Journal of Peace and Conflict Resolution, 5*(2).

Freire, P. (1974). *Pedagogy of the oppressed.* New York: Seabury Press.

Galtung, J. (1996). *Peace by peaceful means: Peace and conflict, development and civilization.* London: Sage.

Harris, I., & Morrison, M. (2003). *Peace education, second edition.* Jefferson, NC: McFarland.

Jacoby, B. 1996. *Service learning in higher education: Concepts and practices.* San Francisco: Jossey-Bass.

Kleiman, P. (2008). Towards transformation: Conceptions of creativity in higher education. *Innovations in Education and Teaching International, 45*(3), 209–217.

Lin, J., Brantmeier, E., & Bruhn, C. (2008). *Transforming education for peace.* Charlotte, NC: Information Age Publishing.

McCarthy, C. (2002). *I'd rather teach peace.* Maryknoll, NY: Orbis.

Pepinsky, H. (2006, December). Peacemaking in the classroom. *Contemporary Justice Review, 9*(4), 427–442.

Peace Education, High School

In 1968, Dr. Martin Luther King, Jr., asked residents of the United States a prescient, urgent, and timely question: Where do we go from here—chaos or community? Since King's death, more than 1 million Americans have been killed violently here at home, including tens of thousands of children. Behind these shameful numbers are small individual faces and individuals' feelings. We must stop this suffering; we must work together to see that the violence against children is stopped, that schools are turned back into places of nurturing and learning, rather than the war zones which some of them have become. We will not be able to deal with the violence in the United States until we learn to deal with the basic ethic of how we resolve disputes and to place an emphasis on peace in the way we relate to one another.

On May 16, 1995, a student was arrested at the Fritsche Middle School in Milwaukee, Wisconsin, for possession of a gun, which was found in her locker. Students, parents, and teachers alike were stunned. The girl had been a straight-A student, who just one day prior had handed an honorary banner to Reverend Desmond Tutu as part of a peace-promoting rally. Upon leaving the rally, the student was assaulted by a fellow student, and allegedly brought the gun to school the next day in self-defense. This was but one of many violent incidents reported in U.S. schools in the last 20 years. What is notable about Fritsche Middle School is its positive and unified response to the incident: The school responded by incorporating peace education into its curriculum in 1996.

Martin Luther King, Jr., served as a powerful leader spreading the message of peace and nonviolent action during the American Civil Rights Movement. (Library of Congress)

Peace education refers to a social movement within education that seeks to counter all forms of violence and promote peace. Violence is defined by peace educators as "any physical, psychological or structural action that is dehumanizing or intentionally harms another." Peace education involves peace-promoting curriculum, alternative teaching structures, and the creation of a nonviolent learning environment. Peace educators seek to help students to identify violence in their lives and their surroundings, to recognize the sources of such violence, and to equip students to demonstrate nonviolent responses to conflict. Furthermore, peace education involves a more cooperative model of learning, moving away from traditional "top-down" approaches of teaching and instead promoting partnerships in learning.

Peace education was spawned as a response to a global decline in education and an increase in school violence, which has characterized the period from the 1980s to the present. The purpose of peace education is to counter violence of all forms. Pioneers in peace education, such as Maria Montessori, for whom Montessori Schools were named, believed that failure to recognize the disempowering effects of traditional models of education simply exacerbated the violence in schools. Montessori developed her ideas around peace education in the post–World War II era of the 1950s, calling it "the best way to counteract the hatred of fascism." The need for peace education has grown ever more pressing with the passage of time. According to the Children's Defense Fund (1991), children today are exposed to more violence than at any previous time, yet a failure on the part of educators to identify the prevalence of violence in the lives of students limits the influence of peace education.

Nonetheless, many schools throughout the United States and around the globe are taking measures to implement peace education. A curriculum that formerly gave mention to violent historical events without making mention of nonviolent conflict resolution is now emphasizing the work and ideas of peace makers, such as Martin Luther King, Jr., Leo Tolstoy, David Henry Thoreau, Mother Theresa, Cesar Chavez, Nel Noddings and bell hooks. Today, class discussions in many high schools include issues such as national disarmament, human rights, domestic violence, refugee relocation, economic inequalities, and ecological concerns. Furthermore, many schools—like the Fritsche Middle School in Milwaukee—are experimenting with different classroom approaches that are conducive to partnership and cooperation. Block scheduling is a revised system of class scheduling in which students attend fewer class periods, with each class spanning a longer period of time than the traditional 48-minute periods and each covering an integrative curriculum that incorporates reading, English, mathematics, language arts, social studies, and sciences. After implementing block scheduling, Fritsche Middle School reported improvement in standardized test scores, improved attendance, a decreased number of incident reports, and a drastic increase in community involvement on the part of students.

Many different peace education models are being successfully implemented today. A few example suffice to demonstrate their breadth:

- *Afghan Sister Project at Carolina Friends School:* The Carolina Friends School in North Carolina established a partnership with a school in Afghanistan, with children in the two schools becoming pen pals, writing journals of their day-to-day life for 10 days and then exchanging the journals to learn about one another's lives, and making crafts to share with one another. The journal project included sending disposable cameras to Afghanistan, so that the children there could take photographs of their daily lives and send them back to the United States. In turn, U.S. students took photos of their daily lives and sent them to Afghanistan. Along with these international exchanges, the Carolina Friends School invited special guest speakers from Afghanistan to speak in their schools. Extracurricular community events were planned featuring music and food from Afghanistan, and parents, teachers and members of the community came together to learn. High school students hosted fundraising events and raised local awareness about the difficulties of accessing clean water in Afghanistan. The money that was raised went to repairing a broken water pump in an Afghan village. The reported effect on students and teachers involved in the project was increased engagement, a sense of contributing to peace efforts in a war-torn region of the world, and a connection across two very distinct cultures.

- *Resolving Conflict Creatively Program (RCCP):* The Resolving Conflict Creatively Program is an approach that places as much importance on the emotional quotient of students as on the intellectual quotient. The emotional quotient, or "emotional intelligence," is measured according to five factors:

    1. Self-awareness, or the ability to recognize what one is feeling
    2. Self-control, or the ability to handle one's emotions
    3. Self-motivation, or the ability to maintain drive in the face of frustration
    4. Empathy, or the ability to imagine and understand the emotions of others
    5. Social competency, or the ability to handle the emotions of others

Studies indicate that the emotional intelligence of American children has been in steady decline since the mid-1970s and, therefore, is correlated with a decline in school performance and an increase in school violence. Moreover, studies show that the emotional center of the brain—the cerebral cortex—is still actively developing until mid to late adolescence. On the basis of this information, the RCCP proposes that schools become centers of learning not only of academic material but also of critical life skills in emotional and social competency. Thus the fostering of self-control and self-regulation skills, social awareness and group participation skills, and social decision-making and problem-solving skills are incorporated into the curriculum of the program. Teachers in schools that have implemented RCCP report less violence in their classrooms, children's spontaneous use of conflict resolution skills, improved self-esteem, and more caring and accepting behavior among students.

- *Comer School Development Program (SDP):* The Comer School Development Program is a three-tiered program, involving parents, teachers, and students. The first component of the program is a planning committee made up of parents and school staff, where decisions are made about school policies, school environment, and specific programs. The second component comprises a team of students and staff members including trained professionals, such as guidance counselors, developmental psychologists, and pediatricians, who determine socially and developmentally appropriate responses to issues facing students. The third component is a program designed to give parents specific and meaningful involvement in the school. The program specifies 12 areas of emphasis:

  1. Order and discipline
  2. Respect, trust, and kindness among students
  3. Caring and sensitivity on the part of school personnel
  4. Fair and equal treatment for all students
  5. Equal access to resources
  6. High expectations for student achievement
  7. Parental involvement
  8. Maintenance of the school building's physical appearance
  9. Academic focus
  10. Collaborative decision making
  11. Productive school–community relations
  12. An absence of finger pointing (between students, teachers, parents, and members of the administration)

These 12 areas of emphasis are thoughtfully and cooperatively implemented by the three teams—the staff and parent committee, the student and professional staff team, and the parental team. Together and with the preceding emphases in mind, the teams work to enhance the environment within the school, to increase the level of support for students, and to find innovative ways to resolve conflicts. For example, in one school where SDP was implemented, it was found that many of the violent incidents at school took place after the final bell, when halls were crowded and students were rushing to go. The parental team of the SDP recommended that dismissal times for the various classes be staggered, so as to decrease congestion in the halls and reduce violent incidents. The school board agreed to a week's trial period, which proved wildly successful and led to implementation of a permanent policy. This child-centered approach can be simply implemented in traditional school settings and has had a transformational effect on students, parents, and teachers alike, with particular effectiveness in schools in poverty-stricken urban areas.

Megan Barnes

Further Reading

Haynes, N. (1996). Creating safe and caring school communities: Comer School Development Program. *Schools, 3,* 308–314.

Lantieri, L., & Patti, J. (1996). Educating children in a violent society. *Journal of Negro Education, 65*(3), 356–368.

Lin, J., Brantmeier, E., & Bruhn, C. (2008). *Transforming education for peace.* Charlotte, NC: Information Age Publishing.

Marion, M., Rousseau, J., & Gollin, K. (2009). Connecting our villages: The Afghan sister schools project at the Carolina Friends School. *Peace & Change, 34*(4), 548–570.

Mortenson, G. (2009). *Stones into schools: Promoting peace with books, not bombs, in Afghanistan and Pakistan.* New York: Viking Press.

Pennington, Douglas

On September 2, 2006, Douglas Pennington, age 49, drove two hours from his home and entered the campus of Shepherd University in West Virginia. He was ostensibly there to visit his two sons, Logan Pennington, age 26, and Benjamin Pennington, age 24, who were both seniors and roommates at the university. Instead, at approximately 2 p.m., the elder Pennington used a .38-caliber revolver to shoot his two sons outside between two buildings before shooting himself. Witnesses say they saw Pennington fire at one son, then shoot the other as he tried to run away. Students reported seeing the three bodies lying on the ground as rescuers attempted to administer cardiopulmonary resuscitation. All three were taken to nearby medical facilities, where they were pronounced dead. State Police Sergeant C. C. Morton initially labeled the event the outcome of a family issue. University President David L. Dunlop announced that the entire community was stunned, yet also spoke out quickly to convince students there was no other threat. Counseling was offered to students who were interested in seeing someone to discuss the emotional ramifications of the matter.

Pennington left several notes in the car that he drove to the university, and investigators found a notebook in his home. In both, he discussed internal battles, feelings of guilt and pain, and his love for his family. Pennington wrote that he always lost those he loved and feared he would lose his family as well. He articulated that he was "forced" to do something to them before someone else could, writing, "I must do the unthinkable." He had been under the care of a mental health physician, Dr. Michael Ehlers, at Western Maryland Health Systems, but had missed two appointments with Dr. Ehlers. His mother, Mary Pennington, told police that her son had been experiencing negative side effects from his medication and that the medication seemed to make him "senile." Family members also said they had tried to have Pennington hospitalized for his mental illness, but their efforts had failed. Others noticed that Pennington was acting strangely and had visited his sons more frequently leading up to the shootings. Pennington purchased his gun only two days before the shooting incident.

Laura L. Finley

Further Reading

Laris, M., & Samuels, R. (2006, September 3). Man kills self, two sons at university in W.Va. *Washington Post.* Retrieved May 4, 2010, from http://www.washingtonpost.com/wp-dyn/content/article/2006/09/02/AR2006090201223.html

Smoot, N. (2007, March 20). Shepherd shooting motive revealed. Retrieved from http://ssristories.com/show.php?item=1663

Police and Surveillance, College

On May 6, 2008, in the largest drug operation on a college campus in U.S. history, the Drug Enforcement Administration (DEA) announced that after a six-month-long undercover investigation on the campus of San Diego State University (SDSU)—one of the largest schools in California's state university system, with approximately 34,000 students—96 people had been arrested, including 75 students, on state and federal drug distribution charges. Operation Sudden Fall targeted large-scale marijuana, cocaine, and ecstasy distribution at SDSU. It involved the use of police surveillance, including intercepted text messages between university students, along with video surveillance. In addition, undercover police officers posing as college students made more than 130 drug purchases on campus. According to the DEA, the seized evidence included 4 pounds of cocaine, 50 pounds of marijuana, 48 hydroponic marijuana plants, 350 ecstasy pills, 30 vials of hash oil, methamphetamine, psilocybin (mushrooms), various illicit prescription drugs, a shotgun, three semi-automatic pistols, three brass knuckles, and $60,000 in cash.

These types of incidents are more frequently occurring on college campuses across the United States. Over the past several years, due to escalating crime rates on college campuses, police activity at these sites has dramatically increased. According to

Campus Carry, an organization that advocates for the availability of concealed weapons on campuses, 71% of college campuses across the United States are patrolled by armed police officers. In 2008, 13 students were murdered on college campuses across the country. In 2007, 12 student murders occurred—although this statistic does not include the shooting spree at Virginia Tech, which resulted in the deaths of 32 students and the wounding of an additional 21 students. In addition, in 2007, 52,744 alcohol-related arrests, 21,948 drug-related arrests, and 1803 illegal weapons arrests occurred on college and university campuses across the United States. Due to the Jeanne Clery Disclosure of Campus Security Policy and Campus Crime Statistics Act, better known as the Clery Act (20 USC § 1092(f)), all colleges and universities that participate in federal financial aid programs must keep and disclose information about crime on and near their respective campuses. On August 14, 2008, the Clery Act was amended—largely due to the Virginia Tech shootings—to require college campuses to develop and implement emergency response plans.

Domestic terrorism is also a major issue at U.S. universities today, and is another factor that is leading to an increased police presence on college campuses. To date, ecoterrorists and animal rights extremist groups such as the Earth Liberation Front (ELF) and the Animal Liberation Front (ALF) have been responsible for more than 2,000 crimes and more than $110 million in damages due to bombings and arsons across the United States. On collegiate campuses, these groups have attacked and destroyed laboratories at the University of Iowa, the University of Michigan, the University of Minnesota, Louisiana State University, and the University of Wisconsin.

Additionally, law enforcement has gotten involved in cases in which professors have been accused of terrorism. On February 20, 2003, University of South Florida professor Dr. Sami Al-Arian was arrested and charged with raising funds and managing the finances of an international terrorist organization that perpetrates violence, largely in Israel. The Justice Department named Al-Arian as the financial director of the Palestinian Islamic Jihad (PIJ) in a 50-count indictment. At the time, U.S. Attorney General John Ashcroft named the PIJ as one of the most violent terrorist groups in the world. Al-Arian was charged, along with seven other individuals, with operating a racketeering enterprise since 1984 and using charitable and educational organizations as front groups for money laundering for the PIJ. In the wake of these charges, *Fox News* commentator Bill O'Reilly called attention to Al-Arian's sometimes inflammatory speeches.

Al-Arian's arrest resulted in a backlash against the University of South Florida, with some referring to it as "Jihad University." The almost immediate result was threats of violence, cancelled classes, and a 5% drop in alumni support. On December 19, 2001, the USF Board of Trustees voted to suspend Al-Arian without pay. In turn, some students rallied to his defense, even circulating petitions for the professor's reinstatement.

A wiretap on his phone, however, seemed to prove Al-Arian's guilt. A series of calls, faxes, and bank transactions demonstrated he had been involved with money transfers involving the PIJ, the Iranian and Syrian governments, Hamas, and other sources in Sudan. Records also showed that Al-Arian arranged to obtain false documentation for known terrorists who entered the United States and helped them to avoid government scrutiny. In all, the federal government, using provisions of the USA Patriot Act, gathered 20,000 hours of phone conversations and faxes, some as old as 1993, as evidence against Al-Arian.

On December 7, 2005, Al-Arian was acquitted of conspiracy to aid PIJ. The Tampa jury deliberated for 13 days before rejecting the prosecutor's arguments. Between 2006 and 2008, Al-Arian was sub poenaed to testify in three terrorism-related investigations. He refused to testify each time and was imprisoned for 13 months for criminal contempt.

The increased use of police and electronic surveillance on college campuses has not gone without criticism. The American Civil Liberties Union (ACLU), citing concerns about free speech on campus, has filed Freedom of Information Act requests seeking details on government surveillance of college professors and students nationwide. The concern is that this type of surveillance will impede academic freedom and stifle the dissent that is a hallmark of campuses across the nation.

Tony Gaskew

Further Reading

Campus crime statistics: http://www.ed.gov/admins/lead/safety/arrests2005-07.pdf

Campus law enforcement statistics. (n.d.). Bureau of Justice Statistics. Retrieved from http://www.ojp.gov/bjs/cample.htm

Citing free speech concerns. (2002). American Civil Liberties Union. Retrieved from http://www.aclu.org/safefree/general/17079prs20021212.html

FBI charges Florida professor with terrorist activities. (2003, February 20). *CNN*. Retrieved May 26, 2010, from http://www.cnn.com/2003/US/South/02/20/professor.arrest/

Inside security. (2008). National Association of Colleges and Business Officers. Retrieved from http://asumag.com/security/inside_security_nacubo/

Kay, J. (2005, December 8). Palestinian activist Sami Al-Arian acquitted on charges in Florida. *World Socialist Web Site*. Retrieved May 6, 2010, from http://www.wsws.org/articles/2005/dec2005/aria-d08.shtml

Kline, M. (2006, June 29). Eco-terrorism in higher education. Retrieved May 6, 2010, from http://www.academia.org/eco-terrorism-in-higher-education/

NSSC works to promote safety on college and university campuses. (n.d.). Retrieved from National School Safety Center: http://www.schoolsafety.us/

Ward, D., & Lee, J. (2005). *The handbook for campus crime reporting*. Retrieved May 6, 2010, from http://www.campusreportonline.net/main/articles.php?id=1054

Police and Surveillance, High School

Historically, school crimes generated very little interest among policymakers until the late 1980s and early 1990s, when a rash of school shootings and the ushering in of crack cocaine afflicted schools across the United States. In fact, during the past decade, more than 300 school-associated violent deaths occurred on or near school campuses in America. In 1992–1993 alone, 42 student homicides occurred on school premises throughout the United States. According to the National Center for Education Statistics, 78% of schools experienced one or more incidents of violent crime in the 2005–2006 school year. Seventeen percent experienced one or more serious violent incidents, 46% experienced one or more thefts, and 68% experienced another type of crime.

In fact, since the shootings at Columbine High School, police departments across the country have drastically changed their response tactics to shooting incidents occurring on high school campuses. Police officers now employ active shooter response tactics when responding to shootings at a high school. The active shooter tactic requires the initial responding officers at the scene of a school shooting to immediately pursue and establish contact with the shooter, so as to contain, capture, or neutralize the shooter. This approach represents a dramatic shift in police response tactics for violent incidents occurring at school settings. Historically, the initial officers arriving at a school shooting would simply secure the scene until specially trained officers, such as SWAT (Special Weapons and Tactics) team members, were deployed to the site. One of the fatal lessons learned form the Columbine High School shootings is that it is imperative for responding officers to react immediately and without delay to school shootings so as to minimize casualties.

As a result of the dramatic rise in school violence in the 1990s and early 2000s, policymakers across the United States intensified their efforts to enhance school safety measures and implemented a variety of security tactics, including the use of metal detectors, zero-tolerance security polices mandating expulsion or suspension for violations of school safety policies, the use of electronic surveillance cameras, and the assignment of sworn police officers to patrol schools. Among these new school safety measures, the use of armed police officers and video surveillance cameras are arguably the most significant because of their authoritarian and intrusive nature.

The issue of police and the use of electronic surveillance in school settings has always been a matter of intense legal debate. In many states, juveniles are required by law to attend high school until they reach maturity, which is generally considered 18 years of age. Within this legal mandate, juveniles are required to report to school for the majority of the year, normally 5 days per week, where they are subjected to a variety of intrusive school policies, rules, and regulations, which may include the use of metal detectors, electronic surveillance cameras, and the search and seizure of their persons and property, including lockers. In the case of *New Jersey v. T.L.O.* (1985), the U.S. Supreme Court ruled that although students do not forfeit all Fourth Amendment rights to be secure from unreasonable search and seizure at school, school officials do not need a search warrant to search a student or a student's possessions. Additionally, the Supreme Court established that school officials need only reasonable suspicion that the search will produce evidence the student violated a state law or school policy before engaging in such a search. In summary, high school students are legally required to attend school, where they have little or no legal authority to refuse to comply with school-mandated security tactics.

Currently, more than 75% of all new schools in the United States are being equipped with video surveillance systems. The most popular school surveillance devices are digital or analog cameras for video recording, but other technologies in use in this setting include metal detectors, ID cards, Internet tracking, biometrics, transparent lockers and book bags, electronic gates, and two-way radios. On September 17, 2008, the School Safety Enhancements Act was passed. The bill includes a $50 million initiative to purchase closed-circuit surveillance equipment for schools.

Although it is difficult to ascertain the exact number of police officers assigned to high schools across the United States, according to Law Enforcement Management and Administrative Statistics (LEMAS) data, more than one-third of all sheriffs' offices and almost half of all local police departments have sworn officers in schools. It is estimated that more than 17,000 school resource officers (SROs) are assigned permanently to schools. In a survey of U.S. public schools, more than 68% of high schools with 1,000 or more students reported the presence of an SRO on campus. The official duties of an SRO—who is considered a hybrid of educational, correctional, and law enforcement official—vary. According to the National Association of School Resource Officers (NASRO), their responsibilities may include assisting in delinquency prevention programs such as Drug Abuse Resistance and Education (D.A.R.E.), patrolling the school grounds, traffic supervision, assisting with the control of disruptive students, intelligence gathering for criminal investigations, attending parent and faculty meetings, and providing in-service training to faculty and staff personnel.

Today, the new question facing high schools across the United States is how far schools must go to create a safe and secure environment for students in an era of global terrorism. Currently, the Department of Homeland Security (DHS) is conducting training at high schools across the country, educating faculty and staff on crisis response and emergency management techniques in preparation for potential terrorist attacks occurring at or near high school campuses.

Tony Gaskew

Further Reading

Brown, B. (2006). Understanding and assessing school police officers: A conceptual and methodological comment. *Journal of Criminal Justice, 34*, 591–604.

Indicators of school crime and safety. (2007). Bureau of Justice Statistics. Retrieved from http://www.ojp.gov/bjs/abstract/iscs07.htm

Managing your schools: Under threat of terrorism. (n.d.) National School Safety Center. Retrieved from http://www.schoolsafety.us/

Policies and Campus Violence Laws

There are approximately 16 million students enrolled in 4,200 colleges and universities in the United States. Approximately 479,000 students between the ages of 18 and 24 were victims of violence-related crimes on campus between 1995 and 2002. Many college and university students have become victims of crimes, such as campus shootings; murder-suicides; homicides; hate crimes based on students' and employees' gender, race, or sexual orientation; bullying; hazing; robbery; assault; and arson. Statistics on campus violence compiled by the American College Health Association (ACHA) indicate that approximately 15% to 20% of female college students have been rape victims; one out of every 14 men in college has been assaulted by an intimate partner; 8% of men and 1% of women possess firearms on campus; 7% of students have been in a physical fights and 4% have been physically assaulted. ACHA also found that only 35% of violent crimes on campus were reported to the police. In spite of the fact that violence in school has declined since the late 1990s, serious violent occurrences on campuses have prompted colleges and universities to act.

In recent years, several school shooting cases on college campuses (for example, the Virginia Tech University and Northern Illinois University shootings) have prompted calls for additional precautionary measures in colleges and universities across the country. Most campuses have counseling centers and trauma-based interventions for survivors of sexual assault, date rape, stalking, and homicide. Some institutions, such as Illinois State University, have enacted a campus safety policy that would ensure a secure environment for all students, employees, and visitors affiliated with the university; violation of the campus safety policy may result in disciplinary action up to and including expulsion, termination of employment, and pursuance of civil and criminal penalties. In conjunction with campus policies concerning violence, federal legislation targeting this problem has been enacted, including the Campus Sexual Assault Victims' Bill of Rights (1992), the Jeanne Clery Disclosure of Campus Security Policy and Campus Crime Statistics Act (1998), the Campus Sex Crime Prevention Act (2000), and the Family Educational Rights and Privacy Act (FERPA). State legislation has also

Police officers run from Norris Hall on the Virginia Tech campus. (AP/Wide World Photos)

been enacted, such as the Michael Minger Act (2000) passed by Kentucky lawmakers.

The Campus Sexual Assault Victims' Bill of Rights was passed by the U.S. Congress in 1992 as a part of the Higher Education Amendments of 1992 (Public Law: 102-325, section 486[c]). This law mandates that all higher education institutions (both public and private) participating in federal student aid programs grant sexual assault victims certain basic rights. Schools are also required to notify sexual assault victims of their option to report their assault to law enforcement. Schools that violate this law may be fined as much as $27,500 or lose their eligibility to participate in federal student aid programs. In accordance with the law, universities are required to provide educational programs on rape and sexual assault awareness; to enforce sanctions for rape and sexual assault on campus; to provide students with information on procedures to follow should sexual assault occurs; and to inform students of on-campus disciplinary action.

The Clery Act [20 USC § 1092(f)] is a federal law, also known as the Campus Security Act, that requires colleges and universities in the United States to disclose information about crime on and around their campuses. This legislation was named in memory of Jeanne Ann Clery, a 19-year-old Lehigh University student who was raped, sodomized, tortured, and murdered in her dormitory room in 1986; after the crime, Clery's parents discovered that Lehigh students were not informed of 38 incidences of violence on campus within three years prior to her murder. Until 1988, only 4% of America's colleges and universities had reported crime statistics to the Federal Bureau of Investigation (FBI). The Clery Act is tied to participation in federal student financial aid programs and enforced by the U.S. Department of Education.

In conjunction with the Clery Act, the Campus Sex Crimes Prevention Act (section 1601 of Public Law 106-386) was enacted in 2000. This federal law mandates tracking of convicted and registered sex offenders who are enrolled as students in a college or university, or working or volunteering on campus.

The Family Educational Rights and Privacy Act (FERPA; 20 U.S.C. § 1232g; 34 CFR Part 99) permits notifications concerning health and safety issues related to students. Although this legislation was designed to safeguard students' privacy, psychologists, psychiatrists, and counselors nevertheless have a duty to warn if threats are made against a particular person by their clients. Courts have ruled that colleges are obligated to take reasonable steps to protect students. The FERPA legislation was amended in the aftermath *of Jain v. State* (2000). In this case, Sanjay Jain, a freshman at the University of Iowa, attempted to commit suicide, but his family was not made aware of the attempt. A second suicide attempt succeeded. Jain's father argued that FERPA, which authorizes disclosure of confidential information to protect the health or safety of a student, required the school to notify Sanjay's family about the student's suicidal behavior. Jain's father unsuccessfully argued that the university violated FERPA by failing to notify him of his son's actions, which constituted an emergency situation.

The Michael Minger Act is a Kentucky state law that requires public and private colleges and universities licensed by the Kentucky Council on Postsecondary Education (CPE) to report crimes on campus to campus employees, students, and the public in a timely manner. It was proposed by Gail Minger, whose 19-year-old son Michael was killed in an arson fire at Murray State University in 1998. Information about an earlier arson fire in Minger's residence hall was not disclosed to students and their parents. The Michael Minger Act was ratified in 2000, and additional provisions dealing with student housing fire safety were passed in 2004. This legislation also requires a crime log to be made available to the public online; this log must record incidents that are known to the police and school officials on campus, as well as make special reports in the instances of ongoing threat to the safety of students and employees. Colleges and universities are also required to submit crime statistics to the CPE annually.

Violence and crimes on college and university campuses are serious problems in the United States, which have prompted implementation of a variety of policies and programs to deter violence on campus. In conjunction with these policies and programs, students, employees, school officials, and law enforcement must adopt a joint collaborative effort to protect students and ensure a safe and secure campus.

Jun Sung Hong

Further Reading

Baum, K., & Klaus, P. (2005). *Violent victimization of college students, 1995–2002* (NCJ Publication No. 206836). Washington, DC: U.S. Department of Justice, Office of Justice Programs, Bureau of Justice Statistics).

Carr, J. L. (2005). *American College Health Association campus violence white paper.* Baltimore, MD: American College Health Association.

Cohen, V. K. (2007). Keeping students alive: Mandating on-campus counseling saves suicidal college students' lives and limits liability. *Fordham Law Review, 75,* 3081–3135.

Security on Campus, Inc. (n.d.). Retrieved June 12, 2009, from http://www.securityoncampus.org

U.S. Department of Education (2002). Integrated postsecondary education data system (IPEDS) enrollment survey, spring 2002. National Center for Education Statistics. Retrieved June 12, 2009, from http://nces.ed.gov/pubsearch/pubsinfo.asp?pubid=2003168

Poulin, Robert

On October 27, 1975, 18-year-old Robert Poulin shot seven people, killing one, at St. Pius X High School in Ottawa, Canada. Prior to the shooting at the school, Poulin had raped and killed a girl, Kim Rabot, in his home. He handcuffed his victim to the bed, sexually assaulted her, and then stabbed her to death. Poulin then set his house on fire and proceeded to the school. He killed himself before he could face justice.

Poulin had a fairly normal upbringing. His father was a former pilot with the Royal Canadian Air Force, who later became a teacher. His mother was a nurse. Poulin had two much older sisters and one younger sister. As a child, he was described as mellow—not the kind of person who was easily upset or frequently in trouble. The family attended church regularly. As a youth, Poulin had several jobs, including delivering newspapers and working in a pizza shop. He was considered a conscientious worker, and he got good grades at school.

Socially, however, Poulin struggled. He was born with a pigeon chest, or a convex chest. His poor vision prevented him from pursuing his dream as a pilot and he wore thick, "Coke-bottle" glasses. He also looked young for his age, hit puberty later than most adolescents, and was slightly overweight. Poulin was shy and particularly awkward with girls. Although he had a lot of friends as a child, he had fewer as a teen. He was not described as a loner, however. One of Poulin's hobbies was playing war games; he and friends played over the telephone, and Poulin played the games alone as well.

Poulin desperately wanted to be in the military. Perhaps one of the pivotal life events that led to his attack occurred when he thought he was accepted for officer training but was later rejected for being immature. Poulin had lied on his application, alleging involvement with sports teams that never happened. He later joined the Cameron Highlanders militia and received military training. In the militia, Poulin first seemed timid but later made friends. He was generally serious, however, and would not talk about his family, like other soldiers did.

Poulin was said to be obsessed with sex and pornography, maintaining an index of several pornographic magazines. After the shooting incident, police found a binder with nearly 1,000 separate entries, all written by Poulin, next to pictures and advertisements. He had a total of 250 pornographic books and magazines. Police also found four pairs of handcuffs in his room, as well as a box of women's clothing, an inflatable sex doll, a vibrator, and a list of the names of 18 girls. Although there is no conclusive proof he was responsible, several of those girls had received obscene telephone calls that stopped after Poulin's suicide. There had also been complaints about assaults and attempted rapes in an apartment building near where Poulin lived, and the descriptions of the assailant fit him. Some women reported that the assailant had woven a balaclava, a scarf-like head covering, and Poulin had written that he would wear a balaclava when he raped a woman.

Leading up the shooting, Poulin had suffered from depression. A diary entry from the previous April describes his suicidal thoughts, although he wrote that he would not act on them until he had engaged in sex with a girl. Poulin also wrote about robbing people and burning down his own home so that his family could suffer. His writing suggests he saw death as something positive, calling it "true bliss." Psychologist Peter Langman has suggested that Poulin was psychotic, based on his lack of empathy and remorse.

Laura L. Finley

Further Reading

Langman, P. (2009). Expanding the sample. Retrieved May 5, 2010, from http://www.schoolshooters.info/expanding-the-sample.pdf

Shooting violence in Canadian schools 1975 to 2007. (n.d.). Retrieved May 5, 2010, from http://www.thestar.com/news/article/217023

Why did he do it? (2007, April 18). *Ottawa Citizen.* Retrieved May 5, 2010, from http://www.canada.com/ottawacitizen/news/story.html?id=e94922ba-eccb-4f19-aaf2- e79170403dfb&k=54359

Prescription Drugs and School Crime and Violence

Many have speculated that either the side effects from taking certain prescription drugs or the withdrawal from taking them has been a factor in school and campus shootings. In particular, a certain class of antidepressant drugs, known as selective serotonin reuptake inhibitors (SSRIs), has been linked to a number of the most serious incidents of violent crime on school and university campuses. This category of drugs includes Prozac, Zoloft, Paxil, Celexa, Lexapro, and Luvox. Newer SSRIs include Remeron and Anafranil. Another similar category consists of the serotonin norepinephrine reuptake inhibitors (SNRIs), which include Effexor, Serzone, Cymbalta, and Pristiq. Dopamine reuptake inhibitors include wellbutrin, which is marketed as Zyban.

Many of these drugs were not tested on young people, yet have been increasingly prescribed to them. Once the U.S. Food and Drug Administration (FDA) approves a drug for use, it can be prescribed to any population, regardless of whether the drug has been formally tested in that group.

SSRIs and other antidepressants are known to cause the following side effects:

- Manic reaction (mania—e.g., kleptomania, pyromania, dipsomania)
- Abnormal thinking
- Hallucinations
- Personality disorder

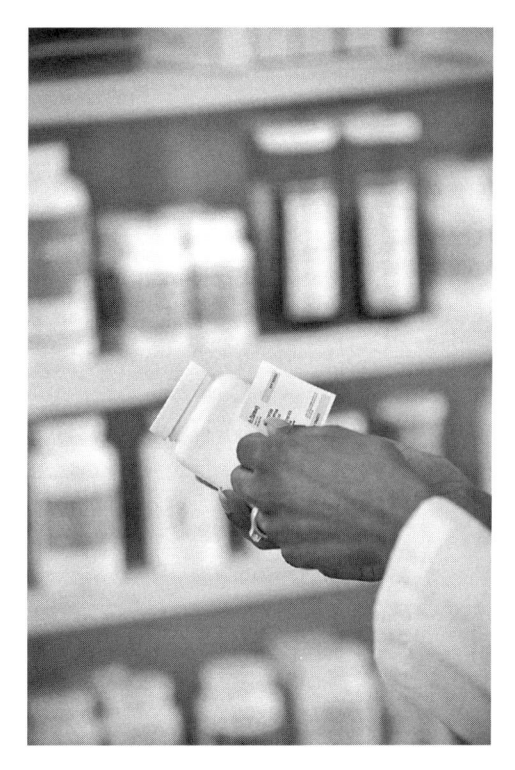

A pharmacist reviews the label on a prescription drug bottle. (iStockPhoto)

- Amnesia
- Agitation
- Psychosis
- Abnormal dreams emotional lability (or instability)
- Alcohol abuse and/or craving
- Hostility
- Paranoid reactions
- Confusion
- Delusions
- Sleep disorders
- Akathisia (severe inner restlessness)
- Discontinuation (withdrawal) syndrome

Following is a partial list of some of the incidents in which a prescription drug has been implicated:

- In 1988, Laurie Dann had been taking Anafranil and lithium when she killed one child and wounded six at an Illinois elementary school.
- Also in 1988, James Wilson, who had been taking Xanax, Valium, and several other drugs, shot and killed two eight-year-old girls and wounded seven others at an elementary school in Greenwood, South Carolina.
- In 1989, Patrick Purdy shot and killed five and wounded 30 other elementary school students in Stockton, California. Purdy had been taking thorazine and amitriptyline.
- Toby R. Sincino shot two Blackville-Hilda High School teachers on October 12, 1995, killing one. Sincino, who killed himself moments later, had been taking the antidepressant Zoloft.
- On May 21, 1998, Kip Kinkel killed four and wounded 23 at Thurston High School in Springfield, Oregon. Kinkel had been taking Prozac.
- On April 20, 1999, Eric Harris and Dylan Klebold killed 13 and wounded 23 others before killing themselves at Columbine High School in Littleton, Colorado. Harris had been taking Luvox.
- On May 20, 1999, T. J. Solomon, who was taking Ritalin, wounded six people at Heritage High School in Conyers, Georgia.
- On March 25, 2005, Jeff Weise killed nine and injured five at Red Lake High School in Red Lake, Minnesota. Weise had been taking Prozac.

- On April 16, 2007, Seung-Hui Cho murdered 32 people at Virginia Tech University, in the deadliest campus shooting ever. Cho had been taking prescription medications.
- In 2006, Duane Morrison shot and killed a girl at Platte Canyon High School in Colorado. Antidepressants later were found in his vehicle.
- On February 14, 2008, shooter Steve Kazmierczak shot 21 people at Northern Illinois University, killing five. He had recently stopped taking Prozac.
- On September 23, 2008, Finnish school shooter Matti Saari killed 10 people and then himself. Saari was taking an SSRI medicinal product as well as a benzodiazepine.
- In November 2009, Christopher Craft, Sr., a graduate of Stissing Mountain Junior-Senior High School, walked into the school around 7:45 A.M., with a concealed disassembled shotgun. After reassembling the weapon in a bathroom, he entered the middle school office and took Principal Robert Hess as a hostage. Craft had been taking Cymbalta for depression.

The federal government has begun to react to what seems by now to be a trend. On September 14, 2008, the FDA mandated that pharmacies provide parents or guardians of patients younger than the age of 18 for whom antidepressants have been prescribed with an Antidepressant Patient Medication Guide. On September 14, 2008, the FDA ordered that a "black box" warning label be placed on antidepressants, describing the risk of suicide for persons younger than age 18 who take these drugs.

Laura L. Finley

Further Reading

Cullen, D. (2010). *Columbine.* New York: Twelve.

Davey, M., & Harris, G. (2005, March 26). Family wonders if Prozac prompted school shootings. *New York Times.* Retrieved April 14, 2010, from http://www.nytimes.com/2005/03/26/national/26shoot.html

Huffington, A. (2007, April 19). Virginia Tech aftermath: Did legal drugs play a role in the massacre? *Huffington Post.* Retrieved May 6, 2010, from http://www.huffingtonpost.com/arianna-huffington/virginia-tech-aftermath-d_b_46280.html

SSRI stories. (n.d.). Retrieved April 14, 2010, from http://www.ssristories.com/index.php

Vossekuil, B., Fein, R., Reddy, M., Borum, R., & Modzeleski, W. (2002). *The final report and findings of the Safe School Initiative: Implications for the prevention of school attacks in the United States.* Jessup, MD: Education Publications Center, U.S. Department of Education.

Prince, Phoebe

On January 14, 2010, Phoebe Nora Mary Prince, an immigrant from Ireland, hung herself on the stairwell leading to the second floor of her family's home. She had endured yet another day of bullying and torment at South Hadley High School in Hadley, Massachusetts, compounded by the fact that the group of girls who harassed her most threw a can of Red Bull out a car window, hitting Prince as she walked home from school.

What emerged in the months following Prince's death was that this abuse had been going on for some time. Kids at the school routinely knocked Prince's books from her hands, threw things at her in the hallway, scribbled her face out of photographs, and even sent her threatening text messages. Particularly ruthless was a group of girls who have been dubbed "the Mean Girls" for their resemblance to the characters in the 2004 movie. They called Prince "Irish slut" and "whore," both in school and on the social networking site Facebook, as well as on Twitter, Craigslist, and Formspring. Evidently the girls started bullying Prince after she briefly dated a popular senior football player at the beginning of her freshman year. Even after Prince's suicide, the girls posted mean comments on the Facebook page that was to serve as a memorial for their classmate.

On March 29, 2010, authorities announced that they had indicted nine teenagers for bullying Prince and prompting her suicide. Seven girls and two boys were charged with a variety of offenses, including statutory rape for the boys, violation of civil rights with bodily injury, criminal harassment, and stalking. The announcement came far too late for some in the community, who were enraged that the girls had seemed to be able to get away with their horrific behavior. Investigators had looked at whether the school should face some blame, given that some officials admitted they knew Prince had been bullied, with some even witnessing it. Investigators found there was no criminal responsibility, but stated that the behavior of some adults was certainly troubling. On April 8, 2010, three of the girls entered "not guilty" pleas to the charges. Reports are that the girls are receiving hateful messages and that social networking sites and message boards have featured calls for them to suffer like Prince did.

Unfortunately, Prince's suicide is not the only recent one related to bullying—an outcome that experts have come to call "bullycide." Only a few months prior to Prince's death, 17-year-old Tyler Lee Long, who suffered from Asperger's syndrome (a mild form of autism), endured similar humiliation at the hands of classmates at Murray County High School in Georgia. The bullying began in fifth grade, when one student began pushing Tyler around. From then on, he faced a torrent of verbal and physical abuse on a daily basis. As in Prince's case, adults were generally indifferent to Long's plight. When the family reported the incidents, the school's response was generally "Boys will be boys." At the beginning of 10th grade, Long was pushed down a flight of stairs, yet the school still took no action against the perpetrators. Long hung himself from his bedroom closet door on October 17, 2009. In March 2010, his parents filed suit against the Murray County School District and Murray High School principal Gail Linder for failing to protect Tyler, even after they had repeatedly told Linder about the bullying. An attorney for the district and Linder has said the defendants had no information to suggest Long was being bullied.

Parents, including the Longs, are growing frustrated with what they have called the "see no evil" approach on the part of schools. They suggest that schools too often characterize bullying as a harmless adolescent rite of passage. Parents have begun to organize anti-bullying campaigns. Groups providing anti-bullying curricula and programs are now sure to include cyberbullying in their materials.

Statistics are not clear about how often bullycide occurs. Bullying itself occurs regularly. Bullying is ultimately about power; it is intentional mistreatment with the goal of obtaining and maintaining power over the victim. In 2009, the National Center for Educational Statistics found that almost one-third of students ages 12 to 18 reported being bullied in school, an increase of more than 20% from 2001. Part of this increase, however, may be the result of more and better reporting.

Cyberbullying may be even more common. A 2008 study in *The Journal of School Health* found that 75% of teens have been bullied online, but only 10% reported the problem to their parents or other adults. It is easier for bullies to harass their victims online than in a face-to-face manner, and they can engage in cyberbullying from anywhere, at any time. Like face-to-face bullying, cyberbullying often targets those who are different, including minorities, children with disabilities, those who are smaller than classmates, or very heavyset kids.

It is clear that bullying has significant negative effects, even if it does not lead the victim to suicide. Victims are often depressed, which leads them to become even more isolated. They may miss school, and their performance is likely to suffer. In addition to the impact on victims, bullying damages the climate of the entire school. Violence prevention and anti-bullying programs are increasingly focusing on how to improve the overall school climate. These considerations include the physical facilities, trust and respect among teachers and students, openness to new ideas, opportunities for all to participate, and much more.

Experts caution against standing up to bullies—the response that is so often presented in film and television. The concern is that bullies tend to have either a size advantage or a cohort of supporters, and maybe both. Further, bullies tend to have above-average self-esteem and see themselves as entitled; thus they are not likely to respond to reasoning.

Experts suggest several elements are critical for dealing with bullies. First, adults must intervene on behalf of the victims. Studies have shown that bullies are most likely to cease harassing victims when adults become involved. Having more adults present is a first step, followed by vigorous enforcement of policy when an incident occurs. Second, children should be empowered to intervene when they are bystanders to bullying. Third, bullies must be punished fairly and consistently. Finally, it is essential that the entire school community, including students, administrators, staff, and parents, receive anti-bullying training.

Laura L. Finley

Further Reading

Clark-Flory, T. (2010, April 8). Phoebe Prince's bullies get bullied. *Salon.* Retrieved May 5, 2010, from http://www.salon.com/life/broadsheet/2010/04/08/phoebe_prince_bullies_get_bullied

Kennedy, H. (2010, March 29). Phoebe Prince, South Hadley High School's "new girl," driven to suicide by teenage cyber bullies. *New York Daily News.* Retrieved April 28, 2010, from http://www.nydailynews.com/news/national/2010/03/29/2010-03-29_phoebe_prince_south_hadley_high_schools_new_girl_driven_to_suicide_by_teenag e_cy.html

Ollove, M. (2010, April 28). Bullying and teen suicide: How do we adjust school climate? Retrieved April 28, 2010, from http://news.yahoo.com/s/csm/20100428/ts_csm/297160_1

Parker-Pope, T. (2007, November 27). More teens victimized by cyber-bullies. *The New York Times,* p. 1–1. Retrieved July 30, 2009, from http://well.blogs.nytimes.com/2007/11/27/more-teens-victimized-by-cyber-bullies/

Professor-Perpetrated Crime and Violence

Crime pervades all areas of human life, and colleges and universities are no exception. Professors are susceptible to the same failings and criminal activity as the rest of society. Professor-perpetrated crimes are linked to crime-related opportunities provided in their employment at colleges. Other crimes of violence are less likely to be related directly to professors' position of authority and trust. Much of the phenomenon of professors as murder victims or as perpetrators has been attributed to the competitive atmosphere and intense performance evaluations for professors, referred to as "publish or perish." By comparison, sexual harassment accusations increased dramatically on college campuses in the 1990s as legislation established stricter guidelines; such events have typically involved a male professor and a younger female instructor or student. Sexual and violence-related crimes are not linked to professors' employment, however, but rather to underlying deviations.

Mishandling of defense secrets is not something that one would normally associate with a college professor. Nevertheless, J. Reece Roth was accused of passing information from a U.S. Air Force contract to two of his foreign research assistants, who were from China and Iran. His actions were considered crimes under the Arms Export Control Act. Roth's materials from his office were seized as well as his computer when he returned from a lecture tour in China. He eventually pleaded guilty to 10 counts of exporting defense-related materials.

An unusual case involving former professor John J. Donovan, Sr., occurred in Cambridge, Massachusetts. Donovan told police that he had been shot and accused his eldest son of arranging the incident. Evidence revealed that Donovan had actually shot himself in the stomach and sprayed bullets around to frame members of his own family. The judge in the case ordered Donovan to stay away from one of his sons, his three daughters, and their spouses. He was also put on probation, ordered to pay $625, perform 200 hours of community service, and undergo a psychiatric evaluation.

Some of the most heinous crimes imaginable involve those that victimize children. Professor Antonio Lasaga faced charges in court for receiving 150,000 pornographic images of children. The images were found on both his home and university computers. Lasaga was also convicted of sexually assaulting and filming the abuse of a young boy. The boy was six when the abuse started, and it lasted for several years. The professor was sentenced to 15 years in prison for the electronic images and 20 years for the rape and videotaping of the assault. Lasagna was ordered to participate in sex offender treatment and register with the sex offender registry upon his release from prison.

Former professor Jack Harclerode pleaded guilty to indecent sexual assault and corruption of a minor. He received a 9- to 30-month sentence and was declared a sexually violent predator. The investigation into Harclerode uncovered 245 sexually explicit photographs of young boys, and he was convicted on 20 counts of possession of child pornography. The trial revealed long-term abuse of boys spanning four decades, according to Harclerode's daughter.

Not all offenders succeed in victimizing children, despite their nefarious intent. Albert Snow, a chemistry professor, received a sentence of 10 years in prison after his conviction for enticement of a minor. Snow talked online to someone he thought was a 15-year-old girl but who was actually a police officer; Snow was arrested when he searched for the girl at an apartment complex. A professor in Hawaii, Marc Fossorier, was arrested for a similar incident. A state investigator was posing as a 15-year-old on the internet when Fossorier talked with her and arranged to have sex. He was sentenced to a year in jail and five years of probation.

Former professor Joshua Young Moon faced a charge of object sexual penetration after assaulting a student in his office. The student suffered from headaches and backaches, and Moon offered to give her a massage. The student fell asleep and awoke to find Moon touching her. Moon pleaded guilty to aggravated sexual battery.

John M. Adams was a college professor in psychiatry. He also saw patients privately. He became aware of a malpractice suit that was being filed against him by a former patient and her husband. Adams claimed that he went to the couple's house to talk about the lawsuit. He shot Bobby Burns and threatened Michelle Burns, but she escaped to a neighbor's house. Adams fled in his own vehicle and then abandoned it a short time later. He then forced two women to drive him to Kentucky. Adams was sentenced to a minimum of 26 years in prison for aggravated burglary, kidnapping, and murder with a firearm specification.

According to the UCR (Uniform Crime Reports), in 2008 34.7% of female murder victims were killed by a husband or boyfriend. In 2009, an argument with his wife spurred Professor George Zinkhan to shoot his wife at a community theater. He also killed two other people who were there and injured an additional two people. His children were waiting in the car at the time. Zinkhan then returned to his car and dropped his children off with a neighbor. He remained missing for two weeks. Zinkhan had committed suicide His body was finally discovered by cadaver dogs in the woods.

Kansas State University Profesor Thomas Murray and his ex-wife had shared custody of their daughter, and it is believed that this arrangement was a source of contention between the two. When Carmin Ross-Murray was found beaten and stabbed to death, investigators looked at Thomas Murray as a suspect. The investigators amassed a large amount of evidence that led them to believe that Thomas Murray was responsible for the murder of his ex-wife. He was ultimately sentenced to life in prison.

In 2004, a professor with a hidden past presented the world of academia with an unusual situation. Paul Krueger had been teaching at Penn State for 15 years, and no one knew of his criminal history. When he was 18 years old, Krueger killed three men who were on a fishing trip, leaving their bullet-ridden bodies behind. Krueger received three life sentences for the crime. Parole commissioners felt that he had been rehabilitated, so he was released after serving only 12 years of his sentence. Krueger went on to graduate school in California, married, and had a son. He eventually become a college professor. When his past was revealed to the public, Krueger resigned.

Recently, Amy Bishop, a professor of neurobiology, opened fire on six of her colleagues after she learned that she had been denied tenure. She killed three of her colleagues and wounded three others. Seven years before this incident, Bishop had shot and killed her brother. At the time the crime was ruled accidental, but in 2010 Bishop was indicted for her brother's death. A 2010 review of a 1993 attempted mail bombing at Harvard Medical School resulted in no charges filed against Bishop.

Crimes perpetrated by professors are difficult for society to grasp due to the trust that parents and students place in these individuals. When these people commit unconscionable crimes such as pedophilia and murder, it is especially horrifying. Violent offenses appear to be precipitated by consistently high stress work environments, highly stressful personal situations, and a final incident that triggers a volatile response. Following the recent rash of college shootings, most states have enacted mandatory removal of professors for threatening physical harm to anyone on campus.

The vast majority of university and college professors are, of course, law-abiding citizens. These individuals spend their lives educating others and creating research that propels our knowledge in all aspects of the sciences and humanities.

Annika Vorhes

Further Reading

Amy Bishop Timeline. Boston Globe. Retrieved March 9, 2011 from http://timelines.boston.com/timelines/amy-bishop

Dewan, S., Saul, S., & Zezima, K. (2010, February 20). For professor, fury just beneath the surface. *The New York Times.* Retrieved from http://www.nytimes.com/2010/02/21/us/21bishop.html

Ellement, J. R. (2007, August 18). Ex-professor found guilty of staging own shooting. *The Boston Globe*. Retrieved from http://www.boston.com/news/local/articles/2007/08/18/ex_professor_found_guilty_of_staging_own_shooting/

Property Crimes, College

Destruction of property is an issue that college campuses continually face. As the United States continues to heal from the wave of school violence that characterized the late 1990s and early 2000s, college campuses have worked to increase the public's confidence in the ability of schools to protect students. While property destruction is not as violent as other types of crimes, it still takes a toll on schools' budgets and on student and staff morale, lessening the control that campus safety officials have over student actions. An examination of factors that may contribute to the occurrence of college property crimes and the transitional nature of college students' lives, an understanding of the theoretical perspectives used to understand crime, and ways those theories can be applied to college property crime will better equip college students and staff to reach students who commit property crimes and prevent these crimes from happening in the first place.

Substance abuse, peer group influence, and economic background are key factors that influence students' decisions to destroy campus property, regardless of individual demographic differences. Substance abuse is a well-known problem for campus law enforcement. The abuse of drugs and alcohol leads to a whole host of problems, from car accidents and battery to the spread of sexually transmitted diseases and unwanted pregnancy. Research has shown that students who engage in regular drinking, taking part in the campus party scene, are significantly more likely to be somehow involved in campus crimes, including crimes against property. It follows logically that while a student is under the influence, with judgment impaired, property destruction may not seem as serious or risky as it would to a student with a sober mindset.

Another external contributing factor to campus property destruction is the student's peer group. A study examining the social influences on criminals cited three specific reasons a person may go along with a group's decisions to commit a crime: "fear of ridicule, status striving, and the diffusion of responsibility within a group" (Hartley, 2011, p. 29). Just as alcohol and drugs can change a student's general view of crime, so peer pressure can temporarily affect a student's judgment. A student's views on the ethics of property destruction while in a psychologically comfortable and secure mindset may change when that same student is scared of rejection. In addition to peer pressure, mere peer presence has an impact. One study addressing self-control and peer influence found that increased time spent with peers created a strong statistical effect that provides evidence of the importance of looking beyond the issues of individual self-control to other external contributing factors—in this case, the peer group. Specifically, destroying property with a group may lower the feeling of personal responsibility an individual student might have.

While substance abuse and peer group are both immediate contributing factors to a student deciding to take part in the commission of a property crime, socioeconomic background may be an underlying factor. A study analyzing the link between poverty and property crime exposure reported that people living in high-crime neighborhoods were five times more likely to witness a property crime being committed than people who do not live in high-crime neighborhoods. Albert Bandura's work demonstrates the strength of modeling—a psychological concept that asserts watching someone do something increases the chance the person watching will then do the same thing, much as children mimic their parents. Continuing along these lines, students who grow up seeing property crimes being committed will be more likely to commit such crimes themselves one day.

The previously described factors are compounded by the transitional nature of being a college student. At a time when their identities are changing, and being formed through various experiences and relationships, students' morals and values are not as absolute as they may have been before these individuals started college and, in many cases, moved out and away from home. A study examining the behavioral changes students experience during the transition from high school to college found that even when controlling for certain demographic characteristics, students experienced similar behavioral changes. Recent research done on college students has found that this transition often brings about heavier episodic drinking, greater marijuana use, more sexual partners, and higher morbidity and mortality rates than found among peers who are the same age but not enrolled in college classes. As students leave their childhood homes, towns, and (in some cases) friends, they are forced to begin making decisions concerning how they spend time that parents or other guardians may have formerly made. This increased independence is only one of the many psychological processes associated with the major transition of moving out and into an institution of higher education.

Social scientists have observed and analyzed these factors contributing to campus property crime through many different theoretical lenses. For example, Travis Hirschi's social control theory holds that people are inherently deviant. An inner connection to society keeps them from committing crimes and weakening that bond. Thus it can be assumed that if a person commits a property crime on a college campus, that individual's bond to society has been somehow weakened. In line with social control theory, the best way to prevent college property crimes would be to strengthen students' ties to the new social environment they find themselves in at the start of their first semester. Strong resident hall programming, mentoring programs, and other social events can help students feel connected to the school and lessen their likelihood of hurting their society by destroying campus property or committing other types of crime.

Another theory commonly applied to the study of crime is Ronald Akers' social learning theory. Akers maintains that people are not inherently deviant or compliant, but rather neutral. He suggests that each person is as likely as the next to be deviant and commit a crime, as determined by that individual's external environment. Rejecting the idea that connectedness to society is the only way to fight an internal tendency to be deviant, Akers points to the various influences on a person as he or she develops into an adult in predicting who will more likely to be deviant and commit a crime. Research analyzing social learning theory links this perspective with Bandura's aforementioned modeling theory, as both point to outside influences as key in a child's future actions. While Akers' theory still places power in the hands of those influencing the developing student, it does not claim that individuals naturally lean toward deviance. Embracing this viewpoint would encourage college staff to pay attention to students' backgrounds. Akers would encourage staff to mentor students, learning which gaps have been left by their upbringing and working to fill those gaps with healthier activities than property crime and other forms of deviance.

Following Akers' reasoning, Bronfenbrenner's ecological systems theory encourages an analysis of the various influences on a person. Bronfenbrenner divides these influences into five systems, each growing in its distance from the individual: the microsystem (closest to the person), the mesosystem, the exosystem, the macrosystem, and the chronosystem (furthest from the person). This approach meshes well with social learning theory, as both perspectives examine what has and is influencing the person in question. By mapping out exactly which influences are acting on the student, it becomes clear which are negative and need to be distanced more from the student, and which are positive and could potentially unite to reach the student and help with the issues he or she is dealing with. For example, a deviant peer group who encourages the student to drink irresponsibly and write graffiti on school buildings can be distanced, whereas friends and resident assistants living in the residence hall who enjoy other legal, healthy activities can be sought out and encouraged to reach out to the student.

Addressing college property crime is a task that requires a deeper understanding of the issues college students are dealing with, the importance of the competing influences on students, and the various theories and the solutions they offer in reducing and eliminating campus property crimes. Students who commit property crimes are expressing themselves in an unhealthy and illegal way for a reason. They have come from a specific home, grown up within a specific culture, and found themselves within a specific peer group at the college campus. A crisis precipitated by a property crime presents college staff with an opportunity to use the contact to intervene and prevent future crimes. College staffs have a difficult task in raising the public's confidence in their ability to maintain safe campuses, as free as possible of all types of crime. The future holds great potential for reaching deviant students at a key point in their lives, thereby helping improve society as whole in doing so.

Meghan McHaney

Further Reading

Bandura, A., & Kupers, C. (1964). Transmission of patterns of self-reinforcement through modeling. *Journal of Abnormal and Social Psychology, 69,* 1–9.

Corbin, W., Fromme, K., & Kruse, M. (2008). Behavioral risks during the transition from high school to college. *Developmental Psychology, 44,* 1497–1504.

Darling, N. (2007). The person on the center of circles. *Research in Human Development, 4,* 203–217.

Jennings, W., Gover, A., & Pudrzynska, D. (2007). A descriptive study of campus safety issues and self-reported campus victimization among male and female college students *Journal of Criminal Justice Education, 2,* 191–208.

Larsson, D. (2006). Exposure to property crime as a consequence of poverty. *Journal of Scandinavian Studies in Criminology and Crime Prevention, 7,* 45–60.

Meldrum, R., Weerman, F., & Young, J. (2009). Reconsidering the effect of self-control and delinquent peers: Implications of measurement for theoretical significance.*Journal of Research in Crime and Delinquency, 46,* 353.

Muuss, R. (1976). The implications of social learning theory for an understanding of adolescent development. *Adolescence, 11,* 61.

Payne, A., & Salotti, S. (2007). Comparative analysis of social learning and social control theories in the prediction of college crime. *Deviant Behavior, 28*, 553–573.

Warr, M. (2002). *Why peers are important/ factors of peer companions in crime: The social aspects of criminal conduct.* Cambridge, UK: Cambridge University Press.

Property Crimes, High School

The term "property crime" typically refers to a crime wherein a piece of property such as a purse, a motor vehicle, or a building is intentionally damaged, stolen, or destroyed. For instance, arson, auto theft, burglary, embezzlement, larceny, shoplifting, and vandalism can be considered property crimes. It is important to note, however, that more precise definitions of what constitutes a property crime vary. There are differences of opinion among criminal justice experts, practitioners, and agencies as to whether all criminal action that involves property should be considered and treated as a property crime.

Students walk toward the outside of the concrete and iron-barred wall of Jordan High School in Los Angeles on October 9, 1996. The high school installed the iron bars on the top of the wall to deter vandalism. (AP/Wide World Photos)

As a case in point, crimes such as the counterfeiting of currency or the forgery of a check involve an economic loss but are not commonly considered to be property crimes. In the annual *Crime in the United States* reports, which is generated using a research program most commonly known as the Uniform Crime Reports, the only types of property crime analyzed by the Federal Bureau of Investigation (FBI) are burglary, larceny-theft, motor vehicle theft, and arson. The FBI does not treat robbery as a property crime because the crime involves either the threat of force or the use of force against the victim. In addition, the FBI does not provide data on many types of property crimes such as fraud and vandalism in the *Crime in the United States* reports.

Whatever definition is used, it is clear that property crimes are more common than violent crimes. For instance, every year in the United States, there are more burglaries than murders. The same holds true for school crimes. Although highly violent school crimes such as school shootings receive a great deal of attention from the media and the general public, such crimes are rare. Likewise, even though many students may be more fearful of being violently attacked by a classmate than of having something stolen from their locker, juveniles are actually more likely to have something stolen from them than to be violently attacked while on school property. However, some research suggests that minor forms of school violence such as bullying and non-injurious assault are as common as property crimes. Among the many types of property crime that may occur at school, such as arson, auto theft, property theft, and vandalism, the most common property crimes are theft and vandalism.

Reports of the prevalence of theft vary, but several scholars have found that the theft of personal property such as clothing, electronic devices (e.g., cell phones), money, and school supplies is a common occurrence in schools. The theft of inexpensive items such as batteries, classroom décor, pencils, and pens is so common that most students, teachers, and administrators probably never even report such incidents. The most recent figures available from the U.S. Departments of Education and Justice show that 86% of high schools and 69% of middle schools experience some type of theft and that 68% of high schools and 43% of middle schools experience thefts that are serious enough that the incidents are reported to the police.

There are no quality state or national data on vandalism in schools. Nevertheless, one can ask any teacher or school administrator about the vandalism of school property, and they will likely say the problem is routine. For instance, graffiti is a common feature in many schools; it can often be found throughout a school on student desks, library tables, laboratory tables, lockers, walls, and bathroom stalls. Another common problem in many schools is the negligent treatment and intentional destruction of school property such as library books, textbooks, computers, calculators, beakers, and microscopes. In addition, common horseplay such as tossing items around in a classroom can result in the destruction of school property such as clocks, light fixtures, and windows and thus may be considered as a type of vandalism.

Although school property crimes do not receive the same attention from scholars or policymakers as do violent school crimes, property crimes on school grounds are a serious problem. In addition to the considerable costs associated with repairing and replacing damaged or stolen property, the general unsightliness of damaged and destroyed property may contribute to an increase in the level of disorder in a school. As originally suggested by Wilson and Kelling (1982) in their classic article "Broken Windows," in areas where the destruction and vandalism of property is not immediately fixed, there is often an increase in such crimes. As the vandalism spreads, the level of disorder increases. When people see that no one cares enough about the property to fix the damage (i.e., that people have no stake in the general well-being of their surroundings), the overall quality of life decreases and the rate of crime increases.

It is hard to take pride in one's community when the streets are littered with abandoned cars, the buildings are covered with graffiti, and the few existing businesses have iron security bars covering their windows. Decent law-abiding citizens who reside in such areas often live in constant fear, while the drug dealers, gang members, pimps, and prostitutes engage in criminal pursuits with impunity. Similarly, when students attend poorly maintained schools that plagued by broken windows and graffiti, they may feel little connection to or concern about their school. It is hard to take pride in one's school when the lockers are broken, the bathrooms are covered with graffiti, and the textbooks are in tatters. Some research indicates that the weaker a youth's bond to the school, the greater the likelihood that the youth will engage in criminal and delinquent activity. As the school environment deteriorates, the learning process suffers because there tends to be an increase in student crime, nondelinquent students become concerned about victimization while at school, and students become fearful of even attending school.

Ben Brown

Further Reading

Brown, B., & Benedict, W. R. (2005). Student victimization in Hispanic high schools: A research note and methodological comment. *Criminal Justice Studies, 18,* 255–269.

Dinkes, R., Cataldi, E. F., Lin-Kelly, W., & Snyder, T. D. (2007, December). *Indicators of school crime and safety: 2007* (NCES 2008-021/NCJ 219553). Washington, DC: U.S. Department of Education, Institute of Education Sciences, National Center for Education Statistics and U.S. Department of Justice, Office of Justice Programs, Bureau of Justice Statistics.

Federal Bureau of Investigation. (2008). *Crime in the United States: 2007.* Washington, DC: U.S. Government Printing Office.

Felson, M. (1998). *Crime and everyday life* (2nd ed.). Thousand Oaks, CA: Pine Forge Press.

Hanke, P. J. (1996). Putting school crime into perspective: Self-reported school victimizations of high school seniors. *Journal of Criminal Justice, 24,* 207–226.

Jenkins, P. H. (1997). School delinquency and the school social bond. *Journal of Research in Crime and Delinquency, 34,* 337–367.

Welsh, W. N. (2003). Individual and institutional predictors of school disorder. *Youth Violence and Juvenile Justice, 1,* 346–368.

Welsh, W. N., Stokes, R., & Greene, J. R. (2000). A macro-level model of school disorder. *Journal of Research in Crime and Delinquency, 37,* 243–283.

Wilson, J. Q., & Kelling, G. L. (1982, March). Broken windows: Police and neighborhood safety. *Atlantic Monthly, 249,* 29–38.

Public Health Approach

Too often, violence in general, and school violence in particular, is handled punitively. Law enforcement personnel are often involved in such cases, and harsh punishments may be doled out to offenders. While there are certainly some benefits to this approach, some advocate for a different focus. A public health approach sees juvenile violence as an epidemic that must be addressed in the same way that an infectious disease or injury would. A public health approach encompasses far more preventive work and entails community collaborations involving activists, educators, social services, mental health and medical professionals, and law enforcement.

It was not until the late 1970s that anyone discussed a public health approach to violence. Mark Rosenberg, director of public health services at the Centers for Disease Control and Prevention (CDC), advocated for the inclusion of community violence in the Surgeon General's national public health agenda (in 1979). One year later, the Federal Alcohol, Drug Abuse and Mental Health Administration organized a symposium on violence as a public health issue. Physicians, psychiatrists, psychologists, and academicians all attended. Five years after the symposium, Surgeon General C. Everett Koop sponsored a conference on the issue, and the U.S. Department of Health and Human Services (HHS) began publishing reports using a public health lens to discuss youth violence.

This idea gained further popularity in 1991 with the publication of Deborah Prothrow-Stith's *Deadly Consequences: How Violence Is Destroying Our Teenage Population and a Plan to Begin Solving the Problem.* Prothrow-Stith, a physician, saw prevention of disease as the highest calling in her field. Troubled by the young people she was seeing in the emergency who had been victims of violence, she was moved to initiate efforts to prevent youth violence. Prothrow-Stith advocates for health education in the classroom, community-based health education, and hospital screenings for risk factors. During the 1990s, she worked with child advocacy groups and community and political leaders to move these ideas into action. She also advised the Children's Defense Fund, helping this organization create the Black Community Crusade for Children's Task Force on violence.

The CDC recommends four steps to a public health approach: (1) define the problem; (2) identify risk and protective factors; (3) develop and test prevention strategies; and (4) assure widespread adoption. Public health professionals use a variety of approaches to help prevent violence. For example, multisystemic therapy (MST) involves closely monitoring the places where a youth spends most of his or her time, such as in the home, in the neighborhood, at school, and with peer groups. Students receive personal counseling, and parents are trained as well. Domestic violence advocates have implemented a public health approach through the DELTA (Domestic Violence Prevention and Leadership Through Alliances) program, which requires funded programs to build a collaborative community response to prevent dating and domestic violence. The California-based Prevention Institute sponsors a number of public health programs designed to prevent violence and reduce injury. Similarly, the Global Campaign for Violence Prevention is a good source of information about a public health approach to violence prevention.

A difficulty with these strategies is that they require tremendous organization and groups willing to collaborate. They are not short-term solutions, but rather require ongoing effort to succeed. Critics contend that they are suitable in urban communities, but not necessarily in rural areas that are less equipped with medical professionals and social services agencies. Politicians may not disapprove of these strategies, but often find it difficult to support a public health approach if it is perceived as being soft on crime.

Laura L. Finley

Further Reading

Finley, L. (Ed.). (2007). *Encyclopedia of school crime and violence.* Westport, CT: Praeger.

Preventing violence and reducing injury. (n.d.). Prevention Institute. Retrieved from http://www.preventioninstitute.org/focus-areas/preventing-violence-and-reducing- injury.html

Prothrow-Stith, D. (1991). *Deadly consequences: How violence is destroying our teenage population and a plan to begin solving the problem.* New York: HarperCollins.

The public health approach. (n.d.). Global Campaign for Violence Prevention. Retrieved from http://www.who.int/violenceprevention/approach/public_health/en/index.html

The public health approach to violence prevention. (2006, September 19). Centers for Disease Control and Prevention. Retrieved May 5, 2010, from http://www.cdc.gov/ncipc/dvp/PublicHealthApproachToViolencePrevention.htm

Punitive Responses, College

College students are at the stage of developmental transition from adolescents to adults. For many, entering college also means moving away from their families and, as a result, fewer restrictions on their activities. For these reasons, the college experience can be associated with increased risk for a variety of psychosocial problems, such as substance abuse. As an additive behavior, alcohol and drug abuse increases the prevalence of campus violence, such as impaired driving, assault, fighting, dating violence, and bias-related violence. Additive behaviors, such as alcohol use and binge drinking, caused negative consequential problems. To limit or reduce alcohol-related harms on college, campuses often implement and enforce policies that restrict and punish use of alcohol (and drugs).

Colleges typically use state and federal laws as a basis for designing their own policies to deal with campus problems. The application of regulatory mandates to college alcohol and drug use started with the federal Drug-Free Schools and Communities Act (DFSCA) of 1989. The DFSCA, which applies to all U.S. colleges, specifies that "as a condition of receiving funds or any other form of financial assistance under any Federal program, an institution of higher education (IHE) must certify that it has adopted and implemented a drug [and alcohol] prevention program" (U.S. Department of Education, n.d.). Therefore, to fulfill DFSCA requirements and retain funding, colleges must provide students with institutional standards of conduct that explicitly prohibit illicit drugs and illegal alcohol use, a description of potential legal and institutional sanctions for substance use violations, a description of health risks posed by drugs and alcohol, and a listing of available treatment options.

The DFSCA mandates that schools must make written drug and alcohol policy available to students on an annual basis, but it did not establish standards for concrete content of these policies. In turn, the contents of such policies vary significantly from institution to institution. In most colleges, alcohol and gambling policies are usually listed both on college websites and in students' handbooks, which are distributed to all incoming freshmen. Generally, those policies include the following aspects:

1. Underage drinking is strictly prohibited.
2. There are rules about where on-campus students can drink and how much alcohol is available.

3. Students with alcohol-related problems are mandated to enter recovery programs.
4. Problematic drinkers can be forced to withdraw from college.
5. College students and employees who commit other acts prohibited by college policy are subject to disciplinary action, up to and including termination of employment or expulsion.
6. College students and employees who commit crimes may be reported to law enforcement authorities.

The ultimate goal of college administrators is to provide a safe atmosphere for students. College punitive policies on alcohol use and other behaviors help control the level of binge drinking and related violence. The punitive reaction to college is also consistent with the American faith in the power of the law to correct bad behaviors. Through the practice of "boundary maintenance" via restrictive and punitive policies, colleges hope to promote a higher degree of conformity among students, while publicizing those behaviors that will not be tolerated. The idea is to deter students from involvement in dangerous behavior. Most campuses have also instituted punitive responses to sexual assault and harassment, with the intent of deterring incidents. Legislation such as the Federal Crime Awareness and Campus Security Act requires colleges and universities to develop appropriate sanctions for students who have committed sexual offenses.

Current college administrators have also noticed the limitations inherent in punitive policies, and many are working on implementing prevention-oriented programs to complement the punishment-oriented policies. Multiple stakeholders, including students, faculty, parents, and counselors, should be recruited to work together for preventing violence. Many campuses have turned to harm reduction campaigns in addition to punitive responses. These campaigns aim to educate students on the prevalence of socially injurious behavior, and to inform them of ways to reduce the impact of this behavior, such as the use of designated drivers. Nevertheless, some types of offenses, such as cyber-related bullying, harassment, and stalking, are less likely to be punished, because not all colleges and universities have kept pace in addressing the threat posed by new technologies.

Hui Huang

Further Reading

Fisher, B., & Sloan, J. (2007, Eds.). *Campus crime: Legal, social, and policy perspectives* (2nd ed.) Springfield, IL: Charles C. Thomas.

Fronius, T., & Kyung-Shick, C. (2009). *Analytical assessment on cybercrime deterrence among college students.* Paper presented at the annual meeting of the American Society of Criminology.

Potter, R., Krider, J., & McMahon, P. (2000). Examining elements of campus sexual violence policies: Is deterrence or health promotion favored? *Violence Against Women, 6*(12), 1245–1362.

Shaffer, H., Donato, A., LaBrie, R., Kidman, R., & LaPlante, D. (2005, February 9). The epidemiology of college alcohol and gambling policies. *Harm Reduction Journal, 2*(1), 1–20.

U.S. Department of Education. (n.d.). Drug-Free Schools and Communities Act (DFSCA) and drug and alcohol abuse prevention regulation. Retrieved December 11, 2010, from http://www.higheredcenter.org/mandates/dfsca

Purdy, Patrick

Patrick Purdy had a history of arrests, mental illness, and alcohol-related problems—but no one could have predicted that he would massacre schoolchildren in the small farm city of Stockton in northern California. On January 17, 1989, Purdy, age 24, fired 106 rounds of ammunition from an AK-47 assault rifle equipped with a 75-round ammunition drum. He sprayed these bullets at Cleveland Elementary School, killing five students, and wounding 29 others plus one teacher, in less than two minutes. The children who died from Purdy's attack were all Southeast Asian refugees. Three girls—Ram Chun, age 8; Sokhim An, age 6; and Oeun Lim, age 8—were Cambodian, as was one boy—Rathanan Or, age 9. The other girl who died, Thuy Tran, age 6, was from Vietnam. At the time of the shooting, the neighborhood in which the school was located was 68.6% Asian.

Purdy was born November 10, 1964. His father, Patrick Benjamin Purdy, was stationed at Fort Lewis, Washington. His mother, Kathleen Toscano, filed for divorce when Purdy was three years old and moved the family to California after her husband threatened her with a weapon. Toscano then married Albert Gulart, Sr., although the marriage lasted just six years. Patrick attended Cleveland Elementary School from kindergarten through third grade.

Twice in December 1973, Child Protective Services took Purdy and his two siblings into custody after a neighbor reported neglect. As a child, Purdy was described as very quiet and lacking coping skills. Neighbors remember him as weird and violent. Joan Capalla, who lived near Purdy when he was a child, recalled the boy chasing her sons with a wooden-handled butcher knife. He developed an alcohol problem as a teenager and was kicked out of his mother's home for hitting his mother when he was 13 or 14. When he was 14 years old, Purdy lived with a foster parent, who told officers she feared him because he had knives and guns. Purdy lived on the streets for a while, attending high school only sporadically.

Between 1980 and the shooting in 1989, Purdy was arrested numerous times. His first arrest was for prostitution. He also was arrested for selling drugs, possessing illegal weapons, receiving stolen property, and being an accomplice to an armed robbery. In 1986, he vandalized his mother's car because she refused to give him money for drugs. When he was almost 22, Purdy told a mental health professional that he had destructive thoughts and was considered to have an antisocial personality. Despite his problems, he never received any long-term mental health intervention. Purdy's friends described him as a nice guy, although they said he was often frustrated and angry.

In fall of 1987, Purdy began taking welding classes at San Joaquin Delta College. He complained that there were too many Southeast Asian students there. In 1988, Purdy held a series of jobs and drifted from Oregon, to Texas, to Connecticut, to Tennessee, before returning to Stockton and renting a room at the El Rancho Motel on December 26. It was during these travels, on August 3, that Purdy purchased the AK-47 he used in the shooting, for $349.95.

On January 17, 1989, Purdy dressed himself in a camouflage shirt with the words "PLO," "Libya," and the misspelled "Death to the Great Satin" written on the front. Before leaving his hotel room, he lined up 100 green plastic soldiers and small tanks, weapons, and jeeps in his hotel room, placing them on shelves, on the refrigerator, and elsewhere. He had carved the words "Freedom," "Victory," and "Hezbollah" (a Shiite Muslim group) into his bayoneted rifle.

At approximately noon, Purdy parked his car behind Cleveland Elementary School. He set it on fire with a Molotov cocktail, then entered the school. Purdy hid behind a group of portable classrooms and shot at the students. When he ran out of ammunition, he shot and killed himself with a pistol. The California Attorney General concluded that Purdy hated minorities and blamed them for his horrible life. He selected Southeast Asians simply because he had the most contact with that group. Captain Dennis Perry of the Stockton Police Department said that Purdy was obsessed with the military.

The school opened the following day, with workmen attempting to patch the 60 bullet holes in the building and scrub the bloodstains from the floors. Only one-fourth of the school's 970 students were in attendance. The school brought in psychologists and nurses, as well as interpreters, to assist the traumatized students.

Purdy's rampage prompted legislative efforts—at both state and federal levels—to restrict the use of assault weapons. The California state legislature moved quickly to enact the nation's first ban on assault weapons. This legislation banned the sale, production, and possession of certain types of assault weapons. The Stockton incident, coupled with a deadly shooting at a San Francisco high-rise office building in 1993, also prompted the U.S. Congress to pass the Federal Assault Weapons Ban, which President Bill Clinton signed into law in 1994. This ban was part of a larger crime control bill called the Federal Violent Crime Control and Law Enforcement Act of 1994. It prohibited 19 types of semi-automatic weapons, including the AK-47, Uzi, Colt AR-15, and Street Sweeper, as well as copies or duplicates of these named weapons and ammunition clips that hold more than 10 rounds. Also banned were any weapons with two or more of a list of military features, including grenade launchers and flash suppressors.

A 1999 study by the US Department of Justice National Institute of Justice (NIJ) found that the ban did, indeed, help keep assault weapons away from criminals. According to a 2004 study commissioned by the Brady Center to Prevent Gun Violence, the assault weapons ban reduced the number of deaths from assault weapons by 66%. Despite this research showing its effectiveness, Congress and President George W. Bush allowed the ban to expire in 2004.

Laura L. Finley

Further Reading

Brady Center to Prevent Gun Violence. (2004). On target: The impact of the 1994 Federal Assault Weapon Act. Retrieved July 19, 2009, from http://www.bradycenter.org/xshare/pdf/reports/on_target.pdf

Phillips, R. (2009, January 18). Purdy recalled as bigot and "sick, sick man." Retrieved July 19, 2009, from http://www.recordnet.com/apps/pbcs.dll/article?AID=/20090118/A_NEWS/901170304 /-1/A_SPECIAL0252

Reinhold, R. (1989, January 19). After shooting, horror, but few answers. *New York Times*. Retrieved July 19, 2009, from http://www.nytimes.com/1989/01/19/us/after-shooting- horror-but-few-answers.html?pagewanted=all

Reuters. (2009, January 15). Twenty years since a nightmare: Stockton, CA shooting of 35 led to strengthening of gun laws. Retrieved July 19, 2009, from http://www.reuters.com/article/pressRelease/idUS226787+15-Jan-2009+PRN20090115

Race and School Crime and Violence

Research about victimization trends among racial or ethnic groups has often been hampered by use of different definitions, different measurements, and different samples. Native American and Asian students have rarely been included in such studies, even though the limited research on the subject suggests Native Americans are particularly vulnerable to such crime and violence. According to the U.S. Department of Education, white male high school seniors are twice as likely to bring a weapon to school as black male seniors. Among all major racial and ethnic groups, blacks are the least likely to bring weapons to school. In fact, all of the high-profile rampage school shooters in the 1990s were white males. Despite the fact that school violence had long been an issue of concern in urban districts with largely minority populations, it was not until the problem spread to suburban and rural areas that it was perceived as critical by the general public.

There is very little difference in the levels of victimization at urban, suburban, and rural schools. A recent study found that racial and ethnic groups were victimized at rates similar to their proportion in the population, but that Asian Americans and African Americans were most likely to report being bullied or harassed because of their race. Another exception was that white students were overrepresented as victims of sexual harassment.

Despite these data, the general public often believes that black, urban students are the most violent. One source of this misconception is the media. Research has repeatedly demonstrated that media sources disproportionately highlight cases in which blacks are offenders. When whites are offenders, more time is devoted to explaining why the incident may have occurred than when blacks offend. The implication is that black violence is to be expected, while white violence is unusual and must be explained. Media portrayals of violent minorities may become a self-fulfilling prophecy.

Some evidence suggests that certain educators already assume African American students to be deviant. In May 2009, parents of nine African American students filed suit in Alabama, saying their children were harassed by teachers, who called them "niggers" and "filthy trash," and were told they would not be allowed to run around the school "like a bunch of wild animals." These students had been suspended for multiple days for offenses such as not having their shirts tucked in properly, not wearing a belt or wearing the wrong kind of belt, and wearing the wrong-color undershirt. The staff at the school used corporal punishment against the students when they ran in the halls or talked in class; when their parents complained, the students received even more punishment. The parents were also banned from school and threatened with arrest for complaining. Because the school board in that district prohibits public speaking related to racial discrimination at its meetings, the parents have had trouble bringing the issue to the public's attention.

Research has shown that coverage of school violence differs tremendously when it is minority offenders who are involved. Whereas reports about the Columbine High School massacre, for instance, emphasized that Dylan Klebold and Eric Harris were from "good" families and thus their actions were difficult to explain, coverage of Jeff Weise's shooting on the Red Lake reservation in Minnesota emphasized the overall violence and poverty of the Native American–dominated region.

Although data do not support the contention that black and Hispanic students are more violent than their white counterparts, these groups do face disproportionate rates of punishment. In a nationally representative study conducted by Education Insights at Public Agenda, 19% of white students, 26% of Hispanic students, and 33% of black students reported that their schools were not consistent in applying discipline. According to U.S. Department of Education data, African American students account for 17% of all pupils enrolled in public schools, yet make up 32% of all students who receive out-of-school suspensions. White youth constitute 63% of public school enrollees, but only 50% of those suspended or expelled. In 2001, the American Bar Association (ABA) voted in favor of abolishing zero-tolerance laws in schools, based on these policies' lack of effectiveness and discriminatory application. Almost 90% of public schools in the United States have some form of zero-tolerance policy in place, and evidence shows such policies are most likely to be adopted in districts where the majority of the student body is African American and/or Latino.

On May 20, 2009, Marshawn Pitts, a 15-year-old African American special needs student, was walking down the hallway of his school in Dolton, Illinois, when a school police officer noticed that his shirt was untucked. The officer began shouting at Pitts, who immediately started to tuck in the shirt. He was not fast enough, however: The officer pushed Pitts into a locker, punched him repeatedly in the face, and then slammed him to the ground and pushed his face into the floor. While Pitts lay on the floor, the officer put him in a hold position that has been banned in eight states because it has resulted in more than 20 deaths. Pitts was left with a broken nose and a bruised jaw. Even worse, he and his classmates were left confused, scared, and angry. The entire incident was captured on school video cameras and has been uploaded on YouTube. Pitts was not carrying a weapon, nor did he in any way threaten anyone. Other high-profile cases, like that involving the 1999 Decatur Seven, in which seven African American males were expelled for fighting, and the Jena Six, in which six African American males were criminally charged for beating a white male after nooses (symbolic of lynching) were hung up at the local school, further highlight the racial divide.

One of the consequences of such racially discriminatory policies is what has been called the "school-to-prison pipeline." Between 2000 and 2004, the Denver Public School System saw a 71% increase in the number of students referred to law enforcement, with many of the referrals for nonviolent offenses. Some schools, like those in the Palm Beach County (Florida) system, have created their own police forces. When students are suspended or expelled, it also affects their acquisition of educational credentials, as these students are more likely to drop out of school altogether.

Corporal punishment in the United States disproportionately affects African American students and, in some areas, Native American students. In the 2006–2007 school year, African American students made up 17.1% of the national student population, but 35.6% of those paddled. In the same year, in the 13 states with the highest rates of paddling, 1.4 times as many African American students were paddled as might be expected given their percentage of the total student population. Although girls of all races were paddled less often than boys, African American girls were nonetheless physically punished at more than twice the rate of their white counterparts in those 13 states during this time period.

Laura L. Finley

Further Reading

ACLU lawsuit challenges racial discrimination in Alabama school district. (2008, May 22). American Civil Liberties Union. Retrieved September 23, 2008, from http://www.aclu.org/racialjustice/edu/35436prs20080522.html

Casella, R. (2001). *"Being down": Challenging violence in urban schools.* New York: Teachers College.

Fennin, P., & Rose, J. (2007). Overrepresentation of African American students in exclusionary discipline: The role of school policy. *Urban Education, 42*(6), 536–559.

Ferguson, A. (2000). *Bad boys: Public schools in the making of black masculinity.* Ann Arbor, MI: University of Michigan Press.

Fine, M., Burns, A., Payne, Y., & Torre, M. (2004) Civics lessons: The color and class of betrayal. *Teachers College Record, 106*(11), 219–223.

Giroux, H. (2009). Brutalizing kids: Painful lessons in the pedagogy of school violence. Truthout. Retrieved October 15, 2009, from www.truthout.org/10090912?print

Giroux, H. (2009). Ten years after Columbine. Counterpunch. Retrieved October 15, 2009, from www.counterpunch.org/giroux04212009.html

Giroux, H. (2009), Youth: Beyond the politics of hope. Truthout. Retrieved October 15, 2009, from www.truthout.org/1013092?print

Hyman, I., & Snook, P. (1999). *Dangerous schools.* San Francisco, CA: Jossey-Bass.

Hirschfield, P. (2008). Preparing for prison? The criminalization of school discipline in the USA. *Theoretical Criminology, 12*(79), 79–101.

Kupchik, A., & Ellis, N. (2008). School discipline and security: Fair for all students? *Youth & Society, 39*(4), 549–574.

Leavy, P., & Maloney, K. (2009). American reporting of school violence and "people like us": A comparison of newspaper coverage of the Columbine and Red Lake school shootings. *Critical Sociology, 35,* 273–292.

Miller, J., Like, T., & Levin, P. (2002). The Caucasian evasion: Victims, exceptions, and defenders of the faith. In C. Richey-Mann & M. Zatz (Eds.), *Images of color, images of crime* (2nd ed.), pp. 100–114). Los Angeles, CA: Roxbury.

NAACP Legal Defense and Educational Fund. (n.d.). Dismantling the school-to-prison pipeline. Retrieved September 29, 2008, from http://www.naacpldf.org/content/pdf/pipeline/Dismantling_the_School_to_Prison_Pipeline.pdf

A violent education: Corporal punishment of children in U.S. public schools. (2008). New York: Amnesty International.

Ramsey, Evan

At the age of 16, Evan Ramsey was the perpetrator of a deadly school shooting at Bethel Regional High School in the small town of Bethel, Alaska, on February 19, 1997. On that day, he killed 15-year-old Josh Palacios, a popular student, as well as the school's principal Ron Edwards, age 50. After wounding several other students, Ramsey then threatened to kill himself with the 12-gauge shotgun he had used to kill the two mortally wounded individuals, but he ultimately surrendered to the police instead.

Ramsey did not have a stable family life growing up. The son of a father in prison and an alcoholic mother who was in several abusive relationships, Evan and his two brothers were taken away from home by the Division of Family and

Youth Services. He was in third grade at the time. After that, the brothers were separated and put in different foster homes. Ramsey lived in 11 foster homes as a child, and suffered from sexual and other kinds of abuse in a few of them.

An eerie parallel has been noted between Evan and his father—Evan's father was involved in a similar incident before Evan's school shooting. When the *Anchorage Times* did not publish a political letter Don Ramsey wrote in 1986, he came to the office with an AR 180-223 semi-automatic gun. Both father and son said after their incidents that they had been ready to die. Don also surrendered to police, and was released from prison two weeks before Evan's school shooting took place.

A psychiatrist discovered that Evan had previously tried to commit suicide as a child. By the time he was in high school, Ramsey was smoking marijuana and getting bad grades. His friends told reporters that he was often depressed and quiet, but he would talk a lot when you got to know him. However, Ramsey claimed that no one knew how he felt; they did not know the pain and rejection he had inside him. He described how, throughout most of his student life, he was teased and tormented by other students, who would hang toilet paper on him, spit on his head, and call him names. When the torment first began, Ramsey would tell his teachers and the principal; when the bullying persisted, the principal simply told him to ignore it. Ramsey, however, said he could no longer take the abuse.

Although Ramsey blamed his actions on a number of sources, including the bullying he received, his parents and teachers, and the foster care system, he also said there were certain people he just wanted to kill, comparing his hatred of them to Hitler's hatred of Jews. A 17-year-old witness noted that Ramsey looked like he was enjoying the shooting during the event. In an interview, Ramsey claimed that after the shooting, he felt good and believed that he let go of his pain and hate through his violent actions; he felt like he had worked out his problems. Friends and teachers of Ramsey portrayed him as having uncontrolled anger, noting that he had previously thrown garbage cans, pushed people, and punched a hole in the wall of one of his foster homes.

One factor thought to have contributed to the attack was the video game *Doom*, which was also believed to have played a role in the Columbine massacre and other school shootings. Ramsey and his friends James Randall and Matthew Charles would play *Doom* together for hours after school. In *Doom*, players shoot and kill each other.

His friends Randall and Charles, both age 14 at the time, encouraged Ramsey in his plans to attack the school, and one helped him learn to use the gun. Randall and Charles even told other students of what Ramsey was planning, though no one shared this information with authorities who could have prevented the attack. Instead, Ramsey said students encouraged him to go forward with his plans, even giving him suggestions about which students to target and taking pictures to remember the event. This pattern is not out of the ordinary; according to a study by the Department of Education and the Secret Service, when people know of a possible school shooter, only 4% tell anyone, and 81% of school shooters do tell other people about their intentions.

On the day of the shooting, Ramsey hid the shotgun he had taken from his foster home in his loose pants when he went to school. The details in reported in various sources are inconsistent, but Ramsey claims that many news sources portrayed the shooting in a way different from what really happened. Many sources claimed that Ramsey went after Palacios and shot him, and that he then tracked down the principal at his administrative office and killed him there. Other sources and Ramsey himself say that both people died in a common area in the school, and that he had not picked Palacios specifically as a target. It is unclear whether Ramsey intended to kill the principal.

A number of students came to watch the shooting from an area above the common area, as they knew something bad was going to happen, although it is unclear if they knew exactly what. Ramsey had told these students he was going to have an "evil day," and he told those whom he liked to stay away from the common area that day. Police said part of the rationale for the shooting was for Ramsey to get back his CD player, which the principal had taken away. Ramsey told his friends he would get the device, and then would start shooting.

It was reported that before he started shooting, Ramsey angrily asked everyone in the common area why they would not just leave him alone. Palacios intended to try to stop Ramsey by getting up and talking to him, which incited Ramsey to shoot him. When the principal then came up behind him to see what was going on, Ramsey turned around and shot him. His wife was nearby and cradled him as he died. Ramsey then ran yelling that he did not want to die.

More than 10 years later in an interview, Ramsey said that he had intended only to kill himself; he stated that he wanted to torture his tormentors—by dying in front of them—but not kill them. However, he claimed that his friends convinced him that he might as well kill others if he was going to kill himself. Ramsey also claimed that he did not realize shooting someone would kill the person at the time. He had thought the situation would be like a video game, in that the person would be alive and get back up, instead of dying. He also said later that at the time he did not think of the consequences of his actions, but only of fixing his problem in the present moment.

Now years after the attack, Ramsey has said he regrets his actions on that fateful day. He feels that prison life is worse than his battles when he was dealing with bullies as a teenager. He even wishes that one of his friends who knew about his plan had turned him in, so that the crime would not have happened. Ramsey has stated that he over-reacted about the bullying. Many people now sympathize with Ramsey because he was only a teenager at the time of his crime, but will spend the rest of his life in prison for something he regrets.

In 1998, Ramsey was tried as an adult and charged with two counts of first-degree murder, one count of attempted murder, and 15 counts of assault. On December 2, 1998, he was sentenced to 210 years in prison. James Randall and Matthew Charles were tried as juveniles as both provided support for Ramsey. Both have been released from prison.

Ramsey has received hundreds of letters from other teens who felt the same way he had felt before the shooting. The letters describe teens who were picked on, who felt they had nowhere to turn, and who had no one listening to them. Ramsey told many people that he planned to kill himself, but no one helped or reported his threats. Now he wants to help others avoid his mistakes.

Sharon Thiel

Further Reading

Avila, J., Holding, R., Whitcraft, T., & Tribolet, B. (2008). School shooter: "I didn't realize" they would die. Retrieved December 17, 2008, from www.Abcnews.go.com

Coloroso, B. (2004). *The bully, the bullied, and the bystander.* New York: HarperCollins.

Flowers, R., & Flowers, H. (2004). *Murders in the United States.* Jefferson, North Carolina: McFarland.

Lieberman, J., & Sachs, B. (2008). *School shootings.* New York: Kensington.

Magestro, S. (n.d.). The warning signs: Evan Ramsey—Bethel, Alaska. Retrieved from http://www.susanmagestro.com/SchoolShootings.html

Religion and High School Crime and Violence

The role of religion in high school crime and violence has taken many forms. In some cases, it has been used as inspiration for heinous acts of physical violence and contentious episodes of verbal intolerance. In other instances, religion has functioned as a means of lessening the threat of crime and violence on high school campuses around the country and around world.

Historically speaking, religiously motivated crime and violence at the high school level is by no means a 20th-century or 21st-century phenomenon. Within the American context, Protestants and Catholics, in times past, have clashed over issues of curriculum, often resulting in periods of religious bigotry or even brute violence that enveloped not only a particular school, but in some cases the entire surrounding community.

In today's world, incidents of religiously motivated crime and violence seem few and far between. According to most experts, the vast majority of the current crime and violence at the high school level is attributed to gang activity, hazing,

Confrontation resulting from religious intolerance is often provoked by an outward expression of someone's faith. Muslim women are often targeted because they wear a hijab as part of their faith. (iStockPhoto)

bullying, or simply peer pressure. While acts of high school crime and violence are rarely influenced by religion—at least directly—there have been some incidents in recent history that have had distinctly religious underpinnings.

On April 20, 1999, two high school seniors named Eric Harris and Dylan Klebold walked into the cafeteria of their school in Littleton, Colorado, and opened fire, killing 12 people and injuring 21. What became known as the Columbine massacre forever altered the United States' understanding of school violence. In the aftermath of the killings, law enforcement attempted to reconstruct the ideology of the perpetrators. The official report revealed that on the list of people whom Klebold and Harris disliked—which included working women, homosexuals, racial minorities, and athletes—were Christians. This religious hatred manifested itself during the carnage when, it was reported, Klebold executed self-proclaimed Christians as they professed their faith.

The Columbine shootings are a rare and extreme example of religiously motivated violence at the high school level. Most forms of crime and violence that involve religion are often more verbal than physical. In the increasingly pluralistic societies of the United States and Europe, high schools, and their European equivalents, have become the locations for numerous acts of religious intolerance. While students of many faiths encounter intolerance on a daily basis, Muslim students—especially females—have experienced the brunt of these attacks. More often than not, these moments of confrontation center on the outward expression of many women's Muslim identity, the wearing of the headscarf known as the *hijab*. In countries such as France, the United Kingdom, and post–September 11 America, there have been numerous incidents in which students have chastised a fellow female student for wearing the hijab to classes. There have also been other, more controversial episodes where teachers and school administers have required female Muslim students to remove the hijab before entering the classroom or school facility.

Whether physical or verbal, high school crime and violence has the attracted the attention of many members of America's religious communities. Not only have Muslim American organizations worked hard to fight post–September 11 discrimination, but other groups, including a number of evangelical Christian organizations, have reacted to school crime and violence by petitioning for the reinstatement of school prayer. For many of these evangelicals, the increase in high school crime and violence is directly related to the U.S. Supreme Court's decision to disallow sanctioned prayer in the public school system—one aspect of what they see as a general "removal of God" from the classroom.

Although often overlooked in favor of more quantifiable categories, religion, as either a motivating or reactionary force, has and will continue to inform our conversations on crime and violence at the high school level.

Jonathan William Olson

Further Reading

Benn, T., & Jawad, H. (Eds.). (2003). *Muslim women in the United Kingdom and beyond*. Boston, MA: Brill.

Fraser, J. (1999). *Between church and state: Religion and public education in a multicultural America*. New York: St. Martin.

Juergensmeyer, M. (2000). *Terror in the mind of God: The global rise of religious violence*. Berkeley, CA: University of California Press.

Larkin, R. (2007). *Comprehending Columbine*. Philadelphia, PA: Temple University Press.

Odell-Scott, D. (2004). *Democracy and religion: Free exercise and diverse visions*. Kent, OH: Kent State University Press.

Resolving Conflict Creatively Program (RCCP)

The Resolving Conflict Creatively Program (RCCP) began in 1985 as a collaborative program between the New York Public Schools and the New York City Chapter of the Educators for Social Responsibility. The professionals affiliated with RCCP believe that violence is one of the chief social ills affecting children and their ability to learn. RCCP has two stated goals: to teach children ethical and moral values that emphasize respect for others; and to provide students with the emotional and social skills necessary to handle potentially disruptive situations. Key components of RCCP's approach include the following measures:

- *Conflict Resolution Curriculum:* The RCCP curriculum for elementary schools is built around 51 lessons or workshops. Each workshop includes a warm-up exercise, review of the agenda for the specific lesson, activities, student evaluation of the session, and closing activity. The secondary school curriculum covers material similar to that provided in the elementary school curriculum but with an additional focus on ways of de-escalating volatile situations that might lead to violent confrontations. RCCP lessons include role playing, group dialogue, and brainstorming. The curriculum address root causes of violence by establishing "multicultural classrooms."

- *Peer Mediation:* RCCP seeks to reduce violent incidents in schools through a model of peer mediation. Student mediators facilitate a meeting between those involved in a particular conflict and help both disputants find a mutually satisfactory solution. A good resolution gives both disputants the responsibility for finding a solution.

- *Professional and Parent Training:* RCCP uses both formal training sessions and one-on-one work to teach regular classroom teachers how to present the conflict-resolution curriculum. RCCP instructors provide 20 hours of introductory training in a series of after-school sessions. The training presents the RCCP philosophy and the curriculum; teaches communication, conflict resolution, and intergroup relations skills; and demonstrates "infusion" strategies for integrating these concepts and skills into social studies, language arts, and other academic subjects.

A key to RCCP's success is the follow-up support that teachers receive. Each new teacher is assigned to an RCCP staff developer, who visits between six and 10 times a year, giving demonstration lessons, helping the teacher prepare, observing classes, giving feedback, and sustaining the teacher's motivation. In addition, the staff developer convenes bimonthly follow-up meetings after school so that the teachers can receive additional training, share their experiences, discuss concerns, and plan school-wide events. During a teacher's second year, the staff developer visits only two or three times.

RCCP staff recently launched a Parent Involvement Program, which they piloted and are slowly expanding in Community School District 15 in Brooklyn, where RCCP began. Under this program, a team of two or three parents per school is trained for 60 hours to lead workshops for other parents on intergroup relations, family communication, and conflict resolution.

Wendell Johnson

Further Reading

DeJong, W. (1994). *Building the peace: The resolving conflict creatively program.* Washington, DC: U.S. Department of Justice, National Institute of Justice.

Lantieri, L., DeJong, W., & Dutrey, J. (1996). Waging peace in our schools: The Resolving Conflict Creatively Program. In A. Hoffman (Ed.), *Schools, violence, and society.* Westport, CT: Praeger.

Restorative Justice

Restorative justice, while a relatively recent, and still somewhat marginal, component of modern criminal justice systems, has long been part of efforts to respond to and prevent crime within a variety of local communities. Approaches in criminology, such as restorative justice and peace-making criminology, express the value of collective efficacy or "social capital," in which strong community networks of social support and informal social control contribute to reducing occurrences of crime. Restorative justice emphasizes effective practices for dealing with crime, based on consensual, interactive, and participatory approaches; this perspective stands in contrast to the more familiar adversarial models of justice, based on retribution and punishment, that make up the overwhelming part of criminal justice system practice.

Proponents of restorative justice note that punishment-centered models of crime control are both ineffective and costly, both in human and resource terms. Prisons are wildly expensive systems for containing and managing people who have been targeted for criminalization. Even more disturbingly, incarceration has long been shown to offer few positive or constructive outcomes for those who are so punished. Advocates of restorative justice note that harsh prison sentences, at most, provide victims of crime with a sense of revenge or vindication. Punishment models do little to assist or support victims who may have been multiply impacted by a criminal event or events. Put simply, systems oriented primarily toward punishing offenders offer little to those who have been victimized by crime.

Restorative justice is concerned with rebuilding relationships after an offense, rather than driving a wedge between offenders and the community, such as occurs within criminal justice systems in capitalist liberal democracies. Restorative justice allows victims, offenders, and the community to address the harms done by crime, so that the community, rather than being further torn apart and pitted against itself, can be repaired. Rather than imposing decisions about winners and losers in an adversarial system, restorative justice seeks to facilitate dialogue among those affected by an incident. All parties with a stake in the offense come together to deal collectively with it.

Restorative justice acts on a range of general principles. First is the view that both victim and the community have been harmed by an offender's actions, and this damage causes a disequilibrium that must be addressed to restore relations, lest more social harm be done. Counter to traditional criminal justice system approaches, offenders as well as victims and the community are seen as having a stake in a successful outcome of this process. Second, those who have offended have some obligation to address the harm they have caused. Third, restorative justice emphasizes the healing of both victim and offender. Victims need information, understanding, safety, and social support. Unlike in the standard criminal justice system, offenders' needs are also addressed, including social security, health care, possibly treatment for addictions, and counseling.

Whereas conventional criminal justice focuses on the offense to the state by individuals and does little to deal with the consequences to the community and its members, restorative justice emphasizes rebuilding community trust and "social capital" as means to defend against future conflicts and offenses. As Brennan (2003, p. 2008) suggests, "Restorative justice builds on social capital because it decentralizes the offense from merely the act of an offender breaking the law, to a breach in a community's trust in its members. This in turn allows the community along with the offender and victim to *collectively* look for a resolution."

One particular approach to restorative justice is drawn from the practice of indigenous sentencing circles. Within these healing circles, a broad range of community members are involved in the justice process to reintegrate offenders into the community, rather than pursuing the segregation model of the penal approach. Unlike adversarial processes as are practiced within the court system, sentencing circles seek solutions to the original conflict and possible underlying causes while working cooperatively to repair relationships harmed by the criminal act. Sentencing circles have been adopted within the criminal justice system in Canada as one option available to members of indigenous communities.

Peace-making criminology argues that the idea of making war on crime needs to be replaced with the idea of making peace on crime. Bracewell identifies the motivating themes of peace-making criminology as follows: "(1) connectedness to each other and to our environment and the need for reconciliation; (2) caring for each other in a nurturing way as a primary objective in corrections; and (3) mindfulness, meaning the cultivation of inner peace" (Lanier & Henry, 2004, p. 330). This approach emphasizes the responsibilities that members of society have as active participants in maintaining and restoring positive social relations. Like other versions of restorative justice, it calls upon community members to address issues of crime and community health and safety directly through their own involvement rather than deferring to the power of instituted authorities.

Restorative justice is no utopian wish. In fact, there have been attempts to employ this approach within several jurisdictions as a means to deal with even extremely violent crimes. Research suggests that restorative justice shows clear effectiveness, in terms of both offender accountability and victim healing.

Instead of escalating the violence in an already violent society by responding to violence and conflict with state-sanctioned violence and conflict, through police and penal actions, society needs to de-escalate violence. With this approach, practices of conciliation, mediation, and dispute settlement become preferable options. Peace-making criminologists, including anarchist-influenced Hal Pepinsky, argue that reducing violence requires people's direct involvement in democratic practices. By this, Pepinsky means "a genuine participation by all in life decisions that is only achievable in a decentralized, nonhierarchical social structure."

Providing community support for offenders benefits all in the community and injects fairness into the practice of justice. Restorative justice offers the prospect of escaping the "zero-sum game" of the traditional criminal justice system, whereby what is said to benefit victims must necessarily hurt offenders. In restorative justice, victim, community, and offender all stand to gain in their own ways.

Jeffrey Shantz

Further Reading

Brennan, L. (2003). *Restoring the justice in criminal justice*. Detroit: Wayne State University, Department of Interdisciplinary Studies.

Lanier, M., & Henry, S. (2004). *Essential criminology*. Boulder, CO: Westview Press

O'Grady, W. (2007). *Crime in Canadian context: Debates and controversies*. Don Mills: Oxford University Press.

Parker, L. (2009, May 22). Schools. Retrieved May 5, 2010, from http://www.restorativejustice.org/programme-place/02practiceissues/schools-1

Restorative justice in school. (2007). Retrieved May 5, 2010, from http://www.transformingconflict.org/Restorative_Justice_in_School.htm

Umbreit, M., Coates, R., Vos, B., & Brown, K. (2002). *Victim offender dialogue in crimes of severe violence: A multi-site study of programs in Texas and Ohio*. Minneapolis: Center for Restorative Justice, University of Minnesota.

Roberts, Charles

On October 2, 2006, Charles Carl Roberts IV killed five Amish girls and himself in an Amish school in Lancaster County, Pennsylvania. Roberts was not Amish, although he lived near the Amish community in Lancaster. As part of his job, the 32-year-old milk truck driver would come to Amish farms to pick up milk. A father of three, Roberts tied up the girls in the schoolhouse, allegedly with the intention of sexually molesting them. Instead, he killed them and himself when the presence of the police led him to change his original plan. Eleven out of the

Charles Roberts likely chose to attack an Amish school near his home in 2006 not because of religious prejudice, but rather because of the lack of building security at the school. (Richard Gunion/Dreamstime.com)

26 students at school that day were girls, students aged 6 to 13. Three girls died at the school, and two died later at the hospital. Fatally shot in the head were Marian Fisher, age 13; Anna Mae Stoltzfus, age 12; Mary Liz Miller, age 8; her sister Lena Miller, age 7; and Naomi Rose Ebersole, age 7. Six other girls were in critical condition, some with gunshots in their heads, although none of them died.

The Lancaster County incident was the third fatal school shooting in a week within the United States. The two previous shootings had taken place in high schools: one in Bailey, Colorado, by a 53-year-old man, and one in Cazenovia, Wisconsin, by a student. Many felt Roberts' shooting mimicked the incident in Bailey, as that shooter also was older and not a student, took the students hostage, and kept only the girls in the classroom, allowing the boys to leave. Also, these incidents are the only two school shootings where a sexual intention was involved. However, Roberts bought his supplies before the Colorado shooting took place, and police felt he was only thinking of himself and his internal struggle, so it is unclear if he was really copying the earlier shooting.

Many considered the shooting to be the outcome of an ongoing struggle within Roberts relating to events in his past. During the attack on the school, he talked to his wife Marie over the phone and told her he had sexually abused children related to him 20 years earlier, when he was 12, and stated that he had been thinking about molesting children again. The children involved in the earlier crimes were between the ages of 3 and 5.

According to one of the suicide notes he left for his family, Roberts also seemed intent on carrying out revenge toward God for letting his baby, Elise, die. Roberts and his wife lost their daughter 20 minutes after she was born early in 1997, nine years before the shooting. In the suicide notes, Roberts described how he never really got over Elise's death. He wrote about how frequently he would be sharing happy moments with his family, but then would think about how Elise was not there to share the joy with them and would become angry. Roberts stated that he hated both God and himself, and felt empty.

In the weeks leading up the shooting, his wife did not think Roberts was acting in an unusual manner. His coworkers, however, indicated that Roberts was acting differently the week before the shooting, and that his mood had changed. Despite this, neither the coworkers nor his wife suspected that Roberts had any violent plans. He had no previous criminal record, and he was described by family and neighbors as a nice man. Everyone who knew him thought he was a peaceful man, but they did not know he had secret sexual fantasies related to children. Marie said he was a very good husband and father to their three children, and she had never known about the molestation of his relatives until Roberts told her during the attack.

The Amish community also never expected any incidence of school violence. Because of the peaceful lifestyle of the Amish and the rural nature of the area they live in, they were not prepared for an attack of this nature. They had no security to prevent it, and no one would have even envisioned such a possibility.

The Lancaster County event was not a spur-of-the-moment crime; Roberts thoroughly planned the attack before he carried it out. He had a checklist of the supplies he brought into the school, all of which were checked off. Also, investigators say he bought the items six days before he went to the school.

Although many speculated the attack was a revenge killing, especially because of Roberts' suicide notes, police investigators believed it was a sex crime ending in suicide. Roberts had been watching the school after his shifts at work, and he likely picked an Amish school as a target because he knew it would not have good security. Rather than targeting the Amish community, Roberts likely focused on the presence of young girls—and the Amish school was an easy and nearby mark in that regard. Police believe he began shooting because he panicked when police surrounded the building.

Roberts brought three firearms with him that day—a rifle, a shotgun, and a semi-automatic pistol. He also had knives, an abundance of ammunition, a stun gun, and a bag of tools, suggesting that he was planning to hold the girls for a long time and that he may have intended to sexually assault the girls. Among the items he brought were KY Jelly lubricant and restraints, including a large board with eyebolts spaced apart, seemingly to bind girls to it.

Before the attack, Roberts went to work until about 3 A.M. He took his children to their bus stop, and then went to the Amish school. He closed himself in the school, blocking the doors with pieces of wood he brought with him. No detail was ignored. When he had all of the students in the school together in one classroom, Roberts let all the boys leave and bound the girls' feet. He also let a pregnant teacher leave, along with three other adult women who had infants with them. According to a sociologist, Amish parents are usually the teachers in the schools.

Roberts went into the school at about 10:00 A.M. Two adults who were told to leave the school called 911 at 10:36 A.M. from a nearby farmhouse. Police got to the site at 10:45 A.M. and surrounded the school. At some point during his time at the school, Roberts spoke to his wife on the phone; Marie had found the suicide notes when she came home after attending a morning prayer group. Roberts then called the police, who had surrounded the building, and told them that if they did not leave he would shoot people within 10 seconds. True to his word, he started shooting soon thereafter.

Roberts' wife was shocked by what he did, claiming he was a wonderful husband and father and stating that the incident was unlike him. In a statement, she told the public to pray for the families who lost their children in the attack as well as to pray for her own family.

After the attack, the Amish community reacted much differently than mainstream America has responded to other school shootings. Instead of implementing new laws and stricter preventive measures, the Amish community has been practicing forgiveness.

Eleven days after Roberts attacked the school, the Amish community tore the building down. The Amish community decided to start fresh with the school, just as they had with their lives.

Sharon Thiel

Further Reading

Amish forgive, pray and mourn after shooting. (2006). *CBS*. Retrieved December 14, 2008, from http://cbs13.com
Fifth girl dies after Amish school shooting. (2006). *CNN*. Retrieved December 17, 2008, from http://cnn.usnews.com.
Lieberman, J., & Sachs, B. (2008). *School shootings*. New York: Kensington.
Police: School killer told wife he molested family members. (2006). *CNN*. Retrieved December 17, 2008 from http://cnn.usnews.com.
Turvey, B., & Petherick, W. (2008). *Forensic victimology*. Maryland Heights, MO: Academic Press.

Rural School Violence

Crime and violence in rural schools and communities are widespread, yet occur in relatively minimal amounts in comparison to crime and violence in urban areas. Mistaken beliefs about "crime-free" rural communities and an underdeveloped rural criminology research base pose significant challenges to ensuring school safety in rural locales. Crime and violence rates among young people are highest in rural communities with higher levels of ethnic diversity, female-headed households, and residential mobility. Community size is also positively associated with rural juvenile crime, whereas community poverty level is not a significant predictor of school crime and violence in rural places.

Data from the School Survey on Crime and Safety (SSOCS) show that nearly seven in 10 (69.5%) rural schools reported a violent incident without a weapon during the 2007–2008 school year and 14.4% experienced at least one violent incident with a weapon in that year; almost half (47.1%) of rural schools had at least one theft. Actual violent crimes in rural schools are slightly more common than threats of violent crimes. SSOCS data indicate that more than 8% of rural schools had at least one student threat of physical attack with a weapon in 2007–2008; 42.8% reported a threat of attack with a weapon in that same span.

Several types of nonviolent offenses occur routinely in rural schools. For example, bullying occurs at least weekly in 21.7% of rural schools. Daily or weekly incidents of student racial or ethnic tensions occur in 3.4% of rural schools, sexual harassment occurs daily or weekly in 2.4% of rural schools, and classroom disorder occurs regularly in 2.2% of rural schools. Vandalism occurs at least once per school year in 38.6% of rural schools.

Three percent of rural schools reported a hate crime during the 2007–2008 academic year, and 2.7% reported at least one gang-related incident. Relatively few rural schools have ever experienced extremist activity (2%).

Rural youth use and abuse illegal substances—including drugs, alcohol, and tobacco products—more often and at younger ages than their urban and suburban peers. More than one-fifth (21.2%) of rural schools had at least one incident of distribution, possession, or use of illegal drugs during the 2007–2008 academic year; 13.9% reported at least one incident of alcohol distribution, use, or possession.

Nonverbal disrespect toward a teacher occurs at least once a week in 5.4% of rural schools, while verbal abuse of a teacher occurs daily or weekly in 3% of rural schools. Teachers have been threatened with injury in 6% of rural schools, while physical attacks against teachers have occurred in 3% of rural schools. Thirty-one percent of rural teachers say that student misbehavior interferes with their teaching.

Rural schools employ a variety of violence prevention strategies, including personal counseling (in 89.2% of schools), individual mentoring (85.7%), behavioral modification (84.6%), violence prevention curricula (83%), recreational enrichment activities (80)%, community-building activities (70.3%), and violence prevention hotlines (23%). More than half of rural schools have written crisis response strategies for bomb threats (89.8%), school shootings (80.3%), hostage situations (68.7%), and suicide threats (71.3%). Acts of violence in rural schools are most often punished by out-of-school suspensions, which occur in 43.5% of cases, and very rarely by expulsion without alternative services, which occurs in 6.7% of cases.

Christopher J. Stapel

Further Reading

Dinkes, R., Kemp, J., & Baum, K. (2009). *Indicators of school crime and safety: 2009* (NCES 2010–012/NCJ 228478). Washington, DC: National Center for Education Statistics, Institute of Education Sciences, U.S. Department of Education, & Bureau of Justice Statistics, Office of Justice Programs, U.S. Department of Justice.

Neiman, S., & DeVoe, J.F. (2009). *Crime, violence, discipline, and safety in U.S. public schools: Findings from the School Survey on Crime and Safety: 2007–08* (NCES 2009–326). Washington, DC: National Center for Education Statistics, Institute of Education Sciences, U.S. Department of Education.

Osgood, D. W., & Chambers, J. M. (2003). *Community correlates of rural youth violence. Juvenile Justice Bulletin.* Washington, DC: U.S. Department of Labor.

Van Gundy, K. (2006). *Reports on rural America: Substance abuse in rural and small town America.* Durham, NH: University of New Hampshire, Carsey Institute.

S

Saari, Matti

On September 23, 2008, 22-year-old culinary arts student Matti Saari stormed into Seinajoki University of Applied Sciences in Kauhajoki, Finland, at approximately 10:50 A.M., armed with a Walther .22 pistol and several bombs and wearing a ski mask. He shot and killed 10 people—nine students and his teacher. Three people escaped the classroom. Before committing suicide, Saari called a friend and said he had just murdered 10 people and that, after he died, he wanted to be cremated. He died at Tampere University Hospital several hours later.

The shooting took place during an exam Saari was to be taking. After he shot his friends and teacher, Saari set them on fire. All of the bodies except one were burned beyond recognition. Survivors said that Saari methodically killed the students one by one and appeared to be enjoying it, having a big smile on his face.

A friend who was with the young man the night before said he seemed normal and that the two discussed the exam. Saari did mention that he had been interviewed by police about a YouTube video he had posted of himself firing a gun. Others described Saari as an outsider who was not very social. He spent hours surfing the web and was obsessed with guns. He had also been seeing a psychologist. A friend said that Saari told him that he thought the Virginia Tech massacre and perpetrator Seung-Hui Cho were great. Saari had idolized his brother, who died of a heart attack in 2003. This loss seemed to have triggered the worst in him.

The same friend whom Saari called right after the massacre said he had been talking about killing people for approximately 18 months, but that he assumed Saari was kidding. Investigator Jari Neulaniemi said police had found a message at home saying Saari intended to kill as many people as possible. Police suspected that Saari had been in contact with Pekka-Eric Auvinen, the 18-year-old who shot eight people at Jokela High School in Tuusula, Finland, the previous year. This relationship was later confirmed. The two had played war games together online and plotted their attacks. They were on the same team in an Internet war game called *Battlefield 2,* in which they detonated bombs, shot people, and used headsets to communicate. They even bought their guns at the same weapons store, called Tera-asekeks, a few hundred yards from the school where Auvinen killed eight people and himself in November 2007. Auvinen had also posted a YouTube video about his plans, and both he and Saari has frequently expressed their hatred for humanity.

Subsequent reports revealed that Saari had been kicked out of the army in 2006, after only one month in the service. He scared his superiors and his peers by firing his weapon without orders. Fellow recruits who worked with him described Saari as weird and quiet, and said he had been teased and bullied.

After the massacres, one school was evacuated and others feared copycat shootings. Residents of Kauhajoki were terrified. In response to Auvinen's and Saari's massacres, Finish Prime Minister Matti Vanhanen said he was considering whether tougher gun laws were needed.

Laura L. Finley

Further Reading

Allen, N. (2008, September 26). Finland school shooting: Gunman Matti Saari made phone call during slaughter. *Telegraph.* Retrieved May 6, 2010, from http://www.telegraph.co.uk/news/worldnews/europe/finland/3083996/Finland-school-shooting-Gunman-Matti-Saari-made-phone-call-during-slaughter.html

Anglesey, S. (2008, September 23). "YouTube killer" shoots ten dead in spree at Finnish school. *The Mirror.* Retrieved May 6, 2010, from http://www.mirror.co.uk/news/latest/2008/09/23/youtube-killer-shoots-10-dead-in-spree-at-finnish-school-115875-20749489/

Pettifor, T. (2008, September 25). Finland school gunman Matti Saari shot friends then set them on fire. *The Mirror.* Retrieved May 6, 2010, from http://www.mirror.co.uk/news/top-stories/2008/09/25/finland-school-gunman-matti-saari-shot-friends-then-set-them-on-fire-115875-20751552/

Safe and Drug-Free Schools and Communities Act

The Safe and Drug-Free Schools and Communities Act of 1994 (SDFSCA) is federal legislation designed to help school districts create safe, disciplined, drug-free learning environments. In 1989, President George H. W. Bush and the governors of all 50 states recognized the need for safe schools and set goals to help the United States achieve this in the coming years. When President William J. Clinton took over the White House in 1993, he continued to work on these goals. His administration created goals aimed at achieving schools that were free of the presence of weapons and drugs. The Clinton administration recognized that teachers cannot teach and students cannot learn to their full potential in an unsafe and undisciplined school environment.

Education reform was a key focus during the Clinton administration, as U.S. leaders understood that successful education of citizens is necessary for the country to compete in a global marketplace. Students need to be proficient in subjects such as mathematics and science; for this to happen, however, a safe learning environment for students to study in is required. Students need to be able to come to school without fear. If they worry about the presence of weapons and drugs everyday, or get involved in the use of drugs or weapons, students will not be able to focus properly on their studies. The U.S. Department of Education has worked closely with state educational agencies (SEAs) and local educational agencies (LEAs) to create safer school environments. President Clinton's signing of the SDFSCA bill in 1994 represented a huge step toward achieving these goals.

The SDFSCA provides financial assistance to 97% of all school districts in the United States, delivering funds used for more than 40 million students. These funds are a huge source of support for drug and violence prevention in schools. The SDFSCA also distributes funds to states depending on the state's school-aged population and relative share of Title I funds. Governors spread out these funds for numerous causes. Much of the additional funds are used for preschoolers, school dropouts, juveniles, and teenage parents. The governor of each state must also use a portion of the funds to work with law enforcement agencies. For example, schools often bring in law enforcement officials to educate students on drugs and weapons.

Furthermore, SEAs must distribute their SDFSCA funds to LEAs based on rates of alcohol and drug use among youths, arrests and convictions of youths, illegal gang activity, and other issues in a particular locality. The SDFSCA has specific sections on accountability, mandating that SEAs and LEAs must establish measurable goals for their drug and violence prevention programs. These agencies must also decide how they will report any progress made. When LEAs apply for SDFSCA funding from SEAs, SEAs can reject their applications or place restrictions on the use of given funds if planned activities do not follow the goals of the SDFSCA. SEAs must monitor the activities of LEAs and provide assistance when needed.

The SDFSCA authorizes additional national programs that work to create safe, disciplined, and drug-free schools. One such program is seeking to develop alternatives to expulsion. When a student is expelled for the possession of drugs or weapons, the SDFSCA wants to provide education for these students in a different way. Another program is looking into the pros and cons of establishing school uniform policies. The Department of Education, working with the Center for Handgun Control, had agreed to distribute videos that deal with the consequences of youths handling handguns. The Department of Education has also agreed to work with the Department of the Treasury to trace handguns and eliminate sources of weapons. These programs are just a few examples of many being implemented to achieve safer school environments.

Approximately a year after President Clinton signed the SDFSCA legislation into law, he made a statement announcing that significant progress has been made in schools throughout the United States. He acknowledged that the country still needs good parents and supportive communities to achieve even more, but praised his administration for its commitment to ensuring safety in schools and on the progress it has achieved thus far. Subsequent presidents have continued to support the legislation and have continued funding for the Office of Safe and Drug-Free Schools.

Arthur Holst

Further Reading

Black, S. (2004). Safe schools don't need zero tolerance. *Education Digest, 70*(2), 27–31.

Casella, R. (2003). Zero tolerance policy in schools: Rationale, consequences, and alternatives. *Teachers College Record, 105*(5), 872–893.

Modzeleski, W. (1996). Creating safe schools: Roles and challenges, a federal perspective. *Education and Urban Society, 28*(4), 12–23.

Stader, D. (2006). Zero tolerance: Safe schools or zero sense? *Journal of Forensic Psychology Practice, 6*(2), 65–75.

Safe Schools/GLSEN

At the forefront of the safe schools movement is GLSEN (Gay, Lesbian and Straight Education Network), a national organization founded in 1995 by a former teacher, Kevin Jennings, who served as the group's executive director for its first 13 years. The mission of GLSEN is to ensure safe schools (K–12) for all students by ending harassment and bullying directed at those who are gay, lesbian, bisexual, or transgendered (GLBT). In addition to providing educational resources, the organization sponsors a number of annual national events, conducts or sponsors research on the extent of school bullying and harassment, helps establish or register gay/straight alliances (student clubs), and assists in the passage of Safe Schools laws.

The four annual "Days of Action" coordinated by GLSEN are the Day of Silence, Ally Week, TransACTION, and Martin Luther King Organizing Weekend. The Day of Silence is an empowering exercise for middle and high school students that asks them to be silent by choice—that is, to raise their voice against homophobia by refusing to speak. Ally Week asks students to take a stand against bullying, harassment, name calling, and other offenses directed toward

GLBT students. Students sign pledge cards to not use anti-GLBT language and to safely intervene in situations where harassment is occurring. TransACTION's purpose is to encourage allies for transgendered individuals, through panel discussions, workshops, and other activities. Martin Luther King Organizing Weekend aims to teach coalition building between the safe schools movement and other social action groups.

Besides the four Days of Action, GLSEN and Simon & Schuster Children's Publishing annually organize No Name-Calling Week. Thousands of middle and elementary schools participate in this event, in which teachers use their lesson plans to teach about the consequences of name calling and to work toward its elimination. GLSEN also maintains the ThinkB4YouSpeak website, which encourages its visitors to enter an original alternative in place of the expression "That's so gay."

Two major research publications by GLSEN are *From Teasing to Torment: School Climate in America* and *The 2005 National School Climate Survey: The Experiences of Lesbian, Gay, Bisexual and Transgendered Youth in Our Nation's Schools*. GLSEN's studies have found that the presence of antidiscrimination policies enhances self-reported feelings of safety by students and that sexual orientation ranks second only to one's appearance or body size as the reason for experiencing harassment.

GLSEN has registered approximately 4,000 gay/straight alliances (GSAs)—student clubs dedicated to creating safe and tolerant school climates for every student regardless of sexual orientation or gender identity/expression. The first GSA was formed in 1988 by a straight student with the help of her teacher, GLSEN's founder.

In addition to its work in assisting coalitions in getting safe-schools laws passed, GLSEN has drafted a model law serving as an example of a well-constructed statute enumerating protected classes (among them those defined based on sexual orientation and gender identity/expression). By 2008, 11 states and the District of Columbia had passed safe-schools laws protecting sexual orientation, and seven states and the District of Columbia had such laws regarding gender identity/expression.

Joan Luxenburg

Further Reading

GLSEN: www.glsen.org

Harris Interactive & GLSEN. (2005). *From teasing to torment: School climate in America, a survey of students and teachers.* New York: GLSEN.

Kosciw, J. G., & Diaz, E. M. (2006). *The 2005 national school climate survey: The experiences of lesbian, gay, bisexual and transgender youth in our nation's schools.* New York: GLSEN.

Safford Unified School District #1 v. Redding

In 2009, the U.S. Supreme Court addressed the issue of school-based strip searches, determining that a strip search for ibuprofen had violated a student's constitutional right to privacy. A different student was found with prescription-strength ibuprofen in school and said she received it from Savannah Redding. Redding was a quiet, 13-year-old honor student at the time of the incident. No drugs were found as a result of the search of Redding, which she called "the most humiliating experience of my life." Justice David Souter wrote the majority opinion for the 8-1 decision. The Court held that a strip search was far too intrusive for a violation of school policy. Further, the court determined that while schools have a legitimate responsibility to keep drugs off campus, strip searches are not a legitimate means to do so. Justice Souter observed that the evidence against Redding was weak, there was no specific reason to believe she had contraband stashed in her underwear, and the medication involved was relatively harmless—400-mg ibuprofen pills, equivalent to two Advil tablets.

Based on the accusation by her classmate, school officials first checked Redding's backpack and outer clothes. The court felt these two searches were reasonable, but determined that the school made "a quantum leap" in taking the next step, which involved stripping Redding to her underwear and asking her to shake them out so that her breasts and pelvic area were exposed. Justice Ruth Bader Ginsburg was especially troubled by the trauma a young girl would experience after enduring this type of intrusion at the hands of a trusted official. In making its decision, the Court exempted from liability the assistant principal who ordered the search, asserting that perhaps he did not know his actions were unconstitutional and thus it was a good-faith exception.

Savannah Redding walks down the steps of the U.S. Supreme Court building after her court hearing in Washington D.C., on April 21, 2009. Redding was strip-searched at her school when she was 13 years old, after being accused by another classmate of possessing and sharing prescription-strength ibuprofen. (AP/Wide World Photos)

Justice Clarence Thomas was the lone dissenter. He asserted that school officials acted logically in searching Redding's underpants. He also stated that decision in the case virtually ensured more students would hide drugs in their underwear, as they would now deem it the safest location for contraband.

Prior to the ruling in *Redding,* lower courts had heard numerous cases on strip searches of students, sometimes affirming the procedure and at other times finding it unconstitutional. For instance, a strip search of a female high school student for drugs was found to be lawful based on several factors, including a tip from another student, an incriminating letter found in a classroom, a teacher's report of strange behavior, and her own father's concern about her drug use.

Because the Court's ruling addressed only strip searches for prescription drugs, it left open the question of whether strip searches for other contraband, such as illicit drugs and weapons, were constitutional. In September 2009, the fall after *Redding* was decided, an administrator at Atlantic High School in Atlantic, Iowa, was placed on suspension for authorizing strip searches of five female students. The searches were conducted after a student reported $100 was missing from a purse in her locker. No money was found. Iowa law seems to prohibit strip searches, but some argued there were circumstances under which a strip search could be acceptable. On February 25, 2010, the American Civil Liberties Union (ACLU) of Iowa filed suit requesting the school district make available records indicating what, if any, punishment was imposed on the two school officials who conducted the searches.

Laura L. Finley

Further Reading

Administrator on leave after school strip search. (2009, September 9). *KCCI.* Retrieved April 8, 2010, from http://www.kcci.com/news/20757778/detail.html

Barnes, R. (2009). Student strip search illegal. *Washington Post.* Retrieved April 8, 2010, from http://www.washingtonpost.com/wp-dyn/content/article/2009/06/25/AR2009062501690.html?sid=ST2009062504131

Bravin, J. (2009, June 26). Court faults strip-search of student. *The Wall Street Journal.* Retrieved April 8, 2010, from http://online.wsj.com/article/SB124593034315253301.html

Save the Children

Save the Children is a nonprofit organization that works to ensure lasting, positive changes in the lives of children. The organization works in the United States as well as in Asia, Latin America, the Caribbean, and the Middle East. Save the Children's priorities include helping students be safe, well nourished, and educate.

In particular, the organization focuses on the world' most vulnerable and marginalized children. It reaches out to children at risk, including girls, ethnic minorities, children affected by HIV/AIDS, children affected wars and other catastrophes, and children with disabilities.

Save the Children provides the following services:

- Training community health workers to care for newborns and young children
- Protecting vulnerable children from abuse and exploitation
- Helping communities in at-risk countries to be prepared in advance of natural disasters
- Improving children's health through regular exercise and nutritious food in the United States

Save the Children helps build schools and ensures the education that students receive in them is of the highest quality. The organization focuses largely—though not exclusively—on girls. Two-thirds of the world's 880 million illiterate adults are women, and 70% of the 125 million children who are not attending school today are girls. Girls are far more likely to leave school due to financial reasons, abuse, disease, and cultural and religious beliefs. For instance, in parts of the Horn of Africa, girls are reluctant to walk to school because many have been abducted on their journey. A dowry system is still in place in the Sahel region of Africa and in some parts of the Middle East that requires girls to leave their studies. In southern Africa and in Asia, the AIDS crisis has left many girls as the head of their broken families; to support their siblings, thy often drop out of school to work. Indigenous girls are among those with the least opportunity.

Save the Children works to address these issues, having found that educating girls has a number of benefits:

- Healthier, better-educated children and grandchildren
- Fewer maternal deaths and reductions in the "younger than age five" mortality rate
- Delayed marriage and better parenting skills
- Improved literacy and numeracy skills, leading to greater economic opportunities
- More skills and knowledge enhancing women's self–esteem and the well-being of families

Save the Children works with university-based researchers to obtain information about problems affecting children and the most effective interventions. Members of the Save–University Partnership for Education Research (SUPER) include

Columbia University Teachers College, George Washington University, Harvard University, Stanford University, University of Maryland, University of Massachusetts at Amherst, University of Minnesota, University of Pennsylvania, and University of Wisconsin. Projects undertaken by SUPER have focused on the quality of early childhood programs in the Philippines, the safety of students in Malawi, the cost-effectiveness of community schools in Haiti, and ways to ensure girls' education in Pakistan.

Although the organization worked in Haiti prior to the devastating earthquake of January 2010, it has dramatically expanded its efforts in that country since this natural disaster occurred. Save the Children has initiated school readiness programs and health and hygiene programs for both Haitian students and their parents.

Laura L. Finley

Further Reading
Save the Children: http://www.savethechildren.org/

School Crime and School Climate, College

Over the past several years, the subjects of bullying and school crime have drawn much attention in the United States, especially as they relate to the increasing incidents of violence recently seen at both the high school and collegiate levels. Studies have shown that one important precursor to potentially lethal incidents of school violence was whether the assailant had been bullied in school during some period and thus wanted to seek revenge. Research into this issue in relation to violent incidents taking place on college campuses is particularly limited, however. Several reports have stated that, contrary to popular belief, bullying occurs among adults of all ages, especially in the workplace. In the college setting, it has been shown that the act of taunting or verbally abuse is not just reserved for students, but is also engaged in by professors or other educators.

In a study carried out by Chapell et al., approximately 33.4% of undergraduate college students reported actually seeing one student bully another one to two times, while 29.4% of the sample population reported seeing a professor bully a student one to two times. Nearly 19% of the college students surveyed stated they had personally been bullied by a fellow peer sometime during their undergraduate career. Regardless of age, bullying at any level has been shown to have negative and long-term mental health consequences on a number of levels. Although those persons who are bullied are not always easily identified, it is essential that research and academic communities take the initiative to try to better understand this population.

There are currently more than 16 million college students enrolled in approximately 4,200 universities and colleges in the United States. Within this population, bullying and acts of violence do not take place solely within the "typical" peer relationships found among individuals that were discussed earlier. Instead, these acts have been seen more frequently in recent times within the romantic or dating relationships found between students. Both physical and sexual violence, which have drawn much more attention in the research community as compared to the general topic of bullying, have been shown to be very common on college campuses regardless of size or location.

The incidence of physical dating violence among undergraduate students tends to range anywhere from 16.7% of this specific population to nearly 48% according to past studies. Sexual dating violence rates among college students have been shown to be relatively high as well; indeed, many researchers have claimed that, on average, nearly one in three college women and one in 10 college men has experienced sexual violence at some level. In particular, young women with a family history of physical or sexual violence are more likely to become involved similarly violent intimate relationships during their collegiate years as compared to their adolescent years.

Having a productive and nurturing college climate is essential to the success of all students. Without this support, feelings of stress and anxiety on campuses across the nation will continue to increase exponentially. Currently, many students are in a state of crisis due to the climate or environment found at their respective institutions. For example, 90% of college students have reported feeling stressed, 40% stated that they are stressed so much that it often interferes with both their social and academic functioning, and 10% stated that they have contemplated suicide sometime during their collegiate career.

Approaches such as putting more emphasis on early identification of suicidal and depressive symptoms and increasing social support are essential to enhancing the culture found on college campuses. Another approach that could be efficiently utilized to enhance the climate found at this institutional level includes increasing the communication among those in leadership at the college or university so that they can better serve their student population.

Once supportive approaches, such as those mentioned previously, are deployed, the classroom environment becomes one that encourages learning instead of limiting it. Along with this positive outcome, student motivation may be increased. It might benefit educators to begin to change the mentality that they are the ultimate authority in the classroom as well. If they allow their students to actually have choices and more decision-making privileges, that flexibility can create a self-regulated learning environment during the duration of the course.

Professors should also be aware of the additional needs of minority of students and understand how they relate to the college. In the past, studies have consistently shown that students of color view the general campus climate more negatively than their white counterparts. A closer look at these data reveals that Latinos and African Americans actually have the most negative views. These feelings often surface in minority students who believe that their particular college or university is not doing enough to recognize and celebrate diversity on the campus as well as in those who contend that their administrators are not committed to creating policies to increase diversity. To create a more welcoming college campus, these sensitive issues must be addressed in an in-depth manner.

Ebony Thomas

Further Reading

Carr, J. L. (2005, February). *American College Health Association campus violence white paper.* Baltimore, MD: American College Health Association.

Chapell, M., Casey, D., De La Cruz, C., Ferrell, J., Forman, J., Lipkin, R., et al. (2004). Bullying in college by students and teachers. *Adolescence, 39,* 53–65.

Chapell, M. S., Hasselman, S. L., Kitchin, T., Loman, S. N., MacIver, K. W., & Sarullo, P. L. (2006). Bullying in elementary school, high school, and college. *Adolescence, 41*(10), 839–855.

Flannery, D., & Quinn-Leering, K. (2000). Violence on college campuses: Understanding its impact on student well-being. *Community College Journal of Research and Practice, 24,* 839–855.

Graves, K. N., Sechrist, S. M., White, J. W., & Paradise, M. J. (2005). Intimate partner violence perpetuated by college women within the context of a history of victimization. *Psychology of Women Quarterly, 29,* 278–289.

Murray, C. E., & Kardatzke, K. N. (2007). Dating violence among college students: Key issues for college counselors. *Journal of College Counseling, 10,* 79–89.

Pettitt, J., & Ayers, D. (2002). Understanding conflict and climate in a community college. *Community College Journal of Research and Practice, 26,* 105–120.

Reid, L. D., & Radhakrishnan, P. (2003). Race matters: The relation between race and general campus climate. *Cultural Diversity and Ethnic Minority Psychology, 9,* 263–275.

Young, A. J. (2007). The challenge to change: Shifting the motivational climate of the college classroom for enhancing learning. *College Teaching, 51,* 127–130.

School Crime and School Climate, High School

Although there is not one commonly accepted definition for school climate in high schools, the vast majority of researchers and scholars suggest that school climate, at its heart, reflects subjective experience in school—that is, how safe and nurtured students and, to some extent, parents and teachers, feel in school. Climate particularly reflects the existence (or absence) of a safe and orderly environment in which to learn. Not surprisingly, then, creating environments free of violence and other crimes is a high priority for schools. Given that one of the important factors in climate is safety, students must feel safe in their school environments if they are to achieve the academic and prosocial goals necessary for them to move forward.

Unfortunately, the climates of many of U.S. schools have changed from safe and nurturing to fearful and fraught with violence, both physical and emotional. The reason for these changes is simple: Violence in schools has been increasing in recent years. The potential danger of school violence is exemplified by such incidents as the shootings at Virginia Tech University and Columbine High School. Although these mass shootings have come to define the notion of school violence, they are really only the most egregious examples. Violence in schools is both spectacular, like the aforementioned events, and subtle. The spectacular forms include not only mass shootings, but also gang activity and gang violence. The subtle forms of school violence are exemplified by bullying, both traditional and nontraditional. Nontraditional bullying may take the form of sexual harassment, sometimes resulting in sexual violence, as well as racial and religious harassment. In addition, many young students are bullied and otherwise targeted because of their sexual orientation.

Accordingly, the climate in U.S. high schools has evolved from open environments, where students walked freely through the halls, to something resembling armed camps. In the latter environments, schools are replete with airport-like security checkpoints, with weapons detectors and armed security officers roaming the halls. Increasing the safety of the school climate by changing the environment into the "armed camp" model is one method of dealing with violence. Unfortunately, this type of climate is an extreme measure and is counterproductive. Today's research is seeking to identify which approaches best address physical safety as well as emotional and psychological safety.

The subtle forms of violence may actually be more insidiously threatening to the feelings of safety of students because they occur more frequently and are largely undetectable. Teasing, bullying, and gay bashing are some of the more prevalent problems faced by high school students today. The means to address these problems rely on the creation of safe and nurturing climates, where there are clearly delineated guidelines for behaviors and attitudes. Many schools have sought to make their climates safer by emphasizing prosocial learning, mandating counseling, and increasing parental involvement.

Educators and law enforcement officials are continually looking for new strategies to address violence and are finding that the climate of the high schools is a key factor in this effort. The most important steps a high school can take in preventing violence focus on both the affective and the physical environment. These measures include promoting a positive school climate and culture, teaching and modeling prosocial behaviors, and providing effective intervention when antisocial behaviors occur or when individual students demonstrate a propensity for violence. In addition, school-wide prevention and intervention strategies can mitigate threats.

Indeed, climate is much more than simply the academic environment. Over the last decade, studies from a range of historically somewhat disparate fields (e.g., risk prevention, health promotion, character education, mental health, and social-emotional learning) have identified research-based school improvement guidelines that can predictably create safe, caring, responsive, and participatory high schools.

Over the last two decades, educators and parents alike have learned that school climate—the quality and character of school life—serves to support students' learning and achievement. Research confirms that a safe and supportive school climate, in which students have positive social relationships and are respected, engaged in their work, and feel competent, matters tremendously.

Aviva Twersky Glasner

Further Reading

American Psychological Association. (2003). Presidential task force on prevention, promoting strength, resilience, and health in young people, *American Psychologist, 58*(6–7), 425–490.

Cohen, J. (2006). Social, emotional, ethical and academic education: Creating a climate for learning, participation in democracy and well-being. *Harvard Educational Review, 76*(2), 201–237.

Freiberg, H. J. (Ed.). (1999). *School climate: Measuring, improving and sustaining healthy learning environments.* Philadelphia, PA: Falmer Press.

School climate research summary. (n.d.). Center for Social and Emotional Education. Retrieved May 6, 2010, from http://nscc.csee.net/effective/school_climate_research_summary.pdf

School environment affects the potential for violence. (2008, January 1). National Youth Violence Prevention Resource Center. Retrieved May 6, 2010, from http://www.safeyouth.org/scripts/faq/schoolenviron.asp

School Crime Victimization Survey

The School Crime Victimization Survey, which is a supplement to the National Crime Victimization Survey (NCVS), estimates the number of students victimized by crime at school, on school grounds, or on the way to and from school. The survey is designed to assist policymakers, researchers, and educational practitioners in making informed decisions regarding crime in schools.

The latest report contains data from 6,297 respondents ages 12 to18 who were enrolled in the sixth through the 12th grades in 2005. Four percent of these students reported that they had been victims of a crime during the reporting period: 3% were victims of theft and 1% were victims of violent crime (rape, robbery, assault). The survey discovered a positive correlation between the presence of gangs, drugs, and alcohol in schools and the likelihood that a student in that school would be the victim of a crime. Male and female students were equally likely to be victims, although males were twice as likely as females to be the victims of a violent crime at school. Students at public schools were three times as likely to be the victims of theft as students enrolled in private schools.

Students who have been victimized at school are more likely to fear attacks, avoid specific places at school, and refrain from participating in extracurricular activities than students who have not been attacked. Other major findings include the following:

- The percentage of sixth-grade and seventh-grade (2% and 3%, respectively) victims was higher than the percentage of 10th-grade (1%) victims.
- Students living in households with incomes of less than $34,999 were less likely to be the victims of school crimes than students from more affluent homes.
- A higher percentage of students receiving grades of "mostly" C's were victims than were students who received "mostly" A's or B's.

Comparisons of data from the 1995, 1999, 2001, and 2005 NCVS Crime Incident Reports revealed an overall decrease in the percentage of students reporting at least one instance of criminal victimization at school in the six months prior to the survey.

The American public continues to be concerned about crime in the schools, safety of students, and the ways that victimization at school impedes academic success. Crime in the schools negatively affects not only those directly involved in the incident, but also other students, faculty, and staff, and creates an unfavorable academic environment. Findings in the School Crime Victimization Survey identify the scope of victimization and environmental conditions connected with it, and can help concerned parties develop policies that better address the issue of school crime and violence.

Wendell Johnson

Further Reading

Bauer, L., Guerino, P., Nolle, K. L., & Tang, S. (2008). *Student victimization in U.S. schools: Results from the 2005 School Crime Supplement to the National Crime Victimization Survey* (NCES 2009-306). Washington, DC: National Center for Education Statistics, Institute of Education Sciences, U.S. Department of Education.

Dinkes, R., Cataldi, E. F., Kena, G., & Baum, K. (2006). *Indicators of school crime and safety: 2006* (NCES 2007-003/NCJ 214262). U.S. Departments of Education and Justice. Washington, DC: U.S. Government Printing Office.

U.S. Department of Justice, Bureau of Justice Statistics. (2009). *National Crime Victimization Survey, 2008* [Collection Year Record-Type Files] [Computer file]. ICPSR25461-v2. Ann Arbor, MI: Inter-university Consortium for Political and Social Research [distributor], 2009-09-11. Doi: 10.3886/ICPSR25461

School-to-Prison Pipeline

While federal studies show that the rate of school-related homicides and nonfatal violence has fallen over most of the past decade, over the same period and perhaps in response to highly publicized incidents of school violence such as the shootings at Columbine High School and Virginia Tech, schools across the United States have adopted zero-tolerance policies to address discipline problems. Zero-tolerance policies aimed at reducing school violence and removing children deemed to be "problems" from schools have created alarming levels of school disruption for children—disruption that begins a process moving these children from the school system into the prison system. This process, which entails the criminalizing of childhood classroom disruptions and the increase in attendant school-based arrests, disciplinary alternative schools, and secured detention, marginalizes at-risk youth and denies them the very education that could prevent future incarceration. Put simply, it has created a "pipeline" that moves the most vulnerable of school-aged children from the school system to the prison system.

Poor children, children of color, children who lack access to medical and mental health care, and those who suffer from abuse or neglect begin their school experiences with multiple strikes against them. Government policies such those espoused under the No Child Left Behind Act, which reward schools for academic achievement and restrict funding for under-achievement, create a climate where struggling children are unwelcome. Racial disparities loom large in school discipline as well, with minority children shown to be overrepresented when it comes to harsh sanctions. Black students have been shown to be more than twice as likely as white students to be suspended from school.

In cases of vulnerable populations, learning differences or disabilities may not be detected until the child enters the public school system. Studies have shown that most children who end up in detention facilities have disabilities that would make them eligible for special education services, but only 37% of them have received any kind of services at school, either because the schools failed to identify their disabilities or due to lack of parental awareness of the child's limitations.

Emotional disturbances, which are a qualifier for special education consideration, create particular risks for students, including the worst graduation rates, the highest dropout rates, and higher arrest rates and pregnancy rates than those for these students' peers. Children with emotional disturbances make up seven out of every 10 children in the juvenile justice system and are three times more likely than their peers to be arrested before leaving school. Almost three-fourths of children with emotional disturbances will be arrested within five years of leaving school.

Clearly, the safety needs attached to the very real dangers of school-based violence must be addressed, and real responses are needed for legitimate threats. However, zero-tolerance disciplinary policies represent a "one size fits all" response to school based incidents that impose severe discipline on students without taking into account their individual circumstances. These policies and the resultant suspensions, expulsions, and arrests are often the first step in a child's journey though the school-to-prison pipeline.

Equally concerning are the racial disparities resulting from the enforcement of these zero-tolerance policies. Black children are four times as likely as their white peers to be incarcerated. Black children are almost five times and Latino children more than twice as likely to be incarcerated as white children for drug offenses. Black children are twice as likely as white children to be put in programs for mental retardation, twice as likely to be held back a grade, three times as likely to be suspended, and 50% more likely to drop out of school. While black children make up 16% of the U.S. youth population, they represent 32% of the children in foster care; while minority youth in general make up 39% of the overall youth population, they account for 60% of the children in the juvenile justice system. Studies have reported that as many as three-fourths of all incarcerated children have mental health disorders and one in five has a severe disorder; Latino children show the highest percentage rate of unmet mental health needs. Today 580,000 black males are serving prison sentences in the United States, while fewer than 40,000 black males earn a bachelor's degree each year. Often, poverty is a factor in incarceration; while wealthier families can provide options such as counseling or private rehabilitation programs, drug counseling, or even military school as alternatives to detention, poor families have limited options—another factor that contribute to their disproportionate representation within the justice system.

As early as kindergarten, some children may begin to show signs for potential risk of offending. In particular, the 10% to 11% of children who enter the school system lacking the social skills that would prevent them from arguing or fighting with teachers are at a significantly higher risk for school failure, delinquency, and potential incarceration. Mandatory expulsions for offenses committed by children as young as age five, while intended to make schools safer, may create the unintended consequence of pushing children—often the most vulnerable children—into a trajectory of delinquency and incarceration.

As concerns for safety grow, a growing number of school districts have begun to rely on police officers to patrol hallways and enforce discipline. These officers often focus on using the legal system to discipline students for conduct that might otherwise be addressed by school programs, counseling, or parent education, thereby moving children from the school yard to the prison yard. Once a child enters the juvenile justice system, reentry into traditional schools can be negatively impacted, initiating a trajectory that may lead toward adult incarceration.

Zero-tolerance policies, harsher drug laws, and rigorous gang intervention tactics have all contributed to a broadening of criminal offenses that affect school-aged children. Behavior that historically would have been handled in the principal's office, such as schoolyard fights, is now being attended to by school-based police officers, who move students directly into the local courts and detention centers. While initial offenses such as truancy, defiant behavior, or fighting might result in a minor punishment, these offenses often begin a paper trail or "record" for the offending child; as these offenses add up over time, the courts' and school's reaction to the child's behavior tend to become harsher. Many areas do not have comprehensive rehabilitation and support programs; as a result, incarceration becomes the only option for at-risk youths.

Marginalized children, when labeled by the school system as "deviant" at a young age, may feel that they are not wanted, or valued, or smart—which puts them on a downward spiral from the beginning of their school experiences. Many begin to mentally drop out as early as the third or forth grade, when the academic and behavioral demands of school may outstrip their earlier academic development and home-based support. Lack of mental health support and early intervention for children with severe emotional and behavioral problems and their families, issues of substance abuse, the absence of a positive home-based support system, or a combination of these factors often bring children into the juvenile justice system. The deeper a child gets into this system, the harder it is to get out. Once expelled from the school system, it is difficult for the child to return, making the risk of dropping out of high school a very real possibility. High school dropouts are 63 times more likely to be incarcerated than graduates from four-year colleges, and four times as likely as their peers with a higher education degree to live 125% below the poverty line. The average high school dropout will cost taxpayers more than $292,000 relative to an average high school graduate.

Addressing the harsh realities of the school-to-prison pipeline will require a shift in emphasis from punishment to support. This support is necessary even before high-risk children enter the school system. Resources for at-risk families, including health, nutrition, and mental health support and preschool to give children a more level social and academic entry process into the school system, can contribute to fewer disparities in the classroom. School resources that address the social, developmental, and behavior needs of our most vulnerable children can keep them in school rather than taking them out of the only known indicator for future success. Support for educational deficiencies, combined with a reduction of suspensions, expulsions, and arrests, can minimize disparities in achievement and outcome for all children, but especially those at highest risk. While it is important to keep schools safe for all students, implementing interventions such as mediation, counseling, and conflict resolution as first-line alternatives can contribute keeping all children in mainstream educational environments and help them build the skills they need to realize their full potential.

Doreen Maller

Further Reading

America's cradle to prison pipeline report. (2007, October 10). Retrieved February 26, 2010, from http://www.childrensdefense.org/child-research-data-publications/data/cradle-prison-pipeline-report-2007-full-highres.html

Homeland insecurity. (2009, January). Retrieved February 26, 2010, from http://www.everychildmatters.org/images/stories/pdf/homelandinsecurity3.pdf

School to prison pipeline: Talking points. (2008, June 6). Retrieved February 26, 2010, from American Civil Liberties Union website: http://www.aclu.org/racial-justice/school-prison-pipeline-talking-points

SchooltoPrison.org. (n.d.). Retrieved February 26, 2010, from https://www.schooltoprison.org/

Southern Poverty Law Center launches "school to prison reform project" to help at-risk children get special education services, avoid incarceration. (2007, September 11). Retrieved February 26, 2010, from http://www.splcenter.org/get-informed/news/splc-launches-school-to-prison-reform-project-to-help-at-risk-children-get-special

Search and Seizure, High School

As school officials, parents, and the general public have grown more concerned about crime and violence in schools, one response has been greater use of search and seizure. If students can be searched for contraband, the logic goes, then not only may problems be averted, but the action may serve as a deterrent. While the U.S. Supreme Court ruled in *Tinker v. Des Moines* that students do have privacy rights under the Fourth Amendment, subsequent court decisions have shown that these rights can be limited.

The first Supreme Court case to deal with school searches was *New Jersey v. T.L.O.*, 469 U.S. 325 (1985). In that case, T.L.O., a 14-year-old girl at Piscataway High School in New Jersey, was found standing in a haze of smoke. Another girl who was with her admitted she had been smoking, but T.L.O. denied it. The teacher who had found the pair did not believe her, and demanded that T.L.O. see the assistant principal, Theodore Chaplick. Chaplick asked T.L.O. to empty her purse, where he found cigarettes and rolling papers, which could have been used for marijuana. He proceeded to open a zippered enclosure of her purse, where he found a pipe, plastic baggies, some marijuana, and a list of people who owed T.L.O. money. He then read some personal letters he found in her purse.

In the case brought before the Supreme Court, T.L.O. contended that none of this evidence should have been used to punish her, as it was obtained through an unlawful search. While affirming that students do have some privacy rights in school, the Court said that schools, acting *in loco parentis* (or as parents), must ensure that students are safe and that the educational climate is conducive to learning. Further, the Court maintained that recent increases in crime and violence among youth made it all the more important for schools to intervene. Thus the Court set a new standard for school searches, allowing school officials to search students based on reasonable suspicion, rather than the probable cause needed by police officers to conduct a search. To determine if there is reasonable suspicion to search a student, the Court said that two factors would be considered: whether the search was justified at its inception, and whether the intrusiveness of the search was reasonably related to its objectives. The Court decided that both elements had been met in T.L.O.'s case.

Over the next decade, concerns about student drug use grew, prompting the next Supreme Court case relevant to school searches. This time the issue dealt with school-based drug testing. In *Vernonia School District 47J v. Acton,* the Court held that drug testing of students as a condition of their participation in school sports was constitutional. In 2002, in *Board of Education v. Earls,* the Court again heard a challenge to school-based drug testing. This time, the district's policy was to test all students involved in extracurricular activities. Again, the Court ruled that such testing was not a violation of students' Fourth Amendment rights.

The last school search case that the Supreme Court has heard was *Safford Unified School District #1 v. Redding* in 2009. This case dealt with school-based strip searches. Thirteen-year-old honor student Savannah Redding was stripped down to her underwear and even asked to shake these garments out so that her private parts were exposed. The search was initiated based on the allegation of another student that Redding had an ibuprofen pill that she had not checked in at the school office—a violation of school policy. No drugs were found. The Supreme Court ruled that this strip search was an unconstitutional violation of Redding's Fourth Amendment rights. In particular, the court noted the trauma Redding felt when she was being searched. The decision did not address other strip searches, however.

In other cases, students have been strip searched based on tips and missing items. In one case, a teenage boy was strip searched because school officials thought his genital region looked larger than normal and suspected that he was "crotching" drugs. Although no drugs were found, a court ruled the search was both justified in its inception and reasonable in scope.

In addition to drug testing and strip searches, schools often employ canine searches to detect drugs and weapons. These searches have been considered lawful. Although the dogs cannot sniff at individual students, they can be lead through vacated classrooms, down hallways with lockers, and in school parking lots. Some recent cases have highlighted the fact that these dogs, however well trained, do not always detect contraband.

As more districts employ school police officers, the situation becomes muddier, in that it is not entirely clear whether the reasonable suspicion or probable cause standard should be used. If police give school officials a tip but do not conduct the search, for instance, the school officials are generally held to the reasonable suspicion standard. This practice can clearly help law enforcement get around the need to have probable cause before police engage in a search. It has been called the "silver platter doctrine," in recognition of the fact that law enforcement is handing over the evidence "on a sliver platter" to school officials.

Another type of school search involves using metal detectors, either hand-held or walk-through devices. The Supreme Court has not heard a case on this issue, but lower courts have affirmed that metal detector searches in schools are lawful.

Critics have expressed concern that these measures do little to keep schools safe but might instead increase fear and anxiety. Further, even when courts do not find searches to be unconstitutional, some believe they do indeed infringe on students' privacy rights, with great impact.

Laura L. Finley

Further Reading

Alderman, E., & Kennedy, C. (1997). *The right to privacy.* Santa Rosa, CA: Vintage.

Barnes, R. (2009). Student strip search illegal. *Washington Post.* Retrieved April 8, 2010, from http://www.washingtonpost.com/wp-dyn/content/article/2009/06/25/AR2009062501690.html?sid=ST2009062504131

Beger, R. (2003). The "worst of both worlds": School security and the disappearing Fourth Amendment rights of students. *Criminal Justice Review, 28,* 336–354.

Daniel, P. (1998). Violence and the public schools: Students rights have been weighed in the balance and found wanting. *Journal of Law and Education, 27* (4), 587,

Devine, J. (1996). *Maximum security.* Chicago, IL: University of Chicago Press.

Finley, L., & Finley, P. (2004). *Piss off! How drug testing and other privacy violations are alienating America's youth.* Monroe, ME: Common Courage.

Hyman, I., & Snook, I. (1999). *Dangerous schools.* San Francisco, CA: Jossey-Bass.

Redden, J. (2000). *Snitch culture.* Los Angeles, CA: Feral House.

Security on Campus, Inc.

Security on Campus, Inc. (SOC), is a national nonprofit organization whose aim is to help campuses maintain safe learning environments. It is supported by both corporate and nonprofit sponsors. To date, SOC has helped achieve legislation

Jeanne Ann Clery's father, Howard Clery founded Security on Campus, Inc., to ensure that measures are taken nationwide to keep students safe on college campuses. (Marianne Barcellona/Time & Life Pictures/Getty Images)

relevant to campus safety and annually compiles data on the safety of campuses across the United States. Additionally, this organization has developed materials and hosts programs to train future college students about safety issues. It also provides expert consultation to colleges and universities seeking to enhance their policies related to campus safety and hosts Clery Act training programs to ensure that staff understand and are compliant with this legislation. Finally, SOC provides advocacy and referral services to victims of campus crime.

The first important piece of legislation SOC helped enact was the 1990 Campus Security Act, renamed the Jeanne Clery Disclosure of Campus Security Policy and Campus Crime Statistics Act in 1998 (in memory of Clery, who was murdered in her college dorm room at age 19). The Clery Act requires institutions of higher education to release statistics on campus crime, as well as their security-related policies, to students and staff. This information must be publicized so prospective students can see it as well. Subsequently, SOC helped establish several amendments to the Clery Act. In 1992, the Campus Sexual Assault Victim's Bill of Rights was enacted. In 2000, SOC helped secure an extension of the "Megan's Law" notification of registered sex offenders to cover college campuses. In addition to legislation, SOC pushed Congress to dub September "National Campus Safety Awareness Month" in 2008.

An important element of SOC's work is its searchable database, which features information about safety on campuses across the United States. The database tallies rates of eight offenses called "index offenses": murder/non-negligent manslaughter, negligent manslaughter, forcible sex offenses, nonforcible sex offenses (statutory rape and incest), robbery, aggravated assault, burglary, motor vehicle theft, and arson.

SOC has created several instructional videos to help campuses reduce the amount of sexual assault and stalking that takes place at institutions of higher education and to provide more useful services for victims. Actress Kristen Stewart, star of the *Twilight* film series, is featured in some of the videos and in a public service announcement (PSA) that SOC created.

Laura L. Finley

Further Reading

Security on Campus: Inc.: http://www.securityoncampus.org/

Sexual Assault Crimes, College

Research has shown that sexual assault on university and college campuses is alarmingly common. Estimates suggest that one in four women who attend a college or university will experience some form of sexual assault in their years of study. While women are most frequently the victims of sexual assault, men also experience various forms of sexual violation.

Sexual assault can be defined as a nonconsensual violation of an individual's sexual integrity. It can take the form of sexual harassment, incest, or sexual abuse. Other terms used to refer to sexual violation include "sexual violence" and "rape." Rape is considered to be a specific form of sexual assault and is defined as nonconsensual sexual intercourse. Sexual violence, a term that is used within the majority of academic literature, encompasses a broader range of experiences and levels of violence. The term "sexual assault," in contrast, is used within the legal system to define all attacks that are of a sexual nature, ranging from inappropriate touching to aggravated assault.

Historically, acts of sexual assault were not seen as forms of aggression. Instead, they were considered to be types of seduction. From this perspective, rape was seen as a form of sex. The shift toward seeing nonconsensual sexual acts as a type of assault was pivotal in sexual assault becoming a recognized concern within the criminal justice system and for those engaging in academic research.

The vast majority of research on sexual assault focuses on women's experiences as victims of sexual violation. As some academics have suggested, this emphasis is a result of the feminist literature from the 1970s, which sought to highlight the victimization of women at the hands of men. As a result, relatively little research has focused on male survivors of sexual assault. However, since the 1990s, some research on this topic has begun to appear.

Myths about sexual assault are often portrayed in popular media. Some of these include the contentions that sexual assault is a rare occurrence, sexual assaults are committed only by strangers, and perpetrators of sexual assault are always abnormal or insane. These myths have been shown to have little bearing on the actual occurrences of sexual assault.

As many studies on sexual assault have shown, forms of sexual violation are not rare occurrences, but rather happen frequently, particularly on university and college campuses. Sexual assault has been shown to occur most commonly between acquaintances, friends, spouses, and family members. Despite what the myth of stranger rape dictates, perpetrators of sexual assault are often intimately connected to victims. The term "date rape" has been coined to highlight rape that occurs between individuals who are dating.

Many myths specifically surround male-perpetrated sexual assault against women. Such claims include that women often lie about sexual assault and that women's choices of clothing, manners of walking, and spaces of occupancy are reasons for their assault. These myths have been suggested by many scholars to be heavily rooted in sexism.

There are also many myths about males' experiences of female-perpetrated sexual assault. It is often assumed that the perpetrators of sexual aggression against boys and men are male. However, this is not always the case. Females can and do rape males. Nevertheless, the vast majority of rapes are male perpetrated. Another common myth about male survivors of sexual assault is that they are homosexual. In reality, research suggests that straight men and boys are just as likely to experience sexualized violence as homosexual males.

Rates of sexual assault are problematic to calculate. This difficulty stems from the extremely low numbers of sexually violent acts that are reported to police. Many victims do not report crimes of sexual assault because of embarrassment, self-blame, and fear. On university and college campuses, victims of sexual assault are less likely to report their experience if they were under the influence of alcohol during the assault, they have limited understanding of the university's policies and procedures surrounding sexual assault, and they have limited knowledge of other sexual assaults on their campus.

In addition to these issues of reporting, many researchers have suggested that rates of sexual assault on university and college campuses are often purposefully obscured. These scholars claim that universities and colleges often mask the prevalence of campus sexual assault in an effort to preserve the image of a safe campus community. This focus on public relations rather addressing the actual problem has been suggested to further the difficulties in understanding the true rates of sexual assaults on university and college campuses.

Despite these difficulties in calculating rates of sexual assault, it is generally accepted that sexual assault is one of the most common crimes committed in North America. It has also been recognized that university and college campuses are some of the most prevalent locations for all forms of sexual assault.

Several scholars have attempted to understand why sexual assaults occur so often on university and college campuses. Many have argued that age, alcohol use, and male norms are connected to the heightened rates of campus sexual assaults. As Frintner and Rubinson (1993) demonstrated in their research, women between the ages of 16 and 24—the age group to which most undergraduate students belong—are at the greatest risk of experiencing some form of sexual assault. Others researchers have shown that in places where alcohol use is prevalent—a descriptor that fits most university and college campuses—sexual assaults occur more frequently. In addition to these issues, many scholars have argued that norms surrounding increased sexual activity and male aggression on university and college campuses contribute to the frequency of campus sexual assaults. Research has shown only 5 percent of sexual offenses occurring on campus are reported to police.

Other scholars have examined possible cultural explanations for campus sexual assault. For instance, he predominance of sexual, and sometimes violent, imagery of women in the media has been suggested to play a role in heightening rates of sexual assault. Furthermore, the prevalence of representations of male aggression and female sexuality in the media has been seen as another potential cause of sexual assault. These cultural explanations have been suggested to contribute to the effects of the issues discussed earlier.

In the past 20 years, the awareness of the prevalence of sexual assault has grown. Research specifically directed toward sexual assault on university and college campuses has increased, and public awareness on the issue has expanded. As a result, greater pressure is being placed on universities and colleges to provide proper resources for victims who have experienced sexual assault. Many campuses have established sexual assault centers or women's centers that focus on providing information and counseling services for survivors of violence. In addition, some campuses have begun to hold self-defense classes for students. While these efforts represent improvements to campus life, some scholars have argued that more work remains to be done.

Several groups on university and college campuses in North America have emerged as part of the effort to raise awareness about campus sexual assault. One in Four is an all-male student group that uses peer education to dispel the myths surrounding sexual assault on university and college campuses. SAFE (Sexual Assault Facts and Education) is another student organization that advocates for victims and educate campus communities about the prevalence and nature of sexual assault.

Andrea Quinlan

Further Reading

Brownmiller, S. (1975). *Against our will: Men, women, and rape*. New York: Bantam Books.
Day, K. (1994). Conceptualizing women's fear of sexual assault on campus: A review of causes and recommendations for change. *Environment and Behaviour, 26*(6), 742–765.
Gavey, N. (2005). *Just sex? The cultural scaffolding of rape*. New York: Routledge.
Tarrant, S. (2008). *Men speak out: Views of gender, sex and power*. New York: Routledge.

Sexual Assault Crimes, High School

Sexual violence has long been an issue in American society. According to one study, roughly 1.3 forcible rapes occur each minute in the United States. The socialization of men and women as well as society's presupposed traditional gender roles play pivotal roles in the sexual violence directed at young girls in high school. This essay discusses the prevalence of sexual assault and rape in high school as well as the issues that underlie such crimes.

According to the National Violence Against Women Survey, 54% of the females surveyed were younger than age 18 at the time they were raped. Roughly 32.7%

were between the ages of 12 and 17. Furthermore, in a study conducted in South Dakota, the frequency of date rape among high school girls ranged from 11.8% to 14.9%. In yet another study, 15% of high school participants reported experiencing sexual violence in their dating relationships. In addition, according to studies conducted by the American Association of University Women in 1993 and 2001, roughly 80% of students in public schools have experienced sexual harassment by school administration or personnel or by their peers. In another study on dating violence in high schools conducted by Molidor and Tolman, 46% of the students stated that the dating violence had occurred on school grounds. Moreover, in 2006, the Bureau of Justice Statistics concluded that the rate of rape and sexual assault among 12- to 15-year-olds was 3.4 per 1,000. For 16- to 19-year-olds, the rate was 2.5 per 1,000.

Sexual assault and rape among high school girls are grossly underreported. There are myriad reasons why young girls do not report these crimes. One reason is fear of retaliation, especially if the offender is known to the victim, which is typically the case. For example, according to the Bureau of Justice Statistics, in 2005, seven of every 10 victims of rape and sexual assault had been victimized by someone they knew.

Additionally, shame, guilt, and a lack of faith in the criminal justice system contribute to the issue of underreporting. In essence, because of the nature of such fear-inducing crimes, young girls often concede to living in a world where silence reigns supreme.

While there are several reasons for the prevalence of sexual violence directed at young girls in high school, one major reason is the socialization of men and the traditional gender roles advocated by society. The United States seems to be infatuated with gender and androcentrism. As a consequence, boys incessantly receive messages from parents, siblings, and the media about what it means to be a "real" man. While girls are supposed to be submissive, sexually pure beings, boys are encouraged to be tough, aggressive, and assertive sexual athletes. Such a macho mentality has the side effect of perpetuating sexual violence against young girls.

As studies on sexual violence in high school were published indicating the immense scope of this problem, educational institutions began to implement educational programs aimed at fostering rejection of rape-supportive attitudes, altering aggressive behavior, and ultimately curbing the prevalence of rape and sexual assault in high school. Although little is known about the effectiveness of such programs, as educators, it is incumbent upon a high school's administration and staff to impart the knowledge that is essential to reduce the incidence of sexual violence.

Conclusively, sexual assault and rape are crimes that are generally void of sexual gratification. They begin and end with a sense of entitlement and a craving for power, domination, and control. Moreover, the idea of an aggressive "real" man, which may be disseminated by parents, siblings, and the media alike, plays a crucial role in the sexual victimization of high school girls. Although it is impossible to completely eradicate sexual assault and rape, through education and a gradual abandonment in the detrimental "real" man images, young men and women can collaborate and curtail the occurrence of sexual violence in high school.

Rebecca Ajo

Further Reading

Fineran, S., & Bolen, R. (2006). Risk factors for peer sexual harassment in schools. *Journal of Interpersonal Violence, 21*(9), 1169–1191.

Garland, T. (2005). An overview of sexual assault and rape myths. In F. P. Reddington & B. Wright Kreisel (Eds.), *Sexual assault: The victims, the perpetrators and the criminal justice system* (pp. 5–27). Durham, NC: Carolina Academic Press.

Lanier, C.A. (2001). Rape-accepting attitudes: Precursors to or consequences of forced sex. *Violence Against Women, 7*(8), 876–885.

National Institute of Justice. (2008). Rape and sexual assault are serious problems. In L. I. (Ed.), *Opposing viewpoints: Sexual violence* (pp. 21–27). Detroit, MI: Greenhaven Press.

Prospero, M. (2007). Young adolescent boys and dating violence: The beginning of patriarchal terrorism? *Affilia: Journal of Women and Social Work, 22*(3), 271–280.

Schubot, D. B. (2001). Date rape prevalence among high school students in a rural midwestern state during 1993, 1995, and 1997. *Journal of Interpersonal Violence.* Retrieved from sagepublications.com

Sexual Harassment

The law recognizes two forms of sexual harassment: quid pro quo and hostile environment. Quid pro quo cases ("something for something") must demonstrate that sexual favors were coerced in exchange for some form of favor such as keeping one's job, securing a promotion, or getting a raise. Hostile environment cases must demonstrate that unwanted sexual behaviors created an environment that negatively affected a person's ability to perform his or her duties.

Legal protections in the United States against sexual harassment in the workplace date back to Title IV of the Civil Rights Act of 1964 (P.L. 88-352), which prohibits workplace discrimination on the basis of race, color, religion, sex, and national origin. However, schools did not have legal precedents to guide their responses to incidents of sexual harassment until 1992, when the U.S. Supreme Court ruled in the case of *Franklin v. Gwinnett County Public Schools*. In this landmark decision, a student named Christine Franklin filed a complaint against a coach and teacher at her school, Andrew Hill, for sexual harassment and abuse. Starting in the fall of 1986, when Franklin was in 10th grade, Hill had sexually oriented conversations with her and asked whether she would consider having intercourse with an older man. The behaviors escalated to forcible kissing and excusing Franklin from class and "subject[ing] her to coercive intercourse" (p. 63). The school investigated Hill's behavior and allegedly took no action against him; in addition, it discouraged Franklin from pressing charges against Hill. Hill resigned on April 14, 1988, on the condition that all charges against him be dropped.

Franklin's lawyers used Title IX of the U.S. Education Amendments of 1972 to establish that students in schools that receive federal funding are protected from harassment based on sex and may be awarded financial damages. Although Title IX is most widely known for its impact in reducing disparities between men and women in athletics participation at the collegiate level, it was written so as to protect individuals from being discriminated against by any federally funded educational institution on the basis of sex.

The second important sexual harassment case that affected students in schools was *Davis v. Monroe County Board of Education* (1999). When she was in the fifth grade, a male classmate of LaShonda Davis tried to touch her breasts and told her, "I want to get in bed with you" and "I want to feel your boobs." Davis reported this behavior to her mother and teacher, but the school did not do anything to support Davis or punish the perpetrator. This harassment continued, with Davis being subjected to verbal taunts, leers in class, and unwanted behaviors. Although Davis reported each of these incidents to her teachers, she still had to sit next to the offending student in class and nothing was done to stop the harassment. The incidents stopped six months later when her parents went to the police; they charged the boy with sexual battery, to which he pleaded guilty. During this time, Davis's previously high grades had dropped, and her father discovered that she had written a suicide note. These events led to a second landmark Supreme Court decision that applied Title IX to cases of student-on-student sexual harassment.

In cases of sexual harassment, four main criteria must be met under the application of Title IX:

1. School officials must have *actual knowledge* of the harassment.
2. School officials must demonstrate *deliberate indifference* to harassment or take actions that are *clearly unreasonable*.
3. School officials must have substantial control over both the harasser and the context in which the known harassment occurs.

4. The harassment must be *severe, pervasive, and objectively offensive* such that it can be said to *deprive the victim) of access* to the educational opportunities of benefits provided by the school *(Davis v. Monroe*, 1999).

The combination of actual knowledge with the acts of deliberate indifference is essential in harassment cases brought under Title IX. The Office of Civil Rights has since clarified that the OCR does not make schools responsible for the actions of the harassing student, "but rather for its own discrimination in failing to take immediate and appropriate steps to remedy the hostile environment once a school official knows about it." Finally, it is important to note that in cases decided in favor of the student, federally funded institutions may be held financially liable for damages.

Although Title IX and the OCR provide clear guidelines and protections for students experiencing sexual harassment, legal scholar Gigi Rollini (2003) argues that "the only victims [who] succeed under *Davis* are ones [who] are utterly debilitated by the harassment." This is due to the fourth criterion, which requires students to demonstrate that the harassment was so severe that it deprived them of access to an education. This point shields the legal system from having to handle minor complaints, but it provides minimal protection to students who are experiencing harassment but manage to maintain their academic performance despite the abuse. In addition to protecting students from heterosexual harassment, Title IX has been used to defend the rights of students who have been targeted for sexual orientation harassment.

Title IX protections have been applied more broadly in cases such as *Ray v. Antioch Unified School District* (2000) and *Montgomery v. Independent School District No. 709* (2000). In these cases, separate federal district courts (California and Minnesota, respectively) decided that schools could be held liable under Title IX for acting with "deliberate indifference" toward students who have reported persistent and severe sexual orientation harassment at school. These decisions applied the four criteria established in *Davis v. Monroe*, and held that Title IX could be effectively used to defend students in cases of sexual orientation harassment by their peers.

The case *Henkle v. Gregory* (2001) provides one example of how a student's complaint led to changes in his school district. In this case, the federal district court of Nevada allowed the case, which sought punitive damages for the Title IX sexual orientation harassment of Derek Henkle, to proceed. The school district chose to settle this case and paid $451,000 in damages to the student. Part of the settlement included changes to several district policies on discrimination and harassment to include sexual orientation and gender expression. These cases indicate that students are using existing legal protections to not only find relief from their own sexual harassment, but also educate others and update the policies and practices of their schools to reduce the potential for harassing behaviors to be directed at other students.

Elizabeth J. Meyer

Further Reading

Meyer, E. (2009). *Gender, bullying, and harassment: Strategies to end sexism and homophobia in schools.* New York: Teachers College Press.

Office for Civil Rights. (1997). Sexual harassment guidance: Harassment of students by school employees, other students or third parties. Retrieved April 19, 2008, from http://www.ed.gov/about/offices/list/ocr/docs/sexhar01.html

Rollini, G. (2003). *Davis v. Monroe County Board of Education:* A hollow victory for student victims of peer sexual harassment. *Florida State University Law Review, 30*, 987–1014.

Roth, S. (1994). Sex discrimination 101: Developing a Title IX analysis for sexual harassment in education. *Journal of Law & Education, 23*(4), 459–521.

Sexual Orientation and School Crime and Violence, College

Individuals who identify themselves as gay, lesbian, bisexual, or transgendered (GLBT) tend to report that college campuses are less than fully comfortable places and that they are often fearful of harassment and physical violence. Verbal harassment of such students is extremely common, and physical aggression against them also occurs regularly. Students often report having to hide their identities to feel safe and to avoid intimidation. Violent incidents have been reported in a wide range of schools, including the Ivy League, large state universities, historically black colleges, community colleges, and religious institutions.

Studies indicate that harassment, threats, and violence are commonly directed at college students who are thought to be gay or lesbian. Nearly 5% of gay students report being a victim of a physical assault during their college years, and 16% to 26% indicate that they have been threatened with physical assault during their time on campus. This incidence appears to mirror the rates of anti-gay violence in the larger society. According to FBI statistics, reports of hate crimes based on sexual orientation increased nearly 11% in 2008. It appears that being *perceived* as gay or lesbian by others is more closely related to harassment than actual sexual orientation. Therefore, students who are more gender atypical in their appearance, who acknowledge their sexual orientation earlier, or who are more open in their orientation are more vulnerable to harassment and attack.

In San Francisco, a survey found that offenses against LGBT students by their peers were very common on community college campuses. Nearly one-third

(32%) of male community college students admitted to verbal harassment against someone whom they thought was gay, with 18% reporting they had committed or threatened physical violence against such a person. The motivations for these attacks varied. Assailants were most likely to view homosexuals as predatory and believed that physically assaulting a gay individual whom they believed was flirting with them was a form of self-defense. Having an individual perceived as gay speak to them or smile at them was considered a threat. Others who admitted to physically assaulting gays attributed their behavior to ideology, the goal of punishing those who behave in inappropriate ways, or thrill seeking.

In a large study of 30 colleges conducted by the Policy Institute of the National Gay and Lesbian Task Force, researchers surveyed students, faculty, staff, and administrators, including those who identified themselves as GLBT and those who identified themselves as heterosexual. The vast majority of the respondents from both groups felt that GLBT students were likely to be harassed on their college campus. Of those who identified themselves as GLBT undergraduates, 36% reported having been harassed during the past 12 months, with the abuse generally taking the form of verbal taunts (89%) from fellow undergraduate students (79%). More than half reported that they concealed their sexual orientation or gender identity to avoid harassment, and 20% said they feared physical assault because of their sexuality.

Not surprisingly, GLBT students generally say that they feel that college campuses are less safe and welcoming for them. In addition to verbal harassment and physical violence by their peers, these students report regular demeaning experiences, including derogatory remarks made by professors and coaches, antigay postings on social networking websites and email messages, anonymous notes left under dorm room doors or in mailboxes, vandalism of cars, and jeers. Others have reported that the police and campus officials do not take these incidents seriously. In rare cases, students at colleges supported by conservative religious denominations have been expelled for their homosexuality. Some evidence suggests that harassment of GLBT students may make them less likely to continue their education. Data indicate that gay and lesbian college students are more likely to be sexually assaulted than their peers, and lesbian students report higher rates of sexual harassment on campus.

Elizabeth Kelley Rhoades

Further Reading

Draughn, T., Elkins, B., & Roy, R. (2002). Allies in the struggle: Eradicating homophobia and heterosexism on campus. In E. P. Cramer (Ed.), *Addressing homophobia and heterosexism on college campuses* (pp. 9–20). New York: Harrington Park Press.

Rankin, S. R. (2003). *Campus climate for gay, lesbian, bisexual, and transgender people: A national perspective.* New York: National Gay and Lesbian Task Force Policy Institute.

Rankin, S. R. (2006). LGBTQA students on campus: Is higher education making the grade? *Journal of Gay & Lesbian Issues in Education, 3,* 111–117.

Sexual Orientation and School Crime and Violence, High School

Lesbian, gay, and bisexual (LGB) and other sexual minority young people tend to experience more bullying, violence, and harassment at school than their heterosexual peers. Victimization based on sexual orientation is often exacerbated in the cases of gender-nonconforming and transgendered students, students of color, and rural

Constance McMillen attends an LGBT pride event at the White House on June 22, 2010. Her Mississippi high school cancelled its prom after discovering that McMillen intended to attend with her same-sex partner. (AP/Wide World Photos)

students. To prevent violence against LGB students in schools, many states, districts, and schools have enacted formal, comprehensive anti-bullying policies. Despite these recent policy interventions, bias-motivated crimes against sexual minorities still occur in schools.

Data from the National School Climate Survey, administered by the Gay, Lesbian and Straight Education Network, show that approximately 90% of LGB students hear a negative use of the word "gay" at school on a routine basis and 75% frequently hear other forms of homophobic speech. Sixty percent of these students hear similar remarks from teachers and other school personnel. In addition to negative speech based on sexual orientation, many sexual minority students hear comments challenging their masculinity or femininity.

Nearly nine out of 10 sexual minority students are victims of verbal harassment at school targeting their sexual orientation; many of these individuals are also verbally harassed because of their gender expression. Almost half of all LGB students are pushed, shoved, or nonverbally harassed because of their sexual orientation; one in four sexual minority students has been punched, kicked, or assaulted at school. Sexual minority students are often targets of sexual harassment and web-based bullying as well. While LGB students are disproportionately victims of violence, they have also been shown to witness and perpetrate more violence than their straight peers. Sexual minority males are more likely than sexual minority females to be victims of violence; gender nonconformity and degree of public sexual disclosure ("outness") are both correlates of victimization among LGB students.

Most sexual minority students who are victims of bullying, harassment, or assault at school do not report the incident to an adult because they anticipate that the situation will become worse if they do. When an incident is reported, the most common response by school personnel is to do nothing; only one-third of sexual minority students who are victims of school-based abuse report an effective intervention from school staff. School personnel effectively intervene even less frequently when faced with anti-gay speech in the classroom. Nonetheless, 80% of LGB students can identify a school staff member who they believe is supportive of LGB students.

Common institutional interventions used to protect LGB students from school-based victimization include gay/straight alliances (GSAs), sexual orientation–inclusive curricula, and comprehensive anti-bullying policies. GSAs are present in more than 4,000 schools, and approximately one-third of LGB students participate in such a group. Evidence suggests that GSAs are effective in decreasing the level of homophobic remarks, harassment, and assault in schools and in increasing the sense of school safety and belonging among sexual minority students. Far fewer schools implement curricula inclusive of LGB, gender-nonconforming, and transgendered people. Comprehensive school- and state-level anti-harassment policies, although relatively rare, have been shown to reduce biased language, homophobic remarks, harassment, and assaults targeting LGB students.

Research routinely shows that sexual minority students have lower grade-point averages, higher absentee rates, higher dropout rates, higher course failure rates, and lower bachelor's degree aspirations than heterosexual students. Academic outcomes and attendance rates are lower among those LGB students who report the highest levels of school-based harassment. While fewer than one-third of students attracted to members of the same sex openly disclose their sexuality to their friends—and even fewer disclose their sexuality to adults at school—those who do maintain a greater sense of school belonging than those who do not.

Several high-profile bias-motivated crimes ("hate crimes") based on sexual orientation and gender identity have occurred in schools. The most notable among them is the 2008 murder of a gender-nonconforming bullying victim, Lawrence King, in Oxnard, California. Dozens of sexual minority students have committed suicide because of confirmed incidents of anti-gay bullying at school.

Christopher J. Stapel

Further Reading

D'Augelli, A. R., Pilkington, N. W., & Hershberger, S. L. (2002, Summer). Incidence and mental health impact of sexual orientation victimization of lesbian, gay, and bisexual youths in high school. *School Psychology Quarterly, 17*(2), 148–167.

Kosciw, J. G., Diaz, E. M., & Greytak, E. A. (2008). *2007 national school climate survey: The experiences of lesbian, gay, bisexual and transgender youth in our nation's schools*. New York: GLSEN.

Russell, S. T., Franz, B. T., & Driscoll, A. K. (2001). Same-sex romantic attraction and experiences of violence in adolescence. *American Journal of Public Health, 91*(6), 903–906.

Social Learning Theories

Social learning theories hold that criminal behaviors are learned in interaction with others, particularly (but not exclusively) those within close personal circles such as family, friends, and neighbors. According to this perspective, criminality is not inborn, biological, or genetic, nor is it limited to people of specific backgrounds, resources, or opportunities. Rather, all people are seen as having the potential to engage in criminal or deviant acts, and criminality is a function of the socialization process. Thus social learning theories focus on interactions or socializing processes between individuals, often in a close face-to-face context. Unlike social structural theories, which as macro-structural theories emphasize large-scale, often abstract, social structures and institutions (such as the economy, labor market, education, government, or culture), social learning theories tend to be micro-structural, focusing on relationships within specific settings or environments. Where structural theories speak of labor markets and unemployment, social learning theories examine relationships within specific workplaces or between individuals and the unemployment office.

Social learning theories of crime and deviance found their most influential early expression in the work of University of Chicago sociologist Edwin Sutherland, who developed his differential association theory in the 1930s. For Sutherland, crime was a function of learning that can influence anyone in any culture. Notably, Sutherland avoided the tendency of most of his peers to focus on working-class subcultures or crimes of the poor. Sutherland's work was groundbreaking in focusing attention on professional and corporate crimes, at a time when few researchers considered such offenses worthy of investigation; in fact, Sutherland coined the term "white-collar crime." To understand the learning of crime, Sutherland examined the recruitment and socialization behaviors of elites within their excusive institutions, including corporate offices, private clubs, and professional schools.

Differential association theory suggests that close and trusted relatives and companions teach criminal behavior and attitudes, creating and sustaining a context in which the emphasis on supporting crime outweighs the emphasis on opposing it. Significantly, differential association theory examines not only the learning of deviant acts, specific techniques, or skills from influential peers, but also the ways in which peer networks teach people to deal with criminality psychologically. Thus peers teach people to rationalize or legitimize their activities, thereby helping people to shift from rule-abiding to rule-breaking identities in a way that supports their deviant or criminal choices. Corporate criminals rationalize their activities as "only doing business" or "helping the economy," for example. Youthful deviants justify their acts as "being cool" or "not being square" or "flipping off authority."

The most significant social learning theories of crime are labeling theories, which follow from the work of Howard Becker. These perspectives examine the development of criminal careers from a first act of (possibly harmless) deviance, rather than the causes of crime itself. Labeling theories are influenced by sociological and psychological theories of symbolic interactionism, as expressed in the work of Charles Cooley, George Herbert Mead, and Herbert Blumer. According to symbolic interactionism, people interpret symbolic gestures from others and incorporate them into their own self-image. Thus negative reactions, whether verbal or expressed in body language, could cause individuals to view themselves in a negative light. This insight would prove to be a central tenet of labeling theory, which examined the effect of social signals—including those given by teachers, police, and other justice officials and media—upon adoption of criminal identities.

The formal beginnings of labeling theory date to the early works of Franklin Tannenbaum in the 1930s, particularly *Crime and Community* (1938). Tannenbaum pointed out that many forms of juvenile delinquency are simply normal parts of adolescent street life. They are part of the play, experiment, adventure, and excitement that represent crucial parts of individual and social development. To others, particularly outsiders of different age cohorts, such activities may be seen as threatening or a nuisance. Those individuals may demand the intervention of some form of social control or punishment of the juvenile offender, whether through police or school officials. Such intervention begins a process of change in the manner in which the targeted individuals and their activities are perceived and treated. There is a gradual shift from the definition of specific acts as evil to the redefining of the individual himself or herself as evil. Everything about the individual, his or her friends, clothing, speech, music, and so on is turned into an object of scrutiny and cast as evidence for a delinquent nature. According to Tannenbaum, individuals targeted in this way may eventually learn to view *themselves* as delinquents. This process, which Tannenbaum refers to as the "dramatization of evil," leads to the child or youth being separated out of the surrounding group and subjected to negative treatment. Not only criminals are made deviant in this manner; rather, individuals who simply violate norms or conventions rather than laws, particularly members of youth subcultures, may be subjected to such treatment. Tannenbaum noted that the poor are more likely than the wealthy to get caught up in this process. This point has been developed by critical criminologists and conflict theorists.

Building on these insights, labeling theory attempts to examine the social and interpersonal processes through which acts, attributes, and beliefs come to be constructed as deviant. It attempts to explain how cultural and individual perceptions create and sustain deviant identities. For labeling theories, deviance results from the enforcement of rules rather than specific acts. The deviant person is simply someone to whom the label "deviant" has been successfully applied, not someone who is fundamentally different. Even more, the deviant person is someone who has come to believe the label as it applies to him or her.

Labeling theorists note that most people have engaged in deviant, even criminal, acts but do not consider themselves to be criminals because those events pass without notice or regard. If someone is caught in such an act, however, a process is engaged that shifts the person's self-perception. Being arrested, identified, brought to trial, and perhaps jailed is what labeling theorists call a "degradation ceremony," in which the person subjected to this treatment is initiated into a deviant role and assigned a deviant label. This process often alters a person's self-concept, disrupts personal relationships, and changes life chances and opportunities, including negatively impacting employment, housing, and education. To be publicly defined as deviant is to carry an expectation that you will behave in certain ways. By assigning negative identities, conforming members of society—and those with the power to assign labels—strongly influence offenders' future behavior. People learn to take on behaviors and attitudes consistent with the label. "Stigma" is the term used by Erving Goffman to refer to the mark of disgrace that is associated with deviant or criminal labels.

People are turned into deviants through official procedures that are about the exercise of power and authority within stratified societies rather than strictly expressions of justice. Labeling theories challenge notions of social consensus that propose social order results from broadly agreed-upon goals and values. For social learning theorists, reality is socially constructed or produced through the activities of disparate and varying groups both internally and through their interactions with other, more or less powerful, groups. They stress the importance of power relations within a given society and suggest that it is essential to know who assumes the authority to do the labeling in society. This information helps explain why less harmful acts, such as shoplifting or squeegeeing, which are often carried out by less powerful members of society, are targeted for criminalization and the deployment of criminal justice system resources, whereas more harmful acts such as pollution, product safety, or unfair labor practices, which are typically undertaken by corporate elites, are less likely to leave the perpetrator with a deviant or criminal label. Similarly, labeling theorists might suggest that schoolyard bullying receives proportionally more public attention than a variety of corporate crimes.

Labeling theorists emphasize that some people have the power to make their labels stick, while others cannot. The definition of deviance or crime is a form of social control exerted by more powerful actors over less powerful actors. Labeling is part of a process that excludes subordinate actors from social participation or from power.

Social psychologist Albert Bandura's social learning theory emphasizes modeling and the processes by which people learn not only through direct experience but also by observing others whom they respect or admire. Role models in the media, arts, sports, or music, for example, can influence people to act in desirable or undesirable ways. As Bandura also noted, observation of violent acts, as on television, could be reflected in violent acts by child observers.

Social learning theories are significant in showing that societies' definitions determine whether certain behavior is considered deviant or criminal, and in pointing out that these definitions change over time and place. Often these definitions are the outcome of social struggle, inequality, and exploitation. Furthermore, labeling theory shows that the act of labeling—especially as associated with the activities of schools, police, criminal justice systems, media, and prisons—may actually perpetuate crime rather than reducing it.

Jeffrey Shantz

Further Reading

Bandura, A. (1977). *Social learning theory.* Morristown, NJ: General Learning Press.

Becker, H. (1963). *Outsiders.* New York: Free Press.

Sutherland, E. (1949). *White collar crime.* New York: Holt, Rinehart and Winston.

Social Networking

Social networking involves online groups of people who share some common interests. As part of their interactions, users create webpages in which they can post pictures, videos, information about themselves, articles, and much more. Users then invite people to be their friends, which grants them access to see the pages. MySpace, a social networking site is owned by Fox Interactive Media, has more than 115 million monthly users across the globe. Facebook, another popular social networking site, boasts more than 400 million users worldwide.

An unidentified University of Missouri student looks at a profile on Facebook. Facebook is a popular social networking site for high school and college students. (AP/Wide World Photos)

Students say bullying and harassment often begins on social networking sites. In recent years, reports have documented the rise in cyberbullying, which is often facilitated through social networking sites. Some cases have received national attention. In one case, a teenage girl's mother orchestrated the bullying through MySpace that led to another girl's suicide. When Lori Drew's daughter told her about an argument she had with her best friend, Megan Meier, she also said she thought Megan was saying bad things about her in school and on MySpace. Drew helped create a MySpace page for a fictitious character, Josh, who "friended" Meier and began to create an online relationship with her. After some time, Josh told Meier told her he hated her and that the world would be better without her. In October 2006, Meier hung herself. Drew was indicted in the case and found guilty of three counts of computer hacking. At the time, prosecutors had a difficult time finding appropriate laws they could use to try Drew. Dardenne Prairie, Missouri, became the first town in the United States to pass legislation to make cyberharassment a specific offense.

In another case, when John Halligan's son Josh committed suicide after being cyberbullied, Halligan lobbied for a bullying prevention law in Vermont that would include cyberbullying; the law was passed. In another case, bullies posted a fake profile of Drew McGowan, claiming he was a homosexual. Phoebe Prince, who was bullied on Facebook by a group of girls from her high school, committed suicide in 2009.

Students have also posted "hit lists" of people whom they intend to kill or inappropriate pictures, such as themselves with weapons and drugs. Often these posts lead school administrators or police to intervene before an attack or criminal incident occurs. Police are now trolling the web, including MySpace and Facebook, to look for clues suggestive of potential violence.

Social networking sites are also used by abusive teen partners as a method to control their victims. Teens may post embarrassing pictures or information or threaten their partners via these sites.

MySpace is aware of the concern that it can be used for violent or criminal purposes and has prepared a "School Administrator's Guide" to assist administrators in addressing problems that might arise. The organization reports that, while the majority (78%) of student Internet use occurs off school grounds, parents generally believe that schools have a responsibility to ensure children's Internet safety. More than 40% of parents have reached out to school administrators for advice on this topic. The MySpace guide includes information explaining how to contact MySpace in the event that a false or offensive profile is posted, or in the case of threats, cyberbullying, or suspected underage users. The guide talks parents through how to handle each of these issues.

MySpace says it is committed to protecting users, in particular young ones. New profiles for persons younger than the age of 18 are automatically defaulted to a private setting, which should prohibit uninvited persons from seeing the information. Users are not able to browse for profile pages by persons younger than the age of 16. All users younger than the age of 18 are required to read a list of safety tips before registering, receive warnings before posting any content, and must pre-approve any comments made on their page. Young users are also prohibited from browsing inappropriate pages, such as romance and relationship chat forums, adult message groups, and mature groups.

On January 14, 2008, state attorneys general from 49 states announced an agreement with MySpace that they felt would better protect children and young people. MySpace agreed to take the following steps:

- Create a task force to develop age and identity verification technology to keep underage children off its site
- Set up a registry of blocked email addresses of minors, to be supplied by parents
- Make the profiles of members ages 14–17 "private" by default, meaning they can be seen by friends only
- Establish a "high school" section of the site for users younger than age 18
- Respond within 72 hours to complaints about inappropriate content
- Hire more staff to police such content as photos and discussion boards

The lone holdout from the agreement, Texas State Attorney Greg Abbott, refused to sign the agreement because he claimed that social networking sites could not adequately protect young people.

Like MySpace, Facebook claims to take great precautions to protect users, but has faced criticisms that they are not sufficient.

PBS Frontline has produced two informative episodes about youth in the digital age. *Growing Up Online* and *Digital Nation* examine how technology is being used by young people, explore the risks they face, and suggest ways to keep them safe. Both episodes, which can be viewed online, also include resources for parents and educators.

Laura L. Finley

Further Reading

Associated Press. (2008, May 15). Missouri woman indicted in MySpace cyber bullying case that ended in teen's suicide. *Fox News.* Retrieved May 6, 2010, from http://www.foxnews.com/story/0,2933,356056,00.html

Digital Nation: http://www.pbs.org/wgbh/pages/frontline/digitalnation/

The facts about teen dating violence. (2010). *Violence Against Women Online Resources.* Retrieved May 6, 2010, from http://vaw.umn.edu/documents/inbriefs/teendatingviolence/teendatingviolence.html

Growing Up Online: http://www.pbs.org/wgbh/pages/frontline/kidsonline/view/

Leonard, T. (2007, November 23). MySpace suicide town outlaws online bullying. *The Telegraph.* Retrieved May 6, 2010, from http://www.telegraph.co.uk/news/worldnews/1570308/MySpace-suicide-town-outlaws-online-bullying.html

MySpace agrees to toughen age control. (2008, January 22). *PBS Frontline.* Retrieved May 6, 2010, from http://www.pbs.org/wgbh/pages/frontline/kidsonline/safe/protecting.html

The official school administrator's guide to understanding MySpace and resolving social networking issues. (n.d.). Retrieved May 6, 2010, from http://cms.myspacecdn.com/cms/SafetySite/documents/SchoolAdministratorGuide.pdf

Roberts, E. (2010, April 9). Students invited to give perspective on school violence. *South Florida Sun Sentinel.* Retrieved May 6, 2010, from http://articles.sun-sentinel.com/2010-04-09/news/fl-dff-mayorside-0408-20100409_1_school-violence-john-esposito-deerfield-beach-middle-school

Saulny, S. (2007, March 22). On hitlists, anger finds an outlet. *New York Times.* Retrieved May 6, 2010, from http://www.nytimes.com/2007/03/22/fashion/22HITLIST.html

Whitcomb, D. (2010, March 9). Cyber-bullying cases put heat on Google, Facebook. Reuters. Retrieved May 6, 2010, from http://www.reuters.com/article/idUSTRE6275UG20100309

Zapf, K. (2008, April 28). Student victim of MySpace bullies. *Pittsburgh Tribune Review.* Retrieved May 6, 2010, from http://www.pittsburghlive.com/x/pittsburghtrib/news/s_448311.html

Social Structure Theories

Social structure theories bring a sociological (rather than biological or psychological) approach to studies of crime and deviance. Instead of focusing solely or primarily on individuals, these theories seek to explain how individuals are situated within and experience larger-scale social institutions such as schools, government, the labor market, cultural industries, and the criminal justice system. Over the years, theorists have proposed mainstream or consensus theories of social structure as well as critical or conflict theories of structure. According to mainstream or consensus theories, social structures serve to regulate and socialize individuals to conform to dominant social norms, rewarding some behaviors while penalizing others. In contrast, according to critical social structure theories, social, economic and political power serve as barriers that impede, constrain, or shape what is possible for people in specific societal contexts, largely based on characteristics such as class, ethnicity, gender, or sexuality.

Mainstream or consensus-based social structure theories trace their roots to the work of the French sociologist Emile Durkheim (1858–1917). For Durkheim, crime was a social rather than psychological phenomenon and the product of a specific kind of social order. Specifically, according to Durkheim, a society without shared norms and values will function poorly. Societies are regulated by a *conscience collective*—that is, shared norms, beliefs, rituals, and customs—that holds their diverse members together, providing a shared worldview or value system that defines acceptable and unacceptable social behaviors. This framework shapes and regulates social interactions. For Durkheim, small-scale societies, such as horticultural or agricultural societies, with a low level of social differentiation and a minimal division of labor, where the majority of society share similar life experiences, exhibit the strongest and most durable conscience collective and, therefore, have the fewest occurrences of crime and deviance. Within industrial capitalist societies, which are characterized by a broad and diverse division of labor, the conscience collective is more difficult to sustain given the great social and cultural differences and the vast disparities in wealth and social opportunity. A breakdown of shared values, increased by a growing division of labor, leads to what Durkheim called *anomie*, or a condition of normlessness. Anomie results in increased crime, deviance, and suicide rates.

Durkheim's work has informed a range of social structure theories, including the influential work of Robert K. Merton and Albert Cohen. During the 1950s and 1960s, structural theories represented the dominant sociological perspective on crime and deviance. First among these was Merton's "strain theory." According to Merton, individuals in capitalist societies such as the United States share essentially the same cultural goals—namely, wealth, status, and financial success, collectively dubbed the American Dream. These goals are encouraged and reinforced by the major social institutions, such as schools, government, media, and corporations. In turn, culturally preferred and encouraged means to achieve these goals are defined—education, hard work, thrift, and personal sacrifice. These become culturally valued attributes or practices, expressed in notions such as the "work ethic."

Of course, people have differential means available for achieving these culturally supported goals. Some have blocked opportunities, perhaps because of class location or socioeconomic status, but also because of race, ethnicity, or gender discrimination. As a consequence these individuals are unable to achieve their goals through legitimate means. Society offers members of different social groups very different institutional means of achieving its proscribed goals, such as unequal opportunities for education regardless of ability, fulfilling work, or financial aid. Strain develops from this means–end discrepancy between culturally encouraged goals and structurally available means for achieving them; if intense enough, it can result in deviance. A gap between effort and reward makes it impossible for some people to set realistic, achievable goals or to plan legitimate ways of achieving their goals.

According to Merton, individuals respond to this strain in one of five ways. First, they may engage in conformism, in which they accept the socially encouraged means and ends. These individuals stay in school and sacrifice to become economically successful. The second option is Innovation, in which people accept the goals of wealth and status but reject the socially approved means of obtaining those goals. An example would be drug dealers or corporate criminals who pursue illegal means or cheat to achieve financial success. The third option involves ritualism, in which people become attached to the means but lose sight of the goals. A "professional student" or middle management bureaucrat might be considered examples of ritualism. The fourth possibility is retreatism, in which people reject both the means and the goals. A dropout or someone who pursues subcultural activities might be an example of this response. Finally there are rebels, those individuals who reject the socially defined goals and means but seek to replace them with alternatives. Revolutionaries, anarchists, and countercultural activists would exemplify rebellion. According to Merton, persons of lower socioeconomic status are most likely to experience greater strain and, therefore, to engage in deviant acts, perhaps taking the form of as retreatism or innovation.

Many theorists have developed structural theories building on Merton's work. Albert Cohen focused specifically on working-class youth. He presented the notion of status frustration to explain higher rates of delinquency among youth from less wealthy backgrounds. In his view, frustration results from the fact that poorer youth lack sufficient access to legitimate means to achieve their goals and recognize their limitations. This recognition is expressed in social frustration, and a sense that they will be punished no matter how they behave; it is acted upon through acts of deviance.

Richard Cloward and Lloyd Ohlin suggest that marginalized youth seek alternatives or innovations to seek their goals. According to these theorists, youth face "differential opportunity structures" that limit their life options and possibilities for personal development. As a result, these individuals form and join subcultures to help themselves achieve their goals or develop alternatives. The work of Cloward and Ohlin focuses on the emergence of deviant subcultures among youth.

Over the last few decades. a variety of authors have focused on economic structures and the emergence of deviance. Robert Agnew's "general strain theory" explains deviance as a coping mechanism to help adolescents deal with the negative emotional states related to their experiences of socioeconomic problems. Proponents of "institutional strain theory" note that throughout the neo-liberal era, roughly from the 1980s to the present, economic issues have come to dominate non-economic spheres, weakening the informal control mechanisms exerted by the family, school, church, and communities. In this environment, politics becomes about the economy, trade, and investment, rather than about social policy, civil rights, or democratic practice. School, for example, is now dominated by considerations of the job market, and future employability, rather than concerns about developing critical thought or citizenship. Programs that are viewed as contributing to personal enrichment rather than employability, such as music, drama, art, classical studies, or philosophy, face cuts or cancellation in favor of trades and technology or business training. According to institutional strain theory, the heightened emphasis on success in economic terms increases social strain (anomie). The emphasis on the most expedient path to economic success means that crime may be viewed as the most efficient means to financial gain. The celebrity status achieved by corporate criminals, such as Michael Milken, during the Reagan era provides but one example of institutional strain theory in action.

Other social structure theorists have preferred to examine links between crime and levels of disorganization within specific neighborhoods or communities rather than more abstract cultural values or institutions. Social ecology theories, influenced by the Chicago School of Sociology and the work of Robert Park, suggest that in crime-ridden neighborhoods, local institutions such as schools and social services agencies have broken down and no longer perform their expected or stated functions. Residents experience conflict and despair and antisocial behavior results. High school dropout rates and high rates of youth unemployment are typical characteristics of breakdown leading to deviance and crime. According to "cultural transmission theory," poor neighborhoods are marked by high population turnover rates, which disrupts informal social controls. Such areas are said to give rise to youth crime. Crime will be a constant feature in this environment, regardless of the personal character of the residents, because of existing structural conditions. According to "cultural transmission theory," gang activity and youth deviance are normal and expected responses to adverse conditions in which legitimized alternatives are otherwise not available for youth who perceive themselves to be trapped without options. For these theories, crime is a strategy to deal with destructive social conditions.

More critical or radical proponents of structural theories reject the emphasis that is often placed on street crimes or the crimes of the working class. First, they point out, the most harmful crimes, socially and environmentally, are crimes of elites, such as toxic dumping, unsafe products, unhealthy working conditions, pollution, and food contamination. These crimes, they argue, should be given more attention than the small-scale crimes that consume most of criminal justice system resources. Second, the use of criminal justice statistics, such as police and court records, within some of the structural theories identified previously, misrepresents actual criminal activity. The use of police records in social ecology theories to calculate neighborhood crime rates, for example, reflects police surveillance of those neighborhoods rather than actual rates of criminal activity. Finally, while structural theories do a good job of documenting social inequalities, critical theorists argue that the point is to confront and end inequality.

For critical structural theorists, including those who favor explanations based on structural Marxism and anarchism, the main structures in society that must be understood in reaction to crime and deviance are the state and capital. These institutions fundamentally control social resources and have the power to define specific acts as crimes and certain individuals as criminals, often on the basis of class or other factors. According to the critical structural perspective, the capitalist state and its institutions exist to preserve the interests of the dominant economic class, the capitalist class of those who own and control the means of production. The main concern of this dominant class is the preservation of an economic and social order that maintains their privilege and allows them to continue the accumulation of wealth. Behaviors that threaten the existing socioeconomic regime are most likely to be targeted, ideologically as well as practically, for punishment. As a consequence, most resources of the criminal justice system are directed toward (often minor) property crimes such as petty thefts and shoplifting. Similarly, moral panics are most often directed toward the activities of the working class and poor, particularly working-class youth—for example, raves, squeegeeing, hip-hop music, punk music. By comparison, crimes of elites, such as corporate crime, ecological crimes, and government misconduct, receive far less attention from the criminal justice system and result in fewer, and less severe, punishments.

The main focus of the criminal justice system, according to critical structural theorists, is to prohibit behaviors that threaten the unequal distribution of property under capitalism or the state's monopoly on the use of force. Thus one sees the criminalization of union organizing, strikes, protests, and rebellion. The inherent conflicts that exist within a system of broad socioeconomic inequality are controlled through the structures of government and the criminal justice system in a way that inhibits disadvantaged classes and sustains dominant classes' capacities to rule. For structural Marxists, the state must be taken over and controlled by the working class to serve their needs. For anarchists, the state, as an inherently authoritarian and hierarchical institution, is always a force of domination and cannot be used to achieve equality. Instead, the state must be replaced by community-based direct democracy and participatory decision making.

Jeffrey Shantz

Further Reading

Cohen, A. (1955). *Delinquent boys*. New York: Free Press.
Merton, R. (1949). *Social theory and social structure*. New York: Free Press.
Polk, K., & Schafer, W. (Eds.). (1972). *Schools and delinquency*. Englewood Cliffs, NJ: Prentice-Hall.

Taylor, I., Walton, P., & Young, J. (1988). *The new criminology: For a social theory of deviance*. London: Routledge.

Solomon, T. J.

On May 20, 1999, a 15-year-old sophomore named Anthony Thomas Solomon, Jr. (also known as T. J.), walked into his high school in Conyers, Georgia, and shot six of his classmates, giving all but one of them superficial wounds. The shooting took place before classes at Heritage High School began for the day, while 150 students were gathered in the school's indoor commons area. The United States was shocked by this tragedy because it occurred exactly one month to the day after the Columbine High School massacre. When one realizes that no one was killed, this incident might not be perceived to be as horrifying as what happened at Columbine.

Solomon had arrived at school that day with a .22-caliber sawed-off shotgun and a .357-magnum revolver stuffed in his baggy jeans. He also arrived at school with a pocket full of bullets. That morning, instead of socializing with his friends, Solomon stood alone off to the side. At 7:55 A.M., he pulled out the shotgun and fired all of its rounds. He emptied the gun, aiming low and firing between 10 and 12 shots.

The six students hit were Jason Cheek, a senior who was shot twice; Cania Cullins, an African American sophomore; Drake Hoy; Stephanie Laster, a sophomore; Ryan Rosa, a junior; and an unidentified student. Of the six, only Laster was seriously hurt; in her case, the bullet first hit a hard surface such as a floor, a table, or a wall and then ricocheted into her lower abdomen. Everyone else suffered either flesh wounds or minor injuries. The attack had lasted less than 10 minutes.

After Solomon had emptied the shotgun, he ran out of the commons. He then fell to his knees and put the revolver in his mouth. Before he could shoot himself, the high school's vice principal, Cecil T. Brinkley, calmed Solomon down. According to Brinkley, Solomon grabbed him and started shaking. Solomon said, "Oh, my God, I'm so scared." Brinkley took Solomon outside and handed him over to a deputy from the Rockdale County Sheriff's Department.

That afternoon, after Solomon was arrested, Solomon's mother, Mae Dean Daniele, a secretary for a veterinarian, and his stepfather, Robert W. Daniele, an executive at a trucking firm, arranged for lawyer Edward T. M. Garland to defend him. He was transported by Sheriff Jeff T. Wigington to a youth detention center, where he was met by his parents and Garland. Rockdale County's District Attorney, Richard Read, said he planned to have Solomon's case transferred from the juvenile courts to the Superior Court so that he could be tried as an adult for aggravated assault, cruelty to children, and weapons violations. Nonetheless, because of his age, Solomon was going to be held in a juvenile facility until he reached the age of majority. The hearing for the transfer was placed on a fast track and scheduled for June 1, approximately two weeks later.

The transfer hearing actually did not begin until August 9, and was held in front of juvenile-court judge William Schneider. It lasted two and one half days. On August 11, Judge Schneider determined that Solomon would be tried in Rockdale County Superior Court on 21 felony charges. If convicted of all of the charges, Solomon could have faced up to 351 years in prison. During the hearing, Garland argued that Solomon, who had been taking Ritalin since the fourth grade, had the maturity of an 11-year-old. He further presciently warned that if Solomon was put in the adult system, he would one day try to kill himself. Schneider partly based his decision on the fact that the shooting seemed to be a copycat shooting. Solomon had left a suicide note at home on the morning of May 20, in which he "expressed allegiance to his 'brothers and sisters related to the trenchcoat mafia.'" In his mind, these individuals included Eric Harris and Dylan Klebold, the shooters in the Columbine massacre. When discussing that event with friends at school, Solomon had stated that he was a better gunman than either Harris or Klebold and that such a massacre should have happened at Heritage High School a long time ago.

Read planned to take Solomon's case to Rockdale County's grand jury on September 7. Garland appealed this plan, arguing that Solomon was mentally ill and belonged in a mental institution. In February 2000, the Georgia Court of Appeals in Atlanta ruled that Solomon was not out of touch with reality and could be tried as an adult. At some point in February, Solomon's parents were interviewed on television. They read a letter from him apologizing for the shootings. In that letter, Solomon said, "It is hard to describe how dark and isolated I felt leading up to the date of my mistake. It almost made everything in my life not worth waiting for." In the letter Solomon did not clarify his motives for the shootings. According to some of his friends, he was depressed and upset over a fight and a breakup he had with his girlfriend, Kara Ward. Ward had been the same age as Solomon when the shootings took place. According to Ward, she and Solomon had not broken up but had simply had a fight. The fight was over the fact that, according to Ward, Solomon was uncommunicative. Solomon, however, had perceived this fight as a breakup.

On October 2, 2000, Solomon pleaded both guilty and guilty but mentally ill to all charges against him. He entered two pleas because Read did not want to accept the plea of guilty but mentally ill. Superior Court Judge Sidney Nation set sentencing for November 8.

At the November hearing, Nation sentenced Solomon to 40 years on charges of aggravated assault. Nation told Solomon at the sentencing hearing that he would be eligible for parole in 18 years. The Georgia Board of Pardons and Paroles told Solomon in May that he would not be considered for pardon until he had served 36 years of his sentence.

While he was in prison, Solomon was given Prozac. As Garland had predicted, Solomon tried to commit suicide. In January 2001, he took a one month's supply of Elavil and ended up hospitalized for three months. After his recovery, Solomon was placed under 24-hour suicide watch in the infirmary at Arrendale State Prison.

In August 2001, Nation agreed to hold a post-sentencing hearing. On August 17, the judge reduced Solomon's sentence from 40 years, which would have meant that he would be eligible for parole after 36 years, to 20 years, which means he is eligible for parole after 18 years, around the time of his 33rd birthday in 2017.

In some ways, Solomon was not a typical school shooter. Before he moved to Conyers, Solomon and his family lived in Kernersville, North Carolina. In Kernersville, he was a member of the Boy Scouts, went to the YMCA, and spent a lot of time with his stepfather. Even in Conyers, Solomon had friends, was a Boy Scout, went to church, and was involved in sports. His stepfather also made sure that he took a gun safety classes. Solomon was an excellent shot, which explains why his friends believe that he had no intention to kill anyone on May 20—if he had wanted to kill someone, they say, he had the gun skills to do it.

Scott Sheidlower

Further Reading

Cloud, J. (1999, May 31). Just a routine school shooting. *Time, 153*(21), 34. Retrieved January 19, 2009, from Academic Search Premier, EBSCOhost.

Farber, H., & Stafford, L. (1999, August 11). Parents mystified as to what set off son: Mom, stepdad say Solomon on Ritalin since 4th grade—changed three years ago. *Atlanta Journal-Constitution.* Retrieved January 8, 2009, from Custom Newspapers, Gale.

Roche, T. (2001, May 28). Voices from the cell. *Time*. Retrieved December 18, 2008, from http://www.time.com/time/printout/0,8816,999966,00.html

Tryggsted, E. (2000, March 7). Former principal recalls day of terror. *Savannah Morning News*. Retrieved December 17, 2008, from http://old.savvannahnow.com/stories/030700/LOCconference.shtml

South America and School Crime and Violence

School violence in South America has been a problem endemic to this region for decades. Rates of violence have been growing recently, however, because of a confluence of two factors: The countries of this region have been increasing the rate at which children enroll in school and the period of time for which they remain in the public education programs. In years past, the dropout rate was much higher in South America.

Students dash across the Henrique Forei school yard in Rio de Janeiro on July 12, 2006. This school provides educational services for students in the Fazendinha shantytown and is frequently disturbed by violence from local gangs. It served as a battleground between police and a local gang, in a conflict that resulted in 6 children wounded by bullets and 11 more hurt by shards of glass. (AP/Wide World Photos)

The roots of violence in schools in this region are attributed to the structure of this region's society. Approximately 32% of the residents of South America live in poor urban communities. Often these metropolises are sprawling, unplanned cities in which tens of thousands of people live in substandard housing and are served only sporadically by municipal utilities like running water and electric power. Schools are not seen by the governments of this region as institutions through which to provide education as a right to their citizens, but rather as places to exert control and maintain class formation. A significant number of youth from the lowest economic class drop out of school before finishing their secondary level of education. Many of the males from this sector eventually join gangs and further contribute to the cycle of violence in their own communities. This trend can, in a large part, be explained by the sociological assertion that criminals tend to act in a rational manner. Because South American society offers little social mobility to those born into the poorest class, crime—rather than education—is seen as the most logical path for escaping poverty.

While most countries in South America have officially outlawed corporal punishment in schools, UNICEF reports that this practice remains common. Notably, children and teenagers in this region are exposed to an extraordinary amount of violence compared to their peers in Western society. Violence within the school walls consists of students abusing other students, students abusing teachers, and teachers abusing students. For example, in Argentina, 23% of students in one study reported that they bullied other students at least several times, while 10% stated that they physically attacked their classmates. Students in the same study volunteered that 8% bullied teachers, while an additional 3% attacked their instructors. In Brazil, the numbers are even more alarming: In a study of 12,000 students from 143 schools in six state capitals, 84% described their schools as violent, while 70% stated that they were victims of violence.

In addition to the significant numbers of young men who join gangs, many poverty-stricken school-aged youth are forced to live in the streets. There, they are subject to a wide array of abuses, ranging from crime to prostitution to drug addiction to murder. The problem of child murder is particularly dire in Brazil, a nation that accounts for more than half of South America's total population. Thousands of young people die every year as a result of violent acts, including 45% of the adolescents whose lives end annually in Brazil. Some experts predict that based on current trends, 33,000 adolescents in Brazil will die violently in 2012. Colombia's homicide rate is 84.4 children killed per 100,000 youths. On average, South America has a rate of 26 homicides per 100,000 youths—the third highest rate of any region in the world. To put this figure in perspective, the corresponding rate in the United States is 11 youth homicides per 100,000 population.

The issue of gangs is not a footnote in this situation. On the contrary, this problem is so immense that two of Brazil's largest cities, Sao Paulo and Rio De Janeiro, have been overrun by gang violence. A sizable number of these gang members are "child soldiers" (as they are referred to by authorities), not dissimilar to the situation found in some areas of both Africa and Asia. In fact, in addition to being pressed into gangs, South American youth as young as nine and 10 years old are sometimes forced to bear arms for various rebel militias in places such as Peru and Colombia.

The children who fight in these conflicts and activities are not the only ones affected by this challenging situation. Six million of Colombia's 17 million children are affected by the toll exacted by these war-like conditions. The emotional stress inflicted by the ongoing conflict is yet another factor that impinges on South American children's ability to live the tranquil lives one might expect youths to enjoy.

In addition to the obvious challenges faced by this dysfunctional society, large swaths of the South American continent are governed by drug lords. There, public schools do not exist in adequate numbers, as the virtual warlords do not wish to see such institutions exist. This vacuum is being addressed on a limited basis by the U.S. Agency for International Aid's (USAID) Alternative Development Program, which funds such infrastructure projects in foreign countries as part of the U.S. efforts to reengineer such problematic socioeconomic situations.

Another plague running rampant among portions of South America's school-aged population is child prostitution. This crime varies greatly across the continent, with Brazil being identified as the most notorious center of child prostitution and trafficking. While many countries have laws forbidding such activities, child prostitution as well as sex tourism and associated exploitation have been identified as huge industries in South America. Peru's Amazon region is one where this problem is especially common. Children are often led into this path through the enticement of being offered work. This lure often proves irresistible, as the widespread poverty found throughout South America creates a tremendous pressure on children to contribute to their household's economic survival.

As numerous studies have shown, children who prematurely enter the workforce have a relatively high risk (compared to those who do not follow this path) of becoming delinquent, being involved in criminal activities, and dropping out of school. In addition, much higher rates of alcohol and drug abuse are found among the population of children who are working. The rate of alcoholism in this population has also been found to be greatly out of proportion to the general population. Among 14-year-olds that are working, the average rate of alcoholism has been found to be 30%. In secondary school, it is often found to exceed 50%. This pattern becomes all the more serious when one considers that studies demonstrate a significant number of those persons arrested for committing homicide were intoxicated either during the act or shortly before it.

Drug abuse among South American students is widespread, although the particular substance of choice varies from country to country. For example, ecstasy is used by many students in Colombia, but not those elsewhere in South America; the use of inhalants is popular among Brazilian students, but not among other South American students. Cocaine use is particularly high in Argentina, Colombia, and Brazil, but not in the rest of the continent. Methamphetamine use is prevalent in Colombia, Brazil, Bolivia, and Argentina, but is barely found in Peru, a country with a pattern of very low drug abuse overall. With regard to marijuana, its use among 14-year-olds in South America is relatively minor, though members of Uruguay's general population increase their use of this drug by four times by the time schoolchildren outgrow their adolescent years.

The overall issue of crime and violence in South American schools is a complex one. Currently, although universal elementary and secondary education is officially available to all school-aged children in this area, attendance is not always possible or probable. Inflated enrollment rates are often reported, with the counts including students who are not in fact attending or who do not remain in school for the full day of classes. In addition, many young people of school age who reside in urban slums or shantytowns are not visible in the census records and are ignored by the education establishment. This neglect makes them vulnerable to greater threats related to crime and violence.

Len Lubitz

Further Reading

Buvinic, M., Morrison, A., & Shifter, M. (1999). *Violence in Latin America and the Caribbean: A framework for action.* Technical Study, Sustainable Development Department, Inter-American Development Bank. Retrieved March 10, 2011 from http://www.bvsde.paho.org/bvsacd/cd66/1073eng.pdf

Cardoso, R., & Verner, D. (2006, December). School drop-out and push-out factors in Brazil: The role of early parenthood, child labor, and poverty. Discussion Paper No. 2515. Bonn, Germany: Institute for the Study of Labor (IZA).

Magaly, S. (2006, July). Insecurity and violence as a new power relation in Latin America. *Annals of the American Academy of Political and Social Science, 606,* 178–195.

UNICEF Innocenti Research Centre: http://www.unicef-irc.org/datasets/data_sets_int.html

UNICEF: Key Issues on Child Protection: http://www.unicef.org/lac/Key_info_on_Child_Protection(1).pdf

Southern Poverty Law Center

In 1971, lawyers Morris Dees and Joe Levin created the Southern Poverty Law Center (SPLC) as a civil rights law firm. SPLC's first president was Julian Bond, who is well known for his civil rights work. Bond currently serves on the board of directors. Today, this nonprofit organization is known across the world for its work tracking hate and extremist groups, litigating cases involving white supremacists, and providing educational resources on acceptance through its teaching arm, Teaching Tolerance.

SPLC's Intelligence Project staff monitor the number and activity of white supremacist and other hate groups. This information is then provided on the organization's website as well as disseminated to law enforcement and media. It is also shared with the public through SPLC's quarterly magazine, *Intelligence Report.* Intelligence Project staff also serve as expert witnesses in trials involving hate crimes and at conferences, and they provide training to police, schools, and other interested community groups.

In the 1980s, SPLC helped win several anti-discrimination victories, including equal benefits for women in the armed forces, the establishment of more inclusive hiring practices for police in Alabama, an end to the involuntary sterilization of women receiving welfare, and reform of conditions in prisons and mental health facilities. Its staff have also addressed issues related to worker safety, tax equity, flying of the confederate flag at the Alabama state capitol, medical services for the poor, and equitable education for homeless children. In *Nixon v. Brewer* (a suit brought by SPLC), the U.S. Supreme Court determined that Alabama's districting system was unfair and was not representing black voters. SPLC is currently working on projects related to immigrant justice and the school-to-prison pipeline.

In 1991, SPLC founded Teaching Tolerance as a means to prevent hate. Teaching Tolerance assists K–12 teachers by providing print and online resources for classroom use twice per year. Teaching Tolerance also provides free multimedia kits to educators on topics related to civil rights and anti-bias issues. These resources are used by more than 400,000 educators.

Teaching Tolerance's website (www.tolerance.org) features a searchable index of classroom activities for all levels of the K–12 curriculum. Topics include gay rights, responding to bias in the school, understanding and accepting those with disabilities, environmental justice, and much more. The site also has links for parents that provide information on teaching tolerance in the home, as well as information specific to younger children and teens. Every year in November, Teaching Tolerance sponsors "Mix It Up Day" at lunch, for which it provides free materials and organizational resources for schools hosting the event; this activity is designed to get students to interact with others in the cafeteria. More than 10,000 schools participate in the event each year.

Nick Sciullo

Further Reading

Southern Poverty Law Center: http://www.splcenter.org/index.jsp
Teaching Tolerance: http://www.tolerance.org/about/index.html

Spencer, Brenda

On January 29, 1979, 16-year-old Brenda Spencer killed two and injured nine at Cleveland Elementary School in San Diego, California. The school was located across the street from her house, so Spencer simply shot out of a window in her home while students waited outside for the school gate to open. She killed Principal Burton Wragg as he tried to protect the children. Head Custodian Mike Suchar was killed as he tried to assist Wragg. One police officer was killed as well.

After she fired 30 rounds, Spencer barricaded herself in her home for almost seven hours. Police tried to talk her out, while Spencer claimed that she would come out shooting. In the end, she surrendered to police. Spencer has gone down in infamy as one of the first school shooters, as one of the only female shooters, and for her famous quote on why she committed her crime: "I don't like Mondays."

Spencer had a history of deviant activity. Neighbors claimed she was involved in petty theft and drug abuse, and was chronically truant. She was obsessed with guns—an obsession her father fueled when he bought her a .22-caliber semiautomatic rifle for Christmas in 1978, along with 500 rounds of ammunition. Yet another neighbor who claimed to be a close friend described Spencer as generally happy. A classmate called her nice, but said her fellow students were scared of her because she talked about killing a lot. Spencer told classmates that she was often stoned on LSD, marijuana, or some other drug. At the time of the shooting, Spencer was just 5 feet 1 inch tall and weighed only 90 pounds.

When asked why she shot at the students and officials, Spencer claimed it was fun and a way to liven up the day. It was easy, she said, like "shooting ducks in a pond." She claimed that she enjoyed killing "a pig" (police officer) and wanted to kill more. She later claimed that she had been under the influence of alcohol and PCP but that investigators and prosecutors had conspired to hide her toxicology results. While investigators did find beer and whiskey bottles around her home, they say that results did not show Spencer was intoxicated. Psychologist Jonathan Fast has argued that Spencer suffered from some type of epilepsy, which is two to four times more common among violent offenders than among members of the general population.

Spencer was tried as an adult and pleaded guilty to two counts of murder and assault with a deadly weapon. She was sentenced to 25 years to life in prison, which she is still serving at California Institute for Women in Chico, California. She has been denied parole four times, most recently in 2009. She is not eligible for parole again until 2019. In her 2001 parole hearing, Spencer claimed for the first time that her father had physically and sexually abused her.

Spencer's shooting inspired a song called "I Don't Like Mondays" by the Boomtown Rats, as well as a documentary film called *The Killing of America*. Her famous phrase was also written on a wall in the popular 1980s movie *The Breakfast Club*. One of the students who survived the attack, Chris Stanley, was honored as Teacher of the Year in San Diego in 2007. He claims it was the heroic educators who tried to help that day who inspired him to teach.

Laura L. Finley

Further Reading

Fast, J. (2008). *Ceremonial violence: A psychological explanation of school shootings.* Woodstock, NY: Overland Press.

O'Toole, M. (2000). *The school shooter: A threat assessment perspective.* Quantico, VA: Federal Bureau of Investigation.

Rowe, P. (2007, October 6), 1979 school shootings inspired boy to teach. *San Diego Tribune.* Retrieved May 6, 2010, from http://www.signonsandiego.com/uniontrib/20071006/news_1n6teacher

Spur Posse

On March 18, 1993, the Los Angeles County Sheriff's Department arrested a group of teenage boys in Lakewood, California. Nine members of this group, who called themselves the Spur Posse, were charged with a variety of sex crimes, ranging from lewd conduct with a 10-year-old to rape. As details emerged, it became clear that the boys were seeking infamy for their sexual conquests. The group was estimated to include between 20 and 30 individuals.

One of the founding members of the group named it the Spur Posse because he was a fan of National Basketball Association (NBA) star David Robinson, who had just been traded to the San Antonio Spurs. Members of the group kept points on how many sexual conquests they had, and agreed to wear the jersey of a professional athlete whose number was the same as their amount. They even decided to take on the name of the athlete. Points could be counted only for sexual penetration, and only with a girl one time. Thus the idea was to have as many sexual partners as possible. The girls were referred to as "no-names" and whores, even though many of them really liked the popular boys. One member boasted of having sexual intercourse with 67 girls over a four-year-period. The boys also engaged in group sex so as to rack up more points, and even began videotaping their conquests.

Eventually, prosecutors dropped all but one of the charges, as they deemed most of the acts consensual. One member of the posse was convicted of lewd conduct with a 10-year-old and spent one year in the Kirby Juvenile Detention Center. He later explained that the young girl was selected because he needed more points so he could "make a name for himself." Some of the parents defended their boys, claiming they only did what "any red-blooded American boy" would do.

Once news of the scandal broke, media became obsessed with the Spur Posse. Members of the group appeared on *The Jenny Jones Show,* on the cover of *The New York Times,* and in *Newsweek, Penthouse,* and many other major news and popular culture outlets. This attention gave the boys the notoriety they sought. At the same time, people began referring to Lakewood as "Rapewood."

Interestingly, some of the boys were fairly successful students. Billy Shehan was in the school's gifted program and ended up graduating with honors. Others did go on to commit crimes. Founder Dana Belman was sentenced to 10 years in state prison for burglary and fraud, another member served time for assault, and a third was killed in a street fight.

Laura L. Finley

Further Reading

Faludi, S. (1999). *Stiffed: The betrayal of the American man.* New York: William Morrow.

Finley, L. (Ed.). (2007). *Encyclopedia of school crime and violence.* Westport, CT: Greenwood.

Smolowe, J., & Lafferty, L. (1993, April 5). Sex with a scorecard. *Time.* Retrieved May 6, 2010, from http://www.time.com/time/magazine/article/0,9171,978157,00.html

Steinhäuser, Robert

On April 26, 2002, 19-year-old Robert Steinhäuser opened fire at Johannes Gutenberg secondary school in Erfurt, Germany, killing 13 teachers, two students, and one police officer. He wore a black Ninja-style outfit and a black ski mask. After declaring, "That's enough for today," he committed suicide by turning the gun on himself. The massacre appears to have been motivated by revenge against teachers. Steinhäuser had failed a required university entrance exam in 2001 and was denied the opportunity to retake the exam one year later because he had missed classes and faked excuse notes.

The Erfurt massacre is one of the worst school shootings in history. More people were killed as a result of Steinhäuser's killing spree (16) than were killed at Columbine High School (13) in Littleton, Colorado, 1999. At the time, the minimum age for gun ownership in Germany was 18. Steinhäuser was legally entitled to own firearms and was a member of two gun clubs. He carried two weapons into the school, a 9-mm Glock 17 (a semi-automatic pistol) and a pump-action (slider) shotgun, though he used only the former in the massacre. Steinhäuser had valid licenses for both weapons. According to Blenkinsop (2002), the Erfurt mass killings coincidentally occurred just before the German parliament passed legislation that tightened gun laws. Pump-action shotguns were banned in the new legislation, and the minimum legal age for gun ownership was raised from 18 to 21.

In addition to being a gun enthusiast, Steinhäuser secretly owned a collection of videos that featured "extreme use of weapons" and violent video games, according to a representative of the German police. In the wake of the Erfurt attack, some conservative critics of the German government, such as the leader of the opposition party, called for the banning of such "killer games" and tougher controls on those who sell them.

Gutenburg secondary school access is blocked off by crime scene tape after the deadly shooting that killed 13 teachers, 2 students, and 1 police officer in Erfurt, Germany, on April 26, 2002. (AP/Wide World Photos)

The Erfurt massacre is of one of several such crimes that took place during the 1990s and 2000s, although most happened in the United States. The increase in frequency in school shootings has sparked discussion about what should be done to avoid future massacres. The levels of violence exhibited, the inability to predict such incidents, and their sensational nature have resulted in widespread publicity and speculation on the approaches to thwart future school shooting sprees. Most strategies have focused on "zero-tolerance" approaches—that is, policies that administer punishments for infractions such as possession of drugs and weapons in school. Such policies have also been used as strategies against behaviors such as bullying. Zero-tolerance approaches are controversial. Casella (2001), for example, describes them as responses that do little more than appease the fears of parents and the scrutiny of journalists, rather than attempt to grapple with social explanations of violence such as school shootings.

The proliferation of zero-tolerance policies belies the fact that school shootings, although horrific and captivating of public interest, are exceedingly rare. The degree of reaction—in the form of journalism, research, books, policies, and public discussion—is disproportionate to the actual numbers of school shootings that have taken place in the last few decades. Such preoccupation with school shootings constitutes a *moral panic*—a term that refers to overreactions to a social phenomenon that is extraordinary or unusual but is widely perceived as a threat to social order and norm.

Media coverage of school shootings tends to focus on the upbringing and psychological state of the perpetrator to explain why such massacres happen. For example, according to a BBC report, Steinhäuser was described as "normal" by those who knew him. The report added that

> Faced with this inability to explain Robert Steinhauser's individual psychology, it was left to Interior Minister Otto Schily to pose the wider question: "We must also ask ourselves the deeper question of what actually is going on in our society when a young person causes such disaster in such a way."

To answer that question is difficult, especially if the focus of the question is a gender-neutral "young person." News reports often describe school shooters as "youngsters" or "kids." Sensationalizing the Columbine massacre, *Time* magazine, on its May 3, 1999, cover story, described the perpetrators as "the monsters next door." The driving question of such commentary is simple: Why? Gender-neutral language is perhaps one of the reasons that concrete insights are elusive. It is not generic "kids" or "monsters" who perpetrate school shootings. Rather, the overwhelming majority of school shooters are boys. One notable exception is the case of Brenda Ann Spencer, who, at the age of 16, shot and killed two adults and injured eight students in San Diego, California, in 1979. The shooting inspired the hit song "I Don't Like Mondays" by the British rock group the Boomtown Rats.

Another obvious but mostly overlooked fact about school shooters, including Steinhäuser, is that the majority are not only male, but also white. An exception is Seung-Hui Cho, a 23-year-old South Korean student who killed 32 people at Virginia Tech University in 2007. Wise (2001) argues that whiteness as an unnamed pattern explains why the Federal Bureau of Investigation (FBI) has not created "profiles" of school shooters, as agents would have if the majority of such killers were black. Whiteness as a commonality has mostly escaped meaningful analysis.

The Spencer and Cho cases aside, the perspective that school shootings are perpetrated by disturbed individual youth is "dangerously shortsighted," according to anti-violence activists Jackson Katz and Sut Jhally (1999). They emphasize the gendered nature of school shootings in their argument that school shootings are "not a case of kids killing kids. This is boys killing boys and boys killing girls."

The socialization of boys, Katz and Jhally argue, is heavily invested in reducing boys' emotional capacities in favor of fostering and rewarding aggression, toughness, and individualism. Combined with social norms of masculinity, the mass media are a significant factor in promoting a "tough guise" (Jhally, 1999) to which boys and men are expected to adhere to gain masculine status. From such a perspective, boys are taught to deal with conflict in verbally and physically aggressive ways. Of course, not all boys subscribe to such normalized notions of masculinity. Nevertheless, socially detrimental behaviors such as aggression are glamorized and idealized in various forms of mass-media entertainment aimed at boys. Further, boys who do not or cannot subscribe to socially normative ways of sounding and acting like a boy are typically rejected as sissies, fags, or queers.

The Steinhäuser case, like other cases of school massacres, incited a call not only for tighter gun controls, but also for bans of violent video games and other forms of media. It also compelled many Germans to consider that school shootings are no longer a phenomenon specific to the United States. While theories and strategies have been offered to explain and prevent school shootings, Newman et al. (2004) suggest that doing so requires the development of a theory that is predictive in its capabilities. Most youth are exposed to violent media and many have guns at their disposal, yet school shootings remain extremely rare. Thus any such theory, Newman et al. argue, is highly unlikely to be valid.

Gerald Walton

Further Reading

Bergling, T. (2001). *Sissyphobia: Gay men and effeminate behavior.* Binghamton, NY: Harrington Park.

Blenkinsop, P. (2002, April 27). Shootings to reignite debate on gun control. *Toronto Star,* p. A26.

Caistor, N. (2002, April 28). Profile of a teenage killer: "Why?" is the question many Germans are asking. *BBC News Online.* Retrieved November 24, 2008, from http://news.bbc.co.uk/1/hi/world/europe/1956206.stm

Casella, R. (2001). *At zero tolerance: Punishment, prevention, and school violence.* New York: Peter Lang.

Connell, R. W. (2007). *Masculinities* (2nd ed.). Cambridge, UK: Polity.

Glassner, B. (1999). *The culture of fear: Why Americans are afraid of the wrong things.* New York: Basic.

Helm, T. (2002, April 29). Teenage gunman wove web of deceit, police say: Massacre in Germany: Parents thought he was taking his final exams. *National Post,* p. A12.

Jhally, S. (Director). (1999). *Tough guise: Violence, media, and the crisis in masculinity.* [Motion picture]. Northampton, MA: Media Education Foundation.

Katz, J., & Jhally, S. (1999, May 2). The national conversation in the wake of Littleton is missing the mark. *Boston Globe,* p. E1. Retrieved from http://www.jacksonkatz.com/pub_missing.html

Larkin, R. W. (2007). *Comprehending Columbine.* Philadelphia, PA: Temple University Press.

Murphy, C. L. (2002, April 30). Playing the game: Germany's teenage killer. *BBC News Online.* Retrieved November 24, 2008, from http://news.bbc.co.uk/2/hi/europe/1959632.stm

Newman, C. S., Fox, C., Harding, D. J., Mehta, J., & Roth, W. (2004). *Rampage: The social roots of school shootings.* New York: Basic Books.

Pascoe, C. J. (2007). *Dude, you're a fag: Masculinity and sexuality in high school.* Berkeley, CA: University of California Press.

Wise, T. (2001, March 6). School shootings and white denial. Retrieved November 25, 2008, from http://academic.udayton.edu/race/01race/white08.htm

Stop Bullying Now

Stopbullyingnow.org is a bilingual website (English and Spanish) that was created and is maintained by the U.S. Department of Health and Human Services, Health Resources and Services Administration. Its tagline, "Take a stand. Lend a hand. Stop Bullying Now!", and its youth-friendly graphics and design make it accessible and appealing for youth and educators who are working to reduce bullying in their schools and communities. The primary audience for this website is middle school students (grades 6–9). The website is divided into four main areas: "What bullying is," "What you can do," "Cool stuff," and "What adults can do."

The "What bullying is" section of the website offers basic definitions and examples of bullying in youth-friendly language. According to the site, "Bullying happens when someone hurts or scares another person on purpose and the person being bullied has a hard time defending himself or herself. Usually, bullying happens over and over." There is also a short quiz to help youth reflect on their own behaviors and identify if they have a tendency to bully others.

The "What you can do" section of resources offers tangible suggestions to students who are interested in addressing the problem of bullying in their own school or community. It includes a "Tip sheet for kids" that prompts children to take actions such as the following: write down where and when you see bullying happen, find out how bullying is handled at your school, stop bullying when you see it, and meet with school leaders to talk about your ideas.

The "Cool stuff" portion of the website is the most kid-friendly. It includes animated webisodes that talk about the various issues that students face when dealing with bullying. In addition, a series of games use the characters introduced in the webisodes to reinforce the information presented throughout the website.

The "What adults can do" section of this site provides a list of available resources for any adult interested in addressing the issue of bullying. There are also two specific areas that are designed to provide tailored information for families and for educators. The "family corner" gives information to family members about the role they can play in supporting a child who may be experiencing bullying at school. The "educators corner" offers information for teachers, administrators, and other adults in schools. Administrators are encouraged to educate their staff, document incidents of bullying, and research bullying intervention programs. There is also a guide titled "Misdirections in Bullying Prevention and Intervention" that administrators may find useful. The section for teachers also includes downloadable comic books that build on the storylines from the webisodes as well as teacher's guides that offer hints on implementing these activities in a classroom.

The Stop Bullying Now site is a comprehensive and user-friendly website that can connect students, families, educators, and community members with valuable resources and information to help them address the problem of bullying in their communities.

Elizabeth J. Meyer

Further Reading

www.stopbullyingnow.hrsa.gov

Suburban School Violence

Due to visibility, excessive media coverage, and other factors, very often when we speak of school violence, we picture urban schools and urban violence. This is not a new perception. In 1973, William J. Chambliss published "The Saints and The Roughnecks," a study that compared the delinquency and deviance of an upper-class group of boys and a lower-class group of boys. While the study did not deal with overt violence, it did deal with potentially violent acts of the upper-class boys (the "Saints"), including high-speed, reckless, and drunk driving; playing chicken with the car lights out; and removing barricades and lanterns from hazardous spots in the road. The Roughnecks' lower-class violence involved mostly fighting. Chambliss felt that the Saints' violence was worse than that of the Roughnecks, but the Saints were not thought of as delinquent by either the police, the townspeople, or the school. Chambliss attributes the difference in perception to three factors: visibility (the lower-class Roughnecks hung out on the corner, the upper-class Saints got in their cars and drove out of town, committing their deviance out of sight of their peer adults), demeanor (the Roughnecks expressed hostility and disdain when caught, whereas the Saints were apologetic and penitent when confronted), and bias (the lower-class boy drinking in the alley is perceived as more deviant than the upper-class boy who drinks in a club and then drives drunk). This study reflects the current attitudes of many toward urban and suburban school violence.

Since the advent of horrible school disasters such as the shooting at Columbine High School in 1999, in the nice suburban town of Littleton, Colorado, society has had to rethink the relationship between suburban schools and the potential for violence. Not only was the Columbine massacre a school tragedy of huge magnitude, but, because of live media coverage, people across the United States were able to watch the event unfold in real time. This event put a vivid new suburban face on school violence, or at least on school shootings. During the mid-1970s, while urban school crime leveled off and began to decline, suburban school crime was on the rise, so perhaps instances of suburban school violence should not have caught Americans as much by surprise.

Generally speaking, schools are relatively safe places to be. Although many people believe that overall school violence is currently on the rise, in fact this is not so. In the last decade, types of school violence other than shootings have decreased by approximately 50%. Most students, particularly those in suburban areas, will not experience any type of violence at school, nor will most schools experience a shooting; among homicides where school-aged children are the victims, less than 1% occur at school or while traveling to or from school. School shootings are rare events. In any given year, there may be from 12 to 20 school shootings in the more than 100,000 U.S. schools. The intense fear of school shootings is the result of a "moral panic," fueled by the media, politicians, public concern, special-interest groups, and "triggering events." After the Columbine school shooting, for example, two-thirds of Americans surveyed in a Gallup poll felt that a similar incident was either very likely or somewhat likely to happen in their schools.

According to the U.S. Department of Education and Bureau of Justice Statistics, the percentage of suburban schools experiencing violent incidents is smaller than the percentage of urban or town schools experiencing such events, but larger than the percentage of rural schools subjected to this kind of violence. For example, more than 82% of urban schools experienced violent incidents, as compared to 74% of suburban schools, 80% of town schools, and almost 70% of rural schools (using 2007–2008 data). There is a larger gap in the urban/suburban/ rural rates of gang-related school crime, with urban rates close to 34%, suburban rates close to 19%, town rates nearly 17%, and rural rates less than 11%.

Urban schools reported 35.8 violent incidents per 1,000 students, while suburban schools experienced 22.8 incidents per 1,000 students, and town and rural schools each had 26.4 incidents per 1,000 students. Violent incidents include a broad range of behaviors, such as actual attacks or fights; threats of attacks or fights; robbery, with or without a weapon; and rape or other sexual battery. Serious violent incidents included all of these actions (except threats) that were committed with a weapon, plus robbery committed with or without a weapon. Without the threats category and non-weapon incidents, there is a greater difference between the urban and suburban school violence rates, with urban schools experiencing 1.9 incidents per 1,000 students, and suburban schools experiencing 0.9 incident per 1,000 students. (Town and rural schools rates were 1.2 and 0.8

incidents per 1,000 students, respectively.) Six percent of suburban teachers report that they were threatened with a physical injury by a student, as compared to 10% of urban teachers and 5% of rural teachers.

While urban schools have higher rates of violence, it is interesting to note that suburban schools have higher rates of disciplinary actions taken against students. For example, with regard to removal of students for the remainder of the school year for possession of an explosive device or a weapon other than a firearm, urban schools removed 3.9% of their students, while suburban schools removed 6.2%.

Suburban schools have a slight edge over urban schools when it comes to written plans for responding to certain violent incidents. For example, 84.9% of suburban schools have a plan for shootings, versus 83% of urban schools. Almost 97% of suburban schools, versus almost 95% of urban schools, have plans for bomb threats or incidents. Suburban schools also have a greater edge in regard to drilling students on the various crisis situation plans: 57.5% of suburban schools versus 50.9% of urban schools drilled students on plans for school shootings; 67.4% suburban schools drilled students on bomb threat plans, whereas only 58.3% of urban schools did the same.

With regard to certain safety precautions, 11.6% of urban schools, as compared to 2.5% of suburban schools, conducted random metal detector checks. However, with regard to the random use of drug-sniffing dogs, suburban schools outdid urban schools 16.2% to 11.7%, respectively. Suburban schools also outdid urban schools in the use of security cameras: 57.5% to 53.3%, respectively. It is difficult to speculate on the meaning of these numbers without further data. Do suburban schools have more cause to take action? Are they using more caution, reacting to less severe incidents ("widening the net")? Do they simply have more resources? Or is there some other explanation for these differences?

The Columbine tragedy set off public debates on the effects on teenagers of violent movies and video games and heavy metal music, proper parental supervision of teenagers, the Goth culture, the decline of religion in public education, the availability of weapons and explosives, and the widespread use (many would say overuse) of pharmaceutical antidepressants by teens. Schools, including suburban schools, expressed concern over the issues of school security, emergency communication systems, and the proliferation of bullying in the schools (most, if not all, school shooters have been bullied). In fact, while other types of violence were actually on the decline in the schools, bullying was on the rise. Roughly 30% of students are involved in bullying, as the bully, the victim, or both. There is little variation in bullying rates among urban, suburban, and rural schools. Among urban schools, 27.5% report incidents of bullying; among suburban schools, this rate is 24.6%. In recent years, the number of anti-bullying programs has increased as schools try to counteract this problem.

In Littleton, Colorado, as well as in other suburban settings that have experienced school shootings, people wondered in the aftermath, "How could this happen here?"

Whereas some expect to see violence in the urban schools, the same violence in suburban schools is often described as being a "complete surprise." In reality, school shooters are almost the polar opposite of the "typical" violent juvenile offender. School shooters often attend affluent suburban high schools, belong to the middle class, have not been violent or aggressive in the past, and are white. Recent research indicates that more than 26% of males and more than 8% of females in suburban areas carry weapons for protection or in anticipation of a possible fight. Males in the study who carried weapons appeared to be at risk for negative behaviors or outcomes such as suicide, depression, and stress. Almost half of the suburban students reported a problem with anger management.

It has long been a theory that urban school shootings occur mainly as a result of drug trafficking dynamics, racial segregation, and poverty, with shooters targeting specific individuals. Urban shooters may be in fear of their own lives. In contrast, shootings in suburban school settings, which are devoid of much of the poverty, racial bias, and violent dynamics of the drug trade, have been compared to "rampage shootings"—that is, incidents based on general rather than specific grievances. In the case of the Columbine massacre, for example, it has been hypothesized that the shootings were a deadly reaction to the constant bullying, humiliation, and violence meted out to the outcasts by the dominant elite, particularly athletes ("jocks"). In fact, there really is no consistent profile of the school shooter. Pointing to the moody, depressed, angry, isolated, weird kid with low self-esteem who is harassed, in emotional pain, does not fit in with his or her peers, and dresses funny is not helpful, because most—if not all—youths fit this description at some point during their teen years. School shooters come from all types of family backgrounds, have academic prowess that ranges from failing to honor roll, and may be loners or have many friends. Most have no disciplinary records. Most shooters would not have been identified on any profile. Indeed, with the use of profiling, we run the risk of "net widening"—that is, over-identification of those who stand out because of their behavior, dress, or tastes in music.

After the Columbine shooting and other tragedies, the concept of zero tolerance was further emphasized in the schools. Zero tolerance, an idea that sprang from the 1994 Gun-Free Schools Act's stipulation that any child caught with a firearm at school was to be expelled for a year, was expanded in many schools to include automatic expulsion for any violation of school safety rules.

Corporal punishment, such as spanking, is a behavior that many would regard as violence in the schools; it has been banned in the schools in more than half of the states, and in individual jurisdictions in other states. Nevertheless, this practice persists in many schools, even in states where it has been banned. Corporal punishment has been banned in New York, for example, yet a number of cases are reported each year. Currently, some jurisdictions are attempting to reinstate it. Corporal punishment is used disproportionately on minorities and students from the lower class;

thus, by inference, it is probably used less often in more affluent suburban schools. Some suggest that corporal punishment rates are lower in both urban and suburban schools than in rural schools; this may be a reflection of the rural nature of the states that retain corporal punishment. Five states—Texas, Mississippi, Tennessee, Alabama, and Arkansas—account for 70% of the corporal punishment cases.

School violence may have a different face in the suburbs, but it is certainly present in these areas, and it is of great concern to parents, school personnel, and others across the country. As with other types of crime, the fear is worse than the reality, but the concerns still need to be addressed.

Carol Lenhart

Further Reading

Borum, R., Cornell, D., Modzeleski, W., & Jimerson, S. (2010). What can be done about school shootings? A review of the evidence." *Educational Researcher, 39*(1), 27–37.

Chambliss, W. (1973). The Saints and the Roughnecks. *Society, 11*(1), 24–31.

Dinkes, R., Kemp, J., Baum, K., & Snyder, T. (2009). *Indicators of school crime and safety: 2009.* Washington, DC: U. S. Department of Education, U. S. Department of Justice, Office of Justice Programs.

Hawkins, S., Campanaro, A., Pits, T., & Steiner, H. (2002). Weapons in an affluent suburban school. *Journal of School Violence, 1*(1), 53–65.

Larkin, R. (2007). *Toward a theory of legitimated adolescent violence.* Conference paper, American Sociological Association Annual Meeting (AN34595204) SocINDEX with Full Text.

Muschert, G. (2007). The Columbine victims and the myth of the juvenile super-predator. *Youth Violence and Juvenile Justice*, 351–366. Retrieved from http://yvj.sagepub.com/cgi/content/abstract/5/4/351

Suicide, College

Worldwide, there are more deaths due to suicide than due to homicides and accidents combined. Approximately 30,000 people die by suicide annually in the United States. Every day, an estimated 80 Americans successfully take their own lives and another 1,500 attempt to take their lives. Every 18 minutes in the United States, a person dies by suicide and an attempted suicide is estimated to occur every minute. Today, suicide is the ninth leading cause of death in the United States. Even more disconcerting is the fact that suicide is the second leading cause of death among college students in America. This essay discusses the prevalence of suicide among college students, explanations as to why such tragedies occur, and ways to alleviate the issue.

According to a recent study that surveyed 26,000 college students at 70 U.S. college and university institutions, slightly more than half of American college students contemplate suicide at some point in their lives. In this same survey, 15% of the student sample affirmed they had "seriously considered" taking their own lives. Additionally, more than 5% of the student sample reported actually attempting suicide. This rate suggests that, at an average university or college institution with 18,000 undergraduate students, 1,080 would seriously contemplate taking their lives in any given year. According to the American College of Health Association, 1,100 suicides do, in fact, occur on college campuses annually.

There are several explanations as to why suicide is so prevalent among college students. One explanation points to the overload of stress and lack of available resources to cope with stress in college institutions. According to research, one in five college undergraduate students in America reports being constantly stressed.

For many incoming freshmen, college can be a very tough transition. Many students feel pressured to choose a career and succeed. Others feel lost, confused, lonely, anxious, and inadequate. Additionally, many struggle to adapt to a new environment. All of these factors can lead to stress and can eventually turn into depression.

According to research, "The primary reason for suicidal thoughts is to end emotional or physical pain." The second reason, according to the same study, is issues regarding romantic relationships. The third is a generalized desire or need to end their lives. The fourth is problems with school and academics.

Although all of these explanations play a role in an individual's decision to terminate their life, none is considered the primary reason as to why a college student, or anyone at all, would decide to take his or her own life. Instead, the primary cause for suicide among college students and all suicides in general is untreated depression. Research indicates that half of students who suffer from suicidal thoughts do not seek counseling or treatment for their distress. Explanations as to why students do not seek help include shame, embarrassment, a lack of knowledge about depression and available resources, and despondence.

Depression, as defined by the American Psychological Association (APA), is a mental disorder whereby "people may experience a lack of interest and pleasure in daily activities, significant weight loss or gain, insomnia or excessive sleeping, lack of energy, inability to concentrate, feelings of worthlessness or excessive guilt and recurrent thoughts of death or suicide." According to the APA, "depression is the most common mental disorder." Luckily, it is manageable and treatable through a combination of therapy and medication.

Data obtained through the American Foundation for Suicide Prevention suggest that depression affects at least 19 million Americans aged 18 and older annually. This number represents roughly 10% of U.S. adults. Research indicates that more American adults suffer from depression than coronary heart disease (7 million), cancer (6 million), and AIDS (200,000) combined.

According to the American College of Health Association, 15% of U.S. college students were diagnosed with depression in 2007, an increase of 5% compared to four years earlier. More than 90% of the youth who successfully commit suicide had at least one mental disorder or psychiatric illness at the time of death. Roughly 50% of the time, this disorder was present but often went undetected for at least two years. "The most common diagnosis among youth are depression, substance abuse and conduct disorders."

According to data obtained from the American College Health Association, roughly 16% of college women and 10% of men in college report having been diagnosed by a professional with depression at some point in their lives. Additionally, in a national survey of college professors, 84% saw an increase in students with mental disorders or psychological problems over the previous five years.

Correlated with depression and suicide among both college students and the general population are substance abuse issues. For example, in a survey about binge drinking reported by the Suicide Prevention Resource Center, approximately 44% of students interviewed reported "drinking heavily" within the two weeks before taking the survey. The majority of researchers define binge drinking as "the consumption of at least five alcoholic drinks in a single sitting for men and four for women." In 2005, approximately 10.8 million individuals aged 12–20 (28.2% of this age group) reported drinking alcohol within the previous month. Roughly 7.2 million (18.8%) were considered binge drinkers, and another 2.3 million (6%) were deemed heavy drinkers.

According to the Center for Science in the Public Interest, more males than females report binge drinking—21.3% versus 16.1%, respectively. Moreover, college students ages 18–22 at full-time colleges or universities are more inclined to binge drink or drink heavily than their peers who are not enrolled in an accredited university. Even more alarming is that 48% of college drinkers interviewed in a survey reported that "drinking to get drunk" is an important reason to drink. Nearly one in four of the students in this sample consumed alcohol at least 10 times per month, and another 29% reported being inebriated at minimum 3 times per month. Furthermore, one in three college students and three in five frequent binge drinkers meet the APA's criteria for alcohol abuse; one in 17 college students and one in five frequent binge drinkers meet the criteria for alcohol dependence. Overall, according to the National Epidemiologic Survey on Alcohol and Related Conditions, 19% of college students in the United States aged 18–24 meet the criteria for alcohol dependence or abuse.

After establishing an understanding of suicide prevalence rates among college students, explanations as to why it occurs, and major correlates of suicide, it is important to understand when suicidal indicators typically surface themselves as well as the warning signs one should be cognizant about. According to the Centers for Disease Control and Prevention, suicide typically emerges as a substantial problem during the high school years, increases in frequency among people between the ages of 20 and 24, and shows a persistently increased incidence throughout the next two decades of life. Some warning signals that a person may be contemplating suicide have been identified: a previous attempt at suicide, frequent discussions about suicide, drug and alcohol abuse, feeling despondent and helpless, depression, changes in behavior and personality, giving away favorite possessions, and a loss of interest in friends and hobbies.

Several steps have been taken to reduce the incidence of suicide in young adults, but even more avenues must be explored if we are to further alleviate the risk of suicide among college students. One example of the measures employed to address the issue can be seen in the efforts of the New York Association of School Psychologists (NYASP) in conjunction with the New York State Office of Mental Health (OMH). The NYASP and OMH have developed workshops, known as SPEAK Workshops, that confront the issue of depression and suicide among college suicide. These workshops present information about the prevalence of suicide and depression, signs and symptoms of depression, signs for suicidal behavior, and available resources. The first such workshop was developed to serve faculty, staff and counselors, or other professionals deemed qualified to monitor the behavior of college students. The second workshop utilized trained psychology graduate students to train and educate other students. Having graduate students lead these events has greatly increased acceptance of these workshops, as the students perceive their trainers as classmates and peers as opposed to figures of authority. Fourteen colleges and universities in New York have participated in this workshop training.

Other steps that can be taken include making high school students take a mandatory depression survey annually. Additionally, doctors should discuss depression with high school students when they have an appointment, and pamphlets about depression and suicide should be passed out in high schools and made readily available in physicians' offices. Furthermore, incoming college freshman should be given pamphlets about depression and suicide in their university packets at every school. Most importantly, the stigma of discussing mental health and suicide must be eliminated, and medical professionals along with educational professionals should be at the forefront of this effort. Students should be encouraged to seek help, openly discuss depression and suicidal thoughts, and be reassured that they have nothing to be ashamed of.

Implementation of suicide prevention programs on all college campuses is essential. Ideally, such a program should include leadership to promote suicide prevention and mental health, screening, crisis management, educational seminars, mental health services, life skills development, means restrictions, social marketing, and social network promotion.

Suicide among college students in the United States is clearly a serious issue. It is a problem for a large number of youth and young adults in college as well as those not in college (7.95 suicides per 100,000 15- to 19-year-olds, 11.97 suicides per 100,000 20- to 24-year-olds, and 12.56 suicides per 100,000 25- to 29-year-olds). Untreated depression is the primary cause for suicide. Depression can be managed and treated if someone takes the necessary step to seek help. Finally, college campuses must implement suicide prevention programs and indefatigably work toward educating their students, faculty, and staff members on this crucial issue.

Rebecca Ajo

Further Reading

College student depression and suicide. (n.d.). American Foundation for Suicide Prevention. Retrieved May 7, 2010, from http://www.afsp.org/index.cfm?page_id=05678008-958D-8476-7CD04234DBBBFC69

Durkin, K. F., Wolfe, S. E., & Lewis, K. (2008). Binge drinking on college campus. In A. Thio, T. C. Calhoun, & A. Conyers, A. (Eds.), *Readings in deviant behavior* (5th ed., pp. 233–236). Boston, MA: Pearson Education.

Facts about suicide. (n.d.). American Foundation for Suicide Prevention. Retrieved February 2, 2010. http://www.afsp.org/index.cfm?fuseaction=home.viewpage&page_id=050fea9f-b064-4092-b1135c3a70de1fda

Johnson, H. (2008, August 18). Half of college students consider suicide. *MSNBC.* http://www.msnbc.msn.com/id/26272639/ns/health-mental_health/

Rawe, J. (2008, May 14). When colleges go on suicide watch. *Time.* Retrieved May 7, 2010, from www.time.com/time.magazine/article/0,9171,1194020,00.html

Suicide Prevention Resource Center, U.S. Department of Health and Human Services. (2004). *Promoting mental health and preventing suicide in college and university settings.* (Newton, MA: Education Development Center.

Suicide, High School

Teenagers today are three times more likely to commit suicide compared to teenagers in the era when their parents attended high school. This increased rate reflects the fact that teenagers are facing more stress in the 21st century than their peers of a generation ago. These pressures include, but are not limited to, alcohol and drug use, family divorce, abuse and neglect, teen relationships, unexpected pregnancy, low self-esteem, depression and loneness, academic stress, confusion about being sexually active, cyberbullying, death of a friend or family member, discovering their sexual orientation (realizing that he or she identifies as gay), "fitting in," eating disorders, guilt, and living in a violent environment. According to the Surgeon General of the United States, on average one teenager younger than the age 15 commits suicide every 2 hours.

Some of these issues may seem small or petty to adults, but to a young person they are very real and serious. High school students are less likely to have the same level of maturity and experience as an adult. When teens feel overwhelmed by their problems, they do not understand how to deal with these obstacles, which in effect causes them to fall into a depressive state. Students may feel weighed down by the problems that they face, taking what could be a minor issue and magnifying it into an unrealistic dramatization. Teenagers frequently feel that the pain they are experiencing is never ending.

People who attempt to commit suicide do not really wish to die. Rather, a suicide attempt is a violent cry for help, an act of desperation that seeks attention. Individuals who take this road want someone to become aware of their problems. Because they do not know who to turn to in a time of need, they decide to act on what they know. They know that if they end their life, all of the pain and unbearable suffering that they feel will also end. This can seem like a fair trade for some people. The pain may be so powerful that it seems the only recourse they have for ending their horrific suffering is to end their life. In fact, suicide is not the answer: No pain is so great that it cannot be overcome and worked through. Suicide is often referred to as the easy way out of a difficult situation.

Why do teenagers committee suicide? Teenagers can feel overwhelmed by their current situation and have no outlet to express their emotional struggles. Some teens may feel burdensome to their family, feel worthless, or have no hope for the future. If a teenager has been the victim of physical or sexual abuse, he or she is also more at risk to commit suicide; the same is true of a person who has been bullied in school and a teenager dealing with his or her homosexuality in an unsupportive family, who lacks a support network. Other students may be suffering with untreated depression or may have a medical condition, such as bipolar disorder, making them more likely to take their own life. Depression in its simplest form occurs when a hormonal imbalance in the brain causes an overwhelming feeling of sadness, loneliness, grief, loss of interest, or sense of isolation from the rest of the world. Once a student attempts suicide, he or she is twice as likely to attempt suicide again; the subsequent attempt usually succeeds.

Males are more successful in their attempts to commit suicide, because they tend to use more extreme measures such as strangulation, hanging, and shooting themselves. Females, by comparison, lean toward less extreme measures such as drowning, overdosing on medication, and other forms of drug use. Other means of suicide include drinking poison, inhaling carbon monoxide, suffocation, faking an accident, cutting one's wrists, or jumping from heights.

It is a myth to believe that most suicides are irrational behavior. When persons begin contemplating suicide, they generally have been dealing with their own personal issues for a length of time. It is highly unusual that a troubled person will immediately pick up a gun and decide to end his or her life. More commonly, individuals think long and hard about how they want to die, which method of suicide they will use, and whether to write a suicide note. If written, such a note typically lists the reasons why a person would choose to take their own life.

Most teenagers emit some discreet signals to their family, friends, or teachers, letting them know that they need help. Nevertheless, a small percentage of teenagers show no signs that they are experiencing a struggle. Worrisome signals include a depressed mood, substance abuse, frequently running away, family loss, talking about death, or withdrawal from friends and family. Other signs, according to the APA, include losing interest in things once loved, having difficulty dealing with one's sexual orientation, having an unplanned pregnancy, impulsive or aggressive behavior, and frequent expressions of rage.

Suicide is outlawed by only two states in the United States. Why have more states not outlawed this behavior? History has shown that when the states decided to make this activity illegal, the number of suicide attempts increased. Suicide is a controversial subject. Many people think of suicide as committing murder. Conversely, others feel that it is up to individuals to decide when they want to end their own life and that such a personal decision should not be ceded to the government.

What effect does suicide have on the victim's family members? Losing a family member, friend, or classmate has long-term effects for those who knew the victim. Beyond the obvious feelings of grief and devastation, they may suffer emotionally and physically from this traumatic experience and lose their focus on other important tasks in life. Suicide of a loved one will very likely affect survivors' emotional state of mind for an extended amount of time. Psychotherapy, children-oriented therapy (such as playing or artwork), or physical exercise may help a person cope with these circumstances.

Natasha Abdin

Further Reading

Berman, A., Jobes, D., & Silverman, M. (2005). *Adolescent suicide: Assessment and intervention* (2nd ed.). Washington, DC: America Psychological Association.

Blauner, S. (2003). *How I stayed alive when my brain was trying to kill me.* New York: HarperCollins.

Box, M. (2005). *Suicide.* San Diego, CA: Greenhaven.

Crook, M. (2004). *Teens talk about suicide.* Vancouver, Canada: Arsenal Pulp Press.

Krasny, R. (2010, April 9).Teen suicide puts spotlight on high-tech bullying. Reuters. Retrieved May 7, 2010, from http://www.reuters.com/article/idUSTRE63847420100409

Murphy, J. (1999). *Coping with teen suicide.* New York: Rosen.

Youth suicide fact sheet. (2007, December 27). National Youth Violence Prevention Resource Center. Retrieved May 7, 2010, from http://www.safeyouth.org/scripts/facts/suicide.asp

Systemic/Structural Violence, College

Systemic violence and structural violence are closely related terms. *Systemic violence* refers to institutional practices or procedures that adversely affect groups or individuals psychologically, mentally, culturally, economically, spiritually, or physically. In a school context, such violence is an unwanted interruption of the student's learning process and the quest for full human potential. *Structural violence* refers to the kinds of harm that social structures in general may perpetrate upon individuals. In educational settings, the institution may cause new inequalities or reproduce previous inequalities held over from the student's prior life or school experiences.

Both kinds of violence occur regularly in colleges and universities worldwide. Systemic violence can occur when persons in authority limit the human potential of a student. For example, when academic advisors steer minority students into easier nonprofessional majors such as general studies (instead of the pre-med path), it effectively limits the potential earning power of those students. Structural violence happens when students are marginalized inadvertently by policies or social customs within the university, thereby introducing new inequalities or reproducing previously held disadvantages. With both types of violence, the student injuries can be overt, in the case of physical violence, or they can be hidden psychological and emotional violence.

Almost always, college staff members, professors, and administrators claim their actions are intended to serve the best interests of the students. They never claim to intentionally do violence to any of their students, who are more likely than ever to be treated as "consumers" of a college education. Despite such claims, the intention of their actions is secondary to the outcome. Administrators and other officials claim not to act out of nefarious intent, but the outcome can still be a violent one for the student.

Systemic or structural violence is often committed by the powerful, those protected by the law. Their acts are directed at those with little power in an effort to maintain existing social arrangements. More broadly, their actions can be understood as a deprivation of basic human rights. All people have a basic right as well as a basic need to live without violence. Because violence is socially constructed, it can be reduced significantly, if not totally eliminated. Violence in this broader perspective amplifies the effects of emotional, social, psychological, economic, and religious violence over more overt physical kinds of violence.

Sheer demographics ensure that in many college classes, minority students will account for a slim proportion of the total students. This imbalance is especially significant for those students who come from a predominately minority neighborhood or high school where they did not experience such marginality. For them, such marginalization is a new phenomenon. For other students, this marginalized setting is a continuation of earlier life experiences, when they were in the minority at a white majority school. If such conditions are coupled with an instructor who is intimidated or insensitive to stereotypical remarks or actions, the marginalization of the student increases.

In addition, if faculty members fail to use technological advances in the classroom that may enhance learning by accommodating a diverse range of learning styles, such an action may do violence to some students. By clinging to "lecture-only" formats, for example, instructors treat students as passive recipients who have no voice in what they learn or how they learn it. Passive teaching practices avoid the affective domain, stressing knowledge that is academic but not emotional.

Further, a trend toward standardization of curricula and assessments is a form of systemic violence that assumes that all students can and should be able to perform at the same level at the same time. Such standardized tests are culturally biased according to many studies.

Another factor sustaining marginality is the bureaucracy surrounding financial aid. Understaffing in this vital department means that the amount of time that can be spent with each individual student is severely limited. This barrier is especially frustrating for students whose ability to attend college is critically dependent on receiving financial assistance in a timely manner. Prompt payment in such cases may determine whether the student attends college or not.

Additionally, many social activities at the college level are centered on Anglo-American culture. Although groups such as Black United Students (BUS), Black Accountants, and Black Engineers serve vital socializing roles, they tend to encourage separation between African American and Anglo-American students.

The cost of a collegiate education in this country is growing at a faster pace than the U.S. economy as a whole. To slow the pace of tuition hikes, administrators have cut back on personnel, equipment, and fringe benefits. In particular, the fiscal crisis has strained the university police forces that are given the task of protecting the student body from harm. Cutbacks in security (among other factors) have enabled school shooters such as Seung-Hui Cho at Virginia Tech and Steven Kazmierczak at Northern Illinois University to enter classrooms with weapons and begin killing or injuring scores of students within a matter of minutes. The aftermath of such a shooting is deeply painful for the entire college community. The community lacks the will to move forward with the business of the college, and there is a pervasive fear that the campus is unsafe. There is also widespread mourning for the lives lost and the sense of security that has been shattered in the wake of the tragic event.

As the fiscal crisis deepens, colleges are feeling pressure to reach out to prospective students not traditionally viewed as qualifying for the college experience. Prisons, halfway houses, drug rehabilitation centers, mental health centers, and homeless shelters—once viewed as off limits for recruiting—are now seen as potential revenue streams for the cash-starved college. Agreements between these entities and the college are justified in the name of public service and community involvement. However, as schools recruit from such nontraditional sources, they are likely to encounter a broader stream of public life, including persons acculturated to a street culture that is far removed from the middle-class standard expected in the college environment. Such individuals may have been socialized to more violent means of resolving disputes rather than peaceful ones, and conflicts involving these students can develop that end in overt physical violence.

The effects of systemic or structural violence can be observed in students while they are still enrolled at the university. For example, to compensate for being marginalized, students may show increased sensitivity and self-consciousness concerning matters of race and may report feelings of inferiority and malaise. Some have a more angry reaction, becoming totally absorbed in blaming the system. These students may show open hostility, acts of defiance, or angry withdrawal.

Hoping to channel their response to marginalization in another direction, some students may seek emulation and identification with the dominant culture at all costs, including trying to "pass" as a member of the dominant culture. Another role frequently sought out is that of an emissary, an interpreter, or a go-between for both cultures.

The most violent outcome of all could be the situation where the marginal student comes to accept a permanently marginal status within a marginal culture. Conditioned since birth to the existence of both cultures and having had shared experiences of dealing with both cultures during the developmental years, the end result of the college experience for such an individual is the continuation and reinforcement of such prior beliefs, thus creating a marginal person who exists in a marginal culture and is totally accepting of this outcome.

Humanistic sociology is one area from which collegiate educators and administrators can draw useful alternatives to counteract the violence that is so intimately woven into the fabric of institutions of academe. Humanistic sociology can help educators develop a broader view of their work and can assist them in creating a more healthy school environment, both physically and emotionally. Humanistic sociology emphasizes a nurturing and positive environment that can promote cooperation and creativity. Schools that promote values of empathy, tolerance, and compassion create an atmosphere that might reduce or eliminate systemic or structural violence. In cases where violence may persist, this approach examines how justice may be maximized for all parties.

Stan C. Weeber

Further Reading

Aronson, E. (2000). *Nobody left to hate: Teaching compassion after Columbine.* New York: W. H. Freeman.

Breese, J., & Grant, K. (2004). Policy implications from a study of marginality: Theory and African American students. *Free Inquiry in Creative Sociology, 32*(2), 169–178.

Finley, L. (2006). Examining school searches as systemic violence. *Critical Criminology, 14,* 117–135.

Finley, L., & Hartmann, D. (2004), Institutional change and resistance: Teacher preparatory faculty and technology integration. *Journal of Technology and Teacher Education, 12*(3), 319–337.

Watkinson, A. (1997). Administrative complicity and systemic violence in education. In J. Epp & A. Watkinson (Eds.), *Systemic violence in education: Broken promises* (pp. 3–24). Albany, NY: State University of New York Press.

Systemic/Structural Violence, High School

Few educational settings are exempt from school violence. Violent incidents occur at the primary level and continue all the way through the post-secondary levels of education. School violence has become a fairly popular topic over the last few decades, and a great deal of public opinion concerning school violence is affected by increased media attention regarding incidents that occur on school grounds.

Contrary to popular belief, school violence has been on the decline for at least the past decade. Middle school and high school students are far more likely than elementary school students to perceive danger in multiple school subcontexts. However, students at the high school level are among those most at risk, with public high schools reporting incidents of violence at higher rates than either public middle schools or primary schools.

The causes of high school violence are of critical concern. Which variables increase the likelihood that school violence will occur? Exploring this phenomenon from the individual level is a common approach taken by researchers. However, structural causes of violence are of equal importance. Sociologist James Henslin characterizes social structure as "the framework of society that was already laid out before you were born." Thus researchers must explore the contributions that social and economic forces make to delinquent behavior among high school students to gain insight into the underlying causes of structural violence among this group.

Structural causes for school violence are multifaceted. Dewey Cornell, Professor of Education at the University of Virginia likens exploring this phenomenon to that of airline industry accidents. In the airline industry, it is generally understood that plane crashes rarely have just one cause. Instead, they typically result from an accumulation of factors, such as poor weather, human error, and electrical failure. These factors come together as a whole, with the end result being a crash. The same tends to be true with school violence: Poverty, discrimination, and lack of social support

Standardized testing and standardized curricula can be seen as forms of systemic violence because they assume that all students are able to perform at the same level as everyone else in the class at the same time. (iStockPhoto)

appear to represent the accumulation of factors most responsible for structural violence in U.S. high schools.

Economic inequality has long been positioned the forefront in discussions of structural violence. The United States is home to many of the world's most affluent people. Statistics, however, reveal significant disparities between the rich and the poor, and those affected most by such income and wealth disparities in the United States are children. Long-lasting scarcity among a great deal of U.S. residents has led many to believe that U.S. social class systems now include a permanent underclass. Furthermore, American children face bouts of poverty at rates unprecedented in other industrialized nations.

Economic deprivation places an individual at an increased risk for violence. Research reveals that adolescents' attempts to prevail over their poverty-stricken conditions often result in a variety of challenges. They often have strong aspirations to achieve the "American Dream." Yet, given their limited circumstances, they often find themselves partaking in delinquent behaviors to accomplish these goals. These delinquent behaviors include illegal drug trafficking and gang activity, as well as problematic behaviors on school grounds.

People of color disproportionately occupy the lower-class sector of U.S. society. In fact, blacks and Hispanics significantly outnumber their white counterparts in this realm. As a result, discussions of poverty, to some degree, must be racialized. Thus, in addition to suffering from class discrimination, members of minority groups must cope with racial discrimination. Many people overlook the fact that youth must endure these oppressive conditions. Minority adolescents have spoken directly about the complexity of mentally coping with these conditions. Some have conveyed feelings of hopelessness and powerlessness, while others have reported expressing hostility through physical altercations as a means of protesting society's unjust ways. The implications of this phenomenon often leave the individual feeling socially excluded.

Lack of social support is an additional factor when examining causes of structural violence in high schools. Societal, community, and familial support are all critical aspects of social control. For instance, children exposed to violence in their homes or neighborhoods are more likely to behave violently in school. For most children, home is a safe haven. However, this scenario is becoming less and less common, particularly for those who reside in low-income neighborhoods. Children have reported witnessing shootings and violent gang activity. Contemporary children often witness first-hand the impact of violence and drugs in their neighborhoods and even in their homes, which can have devastating effects. These issues are perpetuated by single-parent households and further worsened if the custodial parent participates in self-destructive behavior.

Community violence resulting from such problems as drug use and gang activity tends to disproportionately afflict lower-class neighborhoods, and children's perpetual exposure to violence plays a significant role in their likelihood of partaking in violent behavior. For example, studies have revealed that children who are exposed to chronic community violence suffer much higher rates of post-traumatic stress disorder. Consequently, their likelihood of developing cognitive and behavioral problems also increases.

The literature suggests that the more violence children are exposed to (whether in the home or in the community), the more likely they are to feel a loss of control. Researchers have also concluded that students are often overwhelmed by these obstacles. Thus their concerns regarding community violence often take precedence over anything happening in school, good or bad, including their behavior. Feelings of hopelessness, frustration, and loss of control make acting out an appealing choice for struggling adolescents.

Clearly, what happens at school is only one segment of a student's life. Students of all ages may struggle with issues of drugs, abuse, and even neglect within the home, and exposure to violence increases a youth's risk of partaking in deviant behavior in the school system. The duration of exposure to structural violence sets adolescents apart from their pre-teen counterparts and could play a role in the higher incident rate of violence at the high school level. Adolescents have likely endured poverty-stricken lifestyles, racial and class discrimination, and associated societal consequences to a longer degree than younger children, and many adolescents have likely tailored their coping mechanisms to fit their circumstances. However, even the most dedicated students can find themselves developing harmful coping skills. It is apparent that environmental circumstances play a significant role in student performance, and a variety of social factors, from social exclusion to inequality, appear to be critical components in discussions of structural violence in U.S. high schools.

Kamesha Spates

Further Reading

Astor, R., Meyer, H., & Pitner, O. (2001). Elementary and middle school students' perceptions of violence-prone school subcontexts. *Elementary School Journal, 101,* 511–528.

Brady, E. (1995). How to survive urban violence with hope. *English Journal, 84,* 43–50.

Cullen, F. (1994). Social support as an organizing concept for criminology: Presidential address to the Academy of Criminal Justice Sciences. *Justice Quarterly, 11,* 527–59.

Harris, I. (1996). Peace education in an urban school district in the United States. *Peabody Journal of Education, 71,* 63–83.

Henry, S. (2000). What Is school violence? An integrated definition. *Annals of the American Academy of Political and Social Science, 567,* 16–29.

Henslin, J. (2001). *Essentials of sociology: A down-to-earth approach*. Boston: Allyn and Bacon.

Kramer, R. (2000). Poverty, inequality, and youth violence. *Annals of the American Academy of Political and Social Science, 567,* 123–139.

Messner, S., & Rosenfeld, R. (1997). *Crime and the American Dream* (2nd ed.). Belmont, CA: Wadsworth.

Randolph, S., Koblinsky, S., & Roberts, D. (1996). Studying the role of family and school in the development of African American preschoolers in violent neighborhoods. *Journal of Negro Education, 65,* 282–294.

Serious violent crime rate in U.S. schools. (2010). Charlottesville, VA: Youth Violence Project, School of Education, University of Virginia. Retrieved February 23, 2010, from http://youthviolence.edschool.virginia.edu/violence-in-schools/national-statistics.html

Statistics: School violence. (2005). New Haven, CT: National Center for Children Exposed to Violence. Retrieved February 18, 2010, from http://www.nccev.org/violence/statistics/statistics-school.html

Towns, D. (1996). "Rewind the world!": An ethnographic study of inner-city African American children's perceptions of violence. *Journal of Negro Education, 65,* 375–389.

Teacher-Perpetrated Crime and Violence, High School

Although most public attention regarding school violence focuses on situations in which students are the offenders, high school teachers and other school personnel are sometimes perpetrators. It is difficult to find solid data on how often educators are the offenders, as no one collects such data in a systemic way. Teacher- or staff-perpetrated violence may take many forms. Teachers may bully their students by being verbally or physically abusive. They may also commit sexual harassment or sexual assault. Corporal punishment is an example of systemic violence, when the violence perpetrated by educational personnel is the result of policies or practices that are supposed to be "for students' own good."

According to McEvoy (2005), bullying by teachers (or other staff, including coaches, who have supervisory control over students) is defined as "a pattern of conduct, rooted in a power differential, that threatens, harms, humiliates, induces fear, or causes students substantial emotional distress." One anonymous survey of teachers at seven elementary schools found 45% admitted to having bullied a student. Teacher-on-student bullying is in many ways similar to student-to-student bullying. Like all forms of bullying, it is rooted in the bully's desire to obtain and maintain power over the victim. Bullying is done deliberately and is intended to distress the victim. It tends to be repeated and, often, bullies face no repercussions for their behavior. The latter point is even more true when the bully is a teacher or school official.

Victims are selected for numerous reasons—because they appear vulnerable, because it is unlikely that other students will support or defend them, or because they have some particular attribute the educator does not value. Teacher bullies often claim their behavior is justified and will even suggest they have been provoked. Others claim their behavior is simply a motivational tactic or a necessary form of discipline. Because they are in positions of power, teacher or other educational personnel are more easily able to deflect complaints about their behavior. They may try to convince victims they are paranoid or crazy. They may assert that victims are simply unhappy with them and, therefore, are making unfair or unwarranted allegations.

Victims of teachers-perpetrated bullying often feel as if there is nowhere to go for help, as it is the very people who are entrusted to help them who are responsible for the abuse. This situation can leave victims depressed and anxious. Many miss school time to avoid the abuse, and then suffer additional repercussions.

Sexual harassment is unwelcome conduct that is sexual in nature. In a school setting, it refers to conduct that denies or limits a student's ability to participate in or benefit from school programs. It might include inappropriate comments or touching, sexual propositions, displaying or distributing explicit materials, telling sexually inappropriate jokes, and spreading sexual-related rumors. Two types of sexual harassment are distinguished: quid pro quo and hostile environment. Quid pro quo refers to unwelcome propositions or suggestions. Hostile environment occurs when a third party (in this case, a school employee or other student) creates a climate that is inappropriate—for instance, by displaying explicit photographs.

Sexual harassment is prohibited by Title IX of the Education Amendments of 1972. Under this legislation, schools are required to have specific policies regarding sex discrimination and sexual harassment and to distribute those policies to students and staff. In 2000, a nation-wide study conducted by the American Association of University Women (AAUW) Educational Foundation found that approximately 290,000 students experienced physical forms of sexual harassment by a public school employee between 1991 and 2000. Another study two years later by the AAUW found that, of students who reported sexual harassment in schools, 38% had been harassed by teachers or school personnel. A 2008 study found that, while more students are bullied in schools, sexual harassment may be more damaging to both girls and boys.

Psychological abuse or maltreatment takes many forms, ranging from ridicule and verbal assaults to use of inappropriate authoritarian discipline measures to failure to intervene when students are being bullied or harassed by peers. Teachers may humiliate students by calling them names, by repeatedly calling on students who are struggling, and by publicly pointing out poor performances. A very common form of psychologically damaging punishment is the denial of restroom privileges. Educators often defend such abusive behavior, arguing that they were either kidding around or that they were responding to inappropriate student behavior.

One of the most vulnerable groups within schools is lesbian, gay, bisexual, transgendered, and questioning (LGBTQ) youth. The 2005 version of the National School Climate study included 1,732 students ages 13 to 20. It found that

75.4% hear the words "faggot" or "dyke" frequently, and 89.2% hear comments like "You're gay," or "That's so gay" frequently. These comments are typically made when faculty and staff are not present, but when they are around, only 16.5% of the sample said such adults intervened frequently. Students said staff are less likely to intervene when they hear this type of remark than when they hear racist or sexist comments. Notably, 18.6% of the sample said staff also made this type of remark.

Systemic violence refers to institutional practices or procedures that adversely affect individuals or groups psychologically, mentally, culturally, spiritually, economically, or physically. It refers to acts of violence that are embedded or institutionalized into the daily life of schools. Rather than being intentionally damaging, systemic violence is usually the result of practices or policies that are supposed to help maintain a safe educational climate but instead do harm to students.

Corporal punishment is an example of systemic violence. According to the American Civil Liberties Union (ACLU), more than 250,000 public school students endure corporal punishment each year. Corporal punishment takes many forms, but in general refers to the imposition of some physical action that is intended to punish students for misbehavior. Paddling is the most common form of corporal punishment used in schools. A 2009 report by the ACLU and Human Rights Watch found students being hit by belts and rulers, as well as a variety of personal attacks including being thrown to the floor, dragged on hard tile, slapped, or slammed into walls. Students with disabilities are most likely to receive corporal punishment—in particular, students with autism. Most major medical bodies, including the Society for Adolescent Medicine and the American Academy of Pediatrics, have condemned this practice, as it can result in serious medical consequences, including muscle injury, blood clotting, and hemorrhaging.

Corporal punishment is banned in most of the world. Today, 106 nations across the globe outlaw corporal punishment in schools, including the United Kingdom, which did so following a ruling by the European Court of Human Rights. In the United States however, 21 states allow corporal punishment in schools, although the practice is prohibited in most juvenile detention centers and foster care settings.

Corporal punishment in the United States disproportionately affects African American students and, in some areas, Native American students. In the 2006–2007 school year, African American students accounted for 17.1% of the total U.S. student population, but 35.6% of those students who were paddled. In the same year, in the 13 states with the highest rates of paddling, 1.4 times as many African American students were paddled as might be expected given their percentage of the student population. Although girls of all races were paddled less often than boys, African American girls were nonetheless physically punished at more than twice the rate of their white counterparts in those 13 states during this time period.

Laura L. Finley

Further Reading

Epp, J. (1996). *Systemic violence: How schools hurt children*. London: Routledge.

Gay, Lesbian, Straight Education Network (GLSEN). (2005). *From teasing to torment: School climate in America*. Washington, DC: Author.

Gruber, J., & Fineran, S. (2008). Comparing the impact of bullying and sexual harassment victimization on the mental and physical health of adolescents. *Sex Roles, 10*, 1–13.

Hyman, I., & Snook, P. (1999). *Dangerous schools*. San Francisco, CA: Jossey-Bass.

Office for Civil Rights, U.S. Department of Education. (2008). Sexual harassment: It's not academic. Retrieved April 1, 2010, from http://www2.ed.gov/about/offices/list/ocr/docs/ocrshpam.pdf

Stephey, M. (2009, April 12). Corporal punishment in U.S. schools. *Time*. Retrieved March 31, 2010, from http://www.time.com/time/nation/article/0,8599,1915820,00.html

A violent education: Corporal punishment of children in U.S. public schools. (2008). New York: Amnesty International.

Technological Responses, High School

Escalating levels of violence in schools and the widespread community fear that school shootings in particular could happen anywhere have led high school administrators to turn to technology to protect their students. Legislative attention in this area has likewise resulted in greater funding for high-tech school security systems. However, technological responses can have unintended consequences that affect perceived safety levels in schools. While metal detectors and video cameras have been present in schools since the 1980s, new digital technologies are providing additional opportunities for both violence and surveillance.

A metal detector is an electronic implement used to detect the electromagnetic field of metallic objects. These devices have been used in schools as part of an attempt to combat violence by detecting the presence of weapons such as guns and knives among the student population. Introduced in response to inner-city drug problems and the surrounding drug trade, metal detectors have been credited with reducing the number of knives brought into these schools.

Two types of metal detectors are used in schools: hand-held devices and machines fixed to the floor through which students walk. A 2000 study of both middle and high schools found that random metal detectors were used in 4% of public schools, while only 1% required students to pass through fixed metal detectors each day. To prevent accusations of favoritism or discrimination, some schools also use automatic mats that blink red or green lights to select patterns of students for random scanning (e.g., every third or fourth student).

Metal detectors are not a favored method of violence control and are usually introduced only in those schools that report a high incidence of weapons-related violence. Their popularity (or recognized potential for success) has risen and declined at significant moments in the last 20 years. For example, at the end of the 1990s—a decade characterized by school shootings—a *CBS News* poll showed that 71% of respondents believed metal detectors should be present in schools as basic security. Conversely, in the last few years, several high school administrators have gone on record discouraging their use.

The effectiveness of metal detectors is highly contested, with a number of empirical studies producing conflicting findings. While Green (1999) of the Department of Justice argues that use of these devices makes schools safer, Schreck, Miller, and Gibson (2003) of the Department of Criminal Justice describe them as ineffective. Mayer and Leone (1999) from the Bureau of Justice Statistics, in conjunction with the National Center for Education Statistics and the Census Bureau, make the case that metal detectors actually increase social disorder in schools. Likewise, Douglas Thompkins (2000), a former member of a Chicago street gang and now a researcher in criminology and criminal justice, suggests that metal detectors simultaneously decrease violence in schools and create an unhealthy culture of fear. An International Communications Research study also found conflicting views among the general population, with 50% of Americans seeing metal detectors as helpful in preventing school violence and 47% believing they would not help.

In a study of school superintendents in Georgia focusing on their strategies for school security, 97% of respondents reported the use of security cameras in their schools. The cameras are placed in specific locations such as hallways, the cafeteria, parking lots, administrative offices, athletic stadiums, and school buses to allow staff to monitor student behaviors in these areas. Digital video technologies have increased the sophistication of this method of surveillance as videos can be monitored live via any internet connection remotely, allowing 24 hours a day, seven days a week surveillance.

The power of video camera surveillance derives from the possibility that someone could be watching. Some students have even confessed to violations of school rules and policies that were not caught on camera. While anecdotal evidence suggests video cameras in schools have decreased the level of vandalism in particular, their effect on violence is unknown. Research shows that in schools without a history of violence, video surveillance can have a detrimental effect on both students' and teachers' perceptions of their personal safety. In schools where gang activity is recorded, gangs are able to capitalize on the culture of fear surrounding surveillance to increase their power and dominance.

Since the high-profile school shootings in the late 1990s, and particularly in the wake of the shootings at Columbine High School, legislative attention has resulted in increased funding for security technology in U.S. schools. Along with metal detectors and video camera surveillance, technological responses to school violence include motion detectors, intruder alarm monitoring systems, two-way radios and walkie-talkies, lapel microphones, locked doors linked to the fire alarm system to restrict entry to and exit from buildings, and ID card machines (which register attendance, lateness, and discipline records). Pocket grenades for use by teachers are in the planning stage in New York schools. Lie detector (polygraph) tests have also been used to determine whether students were complying with drug and alcohol policies. Polygraphs are rarely used with juveniles, however, and in any case their results may not be admissible when considering disciplinary action. John Devine (1995) of the Metropolitan Center for Urban Education at New York University's School of Education argues that school security is a burgeoning industry that aims to introduce these kinds of measures in every school in America.

While the rate of physical violence in schools may have decreased, the incidence of emotional violence in these settings is rising. As students have become more accustomed to and dependent on the use of social networking, instant messaging, and text messaging, the potential for high school students to receive threatening or abusive messages has increased exponentially. Cyberbullying is a very real problem that administrators have struggled to deal with. Many schools have installed firewalls to prevent access to social networking sites from school computers so as to discourage the incidence of bullying online. While this measure addresses the problem during school hours, off-campus cyberbullying continues to run amok. In 2006, a school girl in Missouri committed suicide after fighting with someone whom she thought was a boy online; the girl had actually been talking with the mother of her friend. In response to this incident, several states have passed anti-cyberbullying legislation.

Incidents in a number of countries show that this is an international issue. For example, responses in Australia at both the school and government levels have led to concerns that focusing on specific technologies or sites detracts from the significant abuse suffered by the victims of cyberbullying. For example, YouTube was banned in all schools in the state of Victoria after a video in which a group of 12 boys forced a disabled girl to perform sexual acts and then burned her hair and urinated on her was posted on the popular video-sharing site. In 2008, a high school student in Western Australia was not allowed to sit for his final-year exams because of a speech he gave at a school assembly in which he criticized his principal's and teachers' responses to an accident that killed five students in his class. A video of the speech was posted on YouTube, though nothing happened to the student who put the film on YouTube.

The faith placed in technological solutions such as firewalls may not be warranted, as a 16–year-old Australian student demonstrated by cracking that country's Internet porn filter in less than 40 minutes. A number of private girls' schools have responded to the problem of cyberbullying outside of school hours by implementing programs that involve consultation between the school administrators, the parents, and the girls. Likewise, NetSafe, a nonprofit organization based in New Zealand (www.netsafe.org.nz), encourages the creation of supportive networks between children, parents, schools, community organizations, and businesses. Its website focuses on education, research, and collective collaboration and allows the anonymous reporting of cyber-offenses, which are then investigated. The site also has links directing youths to telephone help lines and counseling services.

Katie Ellis

Further Reading

Anderson, D. (1998). Curriculum, culture and community: The challenge of school violence. *Crime and Justice, 24*(Youth Violence), 317–363.

Ballard, C., & Brady, L. (2007). Violence prevention in Georgia's rural public school system. *Journal of School Violence, 6*(4), 105–129.

Devine, J. (1995). Can metal detectors replace the panopticon? *Cultural Anthropology, 10*(2), 171–195.

Glazer, G. (2007). School violence. *National Journal, 39*(16), 94.

Green, M. W. (1999). *The appropriate and effective use of security technology in US schools: A guide for schools and law enforcement agencies*. Washington: U.S. Department of Justice, National Institute of Justice, Office of Justice Programs.

Jimerson, S. R., & Furlong, M. J. (2006). *The handbook of school violence and school safety: From research to practice*. New York: Routledge.

Mayer, M. J., & Leone, P. E. (1999). A structural analysis of school violence and disruption: Implications for creating safer schools. *Education and Treatment of Children, 22*, 333–356.

Schrek, C. J., Miller, J. M., & Gibson, C. L. (2003). Trouble in the school yard: A study of the risk factors of victimisation at school. *Crime and Delinquency, 49*, 460–484.

Shariff, S. (2008). *Cyber-bullying: Issues and solutions for the school, the classroom and the home*. New York: Routledge.

Theriot, M. (2009). School resource officers and the criminalization of student behavior. *Journal of Criminal Justice. 37*(3), 280–287.

Thompkins, D. E. (2000). School violence: Gangs and a culture of fear. *Annals of the American Academy of Political and Social Science, 567*, 54–71.

Trump, K. S. (2000). *Classroom killers? Hallway hostages?: How schools can prevent and manage school crises*. Thousand Oaks, CA: Corwin Press.

Technology and Campus Crime and Violence

Colleges and research institutions are usually believed to be the birthplace of new technologies. Numerous inventions and discoveries are coming out of laboratories all around the world every year. To enhance the study and research environment, colleges are dedicated to providing students with access to these new technologies. On the one hand, the technologies offer students a great deal of convenience in terms of completing their academic and research requirements. On the other hand, some of them expose students to violence and are used to perpetrate violence. Additionally, various technologies are useful in responding to violent incidents when they occur and, in some cases, preventing such events from occurring.

Most colleges in United States offer Internet access to students in both classrooms and dormitories. Students can easily log into the campus network with their own Net ID and password, which are given to them when they enter college. Given the convenience of Internet and computer access, students tend to spend a large proportion of their time on the Internet.

One of the main attractions online is video games. Many of these games are violent in nature, and incorporate sexist and stereotypical images into their characters. Because college students generally reach the adult age during their matriculation, they are no longer restricted by the ratings assigned to violent games and can access any content they like. As consoles become more powerful and graphics become more realistic, the virtual world gets closer to the reality. Some players who are attracted to this world become obsessed with it. Rather than having players be the passive recipients of human violence, violent video games involve players in performing violence in the virtual world; in this way, they may promote a higher level of aggression among players.

In addition to violent video games, hundreds of websites can be found that display images and videos of stomach-turning violence. Screaming, cursing, beatings, stabbings, shootings, and smack-downs can be found easily online. Because college students can easily avoid the college-imposed filters intended to prevent them from accessing such sites, they have no trouble viewing the images of dead, dying, and mangled human beings.

Network-related security poses an ongoing challenge in the university setting. College students are not always careful about what they post on social networking sites such as Facebook, and may behind all kinds of clues that could identify specific people, including their names, their phone numbers, their birthdays, and even their precise locations. Other publicly listed information is easy to obtain online, making identity theft a growing problem on college campuses.

Meanwhile, advanced technology has also strengthened college students' ability to defend themselves and fight against violence on their campuses. A review of 20 reports and recommendations for colleges and universities recommended a number of safety measures, including the development of an emergency notification system. Colleges in the United States generally set up campus email service systems, in which each student is provided with an email account. College administrators can then send out information to each student via email, such as when there is a threat on campus. Campus police can also send out crime notices to inform students about particular types of dangers as well as ways to avoid becoming a victim. As more students have obtained cell phones that can receive both calls and text messages, colleges and universities have included phone or text messaging as part of their notification systems. Companies such as Omnilert provide this type of service to colleges and universities. Many colleges and universities added more sophisticated notification systems after the Virginia Tech shooting on April 16, 2007. Virginia Tech has been criticized because university officials waited two hours after the shootings began to send the first email notification to students; this statement merely warned students to be cautious and did not instruct them to stay away from the classrooms—even though shooter Seung-Hui Cho had not yet been apprehended at that point. Other notification systems work through intercoms, with messages being be broadcast to specific areas or even to an entire campus.

Technology can also help solve crimes on campus. Some of the same companies that offer notification services have developed electronic tip lines, where students can anonymously submit information about incidents on campus. The popularity of video recording and digital cameras has helped campus officials to capture the details of many crime scenes. Jamal Albarghouti, a Virginia Tech student who witnessed the shooting in 2007, used his cell phone to record the dramatic shooting. Such videos can be used as evidence in court, as can videotapes made from campus-based surveillance cameras.

After the rash of school shootings in the 1990s, many schools installed metal detectors. Most colleges and universities did not, realizing that it would be impossible to use them effectively on their sprawling campus grounds and that they would contrast with the philosophical openness and freedom of campus communities. Additionally, most of the task forces and study groups that have made recommendations for campus security have not suggested greater use of metal detectors. In lieu of metal detectors, most colleges use some type of secure key, often called a prox card, that allows authorized persons to gain access to residence halls. These keys can also be used to track who has entered and left the building. Although the use of this technology has begun to spread to other buildings, most academic halls remain easily accessible, especially during daytime hours. Even so, some oppose using these technologies, as they believe campuses will be viewed as fortresses, not arenas for free movement and thought. Additionally, the most advanced technologies are very expensive and, therefore, are cost-prohibitive for many campuses. Whatever measures are considered, campus officials are urged to be cautious, and to ensure that their reaction to criminal incidents or the fear of them does not unduly impinge on students' rights.

Hui Huang

Further Reading

Anderson, C. (2004). An update on the effects of playing violent video games. *Journal of Adolescence, 27*, 113–122.

Fox, J., & Savage, J. (2009). Mass murder goes to college: An examination of changes on college campuses after Virginia Tech. *American Behavioral Scientist, 52*, 1465–1485.

Rawe, J. (2007, April 16). Can we make campuses safer? *Time*. Retrieved November 17, 2010, from http://www.time.com/time/nation/article/0,8599,1611164,00.html

Schaffhauser, D. (2010, October 28). E2campus bundles campus emergency safety services. *Campus Technology*. Retrieved November 17, 2010, from http://campustechnology.com/articles/2010/10/28/e2campus-bundles-campus-emergency-safety-services.aspx

Teen Courts

Teen courts, also known as youth courts, student courts, and peer courts, are structured alternative forums where youth can adjudicate peer crimes. Teen courts date back to the 1960s, but did not come to national attention until the 1990s. The programs in the 1990s grew out of efforts promulgated by the American Bar Association to hold youth accountable for their actions before they develop a pattern of law-breaking behavior. According to the National Youth Court Database, in 2006, there were more than 1,127 youth court programs in the United States. Unlike traditional juvenile justice systems, teen courts do not fall within the judicial branch of government. Instead, they are intervention and diversion programs meant to prevent future crimes through peer pressure and relevant, but restorative punishments. Youth offenders between the ages of 10 and 17 can qualify for adjudication in teen courts.

The main purpose of most teen court programs is to determine a fair and restorative sentence, taking into account the needs of both the youth defendants and their victims. Most teen courts are administered or sponsored by juvenile courts, probation officers, law enforcement, nonprofit organizations, or schools. All teen courts operate within the parameters of individual state laws, which vary significantly from state to state. Some states have enacted legislation and standards for design, operation, and funding of such courts. Other states include broad legislation that grants county officials, school districts, and local nonprofit groups the discretion to enact teen courts.

In most states, the teen court's authority is informal. First-time youthful offenders agree to judgment by the teen court as part of a diversion program negotiated with the traditional juvenile justice system. Juveniles and their families agree to comply with the teen court program stipulations in exchange for dismissal of delinquency charges. The penalty for noncompliance with the teen court process is that the offending youth must return to the traditional juvenile justice system and face adjudication by a juvenile court judge.

Teen courts operate like regular juvenile courts, except that there are fewer adults involved, and teenagers take the roles of court clerks, bailiffs, attorneys, jurors, and even judges. They accept a range of offenses for adjudication, but typically reject more serious violent crimes. Most youth courts accept crimes related to theft; vandalism; cigarette, alcohol, and drug possession and use; curfew violation; and truancy. Few courts accept crimes related to fraud, harassment, and criminal mischief. Most sentencing options include a combination of community service, oral and/or written apologies, essays, jury duty, monetary restitution, and attendance at educational workshops. Substance abuse offenders' sentences include drug and alcohol testing. Traffic violations result in suspended driver's licenses. Sentences for victim-related crimes include restitution, victim awareness classes, victim/offender mediation, and jail tours. Some former youth defendants are sentenced to work within the teen court process adjudicating other peer offenders.

Teen courtroom models vary from state to state and from program to program. Four general types exist: adult judge, youth judge, youth tribunal, and peer jury. In the adult judge model, young people perform all of the court roles, except for that of the judge. In the youth judge model, young people, with adult supervision and management, perform all roles. Youth tribunals consist of three youth judges who hear the cases presented by the youth attorneys. Peer jury models operate like a grand jury in that the jury of teens can ask the defendant questions directly. All four teen courtroom models require unpaid participation on behalf of the participating youth. Youth who work in teen courts are either volunteers or previous defendants working in the court as a condition of their sentence.

Mary Christianakis

Further Reading

Butts, J., & Buck, J. (2000, October). Teen courts: A focus on research. *Juvenile Justice Bulletin*. Retrieved May 11, 2010, from http://www.ncjrs.gov/pdffiles1/ojjdp/183472.pdf

Butts, J., Buck, J., & Coggeshall, M. (2002, April). The impact of teen courts on young offenders. Urban Institute. Retrieved May 11, 2010, from http://www.urban.org/UploadedPDF/410457.pdf

Herman, M. (2002). Juvenile justice trends in 2002: Teen courts—A juvenile justice diversion program. National Center for State Courts. Retrieved May 11, 2010, from http://www.ncsconline.org/wc/publications/kis_juvjus_trends02_teenpub.pdf

National Association of Youth Courts: http://www.youthcourt.net/

Williamson, D., & Wells, J. (2004). *Making youth court as effective as possible*. Chicago: American Bar Association.

Tinker v. Des Moines School District

A pivotal court case, *Tinker v. Des Moines School District*, 393 U.S. 503 (1969), helped establish the First Amendment rights of public school students. In December 1965, 15-year-old John Tinker; his sister, 13-year-old Mary Beth Tinker; and a friend, 16-year-old Christopher Eckhardt, wore black armbands with

Mary Beth and John Tinker display the black armbands embellished with a peace sign that they wore to school to protest the Vietnam War in Des Moines, Iowa, on March 4, 1968. Both students, along with their friend Christopher Eckhardt, were suspended from school for wearing the armbands. (Bettmann/Corbis)

peace symbols on them to school. Their attire was part of a protest against the Vietnam War and a symbol of support for the Christmas truce in that war that had been proposed by Senator Robert F. Kennedy. School officials had heard of the students' plan in advance; in preparation for the event, days before they were planning to wear the armbands, the officials established a policy banning the wearing of armbands to school. The three wore the bands anyway, and all were suspended, per the new policy.

The Tinker and Eckhardt families, with the support of the Iowa Civil Liberties Union, filed suit in U.S. District Court, which upheld the school's decision. The families next appealed to the U.S. Court of Appeals for the Eighth Circuit, which resulted in a tie vote that allowed the school's decision to stand. The families then appealed to the U.S. Supreme Court directly, and the Court agreed to hear the case. Oral arguments were held on November 12, 1968.

In a 7-2 decision, the Supreme Court held that the First Amendment applies to public school students. While these rights can be limited, the court held that the school district would need a constitutionally valid reason to do so, and this was not it. Writing for the majority, Justice Abe Fortas noted that a valid reason to limit students' free expression must be more than the avoidance of discomfort that comes with the expression of unpopular opinions. He supported allowing schools to forbid conduct that could "materially and substantially interfere with the requirements of appropriate discipline in the operation of the school." Fortas was concerned that schools would become totalitarian in their discipline, and uttered the now-famous phrase that school children do not "shed their constitutional rights to free expression at the schoolhouse gate."

One of the dissenters to this decision, Justice John Marshall Harlan II, wrote that symbolic speech was not constitutionally protected. Justice Hugo Black, the other dissenter, disagreed with the majority and claimed that the Tinkers' and Eckhardt's behavior was indeed disruptive. Black maintained that allowing students this type of free expression would be a slippery slope that would prompt a "revolutionary era of permissiveness" in schools.

Subsequent decisions have generally limited students' free expression. For instance, in *Bethel School District v. Fraser* in 1986, the Supreme Court ruled that a high school student's speech before a school assembly was not constitutionally protected. In this case, the student's speech had included crude sexual double entendres. In part, the Court sided with the school because the assembly took place during the school day. In *Hazelwood v. Kuhlmeier*, the Court ruled that schools can censor student newspapers when those publications are school sponsored, as in the case of a journalism class that produces the paper.

Laura L. Finley

Further Reading

Dautrich, K., & Yalof, D. (2008). *The future of the First Amendment: The digital media, civic education, and free expression rights in America's high schools.* Lanham, MD: Rowman & Littlefield.

Dupre, A. (2010). *Speaking up: The unintended cost of free speech in public schools.* Cambridge, MA: Harvard University Press.

Rohr, M. (2000). How free is the speech of public school students? *Florida Bar Journal, 74*(6), 79.

Tinker v. Des Moines School District, 393 U.S. 503 (1969). Retrieved from http://caselaw.lp.findlaw.com/scripts/getcase.pl?court=us&vol=393&invol=503

Treacy, Wayne

On March 17, 2010, 15-year-old Wayne Treacy brutally attacked classmate Josie Ratley, also age 15, after a text message exchange in Deerfield Beach, Florida. Both were middle school students. In the text message, Ratley made a comment about Treacy's brother, who had committed suicide in October 2009. Treacy assaulted Ratley at a school bus stop, punching her in the head and, when she fell down, slamming her head into the pavement. He also kicked Ratley with his steel-toed boots. Only the arrival of a teacher, Walter Welsh, to pull him off made Treacy stop.

Ratley was in a medically induced coma at Broward General Medical Center for weeks. She has since regained consciousness but has suffered brain damage and still cannot speak. She had endured three surgeries, including one in which surgeons replaced a section of her skull they had removed to relieve pressure when her brain swelled after the attack.

Treacy's parents have said that their son "snapped," and definitely needed mental health counseling. Treacy has been waived to adult court, where he will be tried on attempted murder charges; he faces the prospect of life in prison. Treacy has pleaded not guilty to the charges. Kayla Manson, age 13, has been charged as an accomplice in the crime, albeit in juvenile court. Manson allegedly told Treacy where to find Ratley.

School officials were quick to denounce the attack. Broward County Schools Superintendent Jim Notter introduced a new district anti-bullying theme that is intended to empower students so that they can make a difference. He urged students and parents to report anything suspicious via the tip line, an email, or a text message and emphasized that all reports are anonymous so students should not fear reprisal.

Unfortunately, this incident was not the first high-profile attack involving Deerfield Beach Middle School. On October 12, 2009, a group of boys attacked 15-year-old Michael Brewer, dousing him with rubbing alcohol and then setting him on fire. Brewer suffered second- and third-degree burns but had recovered enough to enroll in a different school by May 2010. He spoke out publicly to encourage Ratley in her recovery. Brewer also spoke about the dangerous climate at Deerfield Beach Middle School, although administrators claim they have many protections in place.

The community has rallied to support Ratley, and before her, Brewer. Numerous groups organized fundraisers to assist the youths in their recovery. Ratley's mother, in particular, has become a vocal advocate of anti-bullying measures.

Laura L. Finley

Further Reading

McLaughlin, J., & Cilli, L. (2010, April 20). Teen pleads not guilty in Josie Ratley beating. *CBS*. Retrieved May 11, 2010, from http://cbs4.com/local/josie.lou.ratley.2.1644414.html

Miller, C. (2010, March 23). Hero teacher Walter Welsh: "Sorry I didn't get there faster . . ." but he rescued Josie Ratley from steel-toed booting. *CBS News*. Retrieved May 11, 2010, from http://www.cbsnews.com/8301-504083_162-20000992-504083.html?tag=contentMain;contentBody

Miller, C. (2010, April 8). Josie Lou Ratley, Michael Brewer attacks spur Broward County anti-bullying campaign. *CBS*. Retrieved May 11, 2010, from http://www.cbsnews.com/8301-504083_162-20002032-504083.html

Olmeda, R. (2010, April 17). Wayne Treacy, 15, charged as adult in Deerfield beating of Josie Lou Ratley. *Miami Herald*. Retrieved May 11, 2010, from http://www.miamiherald.com/2010/04/17/1584121/wayne-treacy-15-charged-as-adult.html

U

United Nations Children's Fund (UNICEF)

The United Nations Children's Fund (UNICEF) is the United Nations' only entity specifically charged with guaranteeing the rights of children and enforcing the Convention on the Rights of the Child. Created in 1946, it received its mandate from the United Nations General Assembly in 1953. It is a nonpartisan group. In 1965, UNICEF won the Nobel Peace Prize "for the promotion of brotherhood among nations."

UNICEF was created to care for and nurture the world's children by helping overcome poverty, violence, disease, and discrimination. Specifically, UNICEF advocates for prenatal and postnatal care so that children can get the best start in life. It also supports education for all, but particularly for girls because research shows that educating girls has a significant impact on the community. This agency helps provide immunizations and nourishment so that children are healthy, and it works to eradicate HIV and AIDS and their devastating impact. Finally, UNICEF provides emergency relief in cases of natural and other disasters and helps ensure children are not exposed to violence or abuse in the home.

The organization's website (www.unicef.org) features a wealth of information about child survival and development, child protection, education, HIV/AIDS, nutrition, water and sanitation, health, and much more. It is searchable by topic and by country.

Also on the website is information about Goodwill Ambassadors, many of whom are celebrities. Actor Danny Kaye was one of the first, and actress Mia Farrow is currently a Goodwill Ambassador. UNICEF partners with numerous other nongovernmental organizations as well as corporations, including American Airlines, Hewlett-Packard, and IKEA.

The 2011 *State of the World's Children* report is also available on the UNICEF website. It contains statistics, pictures, and analysis of all the major indicators

UNICEF measures. Researchers and others can even use the statistics to make custom tables that include specific measures and/or countries.

UNICEF also has a television and a radio station that are accessible via the organization's website. From the site, people can purchase items that support the organization's programs, including holiday cards and handcrafted goods.

Laura L. Finley

Further Reading
UNICEF: www.unicef.org

U.S. Department of Education

The Office of Safe and Drug-Free Schools (OSDFS), which is a division of the U.S. Department of Education, is charged with administering, coordinating, and recommending policy related to the prevention of drugs and violence in schools. OSDFS provides financial assistance for activities and programs designed to prevent drug use and violence and to foster the health and well-being of students in all grades and through college. It operates under the direction of the Assistant Deputy Secretary of the Department of Education and the advisement of the Safe and Drug-Free Schools and Communities Advisory Committee, which was created by the No Child Left Behind Act of 2001. These entities provide direction, coordination, and leadership for five major elements of OSFS strategy: (1) health, mental health, environmental health, and physical education (HMHEHPE); (2) state-level drug and violence prevention programs; (3) national-level drug and violence prevention programs; (4) character and civic education; and (5) policy and cross-cutting programs.

The HMHEHPE element, following on the heels of the Title V of the Elementary and Secondary School Education Act, administers programs that promote the health and well-being for students and families. It provides grants for counseling, physical education, and related programs.

Title IV of the Elementary and Secondary School Education Act authorized financial assistance to state and local entities implementing drug and violence prevention programs and activities in K–12 schools as well as in higher education. Nationally, drug and violence prevention programs are authorized under Title IV, Safe and Drug Free Schools and Community Act (SDFSCA) of the Improving America's Schools Act of 1994. OSDFS provides grants for model alcohol and drug prevention programs on campuses, coalitions to prevent and respond to drug and alcohol use and to prevent high-risk drinking on campuses, school-based drug testing, mentoring programs, and additional challenge grants.

The Character and Civic Education (CCE) group provides programming and grants related to character and civic education. "We the People" is a civic education program that promotes civic competence among elementary and secondary students. Policy and cross-cutting programs provide discretionary grants for cooperative and collaborative prevention programs, as well as for various types of emergency assistance.

In addition, OSDFS administers several provisions of the Elementary and Secondary Act that were amended by the No Child Left Behind Act of 2001. These include the Gun-Free Schools Act, provisions related to the transfer of student disciplinary records, the Pro-Children Act, and the Unsafe School Choice Option.

On its website (http://www.ed.gov/about/offices/list/osdfs/resources.html#facts), OSDFS provides a wealth of information related to drugs and violence. This material includes fact sheets on a number of topics, more-detailed publications and reports, online courses and survey assessment tools, and links to other entities related to drug, alcohol, and violence prevention.

Laura L. Finley

Further Reading

Office of Safe and Drug-Free Schools: http://www.ed.gov/about/offices/list/osdfs/index.html

U.S. Department of Justice

The U.S. Department of Justice is a federal agency overseen by the U.S. Attorney General and charged with a multitude of duties and responsibilities. The mission statement of the U.S. Department of Justice states that the agency has the following goals: "To enforce the law and defend the interests of the United States according to the law; to ensure public safety against threats foreign and domestic; to provide federal leadership in preventing and controlling crime; to seek just punishment for those guilty of unlawful behavior; and to ensure fair and impartial administration of justice for all Americans."

The origins of the U.S. Department of Justice Department date back to the Judiciary Act of 1789, which created the position of U.S. Attorney General. Because the young nation was still in its early stages of development at that time, and had both a small population and limited government, the Attorney General role was originally a part-time position with limited responsibilities. Roughly a century later, in the aftermath of the Civil War, the U.S. Congress passed the 1870 Act to Establish the Department of Justice, which gave the Attorney General the responsibility of overseeing this agency. The newly created agency was charged with attending to the legal matters of the United States, inclusive of criminal matters and the protection of basic civil liberties.

Since its founding, the U.S. Department of Justice has continued to expand and evolve and is now responsible for numerous tasks, including of law enforcement, correctional administration, research, and policy development. To provide a few examples, the U.S. Department of Justice oversees the U.S. Bureau of Prisons and houses several federal law enforcement agencies, including the Federal Bureau of Investigation, the Drug Enforcement Administration, the U.S. Marshals Service, and the Bureau of Alcohol, Tobacco, Firearms, and Explosives. The aforementioned law enforcement agencies perform numerous tasks, such as the investigation of crimes like arson, bank robbery, kidnapping, drug trafficking, and terrorist attacks; the provision of security in federal courthouses and the protection of federal judges; the provision of security for witnesses in federal criminal cases; and the apprehension of federal fugitives.

As to the research and policy development responsibilities of the agency, the Office of Justice Programs within the U.S. Department of Justice oversees several research-focused agencies, such as the Bureau of Justice Statistics, the National Institute of Justice, and the Office of Juvenile Justice and Delinquency Prevention. These agencies fund and conduct research on topics pertinent to juvenile delinquency and criminal activity such as homicide, property crimes, violent crimes, school crime, and drug use. In addition, they serve in advisory roles by providing information to legislators about best practices for the prevention and reduction of crime.

The U.S. Department of Justice also has some offices that do not conduct original research but rather compile research on specific topics, provide advice on the development of national policies, and assist in the development of local, state, and national programs designed to reduce crime. For instance, the U.S. Department of Justice oversees the Office on Violence Against Women, whose primary task is to provide accurate information on domestic and interpersonal violence and to assist local and state governments in their efforts to reduce domestic violence.

Ben Brown

Further Reading

Bureau of Alcohol, Tobacco, Firearms, and Explosives: www.atf.gov
Bureau of Justice Statistics: www.ojp.usdoj.gov/bjs/
Drug Enforcement Administration: www.usdoj.gov/dea/
Federal Bureau of Investigation: www.fbi.gov
Federal Bureau of Prisons: www.bop.gov
National Institute of Justice: www.ojp.usdoj.gov/nij/
Office of Juvenile Justice and Delinquency Prevention: www.ojjdp.ncjrs.gov
Office on Violence Against Women: www.ovw.usdoj.gov
U.S. Department of Justice: www.usdoj.gov
U.S. Marshals Service: www.usmarshals.gov

V

Vernonia School District 47J v. Acton

Vernonia School District 47J v. Acton et ux., Guardians ad Litem for Acton (No. 94-590) 515 U.S. 646, is a case that was argued before the U.S. Supreme Court on March 28, 1995, and decided on June 26, 1995. In it, the Court ruled on the constitutionality of random drug testing of student athletes.

Located in the small logging town of Vernonia, Oregon, Vernonia School District 47J was composed of one high school and three grade schools. Throughout the 1980s, school athletics played a prominent role in the town's life, and student-athletes served as role models. However, in the mid- to late 1980s, teachers and administrators observed student-athletes boasting of drug use, which they believed promoted a drug culture. Simultaneously, disciplinary referrals doubled in number when compared to the early 1980s. Additionally, some athletes suffered injuries because of their own drug use, as well as the use of others.

Initially, the district invited guest speakers, gave presentations, and created special classes to educate students on the dangers of drug use. When the problem persisted, they brought in trained dogs to sniff out drugs on campus, but to no avail.

To address the drug problem among athletes, district officials proposed a student athlete drug policy to the parents, who provided input on the policy and granted unanimous approval for it. The school board approved the policy, the purpose of which was to prevent student-athletes from using drugs, protect their health and safety, and provide drug users with assistance programming.

Under the policy, athletes were tested through urinalysis at the beginning of the season, and then randomly selected for testing once a week throughout the duration of the season. The students' urine samples were sent to an independent laboratory and tested for amphetamines, cocaine, and marijuana. Only the superintendent, principals, vice principals, and athletic directors had access to test results, which were kept for one year only. If a sample tested positive, a second test was administered to confirm the result. If the second test was negative, no further action was taken. If the second test was positive, then the athlete's parents were informed and the athlete could choose one of two options: (1) participate in an assistance program that included weekly urinalysis or (2) be suspended from the remaining athletic season and the next one as well. Second-time offenders were automatically given option 2. Third-time offenders were suspended for the remainder of the season and the next two seasons. The policy required all student-athletes participating in interscholastic sports and their parents to sign a drug testing consent form as a condition for participation in sports.

From left: attorney John Wittmayer, brother Simon, James Acton, mother Judy, father Wayne, and attorney Tom Christ walk from the U.S. Supreme Court building in Washington, D.C., on March 28, 1995. (AP/Wide World Photos)

The policy had been in place for two full years when James Acton, then a seventh grader, was prohibited from playing football because his parents refused to sign the testing consent forms. In 1991, the Actons filed suit, claiming that the district's policy violated Article I, §9, of the Oregon Constitution, as well as the Fourth Amendment of the U.S. Constitution, which argues for "the right of the people to be secure in their persons, houses, papers, and effects, against unreasonable searches and seizures," and the 14th Amendment of the U.S. Constitution, which extends the constitutional guarantee to searches and seizures by state officers including public school officials. After a bench trial, the Vernonia District Court denied the Actons' claims and dismissed the suit. However, the U.S. Court of Appeals for the Ninth Circuit reversed the District Court's ruling, holding that the policy did indeed violate both the Fourth and 14th Amendments to the U.S. Constitution and Article I, §9, of the Oregon Constitution.

In a 6-3 vote, the U.S. Supreme Court affirmed that mandatory drug testing of student-athletes does not violate the Fourth Amendment and, therefore, is constitutional. The Court argued that children in schools have less privacy than free adults. As argued earlier in the *New Jersey v. T.L.O.* case, warrantless searches in school contexts are permitted because schools have what the Court deemed "special needs" to maintain and enforce disciplinary procedures. Teachers, coaches, and administrators stand *in loco parentis* over children; thus they have the custodial and tutelary obligations to protect the children's health and well-being.

Additionally, the majority decision argued that volunteer student-athletes choose to participate in activities that are closely regulated and are informed of the regular intrusion upon the normal rights and privileges of other students, including privacy. For example, they willingly subject themselves to an even higher degree of regulation, as they must submit to a preseason physical examination, show proof of insurance, maintain a minimum grade-point average, and comply with the rules of conduct as determined by the sport.

Mary Christianakis

Further Reading

Andresen, S. A. (2008). A call for drug-testing of high school student-athletes. *Marquette Sports Law Review, 19*(2), 325–335.

Arnold, T. L. (1996). Constitutionality of random drug testing of student-athletes makes the cut ... but will the athletes?" *Journal of Law & Education, 25*(1), 190–198.

Donaldson, J. F. (2006). Life, liberty, and the pursuit of urinalysis: The constitutionality of random suspicionless drug testing in public schools. *Valparaiso University Law Review, 41*(1), 815–854.

Penrose, M. (2003). Shedding rights, shredding rights: A critical examination of students' privacy rights and the "special needs" doctrine after earls. *Nevada Law Journal, 3*(2), 411–451.

Shutler, S. E. (1996). Random, suspicionless drug testing of high school athletes. *Journal of Criminal Law and Criminology, 86*(4), 1265–1303.

Vernonia School District 47J v. Acton et ux., Guardians ad Litem for Acton (No. 94-590) 515 U.S. 646. (n.d.). Retrieved December 28, 2009, from http://www4.law.cornell.edu/supct/html/94-590.ZO.html

Yamaguchi, R., & Hinkle-DeGroot, R. (2002). *The legal and educational issues behind drug testing in school.* Ann Arbor, MI: Institute for Social Research.

Victimless Offenses, College

A victimless offense is an act that is legally defined as criminal, but has no clearly identifiable victim. Victimless offenses can also occur when an illegal act has been engaged in consensually by all individuals involved. Such crimes are sometimes referred to as crimes of consent or consensual crimes. Criminologists and legal officials disagree as to whether such a thing as a victimless crime can exist, as individuals engaging in certain activities might harm or victimize themselves, or unintentionally victimize others. From this perspective, there is always a victim. The term "consensual crime" might be more appropriate, as it does not imply that there are no victims, but rather that any victims consented to the harm that they received or inflicted on themselves.

The most common forms of so-called victimless offenses on college campuses in the United States are the use of illicit drugs and the under-age consumption and distribution of alcohol. In most instances, individuals who consume illicit drugs do so with the knowledge that they might be inflicting harm on their bodies and are placing themselves at risk for serious health issues. Likewise, many minors know that the possession and consumption of alcohol is illegal on college campuses, but their use of the substance does no apparent harm to others. However, laws are in place to curb offenses related to illicit drug use and underage drinking to protect individuals from harms that they might knowingly or unknowingly inflict on themselves.

In the United States, many activities are prohibited to protect individuals from harming themselves, regardless of their consent to the activity. For instance, individuals must wear a seat belt when riding in a motor vehicle. Likewise, a helmet must be worn when riding a motorcycle. In the most extreme example, it is illegal to commit suicide or to assist someone in committing suicide. These laws are in place to protect people from victimizing themselves.

Beyond protecting the individual, each of these activities can have far-reaching consequences on other individuals and society more generally. While the use of illicit drugs such as cocaine might have the most apparent harm on the individual using the substance, it can also hurt those around the substance user, such as children of the user or other family members. The health ramifications of illicit substance abuse can also lead to use of the health care system and other social services, requiring capital resources that could be used for other important means. Likewise, while the apparent target of the harm of not wearing a seat belt is the individual in the event of an accident, he or she might also directly harm other passengers in the car. Harm to the individual could also harm his or her family, and require health care services that might not have been needed otherwise. Thus there may a number of victims in so-called victimless crimes.

Beyond illicit drug use and underage drinking, other common forms of consensual crime on campuses in the United States include violence, hazing, public nudity, and forms of sexual deviance. Many forms of violence cannot be considered consensual crime, such as sexual assault and intimate-partner violence. Many forms of violence on college campuses can, however, be considered consensual crime, such as a fight between two men in the parking lot outside a bar. In this example, while the men might have willingly engaged in the activity knowing the harm that it could result to self and the other combatant, both could still be criminally charged with assault. Although they may have given their consent to the action, it might not form a viable legal defense; thus a crime would have occurred. In contrast, in a college football game on campus, if a player physically maims another, causing serious, even life-threatening injury, the consent defense can be used, resulting in no criminal penalty for the player.

Like violence, hazing on college campuses can be considered a crime regardless of consent. Of the 43 states that have legal statutes against hazing, most do not recognize consent as a viable legal defense. In some states, however, if an individual consents to be hazed, then no penal sanction is sought. The statutes against hazing of many states also include provisions that indicate that no crime has occurred if the hazing is done as part of a college fraternity ritual or on an athletic team. Other charges related to the hazing, such as sexual assault, can be attributed to the perpetrators of hazing regardless of state hazing laws or the consent of the victim.

The act of streaking, or running nude, across college campuses or at college sporting event is a common occurrence in the United States. Regardless of consent, public nudity is typically illegal, especially if children are witness to the activity. However, there are no real victims of this crime; as such, streakers are often treated with leniency in the courts. When public nudity is forced on an individual, such as is common in hazing rituals, it is often considered to be a crime regardless of consent.

Sexual deviance involving sadism and masochism, as well as statutory rape, can also be illegal. Sadism and masochism involve sexual gratification from inflicting suffering onto another person or having pain inflicted on oneself. When sadism and masochism cross certain lines, such as when they involve knife and gun play, these acts can become illegal regardless of consent. Statutory rape occurs when an individual older than the age of consent has sexual intercourse with an individual younger than the age of consent. Regardless if consent is given, it is not treated as legally valid because of the age of the alleged victim.

Victimless crimes, or consensual crimes, are often characterized as being conflictual in the U.S. legal system. Laws are constructed to help protect individuals from harming themselves, but the consequences of the law often do more harm than the acts that have been criminalized. For instance, it can be argued that the criminalization of marijuana use has greater harmful effect on individuals and societies than the actual harm caused by the drug. Individuals' lives, and the lives of their families, are disrupted by the criminalization of marijuana. Furthermore, the legal system and other law enforcement resources are being used in ways that might be better reserved for addressing more serious crimes. Victimless crimes are also considered conflictual as there is little consensus in American society as to whether they should be criminal. Often, laws against victimless crimes encroach on the civil liberties of citizens, which is a prided aspect of American culture and society.

Curtis Fogel

Further Reading

Dubber, M. D. (2002). *Victims in the war on crime: The use and abuse of victim's rights.* New York: New York University Press.

Leitzel, J. (2008). *Regulating vice: Misguided prohibitions and realistic controls.* New York: Cambridge University Press.

Meier, R. F., & Geis, G. (1997). *Victimless crime? Prostitution, drugs, homosexuality, and abortion.* Los Angeles: Roxbury.

Victimless Offenses, High School

A victimless offense can be broadly defined as an offense where the person who is considered the "victim" consents to the act of violence. Often, the offense violates social and community standards rather than having a tangible legal implication. Suicide and self-harm, which are both dangerous and self-directed, can be considered as victimless offenses and have had a longer history of occurrence in schools than other high-profile acts of violence. Unlike suicide and self-harm, hazing is not self-directed; nevertheless, as a form of violent initiation into a group, victims often consent to the hazing-related violence committed against them. Even so, true consent is questionable in such case, given that peer pressure and a desire to belong to a group are involved.

Suicide is the conscious act of ending one's own life. Self-harm likewise refers to a person's intention to deliberately inflict harm on himself or herself, often as a coping strategy. While suicidal behavior consists of thoughts and actions that may lead to serious injury, self-harm can be distinguished from a suicide attempt in that the person who engages in self-harm does not intend to die. It is possible for both behaviors to exist in the one person; thus an individual engaging in self-harm may accidentally cause his or her own death or attempt suicide in a moment of desperation.

Described as a multidimensional malaise or depression by suicide expert Edwin Shneidman, suicide is a desperate solution where the sufferer can see no other alternative. It is the third leading cause of death among American teenagers and young adults between the ages of 16 and 24. A survey of 10,000 U.S. school-aged adolescents showed that 24.1% had serious thoughts about suicide, 17.7% had made a plan for suicide, and 8.7% had already attempted suicide in the last 12 months. Suicide is far less common in younger age groups, with a less than 1% occurrence noted in children aged 5 to 10.

Suicide, as a consequence of a number of distress factors, is framed on an interpersonal level as the only and best solution in a needful individual. Changes to behavior indicating personal crisis can suggest a risk of suicide. The Center for Suicide Prevention has compiled a list of seven indicators of school-aged adolescents at risk of suicide:

- Unexpected reduction of academic performance
- Ideas and themes of depression, death, and suicide
- Change in mood and marked emotional instability
- Significant grief or stress
- Withdrawal from relationships
- Physical symptoms with emotional cause
- High-risk behaviors

Given that peers are more likely to know of a school-aged adolescent's suicidal intention, school-based suicide prevention programs are a key component of attempts to decrease the incidence of teen suicide. Contagion—the phenomenon in which one suicide facilitates suicide in another person—and clustering—a series of suicides that take place at nearly the same time and place—are also of significant concern to schools. Strategies where the initial suicide is not glorified, yet students are encouraged to discuss their feelings about the incident, are encouraged in schools by suicide prevention organizations. While memorial services are encouraged, permanent memorials such as planting a tree, creating a plaque, or dedicating a yearbook to the individual who committed suicide are discouraged.

It is difficult to obtain reliable statistics on people who engage in self-harm, because this behavior is often a private act committed by individuals who are unwilling to seek professional help. The most common form of self-harm is skin cutting, because people can choose to inflict harm parts of the body that can be covered up by clothing. Other methods include burning, self-hitting, scratching, hair pulling, and interfering with wound healing. Eating disorders can also be considered as a form of self-harm. The most extreme methods of self-harm include removal of the eye and amputation of limbs or genitals.

The motivations of people who deliberately and repetitively damage their bodies with little to no suicidal intent often center on religious and sexual themes. According to Favazza and Rosenthal (1993), the behavior acts as a form of rapid relief from psychological distress and often is performed as a means to cope with tension and anxiety, depression and emptiness, feelings of numbness, anger and aggression, feelings of alienation, self-hatred or guilt, and intense emotional pain.

Self-harm is also a method used to gain control over one's body, and to maintain a sense of security or feeling of uniqueness. It may be a continuation of previous abuse patterns or a way to obtain a feeling of euphoria. Finally, self-harm could be a symptom of a more severe mental disorder. One study found that 71% of respondents described it as an addiction.

Research suggests that the practice of skin cutting is most common among high school girls, with adolescents being more likely to engage in this behavior if their friends do. While females report higher incidences of self-harm, this difference may simply reflect the fact that females are more willing to seek help. Self-harming behaviors typically begin at around age 14, peaking in the 16- to 25-year-old age group. Although the practice may continue for decades, treatment may enable adolescents to learn better coping strategies and grow out of their self-harming behaviors.

Hazing is the humiliating initiation into a club or group whereby a person completes a ritualistic test that usually involves physical or emotional injury. It can be divided into three categories: subtle hazing (generally acceptable behaviors that serve to embarrass new members), harassment hazing (behaviors that cause emotional or physical discomfort), and violent hazing. Although not all hazing is violent, 22% of students have participated in dangerous hazing practices. With the exception of Alaska, Hawaii, Montana, Michigan, New Mexico, South Dakota, and Wyoming, each U.S. state has anti-hazing legislation in effect. Despite the widespread existence of such legislation, violent hazing rituals—including extreme alcohol consumption, savage beatings or paddling, burning, bondage, and exposure to extreme weather conditions—persist in many high schools.

There has been a long tradition of hazing in group initiation. Supporters claim the practice promotes team bonding, which in turn allows teams to work together more effectively; people who do not become truly committed to the endeavor through hazing are likely to have weaker bonds to the group, it is argued. While there is very little research in support of this theory, Stephen Sweet, a sociology professor at New York State University, argues that hazing is not illogical and satisfies a need to belong, thereby counteracting the sense of isolation felt by many students.

Although thought to take place mainly among male college students who are members of athletic teams or fraternities, research shows that dangerous practices of hazing are as prevalent among high school students (22%) as they are among college students (21%). While males are more at risk of hazing, this practice is actually common among high school students of both genders. A recent study found that 48% of U.S. high school students had undergone a hazing ritual so as to join a group or organization, with 24% joining an athletic team; 16% a peer group or gang; 8% a music, art, or theater group; and 7% a church group. Despite the large number of students who engaged in this behavior, only 14%

recognized the activity as hazing. Although it may be framed as a bonding experience by the perpetrators, hazing can be a dangerous activity and cultural norms often prevent victims from speaking out or refusing to participate.

Katie Ellis

Further Reading

Allan, E. J., & Madden, M. (2008). Hazing in view: College students at risk. Retrieved June 7, 2009, from http://www.hazingstudy.org/publications/hazing_in_view_web.pdf

Center for Suicide Prevention. (1998). Considerations for school suicide prevention programs, p. 32. Retrieved from http://www.suicideinfo.ca/csp/assets/alert32.pdf

Center for Suicide Prevention. (2001). A closer look at self-harm, p. 43. Retrieved from http://www.suicideinfo.ca/csp/assets/alert43.pdf

Center for Suicide Prevention. (2004). School memorials after suicide: Helpful or harmful?, p. 54. Retrieved from http://www.suicideinfo.ca/csp/assets/alert54.pdf

Favazza, A. R. (1989). Why patients mutilate themselves. *Hospital & Community Psychiatry, 40*, 137–145.

Favazza, A. R., & Rosenthal, R. J. (1993). Diagnostic issues in self-mutilation. *Hospital & Community Psychiatry, 44*(2), 134–140.

Finkelman, P. (2006). *Encyclopaedia of American civil liberties*. New York: Routledge.

Hoover, N. C., & Pollard, N. J. (2000). High school hazing. Retrieved June 7, 2009, from http://www.alfred.edu/hs_hazing/

Nuwer, H. (1998–2005). Stop hazing: Educating to eliminate hazing. Retrieved June 6, 2009, from http://www.stophazing.org/

Nuwer, H. (2004). *The hazing reader*. Bloomington, Indiana: Indiana University Press.

Shneidman, E. (1993). *Suicide as psychache: A clinical approach to self-destructive behavior*. Lanham, MD: Rowman & Littlefield.

Sweet, S. (2004). Understanding fraternity hazing. In H. Nuwer (Ed.), *The hazing reader* (pp. 1–13). Bloomington, Indiana: Indiana University Press.

Video Games

In the search for explanations when school shootings occur, many have pointed to violent video games as culprits. A number of school and campus shooters were obsessed with playing violent video games, which some experts say are designed to teach people to kill. Others maintain that while playing video games is not the healthiest habit, scores of people do it every day and do not perpetrate acts of violence.

Michael Carneal was a fan of the violent games *Doom, Quake*, and *Mortal Kombat*. The families of some of his Paducah, Kentucky, victims filed suit against the makers of these games in the aftermath of his crimes, claiming they were an influence on Carneal. The suit was not successful. Eric Harris and Dylan Klebold, the Columbine High School shooters, were avid players of *Doom*, and Harris had even written programs for the game. Seung-Hui Cho, the Virginia Tech shooter, was also said to have been a gamer, preferring *Counterstrike*.

An article in the American Psychological Association's *Journal of Personality and Social Psychology* reported on two studies related to video games and violence. In the first, 227 college students completed a survey on their aggressive behaviors and video game playing. Those who played more reported both more aggressive behavior and lower grades in college. In the second study, 210 college students played either a violent video game (*Wolfenstein 3D*) or a nonviolent video game (*Myst*). Afterward, they were asked to "punish an opponent" by pressing a

Teens surround computer screens as they play the game *Counter-Strike* at a Los Angeles cybercafé. These kinds of games are often seen as catalysts to physical violence. (AP/Wide World Photos)

button that made a loud noise. Those who had played the violent game pushed the button longer.

A 2004 study of 607 eighth- and ninth-grade students found that those who played video games were more hostile, got into more physical fights as well as more arguments with teachers, and had lower grades. A 2004 meta-analysis (a review of previous studies) found a causal link between exposure to violent video games and aggressive affect, aggressive behavior, and decreases in helping behavior.

Henry Jenkins, Massachusetts Institute of Technology Professor and Director of Comparative Studies, has listed eight myths about video games. First, he maintains that widespread availability of video games does not correlate with any spike in juvenile violence. Rather, rates of juvenile violence have deceased at the same time more kids are playing video games. Jenkins notes that it makes sense that many of the school shooters have been game players, given that 90% of boys and 40% of girls in the general public play video games.

Second, Jenkins points out the lack of scientific evidence linking the playing of violent video games to acts of aggression. While more than 300 studies have addressed media violence, many have been critiqued for methodological concerns, are not conclusive, or are not contextualized.

Third, Jenkins explains that the primary target market for video games has shifted. Whereas marketing was once focused on children, it is now directed at people older than the age of 18. Fourth, while boys still outnumber girls, there have been dramatic increases in the number of girls playing video games.

Fifth, even if Grossman and others are correct that video games were created and are used to train soldiers to kill, there is no reason to believe the same effect occurs with young people who play them in their homes rather than through military training. Sixth, many video games offer players practice in making ethical or moral choices, which can be important practice for real-world experiences.

Seventh, Jenkins maintains that video games are generally played in groups, with 60% of young people saying they play with friends. Thus games are not necessarily socially isolating, as some contend. Finally, Jenkins argues that rather than desensitizing young people, video games are an important part of young people's play activities.

Laura L. Finley

Further Reading

Anderson, C. (2004). An update on the effects of playing violent video games. *Journal of Adolescence, 27*(1), 113–122.

Anderson, C., & Dill, K. (2000). Video games and aggressive thoughts, feelings and behavior in the laboratory and in life. *Journal of Personality and Social Psychology, 78*(4), 772–790.

Benedetti, W. (2007, April 20). Were video games to blame for massacre? *MSNBC.* Retrieved May 11, 2010, from http://www.msnbc.msn.com/id/18220228/

Gee, J. (2001). *What video games have to tell us about learning and literacy.* New York: Palgrave.

Gentile, D., Lynch, P., Linder, J., & Walsh, D. (2004). The effects of violent video game habits on adolescent hostility, aggressive behaviors, and school performance. *Journal of Adolescence, 27*(1), 5–22.

Grossman, D. (1995). *On killing: The psychological cost of learning to kill in war and society.* New York: Little, Brown.

Jenkins, H. (n.d.). Reality bytes: Eight myths about video games debunked. *PBS.* Retrieved May 11, 2010, from http://www.pbs.org/kcts/videogamerevolution/impact/myths.html

Jones, G. (2002). *Killing monsters: Why children need fantasy, superheroes, and make believe violence.* New York: Basic.

Laidman, J. (1999, April 27). Video games figure in school shootings. *Pittsburgh Post-Gazette.* Retrieved May 11, 2010, from http://www.post-gazette.com/headlines/19990427games4.asp

Violent Nonsexual Crimes, College

Before the 1960s, institutions of higher learning were regarded as sanctuaries—places where crime and criminal justice did not intrude. The 1970s marked one of the most significant decades in the evolution of violence-related crime in higher education. Since the deaths of four students at Kansas State University, the incidence of violent crimes on campus has increased and the types of violence have proliferated.

Crimes on U.S. college campuses have also been influenced by political implications. For example, some citizens have advocated for fewer guns and more stringent gun control laws, while gun advocates have called for legislation permitting students and faculty to carry concealed weapons on campus.

Crimes in postsecondary institutions (including murder, aggravated assault, hazing, and alcohol and drug abuse) have both threatened campus safety and affected students' quality of life. The subject of violent crime in colleges has received significant attention by Congress and educational officials during the last two decades. In 1990, Congress enacted the Campus Security Act and the Student Right-to-Know Act, mandating that all postsecondary institutions make crime statistics available to the campus community, prospective students, and their parents. In 1991, the law was renamed in memory of Jeanne Clery, a Lehigh University student who was murdered on campus in 1986. Institutions are also required to develop safety measures and procedures for notifying the authorities when a crime occurs.

While criminal acts are not new in higher education, the frequency and magnitude of violent crimes at some American college campuses have been highlighted by the media. A survey that was conducted after the enactment of the 1990 legislation reported 30 murders in 2,400 institutions of postsecondary education. Equally disturbing, other types of violent crimes occurred on these campuses as well during the 1991–1992 academic year. In 1998, the *Chronicle of Higher Education* reported 19 murders on four-year college campuses. Over a three-year period (1998–2000), the Department of Education reported 53 murders at U.S. colleges and universities. The report also noted 3,822 aggravated assaults in 1998, 3,606 aggravated assaults in 1999, and 3,644 aggravated assaults in 2000. In 2002, the Department of Education reported 23 murders on college campuses, up from 17 in 2000.

Concealed weapons pose one of the greatest dangers to higher education communities. Over the past two decades, there have been approximately 14 major shootings on college campuses nationwide: Three were committed by campus outsiders, one by a visiting parent, and eight by current or former graduate students (in nursing, medicine, or law). Violent crime on college campuses is prevalent, but several murderous incidents have shocked the country over the years. At the University of Texas in Austin in 1966, 16 people were killed and 32 were hospitalized. Ten years later, at California State University in Fullerton, 7 people were executed and 2 others wounded. In 1991, at the University of Iowa, 5 people were murdered and another paralyzed before the gunman committed suicide. At Northern Illinois University on Valentine's Day in 2008, 5 people including the gunman died; another 18 were wounded. The shootings at Virginia Tech in April 16, 2007, which claimed 33 lives (including the shooter, Seung-Hui Cho), had deep resonance at the University of Texas, where the first university massacre occurred. Aside from those killed, the gunman wounded 17 more people, making it the bloodiest massacre by a single person in U.S. history.

Several other acts of violence were committed by students in the 1990s. At Simon's Rock College, two people were killed and four others wounded in 1992; at San Diego State University, three professors were murdered in 1996. In 1998, at Wayne State University, a professor was murdered. In 1995, a student conspired to commit murder at Florida State University, while a shooting spree occurred at the University of Arizona but no one was injured.

Between 2000 and 2001, four people were murdered by former students: one at the University of Arkansas, and three at Appalachian School of Law. In 2005, four more people died (including the gunman) at Arizona State University, and a debate coach at Stanford University in Alabama stabbed a student to death in 1989. Other college incidents include a professor at Louisiana Tech University who attacked a colleague with a hammer; a Tidewater Community College professor who conspired to kill a colleague in 2006; and a professor at the University of Massachusetts in Lowell who was attacked with a knife. While many incidents involved students and teachers, other assaults were committed by strangers, such as when Julian Robbins killed one Penn State student and wounded another. At Indiana University, an armed stranger assaulted a professor.

There are approximately 16 million students enrolled in 4,200 colleges and universities in the United States. Although violent crimes are a small fraction of all crimes committed on campus (hovering at less than 1% in many instances), there is still a good reason to be concerned. Currently, the number of violent crimes being reported in postsecondary institutions is moving upward, a trend that appears likely to continue unabated into the immediate future.

After the deadly 2007 Virginia Tech shootings, campus security became a highly visible issue, and the search for effective methods to curb violent crimes was highlighted. Institutions around the nation took a hard look at their campus security measures and considered how they could be upgraded. Following other incidents of violent crimes on college campuses, some institutions (including those in Colorado, Delaware, Illinois, Louisiana, New York, and Mississippi) focused on improving communications and security systems inside the campuses. In September 2007, Delaware State University in Dover earned praise for responding quickly to a shooting incident on the campus. Three day earlier, the University of Maryland at College Park had successfully alerted students by cell phones, warning them of imminent danger on the campus.

Hazing and alcohol-fueled incidents are another form of violent crime on campus that has become more prevalent. Fraternities and sororities also contribute to excessive (and frequently dangerous) drinking on college campuses. While fraternities promote self-improvement, they may also promote dangerous behavior such as binge drinking, hazing and other forms of physical abuse, and other life-threatening activities. Research shows that at least one college student has died from alcohol poisoning–related initiations every year from 1970 to 2005. An infamous hazing incident at Alfred University in 1978 led to the death of a 20-year-old freshman. Other hazing-related deaths occurred at Massachusetts Institute of Technology in 1997, where a freshman died; at Auburn University, where Chad Saucier died; and at Wabash College, where an 18-year-old freshman died in 2008. At St. Louis University, a student died after receiving electrical shocks while his skin was coated with flammable chemicals. Another student at the State University of New York died in 2003 after he was forced to drink excessive amounts of water for 10 days.

In other cases, students have suffered permanent damage to their organs from hazing. For example, in 1988, five hockey players at Kent State University were forced to drink a mixture of alcoholic beverages and one student was hospitalized.

At the University of Northern Colorado in 1990, a baseball player was paralyzed after sliding into a pool of mud. During the 1999–2000 academic year, nine hockey players at the University of Vermont were badly injured in hazing. Members of the band at Southern University in Baton Rouge were beaten (and two victims were hospitalized) in 1983. A University of Michigan student suffered kidney failure after being deprived of food, and Ivery Lucky of Florida A&M University suffered renal failure after being beaten as part of a hazing ritual. This deadly behavior led to the growth in the number of states with anti-hazing statutes, from 25 in 1990 to 44 in 2006.

Hate-motivated crimes are intended to hurt and intimidate someone because of that person's race, national or ethnicity origin, religion, disability, or gender/sexual orientation. Hate-motivated crime that targets students, staff, and faculty deprives everyone on the campus of a chance to live and learn in an atmosphere free from fear and intimidation. In 2007, three football players assaulted Palestinian students at the Quaker-affiliated Guilford College campus in North Carolina. While they almost certainly occur frequently, hate crimes are often under-reported on campuses because victims are reluctant to come forward, due to fear of retaliation and repercussions.

The Virginia Tech massacre led many campuses to develop plans to alert students, staff, and faculty of safety threats in minutes, using cell phone and text messaging technology. The University of Maryland is among the hundreds of colleges that have signed contracts with vendors to help with text and voice alerts to students' cell phones in the event of emergencies. Institutions have also increased the security presence on their campuses. For example, in 1988, the University of Illinois at Urbana–Champaign campus employed 37 police officers. Colleges and universities are expected not only to protect the campus community from intruders, but also to take active steps to reduce the major risk factors associated with campus violent crimes. A more productive approach would focus on breaking the culture of silence that prevents students from reporting when a threat is imminent and reaching out to students before they commit violent crimes. Substance abuse and acts of violence should never be tolerated or accepted as forms of coping on campus. Each campus should be prepared to handle emergencies in a timely manner through ongoing education and development of a responsive culture involving staff, faculty, and students. While campuses are relatively safe, coordinated planning will ensure preparation for all future emergencies.

Njoki-Wa-Kinyatti

Further Reading

Jost, K. (2007, May). Gun violence: Are stronger measures needed to protect society? [Electronic version]. *CQ Researcher, 17*(20), 1–33.

Lavant, B. (2000). *Faces of violence: Psychological correlates, concepts and intervention strategies*. Huntington: Nova Science.

Wood, P. (2007). Homicide in higher education: Some reflections on the moral mission of the university [Electronic version]. *Academic Questions, 20*, 277–294.

Violent Nonsexual Crimes, High School

In general, the term "violent crime" refers to any criminal action wherein one or more offenders use either physical violence or the threat of physical violence against one or more victims, as in the case of aggravated assault or armed robbery. Government agencies that study violent crimes, such as the Bureau of Justice Statistics and the Federal Bureau of Investigation, typically treat the following offenses as violent crimes: aggravated assault, simple assault, rape, robbery, homicide, and non-negligent manslaughter. However, a broader definition could include other forms of violence such as psychological violence as in the cases of bullying, harassment, and stalking.

As to the prevalence of violent school crimes, all of the available evidence indicates that schools are relatively safe places. For example, an analysis of National Incident-Based Reporting System data on more than 17 million offenses that occurred from 2000 to 2004 showed that fewer than 1 out of 20 crimes (3.3%) occurred at schools. In other words, more than 95% of crime occurs somewhere other than on school properties. Although highly violent school crimes that result in multiple fatalities—such as the 1997 shootings at Heath High School in West Paducah, Kentucky; the 1998 shootings at Thurston High School in Springfield, Oregon; the 1999 shootings at Columbine High School in Littleton, Colorado; and the 2005 shootings at Red Lake High School in Red Lake, Minnesota—receive a great deal of attention from the media and the general public, such incidents are rare. The fact is that the chances of a youth being feloniously killed by a classmate while at school are less than one in 1 million. For instance, data from the U.S. Departments of Education and Justice show that during the 2005–2006 school year, there were 14 homicides of youths between the ages of 5 and 18 on school properties. In other words, during the 2005–2006 school year there was one student homicide per every 3.8 million students. Research conducted by the U.S. Departments of Education and Justice also shows that during the 2005–2006 school year, only 1% of students reported having been the victim of a violent crime and less than 0.5% of students reported being the victim of a serious violent crime at school such as aggravated assault, rape, or robbery.

Nonetheless, the potential for serious school violence is omnipresent. One problem that contributes to this risk is the presence of weapons in schools.

Research has consistently shown that many students bring weapons such as guns and knives to school. The most recent data available from the U.S. Departments of Education and Justice show that during the 2005–2006 school year, roughly one out of every 10 males reported having carried a weapon to school.

Another factor that contributes to the widespread potential for serious violence in schools is gang activity. Research has shown that gang youths engage in more violent activity than youths not involved with gang activity and that youth gang activity at school increases the potential for school violence. As to the extent of gang activity in schools, the most recent figures available from the U.S. Departments of Education and Justice show that 24% of students reported gangs were present in their school, with 17% of principals reporting problems with gang activity at school.

The good news is that violence in the schools has substantially decreased since the mid-1990s. For example, during the 1990s there were roughly 30 youth homicides per year at schools; by comparison, during the 2005–2006 school year, there were only 14 homicides of youths at school. That is a 50% decrease in school-associated homicides in less than a decade. The rates of nonfatal victimization dropped over this period as well. However, even though there are far fewer violent crimes than property crimes at school and even though the rates of violent crimes at school have substantially decreased since the 1990s, the majority of public schools still experience some type of violent crime.

Research conducted by the U.S. Departments of Education and Justice shows that during the 2005–2006 school year, 78% of all public schools reported at least one incident of violence and that 17% of all public schools reported at least one serious violent offense such as rape or weapons-related assault. It is important to keep in mind that the aforementioned figures on school violence pertain to physical violence such as assaults. As previously discussed, some nonphysical behaviors such as verbal threats and bullying can be considered as forms of violence. The research on school violence suggests that these types of violence occur in schools on a daily basis. For example, a report from the U.S. Departments of Education and Justice indicates that during the 2005–2006 school year, roughly one-third of students (28%) had been bullied; moreover, almost one-fourth of public schools (24%) reported that bullying among students was a daily or weekly occurrence. These figures probably underestimate the true extent of nonphysical aggression.

In a qualitative study of bullying among males, Phillips (2007) used the term "punking" to describe the practice of verbal and physical humiliation, shaming, and violence that males use (typically against one another) in an effort to demonstrate their masculinity. According to the boys interviewed by Phillips, "punking" is a common practice. To provide another example, in a study of female aggression based on interviews with adolescent and adult females, Simmons (2002) argues that females frequently use aggressive intimidation tactics against one another, not by means of threatening violence but through the use of gossip, networking, and social isolation. Simmons contends that school-aged girls are in constant competition with one another for social status and utilize a variety of forms of bullying to achieve and maintain social standing.

A review of the research on bullying and intimidation suggests that there are a few important gender differences between such forms of aggression. First, males tend to be more physical when bullying other males and the bullying may evolve from verbal threats to physical violence. Research conducted by the U.S. Departments of Education and Justice shows that, among students who reported being the victim of bullying, males were almost twice as likely as females (31% versus 18%) to have been injured during incidents of bullying. Second, in contrast to aggression among males wherein the victim is typically an enemy of the perpetrator, Simmons' research on female aggression indicates that females tend to target girls in their own circle of immediate friends. Finally, whereas male bullying tends to be overt, female bullying tends to be covert. For example, whereas the practice of male "punking" often occurs in public with the goal being the public humiliation and intimidation of the victim, female bullying is often subtle and conducted in private among a female clique wherein only the victim and those who are bullying her are aware of the incidents.

In summary, although the rates of school violence have decreased since the 1990s, violence remains a problem in schools. Fatalities stemming from violence are relatively rare occurrences in schools, and serious physical violence is far less common than other types of crime such as theft and vandalism. Nevertheless, owing to the presence of weapons and gangs in schools, there is always the possibility of serious physical violence. In addition, threats of physical violence and psychological violence such as bullying and intimidation are common occurrences in schools. Violence in schools is a problem not only because it can result in serious physical injury and death, but also because it negatively affects the quality of education afforded to the nation's youth. Students who are attacked, bullied, or constantly fearful of being violently victimized may have difficulties concentrating on their studies and in some cases even skip school due to fear. Likewise, teachers who are concerned about the physical safety of their students and themselves may be unable to provide effective instruction. For their part, administrators may devote excessive amounts of time and energy to dealing with violence and threats of violence, which in turn detracts from their abilities to focus on the quality of education afforded to the students. Concisely stated, school violence can have a negative impact on the entire school environment.

Ben Brown

Further Reading

Brown, B. (2004). Juveniles and weapons: Recent research, conceptual considerations, and programmatic interventions. *Youth Violence and Juvenile Justice, 2,* 161–184.

Dinkes, R., Cataldi, E. F., Lin-Kelly, W., & Snyder, T. D. (2007, December). *Indicators of school crime and safety: 2007* (NCES 2008-021/NCJ 219553). Washington, DC: U.S. Department of Education, Institute of Education Sciences, National Center for Education Statistics, & U.S. Department of Justice, Office of Justice Programs, Bureau of Justice Statistics.

Esbensen, F. A. (2008). In-school victimization: Reflections of a researcher. *Journal of Contemporary Criminal Justice*, 24, 114–124.

Howell, J. C., & Decker, S. H. (1999, January). *The youth gangs, drugs, and violence connection* (NCJ 171152). Washington, DC: U.S. Department of Justice, Office of Justice Programs, Office of Juvenile Justice and Delinquency Prevention.

Howell, J. C., & Lynch, J. P. (2000, August). *Youth gangs in schools* (NCJ 183015). Washington, DC: U.S. Department of Justice, Office of Justice Programs, Office of Juvenile Justice and Delinquency Prevention.

Noonan, J. H., & Vavra, M. C. (2007, October). *Crime in schools and colleges: A study of offenders and arrestees reported via National Incident-Based Reporting System Data*. Washington, DC: U.S. Department of Justice, Federal Bureau of Investigation, Justice Information Services Division.

Phillips, D. A. (2007). Punking and bullying: Strategies in middle school, high school, and beyond. *Journal of Interpersonal Violence*, 22(2), 158–178.

Simmons, R. (2002). *Odd girl out: The hidden culture of aggression in girls*. New York: Harcourt.

Virginia Tech Massacre

In the deadliest mass shooting in U.S. history, Virginia Tech student Seung-Hui Cho, age 23, killed 27 students, five professors, and then himself on April 16, 2007. At 7:15 A.M., Cho shot a man and a woman in West Ambler Johnston dormitory. He ran away before the police arrived; when the police came, they focused on the boyfriend of one of the victims as the would-be shooter. Approximately 2½ hours later, Cho entered a classroom in Norris Hall, an engineering building, where he gunned down students in an advanced hydrology class as well as in other classrooms. When police responded to a 911 call, they found that three of the entrances to the building had been chained shut. They finally got into the building 11 minutes after Cho began his attack there, by shooting the lock out of the door to a machine shop. A student who was in one of the classrooms, Trey Perkins, told *MSNBC* that Cho never said a word—he simply entered the room and began firing. In addition to the fatalities, at least 15 students were wounded. Others sustained injuries as they leapt to safety from their classroom windows.

The shootings followed two weeks of bomb threats at the university, although these threats do not appear to have been the work of Cho. The university and police waited two hours after the shootings began to send the first email notification to students. This message simply warned students to be cautious and did not instruct them to stay away from the classrooms—even though Cho was still at large at the time.

The university canceled classes for the remainder of the day on Monday and for the following day. It set up a meeting place for families to reunite with their children at a local hotel, and brought in extra counselors to assist the grieving, confused, and angry students. Virginia Governor Timothy Kaine returned early from a trip to Asia and declared a state of emergency in Blacksburg, the city where the university is located.

Approximately one year after the shooting, Governor Kaine announced that a fund of $100,000 had been set up to assist the families of students killed. Each was also offered counseling and medical expenses, as well as the chance to question the governor and university officials about the shooting. Additional funds were made available to the dozens of survivors of the rampage. Families and survivors accepting the settlement had to agree to forego the right to sue the university. Almost two years later, the university re-opened the wing of Norris Hall where the shooting occurred. A ceremony celebrated the opening of the Center for Peace Studies and Violence Prevention.

Cho was born in South Korea, and his family immigrated to the United States when he was eight years old. Lucinda Roy, a former Virginia Tech professor, authored a book called *No Right to Remain Silent* in spring 2009, in which she argued that she, and others, saw warning signs that Cho was dangerous. As co-chair of the English Department in fall 2005, Roy was told by a colleague about Cho's disturbing writing and behavior. Classmates were afraid of Cho, who would take pictures of them with his cell phone camera from under the desks. Roy began to tutor Cho privately, and found him to be generally unresponsive. Roy said she tried to alert those on campus who might help the clearly troubled student, contacting four different departments including the university police and counseling center, but no one offered Cho the help he needed. They maintained that no one could coerce a student to get counseling; thus, until Cho came in voluntarily or actually threatened himself or someone else overtly, there was nothing they could do.

When Cho threatened suicide, he did get some help from a psychiatric facility off campus. Once he was deemed no longer a threat, however, he was released. Cho contacted the school's mental health counseling center later that year, but records from these sessions remained missing until July 2009, when they were found at the home of a former university counseling official, Dr. Robert C. Miller. It is still unclear why Miller took the records home more than a year before Cho's massacre. Parents of children who were killed or wounded in the rampage were outraged at this finding, suggesting that it indicates further lapses on the part of the university and the police, and even that it hints at deception. Roy said that Cho went to the center multiple times, but never received a thorough examination. Because Cho was older than the age of 21, his parents were never contacted about any of these matters.

A state panel that was convened after the shooting determined that the university had misinterpreted privacy laws. Further, the panel determined that the school did not notify students fast enough once the shooting began. Many victims' parents have expressed a belief that their children would still be alive if the university had responded to Cho's obvious distress earlier. Since the shootings, Virginia Tech has hired new counselors and created a risk assessment team to identify and work with troubled students.

Prior to Cho's rampage, the most deadly university shooting had occurred in 1966 at the University of Texas. In that attack, Charles Whitman killed 16 people from the observation deck of a 28-floor clock tower before he was shot by police.

Laura L. Finley

Further Reading

Agger, B. *There is a gunman on campus: Tragedy and terror at Virginia Tech*. Lanham, MD: Rowman & Littlefield.

Brezina, C. (2000). *Deadly school and campus violence*. New York: Rosen.

Gelineau, K. (2008, March 25). Va. offers Tech shooting victims' families $100,000 each, chance for questions in settlement. *Daily Journal Online*. Retrieved July 21, 2009, from http://dailyjournalonline.com/articles/2008/03/25/news/doc47e9107404fd7232010633.txt

Goldner, D. (2009, April 11). Site of Virginia Tech shooting rampage reopened as Center for Peace Studies and Violence Prevention. *New York Daily News*. Retrieved July 21, 2009, from http://www.nydailynews.com/news/us_world/2009/04/11/2009-04-11_site_of_virginia_tech_shooting_rampage_reopened_as_center_for_peace_studies_and_.ht ml

Johnson, A. (2007, April 17). Worst school shooting ever kills 33 on Va. campus. *MSNBC*. Retrieved July 21, 2009, from http://www.msnbc.msn.com/id/18134671/

Lindsey, S. (2009, July 23). Killer's health records found. *Miami Herald*, p. 3A.

Roy, L. (2009). *No right to remain silent: The tragedy at Virginia Tech*. New York: Harmony.

Warning signs ignored in Va. Tech shooting. (2009, April 7). *CBS Evening News* [online]. Retrieved July 21, 2009, from http://www.cbsnews.com/stories/2009/04/07/eveningnews/main4927476.shtml

W

Weise, Jeff

On March 23, 2005, six years after the infamous Columbine High School massacre, another tragic high school shooting occurred, this time in Minnesota. On that day, Jeff Weise, a 16-year-old adolescent, killed two family members—first his sleeping grandfather, and later his grandfather's life partner—in their home. He then drove his grandfather's police cruiser to nearby Red Lake High School. He was armed with three weapons. Surprising a school security guard, whom he shot and killed, as students and teachers tried to flee. Using his murdered gradnfather's handgun and shotgun, Weise shot randomly at surprised students and teachers who had crowded into a room. He attempted to enter other classrooms, but was encountered Red Lake Police, with whom he exchanged gunshots. Weise was wounded several times and escaped back into a school room, where he committed suicide. The violence, which was over in 10 minutes, left seven students wounded and 10 dead, including Weise.

Red Lake is a fairly remote town populated by residents of the Red Lake American Indian Reservation. It is located in northern Minnesota a few hundred miles from the Canadian border. Weise was a Chippewa Native American Indian, and learned about his indigenous ethnic identity while living on the reservation. At the age of nine, Weise lost his father; the elder Weise was apparently despondent and committed suicide. Jeff moved to Red Lake following the incapacitation of his mother in 1999. Essentially orphaned, Weise moved in with his grandmother, who raised him.

Following the shooting, it was reported that 100 FBI agents worked the case to determine the characteristics of the crime. At the same time that community and tribal leaders mourned the loss of life, the media descended on the town, issuing with numerous news reports covering the massacre. One British reporter counted thousands of Google Internet hits on Jeff Weise's name in a matter of weeks.

The media reported many descriptions of Weise that provided numerous clever story lines concerning his family, personal history, and potential reasons why he committed the shootings. Among them were Weise's unstable family history. Later, concerns about his medication and counseling were highlighted. Reports about Weise's writings about zombies, his identification as a Goth (a teen subculture interested in dark and dangerous images), his dressing in black clothing including trench coats (associating him with the Columbine murders), and his involvement and posts supporting Hitler on neo-Nazi websites—all supposedly links to obsessions with violence and power. Other factors cited in his attack included video games (*Grand Theft Auto* was mentioned) and the movie *Elephant* (about a shooting). In all of these cases there were appealing descriptions and plausible arguments about Weise's motives, but no evidence was given about any direct links that produced the loss of life.

While general patterns in school shootings have been established by researchers who study data on such events, there is no single motive that causes this rare form of violence. Extensive research concerning school shootings has reached the conclusion that while specific risk factors may be involved, the specific constellation of factors that prompt a mass murder or a murder-suicide in a school is unique to each unfortunate incident. Such is the conclusion reached in the National Research Council Institute of Medicine's 2003 book, *Deadly Lessons: Understanding Lethal School Violence*.

The school shooting incident at Red Lake is classified as a rural murder-suicide. Such incidents are quite rare, and the factors in such events that are cited by behavioral scientists include a mix of the most influential variables that can be used to develop a model that explain the murders. The following scenario has been proposed to explain Weise's high school massacre.

Weise's family history reveals some mental illness, given his father's suicide in 1997; there also appear to be genetic dispositions toward despondency, given that Weise was prescribed an antidepressant for diagnosed depression. Researchers also report that some high school shooting perpetrators learn about suicides in high school shootings through multiple media reports, television news, newspaper articles, magazines, and the movie industry. If this exposure coincides with a triggering event or incident, perpetrators may impulsively reason that their violent plans will likewise resolve their own dilemma. The tendency for suicides to cluster following media reports is referred to as the copycat phenomenon.

Orphaned at age 11, Weise experienced two major stressful life events—first parental loss and then moving hundreds of miles to live with his grandmother in Red Lake. Weise lived with her from age 11 to about age 15; it is unclear how long he lived with his grandfather. Research has shown that family bonds are important insulators from delinquency. It appears that Weise's family support was mediocre at best.

As Weise matured during adolescence, his behavior became problematic to school officials. This conflict eventually led to a stressful event in his life: He was expelled from school for misbehavior. The punishment produced an even greater lack of involvement in high school activities and further insulation from friends and teachers. While Weise apparently accepted home schooling, this experience may have affected him detrimentally.

During high school, Weise was reported to be involved in blogging on a number of Internet websites, including a neo-Nazi website that discussed racial purity theories. Research documents that Weise was alarmed by the dilution of his classmates' tribal heritage, symbolized by their listening to rap music. According to Weise, only weak students embraced rap music, which ruined their Native American Indian racial purity. Apparently Weise had read material on websites that discussed Adolph Hitler's politics of authoritarianism and nativism, views that can be appealing to an idealistic and alienated adolescent male. One theme that emerges from this ideology is racial decline. It appears that this distorted racist ideology exacerbated paranoia in Weise (after all he was expelled) and heightened his distrust and perhaps rejection of classmates. This further removed him from group affiliation. Indeed, records show he reported himself as a complete loner, without any friends.

In a context of depression and paranoia and then rejection by the school, Weise's attack appears to be his way of seeking redress for a series of private irritations from his past treatment. Lacking any loyalty to significant others, Weise had little to constrain his conscience and formed a faulty sense of righteousness in his causes. The murder of his grandfather reveals the extent of family disassociation: In most families, a bond of love and loyalty forms among family members.

For the most part, youth tend to communicate their angst to others. Weise did not say much about his frustrations, although his cousin, Louis Jourdain, was later arrested and charged with conspiracy in the Red Lake shootings. Investigators found that Weise had shared some of his personal conflicts with the school and classmates with Jourdain, who had himself engaged in making general threats to the school. Other students also indicated that Weise made vague allusions to violence that might occur at the school. This behavior supports the contention that Weise's paranoid ideation and revenge plans were partially concealed. In most cases, friends of high school shooters report that they learned about some part of their plan prior to its implementation. Given this fact, media organizations have set up hotlines to encourage anonymous reporting (e.g., 1-866-SPEAK-UP) of possible violence. As part of the move to stem the tide of high school murders, current laws allow for prosecution of students who have communicated with others about violence and of anyone who may support or conceal the students' secret, lethal plans. High schools across the country have established safety procedures and encourage students' reporting of any potential violence to them.

In Weise's case, it appears that a combination of distorted perceptions, paranoid and suicidal thinking that increased after his expulsion from school, and possibly conflict with his disciplinarian grandfather (a police officer on the reservation) fueled his plans. Some of the distortions were encouraged by extremist Internet websites and may have led to rejection by, and perhaps contempt of, his Indian classmates owing to Weise's sense of superiority. Probably other unspecified conflicts were taken as personal slights that offended him. For isolated and lonely youth, the best solution may appear to be exacting revenge on those who they perceived have hurt them. For Weise, that meant his grandfather (living with his partner), the school, and his classmates. Following his horrible deeds, he chose to mimic the actions of other murderers before him and commit suicide. The unfortunate postscript to the story of Jeff Weise, and the legacy of high school shooters in general, is that by talking about their frustrations with adults, they might have come to understand that their irritations could be greatly reduced through peaceful means.

James Steinberg

Further Reading

Fox, J., & Levin, J. (2005). *Extreme killing: Understanding serial and mass murder.* Thousand Oaks, CA: Sage.

Marzuk, P., Tardiff, K., & Hisch, C. (1992). The epidemiology of murder-suicide. *Journal of the American Medical Association, 267*(23), 3179.

Whitman, Charles

On August 1, 1966, Charles Joseph Whitman, age 25, perched himself on the observation deck of Austin's 231-foot University of Texas (UT) tower. For 96 minutes, he fired upon unsuspecting strangers below. Earlier that morning, Whitman had murdered his mother and his wife at their residences, supposedly to spare them the embarrassment of what he was about to do from atop the tower. Before he was shot to death by police, he had left people wounded and dead on the stairway and reception area of the observation deck and over a four-block area below. The death toll amounted to 14 people (not including Whitman, his mother, and his wife), with 32 others wounded.

Mass murders were a rare occurrence in the United States in 1966. Whitman's was a very public and random attack by someone who appeared to be the all-American boy. At the time, the nation was still recovering from a shock that had occurred two weeks earlier, when eight student nurses were brutally stabbed and strangled in their shared Chicago townhouse in July 1966 by a down-and-out drifter, and sometime merchant marine, named Richard Speck. Speck had the lifestyle and demeanor of the public's stereotype of someone who would harm innocent strangers. In contrast, the 6-foot-tall, 198-pound, blonde-haired Whitman had the background and appearance of the proverbial "boy next door."

Whitman, the eldest of three boys brought up in an intact upper middle-class home, was a former altar boy and, at age 12, the youngest Eagle Scout in the country. He studied piano and excelled at that activity at an early age. He graduated seventh in a class of 72 from a Catholic high school in West Palm Beach, Florida. His father (C. A. Whitman), the owner of a successful plumbing business in Lake Worth, Florida, was a strict disciplinarian toward his sons and physically abusive toward his wife. C. A. Whitman taught his sons to use guns at an early age. In a photograph (now widely viewed) of Charles Whitman taken at age two, he could be seen holding a rifle upright in each hand; the rifles stood taller than the toddler.

Three days after Whitman's 18th birthday, he enlisted in the Marines, reportedly to escape his domineering father. His time in the Marine Corps had its ups and downs. He won a highly competitive Naval Enlisted Science Education Program scholarship and entered UT-Austin as a mechanical engineering major. However, Whitman dropped out of school and returned to active duty after a year and a half when the military withdrew the scholarship, due to declining grades and prankish behavior (e.g., poaching a deer and then butchering it in a dorm shower). Later, there were also a court martial, time spent in confinement, and a demotion in rank (from lance corporal to private) for lending money to fellow Marines at usurious rates, threatening a Marine, and possessing a personal firearm on base. On the plus side of his experience in the Marines, Whitman received a sharpshooter badge and an honorable discharge.

During his initial enrollment at UT-Austin, Whitman (then age 21) met and married fellow student Kathy Leissner (age 19). After his discharge from the service, Whitman reenrolled at UT, this time majoring in architectural engineering. Upon her graduation, Kathy began teaching high school biology, providing the majority of the household income. Whitman continued to receive financial support from his father, while holding various jobs including that of bill collector and bank teller. Although he obtained a real estate license and became bonded as an insurance salesman, he did not actually sell any real estate or insurance. His last job was that of a research assistant for a civil engineering professor's highway traffic flow study.

A panel of experts, commissioned by then Texas Governor John Connally, searched for answers to what could have caused the massacre they had at their disposal notes written by Whitman that were left at his home and his mother's apartment, diary entries that Whitman was in the habit of writing, the records of the psychiatrist he had visited in March 1966 (who also served on the

Commission), and, most importantly, the results of an autopsy that Whitman himself had requested be performed. The months preceding the shooting found Whitman overworked at school and stressed by his parents' marital discord. His grades had been declining and he had been spreading himself too thin, although he did give up a scout master position that he had held for a year. In the spring 1966 semester, he had been carrying a heavy course load, had helped to move his mother from an abusive marriage in Florida to her own apartment in Austin, and was under pressure from his father's frequent phone calls asking the younger Whitman to convince the mother to move back with the father. During this time he had severe headaches, chewed his fingernails, ate a lot, and gained weight. He took Dexedrine (an amphetamine) to stay awake during long periods of studying for exams and he took two large bottles of Excedrin in a three-month period, for frequent headaches.

In his only session with UT psychiatrist Dr. Maurice Dean Heatly, Whitman admitted that he had hit his own wife on two occasions, hated his father, and had thoughts of shooting people from the tower with a deer rifle. Dr. Heatly made note of these comments and evaluated Whitman as full of hostility, but had no reason to suspect that Whitman would follow through on his thoughts about the tower.

By the summer, Whitman was enrolled in 14 hours of coursework and working at the research job, while his wife took a summer job at the phone company. Apparently Whitman reached his breaking point and began planning the murders. On July 31, he put the plan into action by taking his mother's life around midnight. It has been reported that, according to the mother's brothers, the elder Whitman had financially cut off Whitman and his mother effective July 30. If that information is accurate, it could explain Whitman's timing.

Shortly after 12:00 A.M. on August 1, Whitman apparently strangled his mother, shot her in the head, stabbed her in the chest, and crushed her left hand so severely that the diamond popped out of her engagement ring and a deep impression was left on her finger by her wedding ring. He then left a note expressing his love for her. He posted a forged a note on her door asking that she not be disturbed. Later that morning, he phoned his mother's employer to say she was ill and would not be in.

At his own home, Whitman stabbed his sleeping wife several times in the chest and left a note dated 3:00 A.M. professing his love for her. He left notes for his brothers and his father. Later, he called his wife's employer to report that she was ill and would not be in. Among the errands he ran later that morning were purchases of weapons and ammunition, adding to the stockpile of weapons he already owned. The arsenal Whitman brought with him to the tower that day included a 6-mm Remington 700 bolt-action rifle with four-power scope, a 12-gauge sawed-off shotgun, a .30-caliber M-1 carbine rifle, a .35-caliber pump-action Remington rifle, a 9-mm Luger pistol, a .357 magnum Smith and Wesson revolver, a 6.35-mm Galesi-Brescia pistol, about 700 rounds of ammunition, a machete, a hatchet, and three hunting knives.

When he drove onto the campus with coveralls over his clothing and showed his research assistant identification card, he received a loading zone permit. At the tower building, he used a two-wheel dolly (rented earlier that morning) to transport his gear, most of which was in his Marine footlocker. In addition to the weapons, Whitman had food, water, a transistor radio to monitor news reports, a flashlight, batteries, and an assortment of other necessities (including toilet paper). He took the elevator to the 27th floor and hauled everything up the rest of the stairs to the observation deck. He eliminated one obstacle—the 28th-floor receptionist—by hitting her on the back of her head with a rifle butt and later shooting her. After encountering the receptionist, he was then greeted by a young couple exiting the observation deck. Whitman returned the greeting and let them pass by. But the next group he encountered presented interference, because they were on their way to the observation deck. He shot and killed two of this group (a woman and her teenage nephew), while wounding the other nephew and his aunt, as the husbands lagged a flight of stairs behind and escaped injury.

The sniping from the tower began at 11:48 A.M. The height of the building, combined with the elevation of the land it was on, gave Whitman about a 300-foot vantage point. Whitman's gunfire could be seen coming from the parapet surrounding the clock tower, but Whitman himself was hardly a visible target to those on the ground. The dead, shot on campus that day and across the street from campus at a business strip, included the following individuals: Edna Townsley, the 28th-floor receptionist; Margaret Lamport and her nephew, Mark Gabour, who were on their way to the observation deck; Tom Eckman, who was leaning over his wounded girlfriend (who survived, but lost their eight-month-old unborn child); Robert Boyer, a physics professor; Thomas Ashton, a Peace Corps trainee on his way from class; Thomas Karr, a student; Billy Speed, a police officer; Harry Walchuk, a community college professor working on his doctoral degree; Paul Sonntag and his girlfriend, Claudia Rutt, recent Austin high school graduates running errands on the Drag (the commercial area near the campus); Roy Schmidt, an electrician; and Karen Griffith, a high school senior walking along the Drag (who died from her injuries after a week in the hospital). Although officers and civilians returned Whitman's fire from the ground and even from a small plane, but it was not until two police officers (accompanied by a deputized civilian) reached the tower that an end was brought to the rampage, when those two officers shot and killed Whitman.

There continues to be speculation about what caused Whitman to terrorize so many complete strangers. His actions may have been meant to express his hatred for his father and thereby embarrass the elder Whitman. He may have had a mental breakdown from the work overload, combined with the pressure to get good grades, while coping with his parents' separation. Amphetamine psychosis has been suggested as well. However, Whitman's careful planning and preparation on the day of the murders are not indicative of a break with reality. Dexedrine and Excedrin were found in his possession. His blood tested negative for alcohol. Because embalming of the body had been performed before urine and stomach contents could be examined, optimal toxicology testing was not possible.

The note Whitman had left after killing his wife asked that an autopsy be done to determine whether he suffered from a disorder. The initial autopsy had misdiagnosed an astrocytoma (tumor) in his brain, but the Connally Commission (which included the doctor who had performed the initial autopsy) found the tumor to be a glioblastoma (highly cancerous). It remains unclear whether the tumor had a direct bearing on Whitman's behavior. The Commission's report was inconclusive on this matter, although the report did say that the tumor could have conceivably played a role. Those who were close to Whitman found comfort in believing that the tumor or his fears of having a brain disorder influenced his otherwise inexplicable actions on that infamous day.

Joan Luxenburg

Further Reading

Douglas, J., & Olshaker, M. (1999). *The anatomy of motive*. New York: Scribner.

LaVergne, G. M. (1997). *A sniper in the tower: The Charles Whitman murders*. Denton, TX: University of North Texas Press.

Levin, J., & Fox, J. A. (1985). *Mass murder: America's growing menace*. New York: Plenum Press.

Wimberley, Teah

On November 12, 2008, 15-year-old Teah Wimberley shot her friend and classmate Amanda Collette, a star on the school hip-hop dance squad, at Dillard High School in Fort Lauderdale, Florida. Collette was also 15 at the time. Wimberley had allegedly been interested in a romantic relationship, and when Collette rebuffed her advances, she became enraged. She shot Collette in between classes. After shooting Collette, Wimberley ran to a local restaurant, where she called 911 to report what she had done. Police arrested her at the restaurant and seized her gun.

Wimberley was charged in adult court and found guilty of second-degree murder and possession of a weapon on school grounds. Her attorneys had offered an insanity defense. Although Wimberley faced life in prison for her crimes, the judge recommended that she be sent to a juvenile facility until she is 21, the minimum sentence possible.

Wimberley had been raised by her grandparents after her parents separated before she was born. Her father, Jevon Wimberley, is in prison serving a 25-year sentence for second-degree murder. Wimberley had been abused as a child. During her trial, experts testified that she was very troubled and needed mental health counseling. Wimberley claimed she did not want to kill Collette, but simply sought to make her feel the same pain she had felt when Collette rejected her.

In April 2010, Collette's family filed suit against the Broward County Schools, arguing that their daughter's death could have been prevented. The suit alleges that a teacher was told that a student had a gun on campus and the teacher failed to respond. Allegedly the student said Wimberley had pulled out the gun in science class and said she planned to use it to "make Collette feel pain." After the class the student told his teacher, Hugues Douyon, but was sent back to his seat. Douyon has claimed he was never told about a gun. The family's suit also criticizes the hand-held metal detectors the family claims were present but not in use.

Laura L. Finley

Further Reading

Associated Press. (2008, November 13). Florida girl, 15, fatally shot during argument at high school. *Fox News*. Retrieved May 11, 2010, from http://www.foxnews.com/story/0,2933,450758,00.html

Figueroa, L. (2009, December 9). Teah Wimberley found guilty in Dillard High slaying. *Miami Herald*. Retrieved May 11, 2010, from http://www.miamiherald.com/2009/12/09/1374563/teah-wimberley-found-guilty-in.html

Johnson, A. (April 8, 2010). Victim's family suing school board over Dillard High School shooting. *Miami Herald*. Retrieved May 11, 2010, from http://articles.sun-sentinel.com/2010-04-08/news/fl-wrongful-death-lawsuit-collette-20100408_1_joyce-collette-metal-detectors-teah-wimberley

Wimberley to victim's mom: "I robbed you of Amanda." (2010, March 26). *WPLG Local 10*. Retrieved May 11, 2010, from http://www.justnews.com/news/22963212/detail.html

Woodham, Luke

On October 1, 1997, Luke Timms Woodham went on a school shooting spree after murdering his mother. Before this event, the 16-year-old from Pearl, Mississippi, had never been in trouble with the police or at school. This school shooting is noteworthy for several reasons: because it was the first of several such shootings that plagued the United States in the late 1990s, because so many people were shot, and because it involved a conspiracy investigation. The possibility of cult activity in this case sparked the national media's attention, but in the end the allegations were unproven. Only two of the seven students arrested were sentenced: Luke Woodham, the only gunman, will remain in prison for the rest of his life, and friend Grant Boyette, who pleaded to a lesser charge, is now on supervised probation after serving time in a boot camp–style prison program.

Although a troubled early life does not justify violence, Woodham certainly did not have an easy childhood or adolescence. His parents, Mary Ann and John Woodham, split up when Luke was seven years old. Mary Ann, who had always been very particular about her children's clothing and activities, became even more overbearing. Luke's older brother, John Jr., began staying away from home as much as possible, so Mary Ann assigned more chores to Luke. She also micromanaged what he ate and did while they were home together and was verbally abusive, calling him fat and saying that he would never amount to anything. When John Jr. was around, he would pick on Luke. With an absent father and brother, Luke was left to fend for himself against an abusive and emotionally needy mother. Although Woodham resented the situation, he mostly tried to please his mother when he was younger and silently protested against chores or meals only when he got older.

As an awkward, overweight adolescent with few friends, Woodham's school experiences were no better. Mary Ann insisted that he wear thick glasses, unstylish clothing, and an outdated hairstyle. Also humiliating for someone his age was his mother's daily ritual of driving him to school and making him kiss her on the cheek—actions that provoked jokes. One time Woodham retaliated when an incest joke was directed at him and may have seriously injured his tormentor if other students had not pulled him away. His luck began to change, however, when he turned 15 and a new girl named Christina Menefee moved to town.

Menefee was kind and seemed to appreciate Woodham's gentle manners; they went on three dates over the course of one month. Mary Ann always tagged along, something the Menefee family noticed and thought odd—Mary Ann even supervised the couple once while they sat on the couch. Christy broke off their relationship, confiding to a friend that Luke had gotten too controlling and that she found it embarrassing to have his mother present during dates. The breakup devastated Woodham.

In early 1997, Woodham began working at Domino's as a pizza delivery boy, where he was praised as a courteous employee destined for manager training. He also made a friend. Donald Brooks invited him to participate in a role-playing game group to which he belonged. The group of misfit teenagers, led by an older teen named Grant Boyette, formed their own family and called themselves the "Kroth." The boys were capable students who came across as good Christians, two important attributes in evangelical Pearl, Mississippi. Boyette was especially considered devout, attractive, and charismatic, but he actually had a dual identity. When with his friends, he was fixated on Hitler, Satan, and spell books. With Woodham, he cast spells on his perceived "enemies." Woodham believed that Boyette had special powers and the pair formed a close relationship. Friends within the Kroth must have noticed escalating signs of violence, but only Brooks did anything about it.

Teachers, neighbors, and fellow students were among those who may have seen indicators of a disturbed teen. Woodham wrote several suspicious in-class essays, one stating that he would go on a killing spree if he could be teacher for the day. The teacher did not report these disturbing pieces of writing. Other school officials doubtless witnessed some of the bullying that continue to plague Woodham. Still other events leading up to the matricide and school shooting should have drawn some attention, too. In the year between his breakup with Menefee and the school shooting, Woodham twice threatened to commit suicide. Each time, a classmate stopped him, but it is unclear if either of the students reported the incident to an adult.

Neighbors had long ago stopped inviting the Woodham boys over to play because of their over-aggressiveness, but one neighbor witnessed Woodham and Boyette viciously beat Sparkle, the Woodham family's Shih Tzu. In April 1997, this neighbor watched through his fence as the boys beat the dog with a stick until she could barely walk. Later, John Jr. noticed Sparkle limping and told Luke to bring her to the veterinarian. Instead, Woodham and Boyette beat her again, put her in a bag, set her on fire, and threw her into a pond while she was still alive and whimpering. Rather than show remorse for what he had done to his "dear . . . loved" family dog, Woodham was pleased. He wrote in his diary about his "first kill" and described how satisfying the experience had been.

Because of the pleasure these two boys got from killing, several members of the Kroth distanced themselves from the group at this time. Brooks was among them, especially after Boyette suggested that Brooks kill his father for grounding him. Brooks reported the discussion to the authorities, who did not take the threat seriously. When Woodham told his role-playing friends how upset he was that Menefee would not date him again, Boyette suggested he kill her. Unlike Brooks, Woodham this suggestion seriously. Regardless of who masterminded the plan, Woodham was the one who carried it to its conclusion despite his arguments during his trials about the amount of influence Boyette had over him. Woodham wanted to get back at those who had hurt him, to be remembered forever, and to convince would-be bullies not to pick on others.

On October 1, 1997, Woodham's alarm clock went off at 5:00 A.M. and his violent plan began. He snuck down to the kitchen, got a butcher knife, retrieved a baseball bat from his room, and walked toward his mother's bedroom. He had planned to kill Mary Ann while she slept, but she was in the hallway about to go for a jog. The attack began there and ended in her bedroom, where Woodham forced his way in and stabbed and bludgeoned his mother repeatedly. He finally suffocated her with a pillow and cleaned up both the scene and himself. In taped interviews with police, Woodham said that he had "stopped caring about anything" the night before the murders. He lied in his confession, saying that he had brought a butcher knife into his mother's bedroom, put the pillow over her head, and stabbed her to death. In court he also asserted that demons spoke to him that morning and that he remembered getting the knife and pillow but not the actual murder.

Operating under the assumption that he would die in a shootout with the police, Woodham wrote a last will and testament (which the media later labeled his "manifesto"), called Boyette, retrieved his father's .30-.30 hunting rifle from the attic, and drove himself to Pearl High School. Woodham arrived around 8:00 A.M., just when students were milling around the commons area before class. He found friend Justin Sledge and handed him the notebooks, which included his will, to be passed along to Boyette. Sledge guessed what was about to happen and herded some close friends into the safety of the library. Woodham retrieved his rifle from his car, placed it under his trench coat, and returned to the commons area. He walked directly to Menefee and shot her and her friend Lydia Kaye Dew, killing both. Woodham then turned and calmly shot and injured seven other students. His poor eyesight and inexperience with a gun likely saved many from harm. After an 11-minute rampage, Woodham was first tackled by another boy and then fled to the parking lot. Assistant principal Joel Myrick went to his own car, retrieved a gun he had in his glove compartment, prevented Woodham from driving away, and held him until police arrived.

When officers were bringing Woodham to the police station, they noticed his bandaged hand; the youth said that his injuries were incurred while killing his mother. Police sent cars to her home straight away and discovered her body. Woodham was charged with three counts of murder and seven counts of aggravated assault. He waived his right to counsel, wrote a confession, and agreed to a videotaped interview. He confessed to killing his mother in a calm, straightforward voice. However, when he spoke of his motives—that she never loved him and the various things he had to endure from her—and insisted on his sanity, he became emotional. He accurately detailed what he had done from the time he left the house until he was arrested, recalling whom he shot and how he was arrested.

On October 2, Justin Sledge fanned the community's fears by pinning a note to the door of the school that said the Kroth's numbers were diminished but the group was still strong. He tried to defend Woodham's actions by blaming society, and went as far as interrupting a candlelight vigil. People, among them Woodham's neighbor who witnessed the incident with Sparkle, came forward with information that made the police think that the Kroth was a cult that believed in spells, worshipped Satan, killed animals, and planned a takeover of the school and escape to Cuba. By October 7, 1997, police had arrested six of Woodham's friends on conspiracy charges; cult rumors kept both the townspeople's fears and the media's interest alive for months.

Woodham was tried twice, first for the murder of his mother and then for the school shootings. Each case was heard in county court in an effort to obtain an unbiased jury. Experts for the defense diagnosed Woodham with borderline personality disorder; experts for the prosecution insisted he was mentally capable of standing trial. During the first trial, which ended on June 6, 1998, the jury rejected Woodham's insanity defense and found him guilty of first-degree murder. This trial was very dramatic, with Woodham openly weeping, the power failing, and the jury giving their decision in the dark. Woodham accepted the sentence as God's will and, by the start of the second trial the following Monday, he appeared with Bible in hand and claimed a religious conversion.

Woodham's attorneys—and his own testimony—portrayed him as a victim of the influential Boyette, but Woodham was still given a life sentence for each of the two murders, plus 20 years for each of the seven counts of aggravated assault. He again apologized to the families of those he had hurt but said he had no more tears because God had forgiven him. Woodham is currently serving out his sentence at the Mississippi State Penitentiary at Parchman, where he feels remorse about starting the school shooting trend.

The district attorney dropped charges against five of the boys who were arrested in conjunction with this case. The sixth boy was tried in juvenile court and his records sealed. In October 1998, Grant Boyette and Justin Sledge were charged as accessories to murder before the fact, a serious felony. Sledge was freed but Boyette, who had gotten much attention during the trial, accepted a plea bargain from the district attorney. He pleaded guilty to a lesser charge—interfering with a principal's ability to perform his duties—and was sentenced to six months of prison-based boot camp, followed by five years of either prison or supervised probation.

Sandra Gall Urban

Further Reading

Davis, C. A. (2003). Dare to be different: Luke Woodham. In *Children who kill: Profiles of pre-teen and teenage killers* (pp. 67–79). London: Allison & Busby.

Fast, J. (2008). Luke Woodham: Socialization into extreme violence. In *Ceremonial violence: A psychological explanation of school shootings* (pp. 138–171). Woodstock, NY: Overlook Press.

Roche, T., Berryman, A., Barnes, E., Barnes, S., Harbert, N., Liston, B., et al. (2001, May 28). Voices from the cell. *Time, 157*(21), 32–37. Retrieved January 20, 2009, from http://www.time.com/time/magazine/article/0,9171,999966,00.html?iid=perma_share

Wurst, Andrew

Andrew Wurst murdered a science teacher, John Gillette, on the evening of April 24, 1998, at a school dance in Edinboro, Pennsylvania. He also wounded two classmates, Jacob Tury and Robert Zemcik, and Edrye May Boraten, a teacher who was chaperoning the dance. These acts were carried out not at school, but at Nick's Place, a local banquet hall where the end-of-the-year dance was being held. The majority of the eighth-grade class, along with teachers serving as chaperones, was in attendance. The entire incident lasted about half an hour and ended when the owner of the banquet hall confronted Wurst with his shotgun, ordering him to put the weapon down.

Wurst appeared to be in a state of confused transition. He kept Raggedy Ann dolls in his room, yet he had a girlfriend and was interested in sex. He also enjoyed reading and listening to music, although his interests in both magnified the more violent aspects of human nature. His favorite reading material was stories by well-known horror writers Stephen King and Dean Koontz that centered on violent murders and twisted psychopaths. His favorite musicians were Marilyn Manson, Korn, and Nine Inch Nails—all heavy metal bands. Marilyn Manson's music was, by many, considered to incite violence in young people. Wurst also had heroes that most would find disturbing; he professed to people that Adolph Hitler and Napoleon Bonaparte were his idols. As a result of his darker interests, his new group of friends, a much rougher crowd, nicknamed him "Satan."

This change in friends marked a change in Wurst as well. He became quieter and withdrawn, which is not how he was described by his previous acquaintances. By the last part of eighth grade, he was becoming more aggressive and narcissistic. His new friends seemed to have a significant impact on Wurst. One friend in particular seemed to spur murderous thoughts in him. The pair were often heard talking about murdering people or directly telling people that they would kill them. Wurst began bullying his classmates. One day he decided to alternately flirt with and demean a girl in his class. Justin Fletcher stood up for the girl and confronted Wurst. Fletcher's demand that Wurst leave the girl alone proved effective; this single act further emasculated Wurst. He had also begun drinking and using marijuana by this point.

Wurst did have a girlfriend for a short period of time, but his obsessive and odd behavior caused her to end the relationship. Wurst asked her to the eighth-grade graduation dance but she refused. After this rejection, he decided to ask another girl to the dance, but she laughed at him. This rejection was a massive blow to the young boy's ego. Wurst spoke to many people about the dance. He stated that he would not be around afterward and talked about plans to kill people at the dance.

Wurst was the youngest child in his family and had a close, loving relationship with his mother. As a child, he wet the bed until the age of nine. He was terrified of monsters, and his mother would have to check under the bed and in the closet before he would go to sleep. At night she would lay on the bed with Wurst, making sure he was given the affection that she felt he did not get from his father. She knew that Wurst was more immature than his brothers but attributed this status to his being the baby of the family.

The relationship between Andrew and his father was more complicated. Jerome Wurst was disappointed in his son, who had no interest in the family landscaping business. The business took up most of Jerome's time, so that there was little left for his wife and children. He was a strict disciplinarian who showed little emotion. Shortly before the shooting, Andrew and his father had a fight because of a missing report card. Andrew's grades had dropped continuously, until in the eighth grade he was receiving mostly D's and F's. Neither Catherine nor Jerome Wurst was aware of the psychological turmoil that their son was experiencing.

Many precipitating factors contributed to Wurst's crimes. He was having a difficult time transitioning from childhood into adolescence, indicated by the type of items he utilized to express himself. The fascination he had with horror novels and heavy metal music perpetuated his own violent thoughts and self-loathing. He found inspiration in previous school shootings such as those committed in Jonesboro, Arkansas. Fellow classmates heard Wurst joke about the killings there, yet no one took him seriously. Rejection can have an adverse affect on most people, but Wurst appears to have been especially vulnerable. Refusal by the two girls he asked to the dance not only damaged his ego, but likely spurred the already fueled rage within him. His perceived failures as a son merely added to his feelings of self-loathing. Given that Wurst had an already vulnerable state of mind, the use of drugs and alcohol could only serve to perpetuate his violent, suicidal thoughts.

The eighth-grade dance was held at Nick's Place on April 24, 1998. Wurst took his father's .25-caliber semi-automatic pistol with him to the dance. During the dance, door prizes were handed out and announced by John Gillette. Wurst won one of the prizes, but gave it to a friend. At one point in the evening, shortly before he began shooting, Wurst indicated to one of his friends that he had the gun with him. His friend recalled Wurst talking about suicide and was worried. This friend was so concerned that he alerted other friends and gathered them on the back patio to keep an eye on Wurst. Gillette, a science teacher at the middle school, asked everyone to come inside. When he turned to go inside, Wurst shot him twice, killing him. Wurst then went inside, calling for Eric Wozniak, a student he perceived as an energy. As the students and teachers panicked, he fired two more rounds and wounded Edrye May Boraten, who also taught at the middle school. The other shot wounded Jacob Tury, a student. Justin Fletcher, who had a previous confrontation with Wurst, attempted to stand up to him again. Wurst fired at him but hit Robert Zemcik, another student, instead. Wurst then went outside where James Strand, the owner of Nick's Place, confronted him with his shotgun, demanding that Wurst drop his weapon. Strand and two teachers took Wurst to the back of the building until police arrived. Wurst had been saying that "I died four years ago" and "None of this is real." Shortly after this time, Wurst's mother, along with many other parents, arrived to pick up her son, but instead found her son had been arrested. Wurst was arraigned on April 25, 1998, on a charge of criminal homicide.

Wurst underwent psychiatric evaluations by Robert L. Sadoff for the defense and John S. O'Brien for the prosecution, who came different conclusions. Sadoff examined Wurst in a total of four sessions and met with his parents as well. He came to the conclusion that Wurst suffered from "a major mental illness, with psychotic thinking and delusions of persecution and grandeur." Wurst confessed to Sadoff that he had been having suicidal thoughts since he was 10 years old. He also told him that he had not planned on killing anyone other than himself at the dance and was unsure as to why he shot Gillette. At the time of the shooting, Wurst had stated, "None of this is real"; Sadoff used this statement as a staring point to inquire about Wurst's belief system. According to Sadoff, Wurst did not consider killing Gillette to be wrong because he was not a real person. O'Brien, the other psychiatrist, felt that this was not evidence of a fixed belief system, but rather just thoughts that Wurst had. He felt that Wurst did not suffer from delusions and was capable of standing trial.

Wurst was tried as an adult. He faced charges of criminal homicide, aggravated assault, reckless endangerment, possessing instruments of crime, carrying a firearm without a license, and possession of a controlled substance. He eventually pleaded guilty to third-degree murder. Judge Michael M. Palmisano sentenced Wurst on September 9, 1999, to serve 30 to 60 years. He will be eligible for parole when he is 45 years old. Wurst is currently serving his sentence at the State Correctional Institute Pine Grove in Pennsylvania.

Wurst appears to have been suffering from suicidal tendencies in tandem with violent thought processes. He was unable to deal with minor incidents that occurred in his daily life and had a great deal of difficulty relating to girls. Unable to live up to what his father expected of him, he felt like a disappointment. Many teenagers have a difficult time dealing with frustrations. Concerned students need to report threats of violence; they should not assume that the individual is just joking. A hotline has been set up for anyone who needs to speak to someone about such issues (1-866-STAND UP).

Annika Vorhes

Further Reading

DeJong, W., Epstein, J., & Thomas, E. (2003). Bad things happen in good communities: The rampage shooting in Edinboro, Pennsylvania, and Its aftermath. In M. Moore, C. Petries, A. Braga, & B. McLaughlin (Eds.), *Deadly lessons: Understanding lethal school violence* (pp. 70–100). Washington, DC: National Academies Press.

Palattella, Ed. (1999, March 7). A portrait of conflict. *Erie Times-News*. www.goerie.com.

Y

Youth Activism

Too often, young people are considered suspicious for no reason other than their age. Instead of recognizing their creativity, excitement, energy, and skills, adults tend to underestimate children and teens. Young people have powerful voices, however, and throughout history have often taken the lead in making social change. Students have helped change school policies and legislation at the local, state, and federal levels. They have organized campaigns to call attention to important issues and to engage public support. They have joined and formed groups, led and followed.

In one type of youth activism, young people get involved in adult-led organizations or groups. This often occurs in issues related to educational reform and governmental reform, where young people can play an important role as supporters but cannot lead because of their age.

Some adult-led groups have youth branches, where teens or even children take the lead. For instance, the human rights monitor Amnesty International sponsors student groups for high school youth.

An increasingly common type of youth activism is entirely student created, organized, and led. These activities tend to occur at the local level.

The United States has a long history of youth activism, starting in the late 19th century when young people helped organize strikes to protest poor working conditions and low wages. In 1908, Mary Harris "Mother" Jones organized a march involving 100,000 child miners from Pennsylvania to Washington, D.C. In the 1920s and 1930s, the American Youth Congress was an active youth movement that submitted a "Bill of Youth Rights" to the U.S. Congress. It focused on economic exploitation of youth and on the draft. In the 1940s, 1950s, and early 1960s, young people formed the Student Nonviolent Coordinating Committee and many joined other civil rights movements to march, engage in sit-ins, and participate in other forms of nonviolent protest. In the 1960s and 1970s, students were at the forefront

Actor Chace Crawford donates jeans for the "Teens for Jeans" campaign sponsored by DoSomething.org. Such organizations allow teens to involve themselves in the issues affecting the world today. (AP/Wide World Photos)

of the anti-war movement. In the later 1960s and 1970s, some young women joined the women's liberation movement.

The Supreme Court has upheld youth activism as constitutional as long as it does not disrupt the educational climate. In its 1969 ruling in *Tinker v. Des Moines*, the Court held that students were using their constitutional right to free expression when they wore black armbands to school to protest U.S. involvement in Vietnam. Today, young people are involved in many movements, including environmental, peace, animal rights, gay and lesbian rights, and more.

Many important educators have praised youth activism as an important part of learning. Brazilian educator Paulo Freire, media critic Henry Giroux, historian Howard Zinn, and educators Alfie Kohn and Jonathan Kozol have all pointed out the value of allowing students a voice and a role in community and school affairs.

There are a number of activist-oriented organizations that young people can join; most have websites, so it is easy to find out how to get involved. The Freechild Project focuses on providing opportunities for youths and adults to collaborate. Based in Olympia, Washington, it serves as a clearinghouse for information, projects, training, funding, and more. The organization's website (www.freechild.org)

provides a wealth of information on creativity issues (i.e., censorship and music), economic issues, educational issues, identity issues, democracy issues, social issues, and rights issues. Under the "action" heading, it provides examples of various projects that have been launched. The "resources" heading provides links to many other articles, reports, and sites.

Do Something is another resource for young people who want to become involved in an ongoing community or school project or who want to start their own such project. On its website (www.dosomething.org), young people can learn more about issues ranging from animal welfare to war, peace, and politics. Children as young as seven can apply for small grants to start or expand community projects. The organization also encourages students to form "Do Something" clubs and provides tools for organizing. Youth Noise (www.youthnnoise.com) offers similar resources.

Even little children can get involved. Pennies for Peace is a campaign to help raise awareness and funds for schools across the world, in particular in Afghanistan and Pakistan. Children help by collecting pennies, and can host educational events to go with their fundraising efforts.

Another great website is www.whatkidscando.org. It features many resources as well as stories about youth activism that both inform and inspire.

Laura L. Finley

Further Reading

Do Something: www.dosomething.org

Finley, L., & Stringer, E. (Eds.). (2010). *Beyond "burning bras": Feminist activism for everyone*. Santa Barbara, CA: ABC-CLIO.

Free Child, www.freechild.org

Halpin, M. (2004). *It's your world—if you don't like it, change it: Activism for teenagers*. New York: Simon Pulse.

Jones, E., Haenfler, R., & Johnson, B. (2007). *The better world handbook: Small changes that make a big difference*. Gabriola Island, BC: New Society Publishers.

Noguera, P., & Cammarota, J. (Eds.). (2006). *Beyond resistance! Youth activism and community change*. London: Routledge.

Pennies for Peace, www.penniesforpeace.org

What Kids Can Do, http://www.whatkidscando.org/

Youth Noise, www.youthnoise.com

Youth Crime Watch of America

When a crime occurs, it not only affects a given victim, but also deprives many people of their opportunities to work and live in an environment free of fear.

Unfortunately, no community—whether unsuspecting or otherwise—is immune from falling prey to a variety of unlawful actions.

Bearing this in mind, the Youth Crime Watch of America (YCWA) was established 30 years ago with the following purposes: safeguarding public order; preventing and detecting criminal activity; eliminating unwarranted violence; and ensuring the safety of a neighborhood's citizenry. Modeling itself after the Youth Crime Watch of Miami–Dade County, this nonprofit organization was founded by a handful of concerned citizens in Florida in 1978. Born out of a series of heinous sexual crimes in Miami, YCWA was initially housed in a few high schools as pilot programs. Within a year, school substance abuse and theft of student personal property significantly decreased at these sites. As a result of students gradually summoning up the courage to report crimes, these programs gained community momentum, eventually leading to their statewide implementation.

By 1986, YCWA initiatives had sprung up across the United States, culminating with hundreds of programs. Today the YCWA has created more than 2,000 program sites not only across this country, but throughout the world. Indeed, nearly every state has a YCWA chapter, while model programs exist on four continents. All are welcome to join a YCWA program, with an eye toward encouraging youth volunteers. Once a program is established, YCWA-trained leadership ensures that it is run effectively by providing drug and crime prevention education, creating crime reporting systems, and developing mentoring programs. In addition, YCWA programs are responsible for fostering good community and law enforcement agency relations, in part by hosting a number of events that promote youth involvement.

Unlike other meaningful national and international programs, YCWA counters crime, violence, and drug use with team-oriented collaborations between adolescents and adults. Rather than being solely dependent on well-intentioned adults—namely, teachers, parents, or school administrators—YCWA programs impart the wherewithal to enthusiastic youth determined to help solve community problems. Through a hands-on method, young people become passionate participants in the conflict resolution process.

YCWA programs also work closely with public schools and youth recreational centers. In doing so, advisors stress conflict resolution strategies while championing school bus safety.

Beyond local leadership, each year YCWA divisions come together under the auspices of the National Crime Prevention Conference. During this four-day anticrime conference, thousands of educators, law enforcement officers, policymakers, and both youth and adult volunteers share practices and perspectives on preserving community integrity. From workshops to training seminars, this conference presents multilingual materials such as operating manuals, handbooks, DVD directives, and success stories so that attendees can start a program of their own in short order. These essential start-up elements define how to launch, maintain, and expand programs while avoiding obstacles. The annual YCWA gathering also allows chapter counselors an opportunity to exchange contact information, thereby ensuring that newsletter mailings and follow-up sessions are ongoing.

In recent years, YCWA has garnered national attention for its effectiveness in uniting communities to challenge and ultimately deter crime waves. In fact, every U.S. president since the Reagan administration has honored YCWA for its youth leadership development and proactive approach in nurturing positive communities. Equally noteworthy, YCWA has received a number of national awards, including being designated as a U.S. Department of Education Exemplary Program of Excellence.

The level of recognition and sustained success of YCWA has, in turn, influenced higher education. In 2003, YCWA spearheaded College Crime Watch (CCW) programs aimed at reducing campus crime. In conjunction with building security and university police, CCW promotes safety escort services and timely campus patrols.

With an emphasis on hard work, self-reliance, resourcefulness, social responsibility, self-esteem building, good citizenship, and a greater appreciation for the role of police departments, YCWA community chapters help adolescents become increasingly prepared for almost any seemingly insurmountable ordeal.

Darius Echeverria

Further Reading

Guerra, N., & Smith, E. (Eds.). (2006). *Preventing youth violence in a multicultural society.* Washington, DC: American Psychological Association.

Miller, T. (2008). *School violence and primary prevention.* New York: Springer.

Payne, P. (2006). *Youth violence prevention through asset-based community development.* New York: LFB Scholarly Publishers.

Z

Zero-Tolerance Laws

The concept of zero tolerance originated in the military and coincided with the adoption of the law-and-order agenda in criminal justice. It stems from the "broken windows" thesis developed by George Kelling and James Wilson in the 1980s. The broken windows thesis posited that low-level problems in a community cause citizens to disengage from public spaces, thereby allowing offenders greater opportunity to commit additional and perhaps more serious offenses. The idea was that a crackdown on these low-level offenses—in other words, a zero-tolerance approach—could prevent additional acts of deviance.

The notion of zero tolerance spread to schools in the 1990s, as educators, parents, and politicians became fearful of what they perceived as a surge in school violence. The first zero-tolerance laws were enacted as part of the Gun-Free School Zones Act, part of the Crime Control Act of 1990, which required districts to expel students for no less than one year if they knowingly brought a firearm into a school zone. The 1994 Gun-Free Schools Act provided funds for districts to enact policies with mandatory minimum penalties. It did not absolutely mandate suspension or expulsion for studies who committed offenses, but instead required districts to uniformly treat specific offenses, generally those involving weapons, violence, and drugs. All 50 states endorsed this legislation. Consequently, districts set about determining the specific penalties that would be assigned for given offenses. Eighty-seven percent of all schools now have zero-tolerance policies for alcohol and drugs. Ninety-one percent of schools have adopted zero-tolerance policies for bringing a weapon to school.

Although many people believe these laws address only violent or drug-related behavior, that is not necessarily the case. In fact, most states have some type of "catch-all" clause that allows for the imposition of a mandatory minimum sentence for nonviolent behavior, such as "persistent disobedience."

Supporters say zero-tolerance laws are needed to keep schools safe and drug free so that educators can do what they are supposed to—teach. Many others have expressed concern over zero-tolerance laws. Although they are supposed to ensure that all students committing a specific offense are treated the same, in actuality that has not occurred. African American males, while constituting 17% of the total U.S. student population in 2000, accounted for 33% of students suspended from school in that year. This inequity is not generally due to any proclivity to commit more serious violent incidents, but rather the result of the highly subjective "catch-all" clauses.

Although the intent of zero-tolerance policies was to make schools safer by removing students who had weapons or other dangerous items, many students who have been apprehended with these items are still allowed in the school.

Critics point out that this type of blanket policy often ensnares students who have no nefarious intent. In many cases, students have been suspended or expelled for silly things, as in the case of a 10-year-old who was suspended for taking a paintball gun to show-and-tell, the seventh grader who was suspended for chewing and then sharing a piece of caffeine energy gum, and the five-year-old who was suspended for wearing a fire fighter costume that contained a toy ax. Opponents maintain that no policy should be so rigid it cannot respond to these minor issues.

Critics also note that policies such as zero tolerance have led educators to take a hands-off approach to discipline. Instead of discussing critical issues with students and trying to find root causes, educators are increasingly imposing sanctions with no questions asked. Worse, many students who violate zero-tolerance policies are turned over to law enforcement, creating what has been called the school-to-prison pipeline.

Further, critics note that students who are suspended or expelled are far more likely to drop out of school. Although they can be accepted into other districts, this does not often happen. Thus the problem does not go away but instead becomes one for the larger community, not the school. Additionally, opponents of zero tolerance laws note that there is a scarcity of hard data supporting the contention that these policies are effective.

Given these and other criticisms, the American Bar Association (ABA) has called on districts to remove their zero-tolerance policies. Alternatives might include greater use of in-school suspension, counseling, and development of alternative schools that can meet the needs of all students. Further, educators are encouraged to consider the climate in their school and to enact prevention programs that help maintain a safe, drug-free, and creative school community.

Laura L. Finley

Further Reading

Advancement Project and the Civil Rights Project. (2000). *Opportunities suspended: The devastating consequences of zero tolerance and school discipline policies*. Cambridge, MA: Harvard University Press.

American Bar Association. (n.d.). Zero Tolerance policy. *ABA*. Retrieved May 11, 2010, from http://www.abanet.org/crimjust/juvjus/zerotolreport.html

Casella, R. (2001). *At zero tolerance: Punishment, prevention and school violence*. New York: Peter Lang.

Cauchon, D. (1999, April 13). Zero tolerance policies lack flexibility. *USA Today*. Retrieved May 11, 2010, from http://www.usatoday.com/educate/ednews3.htm

Grant, T. (2006, August 31). Back to school: Zero tolerance makes discipline more severe, involves the courts. *Pittsburgh Post-Gazette*. Retrieved May 11, 2010, from http://www.post-gazette.com/pg/06243/717806-298.stm

Skiba, R., Michael, R., Nardo, A., & Peterson, R. (2000). *The color of discipline: Sources of racial and gender disproportionality in school punishment*. Bloomington, ID: Indiana Education Policy Center.

Discussion Questions

1. What seems to be the primary motivation of high school shooters? Of campus shooters? How are the two similar? How are they different?
2. What are the key differences between high school shooters in urban areas and those in suburban or rural areas? Why do you think these differences occur?
3. Do the media generally do a good job covering school crime and violence? Campus crime and violence? In what ways can media improve?
4. Do you believe the media contribute to the problems of violence in schools and colleges? Why or why not?
5. Besides shootings, what do you consider the most pressing safety concern for schools? For campuses?
6. How big a concern is teacher- or professor-perpetrated crime and violence?
7. Identify the pros and cons of each of the interventions described in this volume, including legislation and punitive efforts, technological efforts, increased police/law enforcement and surveillance, and educational programming.
8. What seems to be the best way to prevent school crime and violence? Campus crime and violence?
9. Which organizations seem to be most effective at responding to school crime and violence? To campus crime and violence? Why?
10. Why do you believe there have been so many more school and campus shootings in the United States, compared with other countries?
11. What are the main differences between the crime and violence occurring in U.S. schools and that occurring outside the United States?
12. Which types of school and campus crime are most difficult to measure? Why? Which strategies could be used to better understand the problem?

13. Do you believe that there is a "profile" of the typical school shooter? Of students who engage in drug-related crime? In nonviolent offenses? In dating violence? In cyberoffenses? Is it useful to develop this type of profile? Why or why not?
14. Do you believe that there is a "profile" of the typical campus shooter? Of college students who engage in drug-related crime? In nonviolent offenses? In dating violence? In cyberoffenses? Is it useful to develop this type of profile? Why or why not?
15. Who is most likely to be the victim of school crime and violence? Of campus crime and violence? Why are these groups or individuals most at risk?
16. Which theoretical perspective is most useful in explaining school crime and violence? Campus crime and violence?
17. What, if any, policy changes should the United States enact to address the problems of school crime and violence?
18. Are there any interventions or policies being utilized in other countries that seem to be effective at responding to or preventing school violence? Why do they seem to be effective? Would they work in the United States? Why or why not?
19. What is youth activism? Why is it important? What are some good examples of it?
20. How important are parents in preventing and responding to school and campus crime and violence?

Extension Activities Related to School and Campus Crime and Violence

1. Host a film screening event using one or more of the films listed in the "Recommended Films About School and Campus Crime and Violence" guide. After viewing the film, lead a discussion about the issues brought up in the film.
2. Research, listen to, and analyze music that is connected to the topics of school and campus crime and violence, such as *Jeremy*. Discuss the lyrics, and describe how they might affect listeners.
3. Write your own songs or poems about school and campus crime and violence. Host a contest or public event in which people perform their work.
4. Read fictional works about school violence, such as those described in the "Fiction and School Violence" entry, and consider whether they accurately present the problem. Which theoretical perspective seems to connect to the situation in the book?
5. Analyze news coverage of recent incidents on campus. Does the coverage accurately present the issue? Which theoretical perspective seems to be presented?
6. Debate the pros and cons of specific policies or interventions. Debate topics could include installation of metal detectors, use of video cameras, hiring of school police officers, drug testing programs, and creation of a gay/straight alliance, among many others.
7. Put on a mock trial for one of the shooters who was never tried. Assign people to research key persons involved in the situation and present the case before a mock jury. Alternatively, use an existing mock trial package to address issues of school and campus crime and violence. The Constitutional Rights Foundation (www.crf-usa.org) has a number of mock trials that can be purchased.
8. Interview persons from multiple generations to see how their perceptions of school and campus crime and violence have changed over time.

9. Write a letter to the editor of a local newspaper or a magazine that discusses school crime and violence in your community and recommends solutions.
10. Research any current legislation being considered in your state or in the federal government that is relevant to the topics of school and campus crime and violence.
11. Research any upcoming court cases that deal with school and campus crime and violence.
12. Call or write a letter to your Congressional representative seeking his or her position on how to best prevent and respond to school and campus crime and violence.
13. Search YouTube for videos related to school and campus crime and violence.
14. Get involved with a local, state, national, or international nonprofit or activist organization that helps prevent violence or provides resources to victims. Spread the word, donate your time, or host a fundraiser.
15. Join a club at your school or college that is helping prevent violence. If there isn't one, start it!
16. Start a website, a blog, or a Facebook or MySpace page related to understanding and preventing school and campus crime and violence.
17. Find a pen pal from another country and learn more about school and campus crime and violence in other regions as you correspond.
18. Make posters to put up at school or on campus that discuss various types of school and campus crime and violence and explain where people can get help.
19. Invite guest speakers to share more about some of the topics covered in this book, such as cyberbullying, policing in schools and on campuses, and dating violence.
20. Host an open forum in your community to discuss school and campus crime and violence.
21. Invite the community to participate in a fun awareness event, such as the Clothesline Project (painting T-shirts related to ending domestic violence) or community art.
22. Read books about and discuss peace with young people. There are wonderful lists of peace-related children's books on the Internet.
23. Lobby for your school or college to include peace education in its curriculum.
24. Make recycled art that shows the importance of a safe and drug-free community.
25. Study what seems to have worked in other countries to reduce or prevent school and campus crime and violence.

Appendix 1: Important Federal Legislation Related to School and Campus Crime and Violence

Public Schools

Title IX of the Education Amendments of 1972:
Enacted in 1972, Title IX prohibits discrimination on the basis of sex in any federally funded activity or program. Most known for addressing gender disparities in extracurricular sports.

Comprehensive Drug Abuse Prevention and Control Act (1970):
Made it a federal crime to traffic drugs within 1,000 feet of a school.

Gun-Free Zones Act (1990):
Required states to enact legislation requiring school districts to expel students caught possessing weapons in school for at least one year. Ruled unconstitutional by the U.S. Supreme Court in 1995.

Safe and Drug-Free Schools and Communities Act (1986):
Established by the 1986 Anti-Drug Abuse Act. SDFSCA supports programs designed to prevent drug abuse and violence, involve parents and communities, and collaborate with federal, state, and local organizations.

No Child Left Behind Act (2001):
Amended and reauthorized the Safe and Drug-Free Schools and Communities Act. NCLB authorized funds for drug abuse and violence prevention.

Campuses

Campus Hate Crimes Right to Know Act (1997):
Requires campus security to collect and report data on hate crimes on campus, including those committed on the basis of race, gender, religion, sexual orientation, ethnicity, or disability.

Crime Awareness and Campus Security Act (1990):
Requires campuses to collect, publish, and distribute an annual report detailing certain crime statistics and describing security and law enforcement policies, crime prevention activities, and procedures for reporting offenses.

Buckley Amendment Clarification (1992):
Clarified that records kept by campus police and security for law enforcement purposes are not confidential "education" records under federal law and, therefore, can be shared with relevant persons.

Campus Sexual Assault Victims' Bill of Rights (1992):
Requires colleges and universities to afford campus sexual assault survivors certain basic rights, including assistance in notifying the police. Schools must have policies in place to address campus sexual assault.

Campus Courts Disclosure Provision (1998):
Ensures that the final records in cases of student disciplinary infractions related to violent crimes or non-forcible sex offenses are no longer protected from disclosure under federal student privacy laws. Victim information is still protected.

Jeanne Clery Disclosure of Campus Security Policy and Campus Crime Statistics Act (1998):
Amends the 1990 Campus Security Act to eliminate loopholes and expand reporting requirements. Statistics for certain off-campus areas have to be disclosed, and schools with a security department must maintain a daily crime log.

Campus Sex Crimes Prevention Act (2000):
Provides for the collection and disclosure of information about convicted, registered sex offenders either enrolled in or employed at institutions of higher education.

National Campus Safety Awareness Month (2008):
Establishes September as National Campus Safety Awareness Month.

Higher Education Opportunity Act (2008):
Adds emergency response and notification provisions to the Clery Act. Also includes protections for whistleblowers.

Appendix 2: Primary Source Documents: Sample Legislation: K–12 Public Schools

Most states enacted anti-bullying legislation in the 1990s and 2000s. Such legislation is intended to reduce bullying, to prepare prevention initiatives, and to allow school districts to better respond when bullying occurs.

Florida added its statute in 2009. It is considered model legislation, as it encompasses all forms of bullying, addresses the need for training, and provides for appropriate services and response.

Florida Statute 1006.147
Bullying and harassment prohibited.

(1) This section may be cited as the "Jeffrey Johnston Stand Up for All Students Act."

(2) Bullying or harassment of any student or employee of a public K–12 educational institution is prohibited:

 (a) During any education program or activity conducted by a public K–12 educational institution;

 (b) During any school-related or school-sponsored program or activity or on a school bus of a public K–12 educational institution; or

 (c) Through the use of data or computer software that is accessed through a computer, computer system, or computer network of a public K–12 educational institution.

(3) For purposes of this section:

 (a) "Bullying" means systematically and chronically inflicting physical hurt or psychological distress on one or more students and may involve:

 1. Teasing;

 2. Social exclusion;

 3. Threat;

4. Intimidation;
5. Stalking;
6. Physical violence;
7. Theft;
8. Sexual, religious, or racial harassment;
9. Public humiliation; or
10. Destruction of property.

(b) "Harassment" means any threatening, insulting, or dehumanizing gesture, use of data or computer software, or written, verbal, or physical conduct directed against a student or school employee that:

1. Places a student or school employee in reasonable fear of harm to his or her person or damage to his or her property;
2. Has the effect of substantially interfering with a student's educational performance, opportunities, or benefits; or
3. Has the effect of substantially disrupting the orderly operation of a school.

(c) Definitions in s. 815.03 and the definition in s. 784.048(1)(d) relating to stalking are applicable to this section.

(d) The definitions of "bullying" and "harassment" include:

1. Retaliation against a student or school employee by another student or school employee for asserting or alleging an act of bullying or harassment. Reporting an act of bullying or harassment that is not made in good faith is considered retaliation.
2. Perpetuation of conduct listed in paragraph (a) or paragraph (b) by an individual or group with intent to demean, dehumanize, embarrass, or cause physical harm to a student or school employee by:

   a Incitement or coercion;
   b Accessing or knowingly causing or providing access to data or computer software through a computer, computer system, or computer network within the scope of the district school system; or
   c Acting in a manner that has an effect substantially similar to the effect of bullying or harassment.

(4) By December 1, 2008, each school district shall adopt a policy prohibiting bullying and harassment of any student or employee of a public K–12 educational institution. Each school district's policy shall be in substantial

conformity with the Department of Education's model policy mandated in subsection (5). The school district bullying and harassment policy shall afford all students the same protection regardless of their status under the law. The school district may establish separate discrimination policies that include categories of students. The school district shall involve students, parents, teachers, administrators, school staff, school volunteers, community representatives, and local law enforcement agencies in the process of adopting the policy. The school district policy must be implemented in a manner that is ongoing throughout the school year and integrated with a school's curriculum, a school's discipline policies, and other violence prevention efforts. The school district policy must contain, at a minimum, the following components:

(a) A statement prohibiting bullying and harassment.
(b) A definition of bullying and a definition of harassment that include the definitions listed in this section.
(c) A description of the type of behavior expected from each student and employee of a public K–12 educational institution.
(d) The consequences for a student or employee of a public K–12 educational institution who commits an act of bullying or harassment.
(e) The consequences for a student or employee of a public K–12 educational institution who is found to have wrongfully and intentionally accused another of an act of bullying or harassment.
(f) A procedure for reporting an act of bullying or harassment, including provisions that permit a person to anonymously report such an act. However, this paragraph does not permit formal disciplinary action to be based solely on an anonymous report.
(g) A procedure for the prompt investigation of a report of bullying or harassment and the persons responsible for the investigation. The investigation of a reported act of bullying or harassment is deemed to be a school-related activity and begins with a report of such an act. Incidents that require a reasonable investigation when reported to appropriate school authorities shall include alleged incidents of bullying or harassment allegedly committed against a child while the child is en route to school aboard a school bus or at a school bus stop.
(h) A process to investigate whether a reported act of bullying or harassment is within the scope of the district school system and, if not, a process for referral of such an act to the appropriate jurisdiction.

(i) A procedure for providing immediate notification to the parents of a victim of bullying or harassment and the parents of the perpetrator of an act of bullying or harassment, as well as notification to all local agencies where criminal charges may be pursued against the perpetrator.

(j) A procedure to refer victims and perpetrators of bullying or harassment for counseling.

(k) A procedure for including incidents of bullying or harassment in the school's report of data concerning school safety and discipline required under s.1006.09(6). The report must include each incident of bullying or harassment and the resulting consequences, including discipline and referrals. The report must include in a separate section each reported incident of bullying or harassment that does not meet the criteria of a prohibited act under this section with recommendations regarding such incidents. The Department of Education shall aggregate information contained in the reports.

(l) A procedure for providing instruction to students, parents, teachers, school administrators, counseling staff, and school volunteers on identifying, preventing, and responding to bullying or harassment.

(m) A procedure for regularly reporting to a victim's parents the actions taken to protect the victim.

(n) A procedure for publicizing the policy, which must include its publication in the code of student conduct required under s.1006.07(2) and in all employee handbooks.

(5) To assist school districts in developing policies prohibiting bullying and harassment, the Department of Education shall develop a model policy that shall be provided to school districts no later than October 1, 2008.

(6) A school employee, school volunteer, student, or parent who promptly reports in good faith an act of bullying or harassment to the appropriate school official designated in the school district's policy and who makes this report in compliance with the procedures set forth in the policy is immune from a cause of action for damages arising out of the reporting itself or any failure to remedy the reported incident.

(7) (a) The physical location or time of access of a computer-related incident cannot be raised as a defense in any disciplinary action initiated under this section.

(b) This section does not apply to any person who uses data or computer software that is accessed through a computer, computer system, or computer network when acting within the scope of his or her lawful employment or investigating a violation of this section in accordance with school district policy.

(8) Distribution of safe schools funds to a school district provided in the 2009–2010 General Appropriations Act is contingent upon and payable to the school district upon the Department of Education's approval of the school district's bullying and harassment policy. The department's approval of each school district's bullying and harassment policy shall be granted upon certification by the department that the school district's policy has been submitted to the department and is in substantial conformity with the department's model bullying and harassment policy as mandated in subsection (5). Distribution of safe schools funds provided to a school district in fiscal year 2010-2011 and thereafter shall be contingent upon and payable to the school district upon the school district's compliance with all reporting procedures contained in this section.

(9) On or before January 1 of each year, the Commissioner of Education shall report to the Governor, the President of the Senate, and the Speaker of the House of Representatives on the implementation of this section. The report shall include data collected pursuant to paragraph (4)(k).

(10) Nothing in this section shall be construed to abridge the rights of students or school employees that are protected by the First Amendment to the Constitution of the United States.

Source: Document available at http://faptflorida.org/MidYearHandouts09/Safe%20Schools%2020090302%20Law%20Against%20Bullying_Rumenik.pdf

§§§§

Michigan is one of the few states that, as of November 2010, still did not have specific anti-bullying legislation. The state does have an anti-bullying policy, but critics note that policies are less binding than legislation. Below is the verbiage from a proposed bill that has yet to be enacted.

House Bill No. 4580

March 12, 2009, Introduced by Reps. Byrnes, Cushingberry, Melton, Paul Scott, Rick Jones, Warren, Scripps, Schuitmaker, Miller, Switalski, Geiss, Kennedy, Liss, Bauer, Lisa Brown, Neumann, Barnett, Haase, Mayes, Roberts, Bledsoe, Valentine, Donigan, Polidori, Lipton, Gregory, Meadows, Gonzales, Johnson and Lindberg and referred to the Committee on Education.
A bill to amend 1976 PA 451, entitled
"The revised school code,"

MCL 380.1 to 380.1852) by adding section 1310b.
The people of the state of Michigan enact:
Sec. 1310b.

(1) Not later than 6 months after the effective date of this section, the board of a school district or intermediate school district or board of directors of a public school academy shall adopt and implement a policy prohibiting bullying or harassment at school, as defined in this section. The legislature encourages a board or board of directors to include in its policy provisions concerning education, parental involvement, reporting, investigation, and intervention. Before adopting the policy, the board or board of directors shall hold at least 1 public hearing on the proposed policy. This public hearing may be held as part of a regular board meeting. Not later than 30 days after adopting the policy, the board or board of directors shall submit a copy of its policy to the department.

(2) Not later than 1 year after the deadline under subsection (1) for districts and public school academies to submit copies of their policies to the department, the department shall submit a report to the senate and house standing committees on education summarizing the status of the implementation of policies under this section.

(3) As used in this section:

  (a) "At school" means in a classroom, elsewhere on school premises, on a school bus or other school-related vehicle, or at a school-sponsored activity or event whether or not it is held on school premises. "At school" includes conduct using a telecommunications access device or telecommunications service provider that occurs off school premises if the telecommunications access device or the telecommunications service provider is owned by or under the control of the school district or public school academy.

  (b) "Bullying or harassment" means abuse of a pupil by 1 or more other pupils in any form. The term includes, but is not limited to, conduct that meets any of the following:

   (i) Substantially interferes with educational opportunities, benefits, or programs of 1 or more pupils.

   (ii) Adversely affects the ability of a pupil to participate in or benefit from the school district's or public school's educational programs or activities by placing the pupil in reasonable fear of physical harm or by causing emotional distress.

   (iii) Is reasonably perceived to be motivated by animus or by an actual or perceived characteristic.

(c) "Telecommunications access device" and "telecommunications service provider" mean those terms as defined in section 219a of the Michigan penal code, 1931 PA 328, MCL 750.219a.

(4) This section shall be known as "Matt's Safe School Law."

Source: Document available at http://www.legislature.mi.gov/documents/2009-2010/billengrossed/House/htm/2009-HEBH-4580.htm

§§§§

Some states have enacted specific legislation to address dating violence and sexual assault in schools. Georgia enacted this legislation in order to coordinate prevention efforts.

Bottom of Form
O.C.G.A. § 20-2-314

Georgia Code
Copyright 2010 by The State of Georgia
All rights reserved.

*** Current through the 2010 Regular Session ***

Title 20. Education
Chapter 2. Elementary and Secondary Education
Article 6. Quality Basic Education
Part 14. Other Educational Programs

O.C.G.A. § 20-2-314 (2010)

§ 20-2-314. Development of **rape prevention,** personal safety education, and teen dating violence prevention programs

The State Board of Education shall develop, with input from appropriate experts, such as rape crisis centers and family violence shelters, a **rape prevention** and personal safety education program and a program for preventing teen dating violence for grade eight through grade 12 which are consistent with the core curriculum provided for in Code Section 20-2-140. Local boards may implement such programs at any time and for any grade level local boards find appropriate, and the state board shall encourage the implementation of such programs. In addition, the state board shall make information regarding such programs available to the Board of Regents of the University System of Georgia.

HISTORY: Code 1981, § 20-2-314, enacted by Ga. L. 2000, p. 163, § 1; Ga. L. 2003, p. 915, § 1.

Document available at http://www.lexis-nexis.com/hottopics/gacode/default.asp

§§§§

Rhode Island enacted the Lindsay Ann Burke Act to coordinate dating violence prevention in schools. It was the first of its kind in the United States.

Chapter 490
2007 — S 0875 Substitute B
Enacted 07/03/07
An Act

Relating to Education—Dating Violence: "Lindsay Ann Burke Act"

Introduced by: Senators Lanzi, Paiva-Weed, Perry, Gallo, and Goodwin
Date Introduced: March 20, 2007
It is enacted by the General Assembly as follows:
Section 1. Title 16 of the General Laws entitled "Education" is hereby amended by adding thereto the following chapter:

Chapter 85
Lindsay Ann Burke Act

16-85-1. Short title. This chapter shall be known and may be cited as the "Lindsay Ann Burke Act."

16-85-2. Legislative findings. The general assembly hereby finds, determines and declares that when a student is a victim of dating violence, his or her academic life suffers and his or her safety at school is jeopardized. The general assembly therefore finds that a policy to create an environment free of dating violence shall be a part of each school district. It is the intent of the general assembly to enact legislation that would require each school district to establish a policy for responding to incidents of dating violence and to provide dating violence education to students, parents, staff, faculty and administrators, in order to prevent dating violence and to address incidents involving dating violence. All students have a right to work and study in a safe, supportive environment that is free from harassment, intimidation and violence.

SECTION 2. Chapter 16-21 of the General Laws entitled "Health and Safety of Pupils" is hereby amended by adding thereto the following section:

16-21-30. Dating Violence Policy.
- (a) As used in this section:
    - (1) "Dating violence" means a pattern of behavior where one person uses threats of, or actually uses, physical, sexual, verbal or emotional abuse to control his or her dating partner.
    - (2) "Dating partner" means any person, regardless of gender, involved in an intimate relationship with another primarily characterized by the expectation of affectionate involvement whether casual, serious or long-term.
    - (3) "At school" means in a classroom, on or immediately adjacent to school premises, on a school bus or other school-related vehicle, at an official school bus stop, or at any school-sponsored activity or event whether or not it is on school grounds.
- (b) The department of education shall develop a model dating violence policy to assist school districts in developing policies for dating violence reporting and response. The model policy shall be issued on or before April 1, 2008.
- (c) Each school district shall establish a specific policy to address incidents of dating violence involving students at school by December 1, 2008. Each school district shall verify compliance with the department of education on an annual basis through the annual school health report.
    - (1) Such policy shall include, but not be limited to, a statement that dating violence will not be tolerated, dating violence reporting procedures, guidelines to responding to at school incidents of dating violence and discipline procedures specific to such incidents.
    - (2) To ensure notice of the school district's dating violence policy, the policy shall be published in any school district policy and handbook that sets forth the comprehensive rules, procedures and standards of conduct for students at school.
- (d) Each school district shall provide dating violence training to all administrators, teachers, nurses and mental health staff at the middle and high school levels. Upon the recommendation of the administrator, other staff may be included or may attend the training on a volunteer basis. The dating violence training shall include, but not be limited to, basic principles of dating violence, warning signs of dating violence and the school district's dating violence policy, to ensure that they are able to appropriately respond to incidents of dating violence at school. Thereafter, this training shall be

provided yearly to all newly hired staff deemed appropriate to receive the training by the school's administration.

(e) Each school district shall inform the students' parents or legal guardians of the school district's dating violence policy. If requested, the school district shall provide the parents or legal guardians with the school district's dating violence policy and relevant information. It is strongly recommended that the school district provide parent awareness training.

(f) This section does not prevent a victim from seeking redress under any other available law, either civil or criminal. This section does not create or alter any tort liability.

SECTION 3. Chapter 16-22 of the General Laws entitled Curriculum" is hereby amended by adding thereto the following section:

16-22-24. Dating Violence Education.

(a) Each school district shall incorporate dating violence education that is age-appropriate into the annual health curriculum framework for students in grades seven (7) through twelve (12).

  (1) Dating violence education shall include, but not be limited to, defining dating violence, recognizing dating violence warning signs and characteristics of healthy relationships. Additionally, students shall be provided with the school district's dating violence policy as provided in subsection 16-21-30(c).

  (2) For the purposes of this section:

    (i) "Dating violence" means a pattern of behavior where one person uses threats of, or actually uses, physical, sexual, verbal or emotional abuse to control his or her dating partner.

    (ii) "Dating partner" means any person involved in an intimate association with another primarily characterized by the expectation of affectionate involvement whether casual, serious or long-term.

    (iii) "At school" means in a classroom, on or immediately adjacent to such school premises, on a school bus or other school-related vehicle, at an official school bus stop, or at any school sponsored activity or event whether or not it is on school grounds.

  (3) To assist school districts in developing a dating violence education program, the department of education shall review and approve the grade level topics relating to dating violence and healthy

relationships in the "health literacy for all students: the Rhode Island health education framework."

(4) The provisions of this section shall be amended in the health education curriculum sections of the Rhode Island rules and regulations for school health programs, R16-21-SCHO, and the Rhode Island basic education program at their next revisions.

(b) Upon written request to the school principal, a parent or legal guardian of a pupil less than eighteen (18) years of age, within a reasonable period of time after the request is made, shall be permitted to examine the dating violence education program instruction materials at the school in which his or her child is enrolled.

SECTION 4. This act shall take effect upon passage.

LC01262/SUB B
Source: Document available at http://www.rilin.state.ri.us/PublicLaws/law07/law07490.htm

§§§§

All states have enacted legislation related to school safety, largely as a response to the Safe and Drug-Free Schools and Community Act of 1994. Following is the wording of Texas's statute, which addresses when, how, and under which circumstances students can be removed from schools

Education Code
Title 2. Public Education
Subtitle G. Safe Schools
Chapter 37. Discipline; Law and Order

Subchapter A. Alternative Settings for Behavior Management

Sec. 37.001. Student Code of Conduct.

(a) The board of trustees of an independent school district shall, with the advice of its district-level committee established under Subchapter F, Chapter 11, adopt a student code of conduct for the district. The student code of conduct must be posted and prominently displayed at each school campus or made available for review at the office of the campus principal. In addition to establishing standards for student conduct, the student code of conduct must:

(1) specify the circumstances, in accordance with this subchapter, under which a student may be removed from a classroom, campus, or disciplinary alternative education program;

(2) specify conditions that authorize or require a principal or other appropriate administrator to transfer a student to a disciplinary alternative education program;

(3) outline conditions under which a student may be suspended as provided by Section 37.005 or expelled as provided by Section 37.007;

(4) specify that consideration will be given, as a factor in each decision concerning suspension, removal to a disciplinary alternative education program, expulsion, or placement in a juvenile justice alternative education program, regardless of whether the decision concerns a mandatory or discretionary action, to:

   (A) self-defense;

   (B) intent or lack of intent at the time the student engaged in the conduct;

   (C) a student's disciplinary history; or

   (D) a disability that substantially impairs the student's capacity to appreciate the wrongfulness of the student's conduct;

(5) provide guidelines for setting the length of a term of:

   (A) a removal under Section 37.006; and

   (B) an expulsion under Section 37.007;

(6) address the notification of a student's parent or guardian of a violation of the student code of conduct committed by the student that results in suspension, removal to a disciplinary alternative education program, or expulsion;

(7) prohibit bullying, harassment, and making hit lists and ensure that district employees enforce those prohibitions; and

(8) provide, as appropriate for students at each grade level, methods, including options, for:

   (A) managing students in the classroom and on school grounds;

   (B) disciplining students; and

   (C) preventing and intervening in student discipline problems, including bullying, harassment, and making hit lists.

(b) In this section:

(1) "Harassment" means threatening to cause harm or bodily injury to another student, engaging in sexually intimidating conduct, causing physical damage to the property of another student, subjecting another student to physical confinement or restraint, or maliciously

taking any action that substantially harms another student's physical or emotional health or safety.

   (2) "Hit list" means a list of people targeted to be harmed, using:

      (A) a firearm, as defined by Section 46.01(3), Penal Code;

      (B) a knife, as defined by Section 46.01(7), Penal Code; or

      (C) any other object to be used with intent to cause bodily harm.

(b-1) The methods adopted under Subsection (a)(8) must provide that a student who is enrolled in a special education program under Subchapter A, Chapter 29, may not be disciplined for conduct prohibited in accordance with Subsection (a)(7) until an admission, review, and dismissal committee meeting has been held to review the conduct.

(c) Once the student code of conduct is promulgated, any change or amendment must be approved by the board of trustees.

(d) Each school year, a school district shall provide parents notice of and information regarding the student code of conduct.

(e) Except as provided by Section 37.007(e), this subchapter does not require the student code of conduct to specify a minimum term of a removal under Section 37.006 or an expulsion under Section 37.007.

Added by Acts 1995, 74th Leg., ch. 260, Sec. 1, eff. May 30, 1995. Amended by Acts 1997, 75th Leg., ch. 1015, Sec. 2, eff. June 19, 1997; Acts 2003, 78th Leg., ch. 1055, Sec. 4, 30, eff. June 20, 2003.
Amended by:
Acts 2005, 79th Leg., Ch. 504, Sec. 1, eff. June 17, 2005.
Acts 2005, 79th Leg., Ch. 920, Sec. 3, eff. June 18, 2005.
Acts 2009, 81st Leg., R.S., Ch. 897, Sec. 1, eff. June 19, 2009.

Sec. 37.002. Removal By Teacher.

(a) A teacher may send a student to the principal's office to maintain effective discipline in the classroom. The principal shall respond by employing appropriate discipline management techniques consistent with the student code of conduct adopted under Section 37.001.

(b) A teacher may remove from class a student:

   (1) who has been documented by the teacher to repeatedly interfere with the teacher's ability to communicate effectively with the students in the class or with the ability of the student's classmates to learn; or

   (2) whose behavior the teacher determines is so unruly, disruptive, or abusive that it seriously interferes with the teacher's ability to

communicate effectively with the students in the class or with the ability of the student's classmates to learn.

(c) If a teacher removes a student from class under Subsection (b), the principal may place the student into another appropriate classroom, into in-school suspension, or into a disciplinary alternative education program as provided by Section 37.008. The principal may not return the student to that teacher's class without the teacher's consent unless the committee established under Section 37.003 determines that such placement is the best or only alternative available. The terms of the removal may prohibit the student from attending or participating in school-sponsored or school-related activity.

(d) A teacher shall remove from class and send to the principal for placement in a disciplinary alternative education program or for expulsion, as appropriate, a student who engages in conduct described under Section 37.006 or 37.007. The student may not be returned to that teacher's class without the teacher's consent unless the committee established under Section 37.003 determines that such placement is the best or only alternative available. If the teacher removed the student from class because the student has engaged in the elements of any offense listed in Section 37.006(a)(2)(B) or Section 37.007(a)(2)(A) or (b)(2)(C) against the teacher, the student may not be returned to the teacher's class without the teacher's consent. The teacher may not be coerced to consent.

Added by Acts 1995, 74th Leg., ch. 260, Sec. 1, eff. May 30, 1995. Amended by Acts 2003, 78th Leg., ch. 1055, Sec. 5, eff. June 20, 2003.
Amended by:
Acts 2005, 79th Leg., Ch. 504, Sec. 2, eff. June 17, 2005.

Sec. 37.0021. Use of Confinement, Restraint, Seclusion, and Time-Out.

(a) It is the policy of this state to treat with dignity and respect all students, including students with disabilities who receive special education services under Subchapter A, Chapter 29. A student with a disability who receives special education services under Subchapter A, Chapter 29, may not be confined in a locked box, locked closet, or other specially designed locked space as either a discipline management practice or a behavior management technique.

(b) In this section:

(1) "Restraint" means the use of physical force or a mechanical device to significantly restrict the free movement of all or a portion of a student's body.

(2) "Seclusion" means a behavior management technique in which a student is confined in a locked box, locked closet, or locked room that:

   (A) is designed solely to seclude a person; and

   (B) contains less than 50 square feet of space.

(3) "Time-out" means a behavior management technique in which, to provide a student with an opportunity to regain self-control, the student is separated from other students for a limited period in a setting:

   (A) that is not locked; and

   (B) from which the exit is not physically blocked by furniture, a closed door held shut from the outside, or another inanimate object.

(c) A school district employee or volunteer or an independent contractor of a district may not place a student in seclusion. This subsection does not apply to the use of seclusion in a court-ordered placement, other than a placement in an educational program of a school district, or in a placement or facility to which the following law, rules, or regulations apply:

   (1) the Children's Health Act of 2000, Pub. L. No. 106-310, any subsequent amendments to that Act, any regulations adopted under that Act, or any subsequent amendments to those regulations;

   (2) 40 T.A.C. Sections 720.1001-720.1013; or

   (3) 25 T.A.C. Section 412.308(e).

(d) The commissioner by rule shall adopt procedures for the use of restraint and time-out by a school district employee or volunteer or an independent contractor of a district in the case of a student with a disability receiving special education services under Subchapter A, Chapter 29. A procedure adopted under this subsection must:

   (1) be consistent with:

      (A) professionally accepted practices and standards of student discipline and techniques for behavior management; and

      (B) relevant health and safety standards; and

   (2) identify any discipline management practice or behavior management technique that requires a district employee or volunteer or an independent contractor of a district to be trained before using that practice or technique.

(e) In the case of a conflict between a rule adopted under Subsection (d) and a rule adopted under Subchapter A, Chapter 29, the rule adopted under Subsection (d) controls.

(f) For purposes of this subsection, "weapon" includes any weapon described under Section 37.007(a)(1). This section does not prevent a student's locked, unattended confinement in an emergency situation while awaiting the arrival of law enforcement personnel if:
   (1) the student possesses a weapon; and
   (2) the confinement is necessary to prevent the student from causing bodily harm to the student or another person.
(g) This section and any rules or procedures adopted under this section do not apply to:
   (1) a peace officer while performing law enforcement duties;
   (2) juvenile probation, detention, or corrections personnel; or
   (3) an educational services provider with whom a student is placed by a judicial authority, unless the services are provided in an educational program of a school district.

Added by Acts 2001, 77th Leg., ch. 212, Sec. 1, eff. Sept. 1, 2001. Amended by Acts 2003, 78th Leg., ch. 1055, Sec. 6, eff. June 20, 2003.

Sec. 37.003. Placement Review Committee.
(a) Each school shall establish a three-member committee to determine placement of a student when a teacher refuses the return of a student to the teacher's class and make recommendations to the district regarding readmission of expelled students. Members shall be appointed as follows:
   (1) the campus faculty shall choose two teachers to serve as members and one teacher to serve as an alternate member; and
   (2) the principal shall choose one member from the professional staff of a campus.
(b) The teacher refusing to readmit the student may not serve on the committee.
(c) The committee's placement determination regarding a student with a disability who receives special education services under Subchapter A, Chapter 29, is subject to the requirements of the Individuals with Disabilities Education Act (20 U.S.C. Section 1400 et seq.) and federal regulations, state statutes, and agency requirements necessary to carry out federal law or regulations or state law relating to special education.

Added by Acts 1995, 74th Leg., ch. 260, Sec. 1, eff. May 30, 1995. Amended by Acts 2003, 78th Leg., ch. 1055, Sec. 7, eff. June 20, 2003.

Sec. 37.004. Placement of Students with Disabilities.

(a) The placement of a student with a disability who receives special education services may be made only by a duly constituted admission, review, and dismissal committee.

(b) Any disciplinary action regarding a student with a disability who receives special education services that would constitute a change in placement under federal law may be taken only after the student's admission, review, and dismissal committee conducts a manifestation determination review under 20 U.S.C. Section 1415(k)(4) and its subsequent amendments. Any disciplinary action regarding the student shall be determined in accordance with federal law and regulations, including laws or regulations requiring the provision of:

   (1) functional behavioral assessments;

   (2) positive behavioral interventions, strategies, and supports;

   (3) behavioral intervention plans; and

   (4) the manifestation determination review.

(c) A student with a disability who receives special education services may not be placed in alternative education programs solely for educational purposes.

(d) A teacher in an alternative education program under Section 37.008 who has a special education assignment must hold an appropriate certificate or permit for that assignment.

Added by Acts 1995, 74th Leg., ch. 260, Sec. 1, eff. May 30, 1995. Amended by Acts 2001, 77th Leg., ch. 767, Sec. 6, eff. June 13, 2001; Acts 2001, 77th Leg., ch. 1225, Sec. 1, eff. June 15, 2001; Acts 2003, 78th Leg., ch. 435, Sec. 1, eff. June 20, 2003; Acts 2003, 78th Leg., ch. 1276, Sec. 6.006, eff. Sept. 1, 2003.

Sec. 37.005. Suspension.

(a) The principal or other appropriate administrator may suspend a student who engages in conduct identified in the student code of conduct adopted under Section 37.001 as conduct for which a student may be suspended.

(b) A suspension under this section may not exceed three school days.

Added by Acts 1995, 74th Leg., ch. 260, Sec. 1, eff. May 30, 1995. Amended by Acts 2003, 78th Leg., ch. 1055, Sec. 8, eff. June 20, 2003.

Sec. 37.0051. Placement of Students Committing Sexual Assault Against Another Student.

(a) As provided by Section 25.0341(b)(2), a student shall be removed from class and placed in a disciplinary alternative education program under Section 37.008 or a juvenile justice alternative education program under Section 37.011.

(b) A limitation imposed by this subchapter on the length of a placement in a disciplinary alternative education program or a juvenile justice alternative education program does not apply to a placement under this section.

Added by Acts 2005, 79th Leg., Ch. 997, Sec. 2, eff. June 18, 2005.

Sec. 37.006. Removal for Certain Conduct.

(a) A student shall be removed from class and placed in a disciplinary alternative education program as provided by Section 37.008 if the student:

  (1) engages in conduct involving a public school that contains the elements of the offense of false alarm or report under Section 42.06, Penal Code, or terroristic threat under Section 22.07, Penal Code; or

  (2) commits the following on or within 300 feet of school property, as measured from any point on the school's real property boundary line, or while attending a school-sponsored or school-related activity on or off of school property:

  (A) engages in conduct punishable as a felony;

  (B) engages in conduct that contains the elements of the offense of assault under Section 22.01(a)(1), Penal Code;

  (C) sells, gives, or delivers to another person or possesses or uses or is under the influence of:

   (i) marihuana or a controlled substance, as defined by Chapter 481, Health and Safety Code, or by 21 U.S.C. Section 801 et seq.; or

   (ii) a dangerous drug, as defined by Chapter 483, Health and Safety Code;

  (D) sells, gives, or delivers to another person an alcoholic beverage, as defined by Section 1.04, Alcoholic Beverage Code, commits a serious act or offense while under the influence of alcohol, or possesses, uses, or is under the influence of an alcoholic beverage;

  (E) engages in conduct that contains the elements of an offense relating to an abusable volatile chemical under Sections 485.031 through 485.034, Health and Safety Code; or

(F) engages in conduct that contains the elements of the offense of public lewdness under Section 21.07, Penal Code, or indecent exposure under Section 21.08, Penal Code.

(b) Except as provided by Section 37.007(d), a student shall be removed from class and placed in a disciplinary alternative education program under Section 37.008 if the student engages in conduct on or off of school property that contains the elements of the offense of retaliation under Section 36.06, Penal Code, against any school employee.

(c) In addition to Subsections (a) and (b), a student shall be removed from class and placed in a disciplinary alternative education program under Section 37.008 based on conduct occurring off campus and while the student is not in attendance at a school-sponsored or school-related activity if:

(1) the student receives deferred prosecution under Section 53.03, Family Code, for conduct defined as a felony offense in Title 5, Penal Code;

(2) a court or jury finds that the student has engaged in delinquent conduct under Section 54.03, Family Code, for conduct defined as a felony offense in Title 5, Penal Code; or

(3) the superintendent or the superintendent's designee has a reasonable belief that the student has engaged in a conduct defined as a felony offense in Title 5, Penal Code.

(d) In addition to Subsections (a), (b), and (c), a student may be removed from class and placed in a disciplinary alternative education program under Section 37.008 based on conduct occurring off campus and while the student is not in attendance at a school-sponsored or school-related activity if:

(1) the superintendent or the superintendent's designee has a reasonable belief that the student has engaged in conduct defined as a felony offense other than those defined in Title 5, Penal Code; and

(2) the continued presence of the student in the regular classroom threatens the safety of other students or teachers or will be detrimental to the educational process.

(e) In determining whether there is a reasonable belief that a student has engaged in conduct defined as a felony offense by the Penal Code, the superintendent or the superintendent's designee may consider all available information, including the information furnished under Article 15.27, Code of Criminal Procedure.

(f) Subject to Section 37.007(e), a student who is younger than 10 years of age shall be removed from class and placed in a disciplinary alternative education program under Section 37.008 if the student engages in conduct described by Section 37.007. An elementary school student may not be placed in a disciplinary alternative education program with any other student who is not an elementary school student.

(g) The terms of a placement under this section must prohibit the student from attending or participating in a school-sponsored or school-related activity.

(h) On receipt of notice under Article 15.27(g), Code of Criminal Procedure, the superintendent or the superintendent's designee shall review the student's placement in the disciplinary alternative education program. The student may not be returned to the regular classroom pending the review. The superintendent or the superintendent's designee shall schedule a review of the student's placement with the student's parent or guardian not later than the third class day after the superintendent or superintendent's designee receives notice from the office or official designated by the court. After reviewing the notice and receiving information from the student's parent or guardian, the superintendent or the superintendent's designee may continue the student's placement in the disciplinary alternative education program if there is reason to believe that the presence of the student in the regular classroom threatens the safety of other students or teachers.

(i) The student or the student's parent or guardian may appeal the superintendent's decision under Subsection (h) to the board of trustees. The student may not be returned to the regular classroom pending the appeal. The board shall, at the next scheduled meeting, review the notice provided under Article 15.27(g), Code of Criminal Procedure, and receive information from the student, the student's parent or guardian, and the superintendent or superintendent's designee and confirm or reverse the decision under Subsection (h). The board shall make a record of the proceedings. If the board confirms the decision of the superintendent or superintendent's designee, the board shall inform the student and the student's parent or guardian of the right to appeal to the commissioner under Subsection (j).

(j) Notwithstanding Section 7.057(e), the decision of the board of trustees under Subsection (i) may be appealed to the commissioner as provided by Sections 7.057(b), (c), (d), and (f). The student may not be returned to the regular classroom pending the appeal.

(k) Subsections (h), (i), and (j) do not apply to placements made in accordance with Subsection (a).

(l) Notwithstanding any other provision of this code, other than Section 37.007(e)(2), a student who is younger than six years of age may not be removed from class and placed in a disciplinary alternative education program.

(m) Removal to a disciplinary alternative education program under Subsection (a) is not required if the student is expelled under Section 37.007 for the same conduct for which removal would be required.

(n) A principal or other appropriate administrator may but is not required to remove a student to a disciplinary alternative education program for off-campus conduct for which removal is required under this section if the principal or other appropriate administrator does not have knowledge of the conduct before the first anniversary of the date the conduct occurred.

(o) In addition to any notice required under Article 15.27, Code of Criminal Procedure, a principal or a principal's designee shall inform each educator who has responsibility for, or is under the direction and supervision of an educator who has responsibility for, the instruction of a student who has engaged in any violation listed in this section of the student's misconduct. Each educator shall keep the information received under this subsection confidential from any person not entitled to the information under this subsection, except that the educator may share the information with the student's parent or guardian as provided for by state or federal law. The State Board for Educator Certification may revoke or suspend the certification of an educator who intentionally violates this subsection.

Added by Acts 1995, 74th Leg., ch. 260, Sec. 1, eff. May 30, 1995. Amended by Acts 1997, 75th Leg., ch. 1015, Sec. 3, eff. June 19, 1997; Acts 1999, 76th Leg., ch. 396, Sec. 2.15, eff. Sept. 1, 1999; Acts 2001, 77th Leg., ch. 486, Sec. 1, eff. June 11, 2001; Acts 2003, 78th Leg., ch. 1055, Sec. 9, eff. June 20, 2003. Amended by:
Acts 2005, 79th Leg., Ch. 504, Sec. 3, eff. June 17, 2005.

Sec. 37.0061. Funding for Alternative Education Services in Juvenile Residential Facilities.

A school district that provides education services to pre-adjudicated and post-adjudicated students who are confined by court order in a juvenile residential facility operated by a juvenile board is entitled to count such students in the district's average daily attendance for purposes of receipt of state funds under the Foundation School Program. If the district has a wealth per student greater than the guaranteed wealth level but less than the equalized wealth level, the district in which the student is enrolled on the date a court orders the student to be confined to a juvenile residential facility shall transfer to the district providing education services an amount equal to the difference between the average Foundation School Program costs per student of the district providing education services and the sum of the state aid and the money from the available school fund received by the district that is attributable to the student for the portion of the school year for which the district provides education services to the student.

Added by Acts 1997, 75th Leg., ch. 1015, Sec. 4, eff. June 19, 1997.

Sec. 37.0062. Instructional Requirements for Alternative Education Services In Juvenile Residential Facilities.

(a) The commissioner shall determine the instructional requirements for education services provided by a school district or open-enrollment charter school in a pre-adjudication secure detention facility or a post-adjudication secure correctional facility operated by a juvenile board or a post-adjudication secure correctional facility operated under contract with the Texas Youth Commission, including requirements relating to:

(1) the length of the school day;

(2) the number of days of instruction provided to students each school year; and

(3) the curriculum of the educational program.

(b) The commissioner shall coordinate with:

(1) the Texas Juvenile Probation Commission in determining the instructional requirements for education services provided under Subsection (a) in a pre-adjudication secure detention facility or a post-adjudication secure correctional facility operated by a juvenile board; and

(2) the Texas Youth Commission in determining the instructional requirements for education services provided under Subsection (a) in a post-adjudication secure correctional facility operated under contract with the Texas Youth Commission.

(c) The commissioner shall adopt rules necessary to administer this section. The rules must ensure that:

(1) a student who receives education services in a pre-adjudication secure detention facility described by this section is offered courses that enable the student to maintain progress toward completing high school graduation requirements; and

(2) a student who receives education services in a post-adjudication secure correctional facility described by this section is offered, at a minimum, the courses necessary to enable the student to complete high school graduation requirements.

(d) The Texas Juvenile Probation Commission or the Texas Youth Commission, as applicable, shall coordinate with the commissioner in establishing standards for:

   (1) ensuring security in the provision of education services in the facilities; and

   (2) providing children in the custody of the facilities access to education services.

Added by Acts 2007, 80th Leg., R.S., Ch. 615, Sec. 1, eff. September 1, 2007.

Sec. 37.007. Expulsion for Serious Offenses.

(a) Except as provided by Subsection (k), a student shall be expelled from a school if the student, on school property or while attending a school-sponsored or school-related activity on or off of school property:

   (1) uses, exhibits, or possesses:

      (A) a firearm as defined by Section 46.01(3), Penal Code;

      (B) an illegal knife as defined by Section 46.01(6), Penal Code, or by local policy;

      (C) a club as defined by Section 46.01(1), Penal Code; or

      (D) a weapon listed as a prohibited weapon under Section 46.05, Penal Code;

   (2) engages in conduct that contains the elements of the offense of:

      (A) aggravated assault under Section 22.02, Penal Code, sexual assault under Section 22.011, Penal Code, or aggravated sexual assault under Section 22.021, Penal Code;

      (B) arson under Section 28.02, Penal Code;

      (C) murder under Section 19.02, Penal Code, capital murder under Section 19.03, Penal Code, or criminal attempt, under Section 15.01, Penal Code, to commit murder or capital murder;

      (D) indecency with a child under Section 21.11, Penal Code;

      (E) aggravated kidnapping under Section 20.04, Penal Code;

      (F) aggravated robbery under Section 29.03, Penal Code;

      (G) manslaughter under Section 19.04, Penal Code;

      (H) criminally negligent homicide under Section 19.05, Penal Code; or

      (I) continuous sexual abuse of young child or children under Section 21.02, Penal Code; or

(3) engages in conduct specified by Section 37.006(a)(2)(C) or (D), if the conduct is punishable as a felony.

(b) A student may be expelled if the student:

(1) engages in conduct involving a public school that contains the elements of the offense of false alarm or report under Section 42.06, Penal Code, or terroristic threat under Section 22.07, Penal Code;

(2) while on or within 300 feet of school property, as measured from any point on the school's real property boundary line, or while attending a school-sponsored or school-related activity on or off of school property:

(A) sells, gives, or delivers to another person or possesses, uses, or is under the influence of any amount of:

(i) marihuana or a controlled substance, as defined by Chapter 481, Health and Safety Code, or by 21 U.S.C. Section 801 et seq.;

(ii) a dangerous drug, as defined by Chapter 483, Health and Safety Code; or

(iii) an alcoholic beverage, as defined by Section 1.04, Alcoholic Beverage Code;

(B) engages in conduct that contains the elements of an offense relating to an abusable volatile chemical under Sections 485.031 through 485.034, Health and Safety Code;

(C) engages in conduct that contains the elements of an offense under Section 22.01(a)(1), Penal Code, against a school district employee or a volunteer as defined by Section 22.053; or

(D) engages in conduct that contains the elements of the offense of deadly conduct under Section 22.05, Penal Code;

(3) subject to Subsection (d), while within 300 feet of school property, as measured from any point on the school's real property boundary line:

(A) engages in conduct specified by Subsection (a); or

(B) possesses a firearm, as defined by 18 U.S.C. Section 921; or

(4) engages in conduct that contains the elements of any offense listed in Subsection (a)(2)(A) or (C) or the offense of aggravated robbery under Section 29.03, Penal Code, against another student, without regard to whether the conduct occurs on or off of school property or while attending a school-sponsored or school-related activity on or off of school property.

(c) A student may be expelled if the student, while placed in an alternative education program for disciplinary reasons, continues to engage in serious or persistent misbehavior that violates the district's student code of conduct.

(d) A student shall be expelled if the student engages in conduct that contains the elements of any offense listed in Subsection (a), and may be expelled if the student engages in conduct that contains the elements of any offense listed in Subsection (b)(2)(C), against any employee or volunteer in retaliation for or as a result of the person's employment or association with a school district, without regard to whether the conduct occurs on or off of school property or while attending a school-sponsored or school-related activity on or off of school property.

(e) In accordance with 20 U.S.C. Section 7151, a local educational agency, including a school district, home-rule school district, or open-enrollment charter school, shall expel a student who brings a firearm, as defined by 18 U.S.C. Section 921, to school. The student must be expelled from the student's regular campus for a period of at least one year, except that:

    (1) the superintendent or other chief administrative officer of the school district or of the other local educational agency, as defined by 20 U. S.C. Section 7801, may modify the length of the expulsion in the case of an individual student;

    (2) the district or other local educational agency shall provide educational services to an expelled student in a disciplinary alternative education program as provided by Section 37.008 if the student is younger than 10 years of age on the date of expulsion; and

    (3) the district or other local educational agency may provide educational services to an expelled student who is 10 years of age or older in a disciplinary alternative education program as provided in Section 37.008.

(f) A student who engages in conduct that contains the elements of the offense of criminal mischief under Section 28.03, Penal Code, may be expelled at the district's discretion if the conduct is punishable as a felony under that section. The student shall be referred to the authorized officer of the juvenile court regardless of whether the student is expelled.

(g) In addition to any notice required under Article 15.27, Code of Criminal Procedure, a school district shall inform each educator who has responsibility for, or is under the direction and supervision of an educator who has responsibility for, the instruction of a student who has engaged in any violation listed in this section of the student's misconduct. Each educator shall keep the information received under this subsection confidential from any person not entitled to the information under this subsection, except that the educator may share the information with the student's parent or guardian as provided for by state or federal law. The State Board for Educator Certification may revoke or suspend the certification of an educator who intentionally violates this subsection.

(h) Subject to Subsection (e), notwithstanding any other provision of this section, a student who is younger than 10 years of age may not be expelled for engaging in conduct described by this section.

(i) A student who engages in conduct described by Subsection (a) may be expelled from school by the district in which the student attends school if the student engages in that conduct:

(1) on school property of another district in this state; or

(2) while attending a school-sponsored or school-related activity of a school in another district in this state.

(j) A student may not be expelled solely on the basis of the student's use, exhibition, or possession of a firearm that occurs:

(1) at an approved target range facility that is not located on a school campus; and

(2) while participating in or preparing for a school-sponsored shooting sports competition or a shooting sports educational activity that is sponsored or supported by the Parks and Wildlife Department or a shooting sports sanctioning organization working with the department.

(k) Subsection (k) does not authorize a student to bring a firearm on school property to participate in or prepare for a school-sponsored shooting sports competition or a shooting sports educational activity described by that subsection.

Added by Acts 1995, 74th Leg., ch. 260, Sec. 1, eff. May 30, 1995. Amended by Acts 1997, 75th Leg., ch. 1015, Sec. 5, eff. June 19, 1997; Acts 1999, 76th Leg., ch. 542, Sec. 1, eff. Aug. 30, 1999; Acts 2001, 77th Leg., ch. 486, Sec. 2, eff. June 11, 2001; Acts 2003, 78th Leg., ch. 225, Sec. 1, eff. June 18, 2003; Acts 2003, 78th Leg., ch. 443, Sec. 1, eff. June 20, 2003; Acts 2003, 78th Leg., ch. 1055, Sec. 10, eff. June 20, 2003.
Amended by:
Acts 2005, 79th Leg., Ch. 504, Sec. 4, eff. June 17, 2005.
Acts 2005, 79th Leg., Ch. 728, Sec. 5.004, eff. September 1, 2005.
Acts 2007, 80th Leg., R.S., Ch. 593, Sec. 3.26, eff. September 1, 2007.
Acts 2009, 81st Leg., R.S., Ch. 338, Sec. 1, eff. June 19, 2009.

Sec. 37.008. Disciplinary Alternative Education Programs.

(a) Each school district shall provide a disciplinary alternative education program that:

  (1) is provided in a setting other than a student's regular classroom;

  (2) is located on or off of a regular school campus;

  (3) provides for the students who are assigned to the disciplinary alternative education program to be separated from students who are not assigned to the program;

  (4) focuses on English language arts, mathematics, science, history, and self-discipline;

  (5) provides for students' educational and behavioral needs;

  (6) provides supervision and counseling;

  (7) employs only teachers who meet all certification requirements established under Subchapter B, Chapter 21; and

  (8) provides not less than the minimum amount of instructional time per day required by Section 25.082(a).

(a-1) The agency shall adopt minimum standards for the operation of disciplinary alternative education programs, including standards relating to:

  (1) student/teacher ratios;

  (2) student health and safety;

  (3) reporting of abuse, neglect, or exploitation of students;

  (4) training for teachers in behavior management and safety procedures; and

  (5) planning for a student's transition from a disciplinary alternative education program to a regular campus.

(b) A disciplinary alternative education program may provide for a student's transfer to:

  (1) a different campus;

  (2) a school-community guidance center; or

  (3) a community-based alternative school.

(c) An off-campus disciplinary alternative education program is not subject to a requirement imposed by this title, other than a limitation on liability, a reporting requirement, or a requirement imposed by this chapter or by Chapter 39.

(d) A school district may provide a disciplinary alternative education program jointly with one or more other districts.

(e) Each school district shall cooperate with government agencies and community organizations that provide services in the district to students placed in a disciplinary alternative education program.

(f) A student removed to a disciplinary alternative education program is counted in computing the average daily attendance of students in the district for the student's time in actual attendance in the program.

(g) A school district shall allocate to a disciplinary alternative education program the same expenditure per student attending the disciplinary alternative education program, including federal, state, and local funds, that would be allocated to the student's school if the student were attending the student's regularly assigned education program, including a special education program.

(h) A school district may not place a student, other than a student suspended as provided under Section 37.005 or expelled as provided under Section 37.007, in an unsupervised setting as a result of conduct for which a student may be placed in a disciplinary alternative education program.

(i) On request of a school district, a regional education service center may provide to the district information on developing a disciplinary alternative education program that takes into consideration the district's size, wealth, and existing facilities in determining the program best suited to the district.

(j) If a student placed in a disciplinary alternative education program enrolls in another school district before the expiration of the period of placement, the board of trustees of the district requiring the placement shall provide to the district in which the student enrolls, at the same time other records of the student are provided, a copy of the placement order. The district in which the student enrolls shall inform each educator who will have responsibility for, or will be under the direction and supervision of an educator who will have responsibility for, the instruction of the student of the contents of the placement order. Each educator shall keep the information received under this subsection confidential from any person not entitled to the information under this subsection, except that the educator may share the information with the student's parent or guardian as provided for by state or federal law. The district in which the student enrolls may continue the disciplinary alternative education program placement under the terms of the order or may allow the student to attend regular classes without completing the period of placement. A district may take any action permitted by this subsection if:

   (1) the student was placed in a disciplinary alternative education program by an open-enrollment charter school under Section 12.131 and the charter school provides to the district a copy of the placement order; or

    (2) the student was placed in a disciplinary alternative education program by a school district in another state and:

        (A) the out-of-state district provides to the district a copy of the placement order; and

        (B) the grounds for the placement by the out-of-state district are grounds for placement in the district in which the student is enrolling.

(j-1) If a student was placed in a disciplinary alternative education program by a school district in another state for a period that exceeds one year and a school district in this state in which the student enrolls continues the placement under Subsection (j), the district shall reduce the period of the placement so that the aggregate period does not exceed one year unless, after a review, the district determines that:

    (1) the student is a threat to the safety of other students or to district employees; or

    (2) extended placement is in the best interest of the student.

(k) A program of educational and support services may be provided to a student and the student's parents when the offense involves drugs or alcohol as specified under Section 37.006 or 37.007. A disciplinary alternative education program that provides chemical dependency treatment services must be licensed under Chapter 464, Health and Safety Code.

(l) A school district is required to provide in the district's disciplinary alternative education program a course necessary to fulfill a student's high school graduation requirements only as provided by this subsection. A school district shall offer a student removed to a disciplinary alternative education program an opportunity to complete coursework before the beginning of the next school year. The school district may provide the student an opportunity to complete coursework through any method available, including a correspondence course, distance learning, or summer school. The district may not charge the student for a course provided under this subsection.

(m) The commissioner shall adopt rules necessary to evaluate annually the performance of each district's disciplinary alternative education program established under this subchapter. The evaluation required by this section shall be based on indicators defined by the commissioner, but must include student performance on assessment instruments required under Sections 39.023(a) and (c). Academically, the mission of disciplinary alternative education programs shall be to enable students to perform at grade level.

(m-1) The commissioner shall develop a process for evaluating a school district disciplinary alternative education program electronically. The commissioner shall also develop a system and standards for review of the evaluation or use systems already available at the agency. The system must be designed to identify districts that are at high risk of having inaccurate disciplinary alternative education program data or of failing to comply with disciplinary alternative education program requirements. The commissioner shall notify the board of trustees of a district of any objection the commissioner has to the district's disciplinary alternative education program data or of a violation of a law or rule revealed by the data, including any violation of disciplinary alternative education program requirements, or of any recommendation by the commissioner concerning the data. If the data reflect that a penal law has been violated, the commissioner shall notify the county attorney, district attorney, or criminal district attorney, as appropriate, and the attorney general. The commissioner is entitled to access to all district records the commissioner considers necessary or appropriate for the review, analysis, or approval of disciplinary alternative education program data.

Added by Acts 1995, 74th Leg., ch. 260, Sec. 1, eff. May 30, 1995. Amended by Acts 1997, 75th Leg., ch. 1015, Sec. 6, eff. June 19, 1997; Acts 1999, 76th Leg., ch. 396, Sec. 2.16, eff. Sept. 1, 1999; Acts 1999, 76th Leg., ch. 1112, Sec. 1, eff. June 18, 1999; Acts 2003, 78th Leg., ch. 631, Sec. 2, eff. June 20, 2003; Acts 2003, 78th Leg., ch. 1055, Sec. 11, eff. June 20, 2003.
Amended by:
Acts 2005, 79th Leg., Ch. 504, Sec. 5, eff. June 17, 2005.
Acts 2007, 80th Leg., R.S., Ch. 1171, Sec. 1, eff. June 15, 2007.

Sec. 37.0081. Expulsion and Placement of Certain Students in Alternative Settings.

(a) Subject to Subsection (h), but notwithstanding any other provision of this subchapter, the board of trustees of a school district, or the board's designee, after an opportunity for a hearing may expel a student and elect to place the student in an alternative setting as provided by Subsection (a-1) if:

  (1) the student:

   (A) has received deferred prosecution under Section 53.03, Family Code, for conduct defined as a felony offense in Title 5, Penal Code;

   (B) has been found by a court or jury to have engaged in delinquent conduct under Section 54.03, Family Code, for conduct defined as a felony offense in Title 5, Penal Code;

   (C) is charged with engaging in conduct defined as a felony offense in Title 5, Penal Code;

(D) has been referred to a juvenile court for allegedly engaging in delinquent conduct under Section 54.03, Family Code, for conduct defined as a felony offense in Title 5, Penal Code;

(E) has received probation or deferred adjudication for a felony offense under Title 5, Penal Code;

(F) has been convicted of a felony offense under Title 5, Penal Code; or

(G) has been arrested for or charged with a felony offense under Title 5, Penal Code; and

(2) the board or the board's designee determines that the student's presence in the regular classroom:

(A) threatens the safety of other students or teachers;

(B) will be detrimental to the educational process; or

(C) is not in the best interests of the district's students.

(a-1) The student must be placed in:

(1) a juvenile justice alternative education program, if the school district is located in a county that operates a juvenile justice alternative education program or the school district contracts with the juvenile board of another county for the provision of a juvenile justice alternative education program; or

(2) a disciplinary alternative education program.

(b) Any decision of the board of trustees or the board's designee under this section is final and may not be appealed.

(c) The board of trustees or the board's designee may expel the student and order placement in accordance with this section regardless of:

(1) the date on which the student's conduct occurred;

(2) the location at which the conduct occurred;

(3) whether the conduct occurred while the student was enrolled in the district; or

(4) whether the student has successfully completed any court disposition requirements imposed in connection with the conduct.

(d) Notwithstanding Section 37.009(c) or (d) or any other provision of this subchapter, a student expelled and ordered placed in an alternative setting by the board of trustees or the board's designee is subject to that placement until:

(1) the student graduates from high school;

(2) the charges described by Subsection (a)(1) are dismissed or reduced to a misdemeanor offense; or

(3) the student completes the term of the placement or is assigned to another program.

(e) A student placed in an alternative setting in accordance with this section is entitled to the periodic review prescribed by Section 37.009(e).

(f) Subsection (d) continues to apply to the student if the student transfers to another school district in the state.

(g) The board of trustees shall reimburse a juvenile justice alternative education program in which a student is placed under this section for the actual cost incurred each day for the student while the student is enrolled in the program. For purposes of this subsection:

(1) the actual cost incurred each day for the student is determined by the juvenile board of the county operating the program; and

(2) the juvenile board shall determine the actual cost each day of the program based on the board's annual audit.

(h) To the extent of a conflict between this section and Section 37.007, Section 37.007 prevails.

Added by Acts 2003, 78th Leg., ch. 1055, Sec. 12, eff. June 20, 2003.
Amended by:
Acts 2007, 80th Leg., R.S., Ch. 1240, Sec. 1, eff. June 15, 2007.

Sec. 37.0082. Assessment of Academic Growth of Students in Disciplinary Alternative Education Programs.

(a) To assess a student's academic growth during placement in a disciplinary alternative education program, a school district shall administer to a student placed in a program for a period of 90 school days or longer an assessment instrument approved by the commissioner for that purpose. The instrument shall be administered:

(1) initially on placement of the student in the program; and

(2) subsequently on the date of the student's departure from the program, or as near that date as possible.

(b) The assessment instrument required by this section:

(1) must be designed to assess at least a student's basic skills in reading and mathematics;

(2) may be:
- (A) comparable to any assessment instrument generally administered to students placed in juvenile justice alternative education programs for a similar purpose; or
- (B) based on an appropriate alternative assessment instrument developed by the agency to measure student academic growth; and

(3) is in addition to the assessment instruments required to be administered under Chapter 39.

(c) The commissioner shall adopt rules necessary to implement this section.

Added by Acts 2007, 80th Leg., R.S., Ch. 1240, Sec. 2, eff. June 15, 2007.

Sec. 37.009. Conference; Hearing; Review.

(a) Not later than the third class day after the day on which a student is removed from class by the teacher under Section 37.002(b) or (d) or by the school principal or other appropriate administrator under Section 37.001(a)(2) or 37.006, the principal or other appropriate administrator shall schedule a conference among the principal or other appropriate administrator, a parent or guardian of the student, the teacher removing the student from class, if any, and the student. At the conference, the student is entitled to written or oral notice of the reasons for the removal, an explanation of the basis for the removal, and an opportunity to respond to the reasons for the removal. The student may not be returned to the regular classroom pending the conference. Following the conference, and whether or not each requested person is in attendance after valid attempts to require the person's attendance, the principal shall order the placement of the student for a period consistent with the student code of conduct. If school district policy allows a student to appeal to the board of trustees or the board's designee a decision of the principal or other appropriate administrator, other than an expulsion under Section 37.007, the decision of the board or the board's designee is final and may not be appealed. If the period of the placement is inconsistent with the guidelines included in the student code of conduct under Section 37.001(a)(5), the order must give notice of the inconsistency. The period of the placement may not exceed one year unless, after a review, the district determines that:

(1) the student is a threat to the safety of other students or to district employees; or

(2) extended placement is in the best interest of the student.

(b) If a student's placement in a disciplinary alternative education program is to extend beyond 60 days or the end of the next grading period, whichever is earlier, a student's parent or guardian is entitled to notice of and an opportunity to participate in a proceeding before the board of trustees of the school district or the board's designee, as provided by policy of the board of trustees of the district. Any decision of the board or the board's designee under this subsection is final and may not be appealed.

(c) Before it may place a student in a disciplinary alternative education program for a period that extends beyond the end of the school year, the board or the board's designee must determine that:

   (1) the student's presence in the regular classroom program or at the student's regular campus presents a danger of physical harm to the student or to another individual; or

   (2) the student has engaged in serious or persistent misbehavior that violates the district's student code of conduct.

(d) The board or the board's designee shall set a term for a student's placement in a disciplinary alternative education program. If the period of the placement is inconsistent with the guidelines included in the student code of conduct under Section 37.001(a)(5), the order must give notice of the inconsistency. The period of the placement may not exceed one year unless, after a review, the district determines that:

   (1) the student is a threat to the safety of other students or to district employees; or

   (2) extended placement is in the best interest of the student.

(e) A student placed in a disciplinary alternative education program shall be provided a review of the student's status, including a review of the student's academic status, by the board's designee at intervals not to exceed 120 days. In the case of a high school student, the board's designee, with the student's parent or guardian, shall review the student's progress towards meeting high school graduation requirements and shall establish a specific graduation plan for the student. The district is not required under this subsection to provide a course in the district's disciplinary alternative education program except as required by Section 37.008(l). At the review, the student or the student's parent or guardian must be given the opportunity to present arguments for the student's return to the regular classroom or campus. The student may not be returned to the classroom of the teacher who removed the student without that teacher's consent. The teacher may not be coerced to consent.

(f) Before a student may be expelled under Section 37.007, the board or the board's designee must provide the student a hearing at which the student is afforded appropriate due process as required by the federal constitution and which the student's parent or guardian is invited, in writing, to attend. At the hearing, the student is entitled to be represented by the student's parent or guardian or another adult who can provide guidance to the student and who is not an employee of the school district. If the school district makes a good-faith effort to inform the student and the student's parent or guardian of the time and place of the hearing, the district may hold the hearing regardless of whether the student, the student's parent or guardian, or another adult representing the student attends. If the decision to expel a student is made by the board's designee, the decision may be appealed to the board. The decision of the board may be appealed by trial de novo to a district court of the county in which the school district's central administrative office is located.

(g) The board or the board's designee shall deliver to the student and the student's parent or guardian a copy of the order placing the student in a disciplinary alternative education program under Section 37.001, 37.002, or 37.006 or expelling the student under Section 37.007.

(h) If the period of an expulsion is inconsistent with the guidelines included in the student code of conduct under Section 37.001(a)(5), the order must give notice of the inconsistency. The period of an expulsion may not exceed one year unless, after a review, the district determines that:

  (1) the student is a threat to the safety of other students or to district employees; or

  (2) extended placement is in the best interest of the student. After a school district notifies the parents or guardians of a student that the student has been expelled, the parent or guardian shall provide adequate supervision of the student during the period of expulsion.

(i) If a student withdraws from the district before an order for placement in a disciplinary alternative education program or expulsion is entered under this section, the principal or board, as appropriate, may complete the proceedings and enter an order. If the student subsequently enrolls in the district during the same or subsequent school year, the district may enforce the order at that time except for any period of the placement or expulsion that has been served by the student on enrollment in another district that honored the order. If the principal or board fails to enter an order after the student withdraws, the next district in which the student enrolls may complete the proceedings and enter an order.

(j) If, during the term of a placement or expulsion ordered under this section, a student engages in additional conduct for which placement in a disciplinary alternative education program or expulsion is required or permitted, additional proceedings may be conducted under this section regarding that conduct and the principal or board, as appropriate, may enter an additional order as a result of those proceedings.

Added by Acts 1995, 74th Leg., ch. 260, Sec. 1, eff. May 30, 1995. Amended by Acts 1997, 75th Leg., ch. 1015, Sec. 7, eff. June 19, 1997; Acts 2003, 78th Leg., ch. 1055, Sec. 13, eff. June 20, 2003.

Sec. 37.0091. Notice to Noncustodial Parent.

(a) A noncustodial parent may request in writing that a school district or school, for the remainder of the school year in which the request is received, provide that parent with a copy of any written notification relating to student misconduct under Section 37.006 or 37.007 that is generally provided by the district or school to a student's parent or guardian.

(b) A school district or school may not unreasonably deny a request authorized by Subsection (a).

(c) Notwithstanding any other provision of this section, a school district or school shall comply with any applicable court order of which the district or school has knowledge.

Added by Acts 2003, 78th Leg., ch. 1055, Sec. 14, eff. June 20, 2003.

Sec. 37.010. Court Involvement.

(a) Not later than the second business day after the date a hearing is held under Section 37.009, the board of trustees of a school district or the board's designee shall deliver a copy of the order placing a student in a disciplinary alternative education program under Section 37.006 or expelling a student under Section 37.007 and any information required under Section 52.04, Family Code, to the authorized officer of the juvenile court in the county in which the student resides. In a county that operates a program under Section 37.011, an expelled student shall to the extent provided by law or by the memorandum of understanding immediately attend the educational program from the date of expulsion, except that in a county with a population greater than 125,000, every expelled student who is not detained or receiving treatment under an order of the juvenile court must be enrolled in an educational program.

(b) If a student is expelled under Section 37.007(c), the board or its designee shall refer the student to the authorized officer of the juvenile court for appropriate proceedings under Title 3, Family Code.

(c) Unless the juvenile board for the county in which the district's central administrative office is located has entered into a memorandum of understanding with the district's board of trustees concerning the juvenile probation department's role in supervising and providing other support services for students in disciplinary alternative education programs, a court may not order a student expelled under Section 37.007 to attend a regular classroom, a regular campus, or a school district disciplinary alternative education program as a condition of probation.

(d) Unless the juvenile board for the county in which the district's central administrative office is located has entered into a memorandum of understanding as described by Subsection (c), if a court orders a student to attend a disciplinary alternative education program as a condition of probation once during a school year and the student is referred to juvenile court again during that school year, the juvenile court may not order the student to attend a disciplinary alternative education program in a district without the district's consent until the student has successfully completed any sentencing requirements the court imposes.

(e) Any placement in a disciplinary alternative education program by a court under this section must prohibit the student from attending or participating in school-sponsored or school-related activities.

(f) If a student is expelled under Section 37.007, on the recommendation of the committee established under Section 37.003 or on its own initiative, a district may readmit the student while the student is completing any court disposition requirements the court imposes. After the student has successfully completed any court disposition requirements the court imposes, including conditions of a deferred prosecution ordered by the court, or such conditions required by the prosecutor or probation department, if the student meets the requirements for admission into the public schools established by this title, a district may not refuse to admit the student, but the district may place the student in the disciplinary alternative education program. Notwithstanding Section 37.002(d), the student may not be returned to the classroom of the teacher under whose supervision the offense occurred without that teacher's consent. The teacher may not be coerced to consent.

(g) If an expelled student enrolls in another school district, the board of trustees of the district that expelled the student shall provide to the district in which the student enrolls, at the same time other records of the student are provided, a copy of the expulsion order and the referral to the authorized officer of the juvenile court. The district in which the student enrolls may continue the expulsion under the terms of the order, may place the student in a disciplinary alternative education program for the period specified by the expulsion order, or may allow the student to attend regular classes without completing the period of expulsion. A district may take any action permitted by this subsection if the student was expelled by a school district in another state if:

(1) the out-of-state district provides to the district a copy of the expulsion order; and

(2) the grounds for the expulsion are also grounds for expulsion in the district in which the student is enrolling.

(g-1) If a student was expelled by a school district in another state for a period that exceeds one year and a school district in this state continues the expulsion or places the student in a disciplinary alternative education program under Subsection (g), the district shall reduce the period of the expulsion or placement so that the aggregate period does not exceed one year unless, after a review, the district determines that:

(1) the student is a threat to the safety of other students or to district employees; or

(2) extended placement is in the best interest of the student.

(h) A person is not liable in civil damages for a referral to juvenile court as required by this section.

Added by Acts 1995, 74th Leg., ch. 260, Sec. 1, eff. May 30, 1995. Amended by Acts 1997, 75th Leg., ch. 1015, Sec. 8, eff. June 19, 1997; Acts 2003, 78th Leg., ch. 1055, Sec. 15, eff. June 20, 2003.

Sec. 37.011. Juvenile Justice Alternative Education Program.

(a) The juvenile board of a county with a population greater than 125,000 shall develop a juvenile justice alternative education program, subject to the approval of the Texas Juvenile Probation Commission. The juvenile board of a county with a population of 125,000 or less may develop a juvenile justice alternative education program. For the purposes of this subchapter, only a disciplinary alternative education program operated under the authority of a juvenile board of a county is considered a juvenile justice alternative education program. A juvenile justice alternative education program in a county with a population of 125,000 or less:

(1) is not required to be approved by the Texas Juvenile Probation Commission; and

(2) is not subject to Subsection (c), (d), (f), or (g).

(a-1) For purposes of this section and Section 37.010(a), a county with a population greater than 125,000 is considered to be a county with a population of 125,000 or less if:

    (1) the county had a population of 125,000 or less according to the 2000 federal census; and

    (2) the juvenile board of the county enters into, with the approval of the Texas Juvenile Probation Commission, a memorandum of understanding with each school district within the county that:

        (A) outlines the responsibilities of the board and school districts in minimizing the number of students expelled without receiving alternative educational services; and

        (B) includes the coordination procedures required by Section 37.013.

(b) If a student admitted into the public schools of a school district under Section 25.001(b) is expelled from school for conduct for which expulsion is required under Section 37.007(a), (d), or (e), the juvenile court, the juvenile board, or the juvenile board's designee, as appropriate, shall:

    (1) if the student is placed on probation under Section 54.04, Family Code, order the student to attend the juvenile justice alternative education program in the county in which the student resides from the date of disposition as a condition of probation, unless the child is placed in a post-adjudication treatment facility;

    (2) if the student is placed on deferred prosecution under Section 53.03, Family Code, by the court, prosecutor, or probation department, require the student to immediately attend the juvenile justice alternative education program in the county in which the student resides for a period not to exceed six months as a condition of the deferred prosecution;

    (3) in determining the conditions of the deferred prosecution or court-ordered probation, consider the length of the school district's expulsion order for the student; and

    (4) provide timely educational services to the student in the juvenile justice alternative education program in the county in which the student resides, regardless of the student's age or whether the juvenile court has jurisdiction over the student.

(b-1) Subsection (b)(4) does not require that educational services be provided to a student who is not entitled to admission into the public schools of a school district under Section 25.001(b).

(c) A juvenile justice alternative education program shall adopt a student code of conduct in accordance with Section 37.001.

(d) A juvenile justice alternative education program must focus on English language arts, mathematics, science, social studies, and self-discipline. Each school district shall consider course credit earned by a student while in a juvenile justice alternative education program as credit earned in a district school. Each program shall administer assessment instruments under Subchapter B, Chapter 39, and shall offer a high school equivalency program. The juvenile board or the board's designee, with the parent or guardian of each student, shall regularly review the student's academic progress. In the case of a high school student, the board or the board's designee, with the student's parent or guardian, shall review the student's progress towards meeting high school graduation requirements and shall establish a specific graduation plan for the student. The program is not required to provide a course necessary to fulfill a student's high school graduation requirements other than a course specified by this subsection.

(e) A juvenile justice alternative education program may be provided in a facility owned by a school district. A school district may provide personnel and services for a juvenile justice alternative education program under a contract with the juvenile board.

(f) A juvenile justice alternative education program must operate at least seven hours per day and 180 days per year, except that a program may apply to the Texas Juvenile Probation Commission for a waiver of the 180-day requirement. The commission may not grant a waiver to a program under this subsection for a number of days that exceeds the highest number of instructional days waived by the commissioner during the same school year for a school district served by the program.

(g) A juvenile justice alternative education program shall be subject to a written operating policy developed by the local juvenile justice board and submitted to the Texas Juvenile Probation Commission for review and comment. A juvenile justice alternative education program is not subject to a requirement imposed by this title, other than a reporting requirement or a requirement imposed by this chapter or by Chapter 39.

(h) Academically, the mission of juvenile justice alternative education programs shall be to enable students to perform at grade level. For purposes of accountability under Chapter 39, a student enrolled in a juvenile justice alternative education program is reported as if the student were enrolled at the student's assigned campus in the student's regularly assigned education program, including a special education program. Annually the Texas

Juvenile Probation Commission, with the agreement of the commissioner, shall develop and implement a system of accountability consistent with Chapter 39, where appropriate, to assure that students make progress toward grade level while attending a juvenile justice alternative education program. The Texas Juvenile Probation Commission shall adopt rules for the distribution of funds appropriated under this section to juvenile boards in counties required to establish juvenile justice alternative education programs. Except as determined by the commissioner, a student served by a juvenile justice alternative education program on the basis of an expulsion required under Section 37.007(a), (d), or (e) is not eligible for Foundation School Program funding under Chapter 42 or 31 if the juvenile justice alternative education program receives funding from the Texas Juvenile Probation Commission under this subchapter.

(i) A student transferred to a juvenile justice alternative education program must participate in the program for the full period ordered by the juvenile court unless the student's school district agrees to accept the student before the date ordered by the juvenile court. The juvenile court may not order a period of transfer under this section that exceeds the term of any probation ordered by the juvenile court.

(j) In relation to the development and operation of a juvenile justice alternative education program, a juvenile board and a county and a commissioners court are immune from liability to the same extent as a school district, and the juvenile board's or county's professional employees and volunteers are immune from liability to the same extent as a school district's professional employees and volunteers.

(k) Each school district in a county with a population greater than 125,000 and the county juvenile board shall annually enter into a joint memorandum of understanding that:

(1) outlines the responsibilities of the juvenile board concerning the establishment and operation of a juvenile justice alternative education program under this section;

(2) defines the amount and conditions on payments from the school district to the juvenile board for students of the school district served in the juvenile justice alternative education program whose placement was not made on the basis of an expulsion required under Section 37.007(a), (d), or (e);

(3) identifies those categories of conduct that the school district has defined in its student code of conduct as constituting serious or

persistent misbehavior for which a student may be placed in the juvenile justice alternative education program;

(4) identifies and requires a timely placement and specifies a term of placement for expelled students for whom the school district has received a notice under Section 52.041(d), Family Code;

(5) establishes services for the transitioning of expelled students to the school district prior to the completion of the student's placement in the juvenile justice alternative education program;

(6) establishes a plan that provides transportation services for students placed in the juvenile justice alternative education program;

(7) establishes the circumstances and conditions under which a juvenile may be allowed to remain in the juvenile justice alternative education program setting once the juvenile is no longer under juvenile court jurisdiction; and

(8) establishes a plan to address special education services required by law.

(l) The school district shall be responsible for providing an immediate educational program to students who engage in behavior resulting in expulsion under Section 37.007(b), (c), and (f) but who are not eligible for admission into the juvenile justice alternative education program in accordance with the memorandum of understanding required under this section. The school district may provide the program or the school district may contract with a county juvenile board, a private provider, or one or more other school districts to provide the program. The memorandum of understanding shall address the circumstances under which such students who continue to engage in serious or persistent misbehavior shall be admitted into the juvenile justice alternative education program.

(m) Each school district in a county with a population greater than 125,000 and the county juvenile board shall adopt a joint memorandum of understanding as required by this section not later than September 1 of each school year.

(n) If a student who is ordered to attend a juvenile justice alternative education program moves from one county to another, the juvenile court may request the juvenile justice alternative education program in the county to which the student moves to provide educational services to the student in accordance with the local memorandum of understanding between the school district and juvenile board in the receiving county.

(o) In relation to the development and operation of a juvenile justice alternative education program, a juvenile board and a county and a commissioners court are immune from liability to the same extent as a school district, and the juvenile board's or county's employees and volunteers are immune from liability to the same extent as a school district's employees and volunteers.

(p) If a district elects to contract with the juvenile board for placement in the juvenile justice alternative education program of students expelled under Section 37.007(b), (c), and (f) and the juvenile board and district are unable to reach an agreement in the memorandum of understanding, either party may request that the issues of dispute be referred to a binding arbitration process that uses a qualified alternative dispute resolution arbitrator in which each party will pay its pro rata share of the arbitration costs. Each party must submit its final proposal to the arbitrator. If the parties cannot agree on an arbitrator, the juvenile board shall select an arbitrator, the school districts shall select an arbitrator, and those two arbitrators shall select an arbitrator who will decide the issues in dispute. An arbitration decision issued under this subsection is enforceable in a court in the county in which the juvenile justice alternative education program is located. Any decision by an arbitrator concerning the amount of the funding for a student who is expelled and attending a juvenile justice alternative education program must provide an amount sufficient based on operation of the juvenile justice alternative education program in accordance with this chapter. In determining the amount to be paid by a school district for an expelled student enrolled in a juvenile justice alternative education program, the arbitrator shall consider the relevant factors, including evidence of:

(1) the actual average total per student expenditure in the district's alternative education setting;

(2) the expected per student cost in the juvenile justice alternative education program as described and agreed on in the memorandum of understanding and in compliance with this chapter; and

(3) the costs necessary to achieve the accountability goals under this chapter.

(q) In accordance with rules adopted by the board of trustees for the Teacher Retirement System of Texas, a certified educator employed by a juvenile board in a juvenile justice alternative education program shall be eligible for membership and participation in the system to the same extent that an employee of a public school district is eligible. The juvenile board shall make any contribution that otherwise would be the responsibility of the school district if the person were employed by the school district, and the state shall make any contribution to the same extent as if the person were employed by a school district.

Added by Acts 1995, 74th Leg., ch. 260, Sec. 1, eff. May 30, 1995. Amended by Acts 1997, 75th Leg., ch. 1015, Sec. 9, eff. June 19, 1997; Acts 1997, 75th Leg., ch. 1282, Sec. 1, eff. June 20, 1997; Acts 1999, 76th Leg., ch. 396, Sec. 2.17, eff. Sept. 1, 1999; Acts 2001, 77th Leg., ch. 1225, Sec. 2, eff. June 15, 2001; Acts 2003, 78th Leg., ch. 1055, Sec. 16, eff. June 20, 2003.
Amended by:
Acts 2009, 81st Leg., R.S., Ch. 376, Sec. 1, eff. June 19, 2009.

Sec. 37.012. Funding of Juvenile Justice Alternative Education Programs.

(a) Subject to Section 37.011(n), the school district in which a student is enrolled on the date the student is expelled for conduct for which expulsion is permitted but not required under Section 37.007 shall, if the student is served by the juvenile justice alternative education program, provide funding to the juvenile board for the portion of the school year for which the juvenile justice alternative education program provides educational services in an amount determined by the memorandum of understanding under Section 37.011(k)(2).

(b) Funds received under this section must be expended on juvenile justice alternative education programs.

(c) The Office of State-Federal Relations shall assist a local juvenile probation department in identifying additional state or federal funds to assist local juvenile probation departments conducting educational or job training programs within juvenile justice alternative education programs.

(d) A school district is not required to provide funding to a juvenile board for a student who is assigned by a court to a juvenile justice alternative education program but who has not been expelled.

(e) Except as otherwise authorized by law, a juvenile justice alternative education program may not require a student or the parent or guardian of a student to pay any fee, including an entrance fee or supply fee, for participating in the program.

Added by Acts 1995, 74th Leg., ch. 260, Sec. 1, eff. May 30, 1995. Amended by Acts 1997, 75th Leg., ch. 1015, Sec. 10, eff. June 19, 1997; Acts 2003, 78th Leg., ch. 1055, Sec. 17, eff. June 20, 2003.
Amended by:
Acts 2005, 79th Leg., Ch. 964, Sec. 1, eff. June 18, 2005.

Sec. 37.013. Coordination Between School Districts and Juvenile Boards.

The board of trustees of the school district or the board's designee shall at the call of the president of the board of trustees regularly meet with the juvenile board for the county in which the district's central administrative office is located or the juvenile board's designee concerning supervision and rehabilitative services appropriate for expelled students and students assigned to disciplinary alternative education programs. Matters for discussion shall include service by probation officers at the disciplinary alternative education program site, recruitment of volunteers to serve as mentors and provide tutoring services, and coordination with other social service agencies.

Added by Acts 1995, 74th Leg., ch. 260, Sec. 1, eff. May 30, 1995. Amended by Acts 2003, 78th Leg., ch. 1055, Sec. 18, eff. June 20, 2003.

Sec. 37.014. Court-Related Children—Liaison Officers.

Each school district shall appoint at least one educator to act as liaison officer for court-related children who are enrolled in the district. The liaison officer shall provide counseling and services for each court-related child and the child's parents to establish or reestablish normal attendance and progress of the child in the school. Added by Acts 1995, 74th Leg., ch. 260, Sec. 1, eff. May 30, 1995.

Sec. 37.015. Reports to Local Law Enforcement; Liability.

(a) The principal of a public or private primary or secondary school, or a person designated by the principal under Subsection (d), shall notify any school district police department and the police department of the municipality in which the school is located or, if the school is not in a municipality, the sheriff of the county in which the school is located if the principal has reasonable grounds to believe that any of the following activities occur in school, on school property, or at a school-sponsored or school-related activity on or off school property, whether or not the activity is investigated by school security officers:

  (1) conduct that may constitute an offense listed under Section 508.149, Government Code;

  (2) deadly conduct under Section 22.05, Penal Code;

  (3) a terroristic threat under Section 22.07, Penal Code;

  (4) the use, sale, or possession of a controlled substance, drug paraphernalia, or marihuana under Chapter 481, Health and Safety Code;

  (5) the possession of any of the weapons or devices listed under Sections 46.01(1)-(14) or Section 46.01(16), Penal Code;

  (6) conduct that may constitute a criminal offense under Section 71.02, Penal Code; or

  (7) conduct that may constitute a criminal offense for which a student may be expelled under Section 37.007(a), (d), or (e).

(b) A person who makes a notification under this section shall include the name and address of each student the person believes may have participated in the activity.

(c) A notification is not required under Subsection (a) if the person reasonably believes that the activity does not constitute a criminal offense.

(d) The principal of a public or private primary or secondary school may designate a school employee who is under the supervision of the principal to make the reports required by this section.

(e) The person who makes the notification required under Subsection (a) shall also notify each instructional or support employee of the school who has regular contact with a student whose conduct is the subject of the notice.

(f) A person is not liable in civil damages for reporting in good faith as required by this section.

Added by Acts 1995, 74th Leg., ch. 260, Sec. 1, eff. May 30, 1995. Amended by Acts 1997, 75th Leg., ch. 165, Sec. 12.05, eff. Sept. 1, 1997; Acts 2003, 78th Leg., ch. 1055, Sec. 19, eff. June 20, 2003.

Sec. 37.016. Report of Drug Offenses; Liability.

A teacher, school administrator, or school employee is not liable in civil damages for reporting to a school administrator or governmental authority, in the exercise of professional judgment within the scope of the teacher's, administrator's, or employee's duties, a student whom the teacher suspects of using, passing, or selling, on school property:

(1) marihuana or a controlled substance, as defined by Chapter 481, Health and Safety Code;

(2) a dangerous drug, as defined by Chapter 483, Health and Safety Code;

(3) an abusable glue or aerosol paint, as defined by Chapter 485, Health and Safety Code, or a volatile chemical, as listed in Chapter 484, Health and Safety Code, if the substance is used or sold for the purpose of inhaling its fumes or vapors; or

(4) an alcoholic beverage, as defined by Section 1.04, Alcoholic Beverage Code.

Added by Acts 1995, 74th Leg., ch. 260, Sec. 1, eff. May 30, 1995.

Sec. 37.017. Destruction Of Certain Records.

Information received by a school district under Article 15.27, Code of Criminal Procedure, may not be attached to the permanent academic file of the student who is the subject of the report. The school district shall destroy the information at the end of the school year in which the report was filed.

Added by Acts 1995, 74th Leg., ch. 260, Sec. 1, eff. May 30, 1995.

Sec. 37.018. Information for Educators.

Each school district shall provide each teacher and administrator with a copy of this subchapter and with a copy of the local policy relating to this subchapter. Added by Acts 1995, 74th Leg., ch. 260, Sec. 1, eff. May 30, 1995.

Sec. 37.019. Emergency Placement Or Expulsion.

(a) This subchapter does not prevent the principal or the principal's designee from ordering the immediate placement of a student in a disciplinary alternative education program if the principal or the principal's designee reasonably believes the student's behavior is so unruly, disruptive, or abusive that it seriously interferes with a teacher's ability to communicate effectively with the students in a class, with the ability of the student's classmates to learn, or with the operation of school or a school-sponsored activity.

(b) This subchapter does not prevent the principal or the principal's designee from ordering the immediate expulsion of a student if the principal or the principal's designee reasonably believes that action is necessary to protect persons or property from imminent harm.

(c) At the time of an emergency placement or expulsion, the student shall be given oral notice of the reason for the action. The reason must be a reason for which placement in a disciplinary alternative education program or expulsion may be made on a nonemergency basis. Within a reasonable time after the emergency placement or expulsion, but not later than the 10th day after the date of the placement or expulsion, the student shall be accorded the appropriate due process as required under Section 37.009. If the student subject to the emergency placement or expulsion is a student with disabilities who receives special education services, the emergency placement or expulsion is subject to federal law and regulations and must be consistent with the consequences that would apply under this subchapter to a student without a disability.

(d) A principal or principal's designee is not liable in civil damages for an emergency placement under this section.

Added by Acts 1995, 74th Leg., ch. 260, Sec. 1, eff. May 30, 1995. Amended by Acts 2001, 77th Leg., ch. 767, Sec. 7, eff. June 13, 2001; Acts 2003, 78th Leg., ch. 1055, Sec. 20, eff. June 20, 2003.

Sec. 37.020. Reports Relating to Expulsions and Disciplinary Alternative Education Program Placements.

(a) In the manner required by the commissioner, each school district shall annually report to the commissioner the information required by this section.

(b) For each placement in a disciplinary alternative education program established under Section 37.008, the district shall report:

(1) information identifying the student, including the student's race, sex, and date of birth, that will enable the agency to compare placement data with information collected through other reports;

(2) information indicating whether the placement was based on:

(A) conduct violating the student code of conduct adopted under Section 37.001;

(B) conduct for which a student may be removed from class under Section 37.002(b);

(C) conduct for which placement in a disciplinary alternative education program is required by Section 37.006; or

(D) conduct occurring while a student was enrolled in another district and for which placement in a disciplinary alternative education program is permitted by Section 37.008(j);

(3) the number of full or partial days the student was assigned to the program and the number of full or partial days the student attended the program; and

(4) the number of placements that were inconsistent with the guidelines included in the student code of conduct under Section 37.001(a)(5).

(c) For each expulsion under Section 37.007, the district shall report:

(1) information identifying the student, including the student's race, sex, and date of birth, that will enable the agency to compare placement data with information collected through other reports;

(2) information indicating whether the expulsion was based on:

(A) conduct for which expulsion is required under Section 37.007, including information specifically indicating whether a student was expelled on the basis of Section 37.007(e); or

(B) conduct for which expulsion is permitted under Section 37.007;

(3) the number of full or partial days the student was expelled;

(4) information indicating whether:

(A) the student was placed in a juvenile justice alternative education program under Section 37.011;

(B) the student was placed in a disciplinary alternative education program; or

(C) the student was not placed in a juvenile justice or other disciplinary alternative education program; and

(5) the number of expulsions that were inconsistent with the guidelines included in the student code of conduct under Section 37.001(a)(5).

Added by Acts 1997, 75th Leg., ch. 1015, Sec. 11, eff. June 19, 1997. Amended by Acts 2003, 78th Leg., ch. 1055, Sec. 21, eff. June 20, 2003.

Sec. 37.021. Opportunity to Complete Courses During In-School and Certain Other Placements.

(a) If a school district removes a student from the regular classroom and places the student in in-school suspension or another setting other than a disciplinary alternative education program, the district shall offer the student the opportunity to complete before the beginning of the next school year each course in which the student was enrolled at the time of the removal.

(b) The district may provide the opportunity to complete courses by any method available, including a correspondence course, distance learning, or summer school.

Added by Acts 2003, 78th Leg., ch. 1055, Sec. 22, eff. June 20, 2003.

Sec. 37.022. Notice of Disciplinary Action.

(a) In this section:
   (1) "Disciplinary action" means a suspension, expulsion, placement in an alternative education program, or other limitation in enrollment eligibility of a student by a district or school.
   (2) "District or school" includes an independent school district, a home-rule school district, a campus or campus program charter holder, or an open-enrollment charter school.

(b) If a district or school takes disciplinary action against a student and the student subsequently enrolls in another district or school before the expiration of the period of disciplinary action, the governing body of the district or school taking the disciplinary action shall provide to the district or school in which the student enrolls, at the same time other records of the student are provided, a copy of the order of disciplinary action.

(c) Subject to Section 37.007(e), the district or school in which the student enrolls may continue the disciplinary action under the terms of the order or may allow the student to attend regular classes without completing the period of disciplinary action.

Added by Acts 2003, 78th Leg., ch. 631, Sec. 1, eff. June 20, 2003.
Renumbered from Education Code, Section 37.021 by Acts 2005, 79th Leg., Ch. 728, Sec. 23.001(16), eff. September 1, 2005.
Subchapter B. School-Community Guidance Centers

Sec. 37.051. Establishment.

Each school district may establish a school-community guidance center designed to locate and assist children with problems that interfere with education, including juvenile offenders and children with severe behavioral problems or character disorders. Each center shall coordinate the efforts of school district personnel, local police departments, school attendance officers, and probation officers in working with students, dropouts, and parents in identifying and correcting factors that adversely affect the education of the children.

Added by Acts 1995, 74th Leg., ch. 260, Sec. 1, eff. May 30, 1995.

Sec. 37.052. Cooperative Programs.

The board of trustees of a school district may develop cooperative programs with state youth agencies for children found to have engaged in delinquent conduct.

Added by Acts 1995, 74th Leg., ch. 260, Sec. 1, eff. May 30, 1995.

Sec. 37.053. Cooperation of Governmental Agencies.

(a) Each governmental agency that is concerned with children and that has jurisdiction in the school district shall cooperate with the school-community guidance centers on the request of the superintendent of the district and shall designate a liaison to work with the centers in identifying and correcting problems affecting school-age children in the district.

(b) The governmental agency may establish or finance a school-community guidance center jointly with the school district according to terms approved by the governing body of each entity participating in the joint establishment or financing of the center.

Added by Acts 1995, 74th Leg., ch. 260, Sec. 1, eff. May 30, 1995.

Sec. 37.054. Parental Notice, Consent, and Access To Information.

(a) Before a student is admitted to a school-community guidance center, the administrator of the center must notify the student's parent or guardian that the student has been assigned to attend the center.

(b) The notification must include:

   (1) the reason that the student has been assigned to the center;

   (2) a statement that on request the parent or guardian is entitled to be fully informed in writing of any treatment method or testing program involving the student; and

   (3) a statement that the parent or guardian may request to be advised and to give written, signed consent for any psychological testing or treatment involving the student.

(c) If, after notification, a parent refuses to consent to testing or treatment of the student, the center may not provide any further psychological treatment or testing.

(d) A parent or guardian of a student attending a center is entitled to inspect:

   (1) any instructional or guidance material to be used by the student, including teachers' manuals, tapes, and films; and

   (2) the results of any treatment, testing, or guidance method involving the student.

(e) The administrator of the center may set a schedule for inspection of materials that allows reasonable access but does not interfere with the conduct of classes or business activities of the school.

Added by Acts 1995, 74th Leg., ch. 260, Sec. 1, eff. May 30, 1995.

Sec. 37.055. Parental Involvement.

(a) On admitting a student to a school-community guidance center, a representative of the school district, the student, and the student's parent shall develop an agreement that specifies the responsibilities of the parent and the student. The agreement must include:

   (1) a statement of the student's behavioral and learning objectives;

   (2) a requirement that the parent attend specified meetings and conferences for teacher review of the student's progress; and

   (3) the parent's acknowledgement that the parent understands and accepts the responsibilities imposed by the agreement regarding

attendance at meetings and conferences and assistance in meeting other objectives, defined by the district, to aid student remediation.

(b) The superintendent of the school district may obtain a court order from a district court in the school district requiring a parent to comply with an agreement made under this section. A parent who violates a court order issued under this subsection may be punished for contempt of court.

(c) In this section, "parent" includes a legal guardian.

Added by Acts 1995, 74th Leg., ch. 260, Sec. 1, eff. May 30, 1995.

Sec. 37.056. Court Supervision.

(a) In this section, "court" means a juvenile court or alternate juvenile court designated under Chapter 51, Family Code. The court may delegate responsibility under this section to a referee appointed under Section 51.04, Family Code.

(b) If a representative of the school district, the student, and the parent or guardian for any reason fail to reach an agreement under Section 37.055, the court may, on the request of any party and after a hearing, enter an order establishing the responsibilities and duties of each of the parties as the court considers appropriate.

(c) The court may compel attendance at any hearing held under this section through any legal process, including subpoena and habeas corpus.

(d) If the parties reach an agreement under Section 37.055, and if the written agreement so provides, the court may enter an order that incorporates the terms of the agreement.

(e) Any party who violates an order issued under this section may be punished for contempt of court.

(f) A school district may enter into an agreement to share the costs incurred by a county under this section.

Added by Acts 1995, 74th Leg., ch. 260, Sec. 1, eff. May 30, 1995.
Subchapter C. Law and Order

Sec. 37.081. School District Peace Officers and Security Personnel.

(a) The board of trustees of any school district may employ security personnel and may commission peace officers to carry out this subchapter. If a board of trustees authorizes a person employed as security personnel to carry a weapon, the person must be a commissioned peace officer. The jurisdiction of a peace officer or security personnel under this section shall be determined by the board of trustees and may include all territory in the boundaries of the school district and all property outside the boundaries of the district that is owned, leased, or rented by or otherwise under the control of the school district and the board of trustees that employ the peace officer or security personnel.

(b) In a peace officer's jurisdiction, a peace officer commissioned under this section:

　(1) has the powers, privileges, and immunities of peace officers;

　(2) may enforce all laws, including municipal ordinances, county ordinances, and state laws; and

　(3) may, in accordance with Chapter 52, Family Code, take a juvenile into custody.

(c) A school district peace officer may provide assistance to another law enforcement agency. A school district may contract with a political subdivision for the jurisdiction of a school district peace officer to include all territory in the jurisdiction of the political subdivision.

(d) A school district peace officer shall perform administrative and law enforcement duties for the school district as determined by the board of trustees of the school district. Those duties must include protecting:

　(1) the safety and welfare of any person in the jurisdiction of the peace officer; and

　(2) the property of the school district.

(e) The board of trustees of the district shall determine the scope of the on-duty and off-duty law enforcement activities of school district peace officers. A school district must authorize in writing any off-duty law enforcement activities performed by a school district peace officer.

(f) The chief of police of the school district police department shall be accountable to the superintendent and shall report to the superintendent or the superintendent's designee. School district police officers shall be supervised by the chief of police of the school district or the chief of police's designee and shall be licensed by the Commission on Law Enforcement Officer Standards and Education.

(g) A school district police department and the law enforcement agencies with which it has overlapping jurisdiction shall enter into a memorandum of understanding that outlines reasonable communication and coordination efforts between the department and the agencies.

(h) A peace officer assigned to duty and commissioned under this section shall take and file the oath required of peace officers and shall execute and file a bond in the sum of $1,000, payable to the board of trustees, with two or more sureties, conditioned that the peace officer will fairly, impartially, and faithfully perform all the duties that may be required of the peace officer by law. The bond may be sued on in the name of any person injured until the whole amount of the bond is recovered. Any peace officer commissioned under this section must meet all minimum standards for peace officers established by the Commission on Law Enforcement Officer Standards and Education.

Added by Acts 1995, 74th Leg., ch. 260, Sec. 1, eff. May 30, 1995.

Sec. 37.082. Possession of Paging Devices.

(a) The board of trustees of a school district may adopt a policy prohibiting a student from possessing a paging device while on school property or while attending a school-sponsored or school-related activity on or off school property. The policy may establish disciplinary measures to be imposed for violation of the prohibition and may provide for confiscation of the paging device.

(b) The policy may provide for the district to:

(1) dispose of a confiscated paging device in any reasonable manner after having provided the student's parent and the company whose name and address or telephone number appear on the device 30 days' prior notice of its intent to dispose of that device. The notice shall include the serial number of the device and may be made by telephone, telegraph, or in writing; and

(2) charge the owner of the device or the student's parent an administrative fee not to exceed $15 before it releases the device.

(c) In this section, "paging device" means a telecommunications device that emits an audible signal, vibrates, displays a message, or otherwise summons or delivers a communication to the possessor. The term does not include an amateur radio under the control of an operator who holds an amateur radio station license issued by the Federal Communications Commission.

Added by Acts 1995, 74th Leg., ch. 260, Sec. 1, eff. May 30, 1995.
Amended by:
Acts 2007, 80th Leg., R.S., Ch. 258, Sec. 2.02, eff. September 1, 2007.

Sec. 37.083. Discipline Management Programs; Sexual Harassment Policies.

(a) Each school district shall adopt and implement a discipline management program to be included in the district improvement plan under Section 11.252. The program must provide for prevention of and education concerning unwanted physical or verbal aggression, sexual harassment, and other forms of bullying in school, on school grounds, and in school vehicles.

(b) Each school district may develop and implement a sexual harassment policy to be included in the district improvement plan under Section 11.252.

Added by Acts 1995, 74th Leg., ch. 260, Sec. 1, eff. May 30, 1995.
Amended by:
Acts 2005, 79th Leg., Ch. 920, Sec. 4, eff. June 18, 2005.

Sec. 37.0831. Dating Violence Policies.

(a) Each school district shall adopt and implement a dating violence policy to be included in the district improvement plan under Section 11.252.

(b) A dating violence policy must:

(1) include a definition of dating violence that includes the intentional use of physical, sexual, verbal, or emotional abuse by a person to harm, threaten, intimidate, or control another person in a dating relationship, as defined by Section 71.0021, Family Code; and

(2) address safety planning, enforcement of protective orders, school-based alternatives to protective orders, training for teachers and administrators, counseling for affected students, and awareness education for students and parents.

Added by Acts 2007, 80th Leg., R.S., Ch. 131, Sec. 1, eff. May 18, 2007.

Sec. 37.084. Interagency Sharing of Records.

(a) A school district superintendent or the superintendent's designee may disclose information contained in a student's educational records to a juvenile justice agency, as that term is defined by Section 58.101, Family Code, if the disclosure is under an interagency agreement authorized by Section 58.0051, Family Code.

(b) The commissioner may enter into an interagency agreement to share educational information for research and analytical purposes with the:

(1) Texas Juvenile Probation Commission;

(2) Texas Youth Commission;

(3) Texas Department of Criminal Justice; and

(4) Criminal Justice Policy Council.

(c) This section does not require or authorize release of student-level information except in conformity with the Family Educational Rights and Privacy Act of 1974 (20 U.S.C. Section 1232g), as amended.

Added by Acts 1999, 76th Leg., ch. 217, Sec. 2, eff. May 24, 1999.
Subchapter D. Protection of Buildings and Grounds

Sec. 37.101. Applicability of Criminal Laws.

The criminal laws of the state apply in the areas under the control and jurisdiction of the board of trustees of any school district in this state.

Added by Acts 1995, 74th Leg., ch. 260, Sec. 1, eff. May 30, 1995.

Sec. 37.102. Rules; Penalty.

(a) The board of trustees of a school district may adopt rules for the safety and welfare of students, employees, and property and other rules it considers necessary to carry out this subchapter and the governance of the district, including rules providing for the operation and parking of vehicles on school property. The board may adopt and charge a reasonable fee for parking and for providing traffic control.

(b) A law or ordinance regulating traffic on a public highway or street applies to the operation of a vehicle on school property, except as modified by this subchapter.

(c) A person who violates any rule adopted under this subchapter providing for the operation and parking of vehicles on school property commits an offense. An offense under this section is a Class C misdemeanor.

Added by Acts 1995, 74th Leg., ch. 260, Sec. 1, eff. May 30, 1995.
Amended by:
Acts 2007, 80th Leg., R.S., Ch. 1167, Sec. 1, eff. September 1, 2007.

Sec. 37.103. Enforcement of Rules.

Notwithstanding any other provision of this subchapter, the board of trustees of a school district may authorize any officer commissioned by the board to enforce rules adopted by the board. This subchapter is not intended to restrict the authority of each district to adopt and enforce appropriate rules for the orderly conduct of the district in carrying out its purposes and objectives or the right of separate jurisdiction relating to the conduct of its students and personnel.

Added by Acts 1995, 74th Leg., ch. 260, Sec. 1, eff. May 30, 1995.

Sec. 37.104. Courts Having Jurisdiction.

The judge of a municipal court of a municipality in which, or any justice of the peace of a county in which, property under the control and jurisdiction of a school district is located may hear and determine criminal cases involving violations of this subchapter or rules adopted under this subchapter.

Added by Acts 1995, 74th Leg., ch. 260, Sec. 1, eff. May 30, 1995.

Sec. 37.105. Unauthorized Persons: Refusal of Entry, Ejection, Identification.

The board of trustees of a school district or its authorized representative may refuse to allow a person without legitimate business to enter on property under the board's control and may eject any undesirable person from the property on the person's refusal to leave peaceably on request. Identification may be required of any person on the property.

Added by Acts 1995, 74th Leg., ch. 260, Sec. 1, eff. May 30, 1995.

Sec. 37.106. Vehicle Identification Insignia.

The board of trustees of a school district may provide for the issuance and use of suitable vehicle identification insignia. The board may bar or suspend a person from driving or parking a vehicle on any school property as a result of the person's violation of any rule adopted by the board or of this subchapter. Reinstatement of the privileges may be permitted and a reasonable fee assessed.
Added by Acts 1995, 74th Leg., ch. 260, Sec. 1, eff. May 30, 1995.

Sec. 37.107. Trespass on School Grounds.

An unauthorized person who trespasses on the grounds of any school district of this state commits an offense. An offense under this section is a Class C misdemeanor.

Added by Acts 1995, 74th Leg., ch. 260, Sec. 1, eff. May 30, 1995.

Sec. 37.108. Multihazard Emergency Operations Plan; Safety and Security Audit.

- (a) Each school district or public junior college district shall adopt and implement a multihazard emergency operations plan for use in the district's facilities. The plan must address mitigation, preparedness, response, and recovery as defined by the commissioner of education or commissioner of higher education in conjunction with the governor's office of homeland security. The plan must provide for:

(1) district employee training in responding to an emergency;

(2) if the plan applies to a school district, mandatory school drills and exercises to prepare district students and employees for responding to an emergency;

(3) measures to ensure coordination with the Department of State Health Services and local emergency management agencies, law enforcement, health departments, and fire departments in the event of an emergency; and

(4) the implementation of a safety and security audit as required by Subsection (b).

(b) At least once every three years, each school district or public junior college district shall conduct a safety and security audit of the district's facilities. To the extent possible, a district shall follow safety and security audit procedures developed by the Texas School Safety Center or a comparable public or private entity.

(c) A school district or public junior college district shall report the results of the safety and security audit conducted under Subsection (b) to the district's board of trustees and, in the manner required by the Texas School Safety Center, to the Texas School Safety Center.

(c-1) Except as provided by Subsection (c-2), any document or information collected, developed, or produced during a safety and security audit conducted under Subsection (b) is not subject to disclosure under Chapter 552, Government Code.

(c-2) A document relating to a school district's or public junior college district's multihazard emergency operations plan is subject to disclosure if the document enables a person to:

(1) verify that the district has established a plan and determine the agencies involved in the development of the plan and the agencies coordinating with the district to respond to an emergency, including the Department of State Health Services, local emergency services agencies, law enforcement agencies, health departments, and fire departments;

(2) verify that the district's plan was reviewed within the last 12 months and determine the specific review dates;

(3) verify that the plan addresses the four phases of emergency management under Subsection (a);

(4) verify that district employees have been trained to respond to an emergency and determine the types of training, the number of employees trained, and the person conducting the training;

(5) verify that each campus in the district has conducted mandatory emergency drills and exercises in accordance with the plan and determine the frequency of the drills;

(6) if the district is a school district, verify that the district has established a plan for responding to a train derailment if required under Subsection (d);

(7) verify that the district has completed a safety and security audit under Subsection (b) and determine the date the audit was conducted, the person conducting the audit, and the date the district presented the results of the audit to the district's board of trustees;

(8) verify that the district has addressed any recommendations by the district's board of trustees for improvement of the plan and determine the district's progress within the last 12 months; and

(9) if the district is a school district, verify that the district has established a visitor policy and identify the provisions governing access to a district building or other district property.

(d) A school district shall include in its multihazard emergency operations plan a policy for responding to a train derailment near a district school. A school district is only required to adopt the policy described by this subsection if a district school is located within 1,000 yards of a railroad track, as measured from any point on the school's real property boundary line. The school district may use any available community resources in developing the policy described by this subsection.

Added by Acts 2005, 79th Leg., Ch. 780, Sec. 1, eff. September 1, 2005.
Amended by:
Acts 2007, 80th Leg., R.S., Ch. 258, Sec. 3.02, eff. September 1, 2007.
Acts 2007, 80th Leg., R.S., Ch. 1326, Sec. 2, eff. September 1, 2007.
Acts 2009, 81st Leg., R.S., Ch. 1280, Sec. 6.01, eff. September 1, 2009.
Acts 2009, 81st Leg., R.S., Ch. 1280, Sec. 6.02, eff. September 1, 2009.

Sec. 37.109. School Safety and Security Committee.

(a) In accordance with guidelines established by the Texas School Safety Center, each school district shall establish a school safety and security committee.

(b) The committee shall:
  (1) participate on behalf of the district in developing and implementing emergency plans consistent with the district multihazard emergency operations plan required by Section 37.108(a) to ensure that the plans reflect specific campus, facility, or support services needs;
  (2) provide the district with any campus, facility, or support services information required in connection with a safety and security audit required by Section 37.108(b), a safety and security audit report required by Section 37.108(c), or another report required to be submitted by the district to the Texas School Safety Center; and
  (3) review each report required to be submitted by the district to the Texas School Safety Center to ensure that the report contains accurate and complete information regarding each campus, facility, or support service in accordance with criteria established by the center.

Added by Acts 2009, 81st Leg., R.S., Ch. 1280, Sec. 6.03, eff. September 1, 2009.

Sec. 37.110. Information Regarding Gang-Free Zones.

The superintendent of each public school district and the administrator of each private elementary or secondary school located in the public school district shall ensure that the student handbook for each campus in the public school district includes information on gang-free zones and the consequences of engaging in organized criminal activity within those zones.

Added by Acts 2009, 81st Leg., R.S., Ch. 1130, Sec. 4, eff. June 19, 2009.
Subchapter E. Penal Provisions

Sec. 37.121. Fraternities, Sororities, Secret Societies, and Gangs.
  (a) A person commits an offense if the person:
    (1) is a member of, pledges to become a member of, joins, or solicits another person to join or pledge to become a member of a public school fraternity, sorority, secret society, or gang; or
    (2) is not enrolled in a public school and solicits another person to attend a meeting of a public school fraternity, sorority, secret society, or gang or a meeting at which membership in one of those groups is encouraged.
  (b) A school district board of trustees or an educator shall recommend placing in a disciplinary alternative education program any student under the person's control who violates Subsection (a).
  (c) An offense under this section is a Class C misdemeanor.

(d) In this section, "public school fraternity, sorority, secret society, or gang" means an organization composed wholly or in part of students of public primary or secondary schools that seeks to perpetuate itself by taking in additional members from the students enrolled in school on the basis of the decision of its membership rather than on the free choice of a student in the school who is qualified by the rules of the school to fill the special aims of the organization. The term does not include an agency for public welfare, including Boy Scouts, Hi-Y, Girl Reserves, DeMolay, Rainbow Girls, Pan-American Clubs, scholarship societies, or other similar educational organizations sponsored by state or national education authorities.

Added by Acts 1995, 74th Leg., ch. 260, Sec. 1, eff. May 30, 1995.
Amended by Acts 2003, 78th Leg., ch. 1055, Sec. 23, eff. June 20, 2003.

Sec. 37.122. Possession of Intoxicants on Public School Grounds.

(a) A person commits an offense if the person possesses an intoxicating beverage for consumption, sale, or distribution while:
   (1) on the grounds or in a building of a public school; or
   (2) entering or inside any enclosure, field, or stadium where an athletic event sponsored or participated in by a public school of this state is being held.
(b) An officer of this state who sees a person violating this section shall immediately seize the intoxicating beverage and, within a reasonable time, deliver it to the county or district attorney to be held as evidence until the trial of the accused possessor.
(c) An offense under this section is a Class C misdemeanor.

Added by Acts 1995, 74th Leg., ch. 260, Sec. 1, eff. May 30, 1995.

Sec. 37.123. Disruptive Activities.

(a) A person commits an offense if the person, alone or in concert with others, intentionally engages in disruptive activity on the campus or property of any private or public school.
(b) For purposes of this section, disruptive activity is:
   (1) obstructing or restraining the passage of persons in an exit, entrance, or hallway of a building without the authorization of the administration of the school;
   (2) seizing control of a building or portion of a building to interfere with an administrative, educational, research, or other authorized activity;

(3) preventing or attempting to prevent by force or violence or the threat of force or violence a lawful assembly authorized by the school administration so that a person attempting to participate in the assembly is unable to participate due to the use of force or violence or due to a reasonable fear that force or violence is likely to occur;

(4) disrupting by force or violence or the threat of force or violence a lawful assembly in progress; or

(5) obstructing or restraining the passage of a person at an exit or entrance to the campus or property or preventing or attempting to prevent by force or violence or by threats of force or violence the ingress or egress of a person to or from the property or campus without the authorization of the administration of the school.

(c) An offense under this section is a Class B misdemeanor.

(d) Any person who is convicted the third time of violating this section is ineligible to attend any institution of higher education receiving funds from this state before the second anniversary of the third conviction.

(e) This section may not be construed to infringe on any right of free speech or expression guaranteed by the constitution of the United States or of this state.

Added by Acts 1995, 74th Leg., ch. 260, Sec. 1, eff. May 30, 1995.

Sec. 37.124. Disruption of Classes.

(a) A person commits an offense if the person, on school property or on public property within 500 feet of school property, alone or in concert with others, intentionally disrupts the conduct of classes or other school activities.

(b) An offense under this section is a Class C misdemeanor.

(c) In this section:

(1) "Disrupting the conduct of classes or other school activities" includes:

(A) emitting noise of an intensity that prevents or hinders classroom instruction;

(B) enticing or attempting to entice a student away from a class or other school activity that the student is required to attend;

(C) preventing or attempting to prevent a student from attending a class or other school activity that the student is required to attend; and

(D) entering a classroom without the consent of either the principal or the teacher and, through either acts of misconduct or the use of loud or profane language, disrupting class activities.

(2) "Public property" includes a street, highway, alley, public park, or sidewalk.

(3) "School property" includes a public school campus or school grounds on which a public school is located and any grounds or buildings used by a school for an assembly or other school-sponsored activity.

Added by Acts 1995, 74th Leg., ch. 260, Sec. 1, eff. May 30, 1995.

Sec. 37.125. Exhibition of Firearms.

(a) A person commits an offense if, in a manner intended to cause alarm or personal injury to another person or to damage school property, the person intentionally exhibits, uses, or threatens to exhibit or use a firearm:

(1) in or on any property, including a parking lot, parking garage, or other parking area, that is owned by a private or public school; or

(2) on a school bus being used to transport children to or from school-sponsored activities of a private or public school.

(b) An offense under this section is a third degree felony.

Added by Acts 1995, 74th Leg., ch. 260, Sec. 1, eff. May 30, 1995.
Amended by:
Acts 2007, 80th Leg., R.S., Ch. 704, Sec. 1, eff. September 1, 2007.

Sec. 37.126. Disruption of Transportation.

(a) Except as provided by Section 37.125, a person commits an offense if the person intentionally disrupts, prevents, or interferes with the lawful transportation of children to or from school or an activity sponsored by a school on a vehicle owned or operated by a county or independent school district.

(b) An offense under this section is a Class C misdemeanor.

Added by Acts 1995, 74th Leg., ch. 260, Sec. 1, eff. May 30, 1995.
Subchapter F. Hazing

Sec. 37.151. Definitions.

In this subchapter:

(1) "Educational institution" includes a public or private high school.

(2) "Pledge" means any person who has been accepted by, is considering an offer of membership from, or is in the process of qualifying for membership in an organization.

(3) "Pledging" means any action or activity related to becoming a member of an organization.

(4) "Student" means any person who:
  (A) is registered in or in attendance at an educational institution;
  (B) has been accepted for admission at the educational institution where the hazing incident occurs; or
  (C) intends to attend an educational institution during any of its regular sessions after a period of scheduled vacation.

(5) "Organization" means a fraternity, sorority, association, corporation, order, society, corps, club, or service, social, or similar group, whose members are primarily students.

(6) "Hazing" means any intentional, knowing, or reckless act, occurring on or off the campus of an educational institution, by one person alone or acting with others, directed against a student, that endangers the mental or physical health or safety of a student for the purpose of pledging, being initiated into, affiliating with, holding office in, or maintaining membership in an organization. The term includes:
  (A) any type of physical brutality, such as whipping, beating, striking, branding, electronic shocking, placing of a harmful substance on the body, or similar activity;
  (B) any type of physical activity, such as sleep deprivation, exposure to the elements, confinement in a small space, calisthenics, or other activity that subjects the student to an unreasonable risk of harm or that adversely affects the mental or physical health or safety of the student;
  (C) any activity involving consumption of a food, liquid, alcoholic beverage, liquor, drug, or other substance that subjects the student to an unreasonable risk of harm or that adversely affects the mental or physical health or safety of the student;
  (D) any activity that intimidates or threatens the student with ostracism, that subjects the student to extreme mental stress, shame, or humiliation, that adversely affects the mental health or dignity of the student or discourages the student from entering or remaining registered in an educational institution, or that may reasonably be expected to cause a student to leave the organization or the institution rather than submit to acts described in this subdivision; and
  (E) any activity that induces, causes, or requires the student to perform a duty or task that involves a violation of the Penal Code.

Added by Acts 1995, 74th Leg., ch. 260, Sec. 1, eff. May 30, 1995.

Sec. 37.152. Personal Hazing Offense.

(a) A person commits an offense if the person:
  (1) engages in hazing;
  (2) solicits, encourages, directs, aids, or attempts to aid another in engaging in hazing;
  (3) recklessly permits hazing to occur; or
  (4) has firsthand knowledge of the planning of a specific hazing incident involving a student in an educational institution, or has firsthand knowledge that a specific hazing incident has occurred, and knowingly fails to report that knowledge in writing to the dean of students or other appropriate official of the institution.

(b) The offense of failing to report is a Class B misdemeanor.

(c) Any other offense under this section that does not cause serious bodily injury to another is a Class B misdemeanor.

(d) Any other offense under this section that causes serious bodily injury to another is a Class A misdemeanor.

(e) Any other offense under this section that causes the death of another is a state jail felony.

(f) Except if an offense causes the death of a student, in sentencing a person convicted of an offense under this section, the court may require the person to perform community service, subject to the same conditions imposed on a person placed on community supervision under Section 11, Article 42.12, Code of Criminal Procedure, for an appropriate period of time in lieu of confinement in county jail or in lieu of a part of the time the person is sentenced to confinement in county jail.

Added by Acts 1995, 74th Leg., ch. 260, Sec. 1, eff. May 30, 1995.

Sec. 37.153. Organization Hazing Offense.

(a) An organization commits an offense if the organization condones or encourages hazing or if an officer or any combination of members, pledges, or alumni of the organization commits or assists in the commission of hazing.

(b) An offense under this section is a misdemeanor punishable by:
  (1) a fine of not less than $5,000 nor more than $10,000; or
  (2) if the court finds that the offense caused personal injury, property damage, or other loss, a fine of not less than $5,000 nor more than double the amount lost or expenses incurred because of the injury, damage, or loss.

Added by Acts 1995, 74th Leg., ch. 260, Sec. 1, eff. May 30, 1995.

Sec. 37.154. Consent Not a Defense.

It is not a defense to prosecution of an offense under this subchapter that the person against whom the hazing was directed consented to or acquiesced in the hazing activity.

Added by Acts 1995, 74th Leg., ch. 260, Sec. 1, eff. May 30, 1995.

Sec. 37.155. Immunity from Prosecution Available.

In the prosecution of an offense under this subchapter, the court may grant immunity from prosecution for the offense to each person who is subpoenaed to testify for the prosecution and who does testify for the prosecution. Any person reporting a specific hazing incident involving a student in an educational institution to the dean of students or other appropriate official of the institution is immune from civil or criminal liability that might otherwise be incurred or imposed as a result of the report. Immunity extends to participation in any judicial proceeding resulting from the report. A person reporting in bad faith or with malice is not protected by this section.

Added by Acts 1995, 74th Leg., ch. 260, Sec. 1, eff. May 30, 1995.

Sec. 37.156. Offenses in Addition to Other Penal Provisions.

This subchapter does not affect or repeal any penal law of this state. This subchapter does not limit or affect the right of an educational institution to enforce its own penalties against hazing.

Added by Acts 1995, 74th Leg., ch. 260, Sec. 1, eff. May 30, 1995.

Sec. 37.157. Reporting by Medical Authorities.

A doctor or other medical practitioner who treats a student who may have been subjected to hazing activities:

(1) may report the suspected hazing activities to police or other law enforcement officials; and

(2) is immune from civil or other liability that might otherwise be imposed or incurred as a result of the report, unless the report is made in bad faith or with malice.

Added by Acts 1995, 74th Leg., ch. 260, Sec. 1, eff. May 30, 1995.
Subchapter G. Texas School Safety Center

Sec. 37.201. Definition.

In this subchapter, "center" means the Texas School Safety Center.

Added by Acts 2001, 77th Leg., ch. 923, Sec. 1, eff. Sept. 1, 2001.

Sec. 37.202. Purpose.

The purpose of the center is to serve as:

(1) a central location for school safety and security information, including research, training, and technical assistance related to successful school safety and security programs;

(2) a central registry of persons providing school safety and security consulting services in the state; and

(3) a resource for the prevention of youth violence and the promotion of safety in the state.

Added by Acts 2001, 77th Leg., ch. 923, Sec. 1, eff. Sept. 1, 2001.
Amended by:

Acts 2009, 81st Leg., R.S., Ch. 1280, Sec. 6.04, eff. September 1, 2009.

Sec. 37.203. Board.

(a) The center is advised by a board of directors composed of:

(1) the attorney general, or the attorney general's designee;

(2) the commissioner, or the commissioner's designee;

(3) the executive director of the Texas Juvenile Probation Commission, or the executive director's designee;

(4) the executive commissioner of the Texas Youth Commission, or the executive commissioner's designee;

(5) the commissioner of the Department of State Health Services, or the commissioner's designee;

(6) the commissioner of higher education, or the commissioner's designee; and

(7) the following members appointed by the governor with the advice and consent of the senate:

(A) a juvenile court judge;

(B) a member of a school district's board of trustees;

(C) an administrator of a public primary school;

(D) an administrator of a public secondary school;

(E) a member of the state parent–teacher association;

(F) a teacher from a public primary or secondary school;

(G) a public school superintendent who is a member of the Texas Association of School Administrators;

(H) a school district police officer or a peace officer whose primary duty consists of working in a public school; and

(I) two members of the public.

(b) Members of the board appointed under Subsection (a)(7) serve staggered two-year terms, with the terms of the members described by Subsections (a)(7)(A)-(E) expiring on February 1 of each odd-numbered year and the terms of the members described by Subsections (a)(7)(F)-(I) expiring on February 1 of each even-numbered year. A member may serve more than one term.

(c) The board may form committees as necessary.

Added by Acts 2001, 77th Leg., ch. 923, Sec. 1, eff. Sept. 1, 2001.
Amended by:
Acts 2005, 79th Leg., Ch. 780, Sec. 2, eff. September 1, 2005.
Acts 2007, 80th Leg., R.S., Ch. 258, Sec. 3.03, eff. September 1, 2007.
Acts 2007, 80th Leg., R.S., Ch. 263, Sec. 4, eff. June 8, 2007.
Acts 2009, 81st Leg., R.S., Ch. 87, Sec. 7.005, eff. September 1, 2009.
Acts 2009, 81st Leg., R.S., Ch. 1280, Sec. 6.05, eff. September 1, 2009.
Acts 2009, 81st Leg., R.S., Ch. 1280, Sec. 6.06, eff. September 1, 2009.

Sec. 37.204. Officers; Meetings; Compensation.

(a) The board shall annually elect from among its members a chairperson and a vice chairperson.

(b) The board shall meet at least four times each year.

(c) A member of the board may not receive compensation but is entitled to reimbursement of the travel expenses incurred by the member while conducting the business of the board as provided by the General Appropriations Act.

Added by Acts 2001, 77th Leg., ch. 923, Sec. 1, eff. Sept. 1, 2001.

Sec. 37.205. Safety Training Programs.

The center shall conduct for school districts a safety training program that includes:

(1) development of a positive school environment and proactive safety measures designed to address local concerns;

(2) school safety courses for law enforcement officials, with a focus on school district police officers and school resource officers;

(3) discussion of school safety issues with parents and community members; and

(4) assistance in developing a multihazard emergency operations plan for adoption under Section 37.108.

Added by Acts 2001, 77th Leg., ch. 923, Sec. 1, eff. Sept. 1, 2001.
Amended by:
Acts 2005, 79th Leg., Ch. 780, Sec. 3, eff. September 1, 2005.

Sec. 37.2051. Security Criteria for Instructional Facilities.

The center shall develop security criteria that school districts may consider in the design of instructional facilities.

Added by Acts 2005, 79th Leg., Ch. 780, Sec. 4, eff. September 1, 2005.

Sec. 37.207. Model Safety and Security Audit Procedure.

(a) The center shall develop a model safety and security audit procedure for use by school districts and public junior college districts that includes:

 (1) providing each district with guidelines showing proper audit procedures;

 (2) reviewing elements of each district audit and making recommendations for improvements in the state based on that review; and

 (3) incorporating the findings of district audits in a statewide report on school safety and security made available by the center to the public.

(b) Each school district shall report the results of its audits to the center in the manner required by the center.

Added by Acts 2001, 77th Leg., ch. 923, Sec. 1, eff. Sept. 1, 2001.
Amended by:
Acts 2007, 80th Leg., R.S., Ch. 258, Sec. 3.04, eff. September 1, 2007.
Acts 2009, 81st Leg., R.S., Ch. 1280, Sec. 6.07, eff. September 1, 2009.

Sec. 37.208. On-Site Assistance.

On request of a school district, the center may provide on-site technical assistance to the district for:

(1) school safety and security audits; and

(2) school safety and security information and presentations.

Added by Acts 2001, 77th Leg., ch. 923, Sec. 1, eff. Sept. 1, 2001.
Amended by:
Acts 2005, 79th Leg., Ch. 780, Sec. 5, eff. September 1, 2005.

Sec. 37.209. Center Website.

The center shall develop and maintain an interactive Internet website that includes:

(1) quarterly news updates related to school safety and security and violence prevention;

(2) school crime data;

(3) a schedule of training and special events; and

(4) a list of persons who provide school safety or security consulting services in this state and are registered in accordance with Section 37.2091.

Added by Acts 2001, 77th Leg., ch. 923, Sec. 1, eff. Sept. 1, 2001.
Amended by:
Acts 2009, 81st Leg., R.S., Ch. 1280, Sec. 6.08, eff. September 1, 2009.

Sec. 37.2091. Registry of Persons Providing School Safety or Security Consulting Services.

(a) In this section, "school safety or security consulting services" includes any service provided to a school district, institution of higher education, district facility, or campus by a person consisting of advice, information, recommendations, data collection, or safety and security audit services relevant to school safety and security, regardless of whether the person is paid for those services.

(b) The center shall establish a registry of persons providing school safety or security consulting services in this state.

(c) Each person providing school safety or security consulting services in this state shall register with the center in accordance with requirements established by the center. The requirements must include provisions requiring a person registering with the center to provide information regarding:

(1) the person's background, education, and experience that are relevant to the person's ability to provide knowledgeable and effective school safety or security consulting services; and

(2) any complaints or pending litigation relating to the person's provision of school safety or security consulting services.

(d) The registry is intended to serve only as an informational resource for school districts and institutions of higher education. The inclusion of a person in the registry is not an indication of the person's qualifications or ability to provide school safety or security consulting services or that the center endorses the person's school safety or security consulting services.

(e) The center shall include information regarding the registry, including the number of persons registered and the general degree of school safety or security experience possessed by those persons, in the biennial report required by Section 37.216.

Added by Acts 2009, 81st Leg., R.S., Ch. 1280, Sec. 6.09, eff. September 1, 2009.

Sec. 37.211. Recognition of Schools.

The center shall provide for the public recognition of schools that implement effective school safety measures and violence prevention.

Added by Acts 2001, 77th Leg., ch. 923, Sec. 1, eff. Sept. 1, 2001.

Sec. 37.212. Interagency Cooperation.

The center shall promote cooperation between state agencies, institutions of higher education, and any local juvenile delinquency prevention councils to address discipline and safety issues in the state.

Added by Acts 2001, 77th Leg., ch. 923, Sec. 1, eff. Sept. 1, 2001.

Sec. 37.2121. Memoranda of Understanding and Mutual Aid Agreements.

(a) The center shall identify and inform school districts of the types of entities, including local and regional authorities, other school districts, and emergency first responders, with whom school districts should customarily make efforts to enter into memoranda of understanding or mutual aid agreements addressing issues that affect school safety and security.

(b) The center shall develop guidelines regarding memoranda of understanding and mutual aid agreements between school districts and the entities identified in accordance with Subsection (a). The guidelines:

(1) must include descriptions of the provisions that should customarily be included in each memorandum or agreement with a particular type of entity;

(2) may include sample language for those provisions; and

(3) must be consistent with the Texas Statewide Mutual Aid System established under Subchapter E-1, Chapter 418, Government Code.

(c) The center shall encourage school districts to enter into memoranda of understanding and mutual aid agreements with entities identified in accordance with Subsection (a) that comply with the guidelines developed under Subsection (b).

(d) Each school district that enters into a memorandum of understanding or mutual aid agreement addressing issues that affect school safety and

security shall, at the center's request, provide the following information to the center:
  (1) the name of each entity with which the school district has entered into a memorandum of understanding or mutual aid agreement;
  (2) the effective date of each memorandum or agreement; and
  (3) a summary of each memorandum or agreement.
(c) The center shall include information regarding the center's efforts under this section in the report required by Section 37.216.

Added by Acts 2009, 81st Leg., R.S., Ch. 1280, Sec. 6.09, eff. September 1, 2009.

Sec. 37.213. Public Junior Colleges.
(a) In this section, "public junior college" has the meaning assigned by Section 61.003.
(b) The center shall research best practices regarding emergency preparedness of public junior colleges and serve as a clearinghouse for that information.
(c) The center shall provide public junior colleges with training, technical assistance, and published guidelines or templates, as appropriate, in the following areas:
  (1) multihazard emergency operations plan development;
  (2) drill and exercise development and implementation;
  (3) mutual aid agreements;
  (4) identification of equipment and funds that may be used by public junior colleges in an emergency; and
  (5) reporting in accordance with 20 U.S.C. Section 1092(f).

Added by Acts 2007, 80th Leg., R.S., Ch. 258, Sec. 3.05, eff. September 1, 2007.
Amended by:
Acts 2009, 81st Leg., R.S., Ch. 1280, Sec. 6.10, eff. September 1, 2009.

Sec. 37.214. Authority to Accept Certain Funds.
The center may solicit and accept gifts, grants, and donations from public and private entities to use for the purposes of this subchapter.
Added by Acts 2001, 77th Leg., ch. 923, Sec. 1, eff. Sept. 1, 2001.

Sec. 37.215. Budget.
(a) The board shall annually approve a budget for the center.
(b) The center shall biannually prepare a budget request for submission to the legislature.

Added by Acts 2001, 77th Leg., ch. 923, Sec. 1, eff. Sept. 1, 2001.
Amended by:
Acts 2005, 79th Leg., Ch. 780, Sec. 6, eff. September 1, 2005.

Sec. 37.216. Biennial Report.

(a) Not later than January 1 of each odd-numbered year, the board shall provide a report to the governor, the legislature, the State Board of Education, and the agency.

(b) The biennial report must include any findings made by the center regarding school safety and security and the center's functions, budget information, and strategic planning initiatives of the center.

Added by Acts 2001, 77th Leg., ch. 923, Sec. 1, eff. Sept. 1, 2001.
Amended by:
Acts 2009, 81st Leg., R.S., Ch. 1280, Sec. 6.11, eff. September 1, 2009.

Sec. 37.2161. School Safety And Security Progress Report.

(a) The center shall periodically provide a school safety and security progress report to the governor, the legislature, the State Board of Education, and the agency that contains current information regarding school safety and security in the school districts and public junior college districts of this state based on:

   (1) elements of each district's multihazard emergency operations plan required by Section 37.108(a);

   (2) elements of each district's safety and security audit required by Section 37.108(b); and

   (3) any other report required to be submitted to the center.

(b) The center shall establish guidelines regarding the specific information to be included in the report required by this section.

(c) The center may provide the report required by this section in conjunction with the report required by Section 37.216.

Added by Acts 2009, 81st Leg., R.S., Ch. 1280, Sec. 6.12, eff. September 1, 2009.

Sec. 37.217. Community Education Relating to Internet Safety.

(a) The center, in cooperation with the attorney general, shall develop a program that provides instruction concerning Internet safety, including instruction relating to:

(1) the potential dangers of allowing personal information to appear on an Internet website;
(2) the manner in which to report an inappropriate online solicitation; and
(3) the prevention, detection, and reporting of bullying or threats occurring over the Internet.

(b) In developing the program, the center shall:
(1) solicit input from interested stakeholders; and
(2) to the extent practicable, draw from existing resources and programs.

(c) The center shall make the program available to public schools.

Added by Acts 2007, 80th Leg., R.S., Ch. 343, Sec. 1, eff. June 15, 2007.
Subchapter I. Placement of Registered Sex Offenders

Sec. 37.301. Definition.
In this subchapter, "board of trustees" includes the board's designee.

Added by Acts 2007, 80th Leg., R.S., Ch. 1240, Sec. 3, eff. June 15, 2007.
Added by Acts 2007, 80th Leg., R.S., Ch. 1291, Sec. 3, eff. September 1, 2007.

Sec. 37.302. Applicability.
This subchapter:

(1) applies to a student who is required to register as a sex offender under Chapter 62, Code of Criminal Procedure; and
(2) does not apply to a student who is no longer required to register as a sex offender under Chapter 62, Code of Criminal Procedure, including a student who receives an exemption from registration under Subchapter H, Chapter 62, Code of Criminal Procedure, or a student who receives an early termination of the obligation to register under Subchapter I, Chapter 62, Code of Criminal Procedure.

Added by Acts 2007, 80th Leg., R.S., Ch. 1240, Sec. 3, eff. June 15, 2007.
Added by Acts 2007, 80th Leg., R.S., Ch. 1291, Sec. 3, eff. September 1, 2007.

Sec. 37.303. Removal of Registered Sex Offender from Regular Classroom.
Notwithstanding any provision of Subchapter A, on receiving notice under Article 15.27, Code of Criminal Procedure, or Chapter 62, Code of Criminal Procedure, that a student is required to register as a sex offender under that chapter, a school

district shall remove the student from the regular classroom and determine the appropriate placement of the student in the manner provided by this subchapter.

Added by Acts 2007, 80th Leg., R.S., Ch. 1240, Sec. 3, eff. June 15, 2007.
Added by Acts 2007, 80th Leg., R.S., Ch. 1291, Sec. 3, eff. September 1, 2007.

Sec. 37.304. Placement of Registered Sex Offender Who Is Under Court Supervision.

(a) A school district shall place a student to whom this subchapter applies and who is under any form of court supervision, including probation, community supervision, or parole, in the appropriate alternative education program as provided by Section 37.309 for at least one semester.

(b) If a student transfers to another school district during the student's mandatory placement in an alternative education program under Subsection (a), the district to which the student transfers may:

(1) require the student to complete an additional semester in the appropriate alternative education program without conducting a review of the student's placement for that semester under Section 37.306; or

(2) count any time spent by the student in an alternative education program in the district from which the student transfers toward the mandatory placement requirement under Subsection (a).

Added by Acts 2007, 80th Leg., R.S., Ch. 1240, Sec. 3, eff. June 15, 2007.
Added by Acts 2007, 80th Leg., R.S., Ch. 1291, Sec. 3, eff. September 1, 2007.

Sec. 37.305. Placement of Registered Sex Offender Who Is Not Under Court Supervision.

A school district may place a student to whom this subchapter applies and who is not under any form of court supervision in the appropriate alternative education program as provided by Section 37.309 for one semester or in the regular classroom. The district may not place the student in the regular classroom if the district board of trustees determines that the student's presence in the regular classroom:

(1) threatens the safety of other students or teachers;
(2) will be detrimental to the educational process; or
(3) is not in the best interests of the district's students.

Added by Acts 2007, 80th Leg., R.S., Ch. 1240, Sec. 3, eff. June 15, 2007.
Added by Acts 2007, 80th Leg., R.S., Ch. 1291, Sec. 3, eff. September 1, 2007.

Sec. 37.306. Review of Placement in Alternative Education Program.

(a) At the end of the first semester of a student's placement in an alternative education program under Section 37.304 or 37.305, the school district board of trustees shall convene a committee to review the student's placement in the alternative education program. The committee must be composed of:

   (1) a classroom teacher from the campus to which the student would be assigned were the student not placed in an alternative education program;

   (2) the student's parole or probation officer or, in the case of a student who does not have a parole or probation officer, a representative of the local juvenile probation department;

   (3) an instructor from the alternative education program to which the student is assigned;

   (4) a school district designee selected by the board of trustees; and

   (5) a counselor employed by the school district.

(b) The committee by majority vote shall determine and recommend to the school district board of trustees whether the student should be returned to the regular classroom or remain in the alternative education program.

(c) If the committee recommends that the student be returned to the regular classroom, the board of trustees shall return the student to the regular classroom unless the board determines that the student's presence in the regular classroom:

   (1) threatens the safety of other students or teachers;

   (2) will be detrimental to the educational process; or

   (3) is not in the best interests of the district's students.

(d) If the committee recommends that the student remain in the alternative education program, the board of trustees shall continue the student's placement in the alternative education program unless the board determines that the student's presence in the regular classroom:

   (1) does not threaten the safety of other students or teachers;

   (2) will not be detrimental to the educational process; and

   (3) is not contrary to the best interests of the district's students.

(e) If, after receiving a recommendation under Subsection (b), the school district board of trustees determines that the student should remain in an alternative education program, the board shall before the beginning of each school year convene the committee described by Subsection (a) to review, in the manner provided by Subsections (b), (c), and (d), the student's placement in an alternative education program.

Added by Acts 2007, 80th Leg., R.S., Ch. 1240, Sec. 3, eff. June 15, 2007.
Added by Acts 2007, 80th Leg., R.S., Ch. 1291, Sec. 3, eff. September 1, 2007.

Sec. 37.307. Placement and Review of Student with Disability.
 (a) The placement under this subchapter of a student with a disability who receives special education services must be made in compliance with the Individuals with Disabilities Education Act (20 U.S.C. Section 1400 et seq.).
 (b) The review under Section 37.306 of the placement of a student with a disability who receives special education services may be made only by a duly constituted admission, review, and dismissal committee. The admission, review, and dismissal committee may request that the board of trustees convene a committee described by Section 37.306(a) to assist the admission, review, and dismissal committee in conducting the review.

Added by Acts 2007, 80th Leg., R.S., Ch. 1240, Sec. 3, eff. June 15, 2007.
Added by Acts 2007, 80th Leg., R.S., Ch. 1291, Sec. 3, eff. September 1, 2007.

Sec. 37.308. Transfer of Registered Sex Offender.
Except as provided by Section 37.304(b), a school district shall determine whether to place a student to whom this subchapter applies and who transfers to the district in the appropriate alternative education program as provided by Section 37.309 or in a regular classroom. The school district shall follow the procedures specified under Section 37.306 in making the determination.

Added by Acts 2007, 80th Leg., R.S., Ch. 1240, Sec. 3, eff. June 15, 2007.
Added by Acts 2007, 80th Leg., R.S., Ch. 1291, Sec. 3, eff. September 1, 2007.

Sec. 37.309. Placement in Disciplinary Alternative Education Program or Juvenile Justice Alternative Education Program.
 (a) Except as provided by Subsection (b), a school district shall place a student who is required by the board of trustees to attend an alternative education program under this subchapter in a disciplinary alternative education program.
 (b) A school district shall place a student who is required by the board of trustees to attend an alternative education program under this subchapter in a juvenile justice alternative education program if:
  (1) the memorandum of understanding entered into between the school district and juvenile board under Section 37.011(k) provides for the placement of students to whom this subchapter applies in the juvenile justice alternative education program; or

(2) a court orders the placement of the student in a juvenile justice alternative education program.

Added by Acts 2007, 80th Leg., R.S., Ch. 1240, Sec. 3, eff. June 15, 2007.
Added by Acts 2007, 80th Leg., R.S., Ch. 1291, Sec. 3, eff. September 1, 2007.

Sec. 37.310. Funding for Registered Sex Offender Placed in Juvenile Justice Alternative Education Program.

A juvenile justice alternative education program is entitled to funding for a student who is placed in the program under this subchapter in the same manner as a juvenile justice alternative education program is entitled to funding under Section 37.012 for a student who is expelled and placed in a juvenile justice alternative education program for conduct for which expulsion is permitted but not required under Section 37.007.

Added by Acts 2007, 80th Leg., R.S., Ch. 1240, Sec. 3, eff. June 15, 2007.
Added by Acts 2007, 80th Leg., R.S., Ch. 1291, Sec. 3, eff. September 1, 2007.

Sec. 37.311. Conference.

(a) A student or the student's parent or guardian may appeal a decision by a school district board of trustees to place the student in an alternative education program under this subchapter by requesting a conference among the board of trustees, the student's parent or guardian, and the student. The conference is limited to the factual question of whether the student is required to register as a sex offender under Chapter 62, Code of Criminal Procedure.

(b) If the school district board of trustees determines at the conclusion of the conference that the student is required to register as a sex offender under Chapter 62, Code of Criminal Procedure, the student is subject to placement in an alternative education program in the manner provided by this subchapter.

(c) A decision by the board of trustees under this section is final and may not be appealed.

Added by Acts 2007, 80th Leg., R.S., Ch. 1240, Sec. 3, eff. June 15, 2007.
Added by Acts 2007, 80th Leg., R.S., Ch. 1291, Sec. 3, eff. September 1, 2007.

Sec. 37.312. Liability.

This subchapter does not:

(1) waive any liability or immunity of a governmental entity or its officers or employees; or

(2) create any liability for or a cause of action against a governmental entity or its officers or employees.

Added by Acts 2007, 80th Leg., R.S., Ch. 1240, Sec. 3, eff. June 15, 2007.
Added by Acts 2007, 80th Leg., R.S., Ch. 1291, Sec. 3, eff. September 1, 2007.

Sec. 37.313. Conflicts of Law.

To the extent of any conflict between a provision of this subchapter and a provision of Subchapter A, this subchapter prevails.

Added by Acts 2007, 80th Leg., R.S., Ch. 1240, Sec. 3, eff. June 15, 2007.
Added by Acts 2007, 80th Leg., R.S., Ch. 1291, Sec. 3, eff. September 1, 2007.
Source: Document available at http://www.statutes.legis.state.tx.us/Docs/ED/htm/ED.37.htm

Appendix 3: Primary Source Documents: Sample Legislation: Colleges and Universities

At the college/university level, legislation has been enacted to require institutions of higher education to institute campus sexual assault prevention and reporting programs. Following is the wording of one such statute.

Statute Text-20 USC § 1092 (f)(8)

(A) Each institution of higher education participating in any program under this subchapter and part C of subchapter I of chapter 34 of Title 42 shall develop and distribute as part of the report described in paragraph (1) a statement of policy regarding—

  (i) such institution's campus sexual assault programs, which shall be aimed at prevention of sex offenses; and

  (ii) the procedures followed once a sex offense has occurred.

(B) The policy described in subparagraph (A) shall address the following areas:

  (i) Education programs to promote the awareness of rape, acquaintance rape, and other sex offenses.

  (ii) Possible sanctions to be imposed following the final determination of an on-campus disciplinary procedure regarding rape, acquaintance rape, or other sex offenses, forcible or nonforcible.

  (iii) Procedures students should follow if a sex offense occurs, including who should be contacted, the importance of preserving evidence as may be necessary to the proof of criminal sexual assault, and to whom the alleged offense should be reported.

  (iv) Procedures for on-campus disciplinary action in cases of alleged sexual assault, which shall include a clear statement that—

    (I) the accuser and the accused are entitled to the same opportunities to have others present during a campus disciplinary proceeding; and

(II) both the accuser and the accused shall be informed of the outcome of any campus disciplinary proceeding brought alleging a sexual assault.

(v) Informing students of their options to notify proper law enforcement authorities, including on-campus and local police, and the option to be assisted by campus authorities in notifying such authorities, if the student so chooses. (vii) Notification of students of options for, and available assistance in, changing academic and living situations after an alleged sexual assault incident, if so requested by the victim and if such changes are reasonably available.

(C) Nothing in this paragraph shall be construed to confer a private right of action upon any person to enforce the provisions of this paragraph.

Implementing Regulations-34 CFR § 668.46 (b)(11)

Annual security report. An institution must prepare an annual security report that contains, at a minimum, the following information:

(1) (11) A statement of policy regarding the institution's campus sexual assault programs to prevent sex offenses, and procedures to follow when a sex offense occurs. The statement must include—

   (i) A description of educational programs to promote the awareness of rape, acquaintance rape, and other forcible and nonforcible sex offenses;

   (ii) Procedures students should follow if a sex offense occurs, including procedures concerning who should be contacted, the importance of preserving evidence for the proof of a criminal offense, and to whom the alleged offense should be reported;

   (iii) Information on a student's option to notify appropriate law enforcement authorities, including on-campus and local police, and a statement that institutional personnel will assist the student in notifying these authorities, if the student requests the assistance of these personnel;

   (iv) Notification to students of existing on- and off-campus counseling, mental health, or other student services for victims of sex offenses;

   (v) Notification to students that the institution will change a victim's academic and living situations after an alleged sex offense and of the options for those changes, if those changes are requested by the victim and are reasonably available;

(vi) Procedures for campus disciplinary action in cases of an alleged sex offense, including a clear statement that—

   (A) The accuser and the accused are entitled to the same opportunities to have others present during a disciplinary proceeding; and

   (B) Both the accuser and the accused must be informed of the outcome of any institutional disciplinary proceeding brought alleging a sex offense. Compliance with this paragraph does not constitute a violation of the Family Educational Rights and Privacy Act (20 U.S.C. 1232g). For the purpose of this paragraph, the outcome of a disciplinary proceeding means only the institution's final determination with respect to the alleged sex offense and any sanction that is imposed against the accused; and

(vii) Sanctions the institution may impose following a final determination of an institutional disciplinary proceeding regarding rape, acquaintance rape, or other forcible or nonforcible sex offenses.

Source: Available at http://www.securityoncampus.org/index.php?option=com_content&view=article&id=133&Itemid=27

§§§§

The Jeanne Clery Act required that institutions of higher education report to students, faculty, staff. and the general public about crime occurring on campus. Following is the wording of this legislation, as well as the revisions enacted in 2008.
Jeanne Clery Act Text
As Amended Through 2008

20 U.S.C. § 1092(f) Disclosure of campus security policy and campus crime statistics

(1) Each eligible institution participating in any program under this title, other than a foreign institution higher education, shall on August 1, 1991, begin to collect the following information with respect to campus crime statistics and campus security policies of that institution, and beginning September 1, 1992, and each year thereafter, prepare, publish, and distribute, through appropriate publications or mailings, to all current students and employees, and to any applicant for enrollment or employment upon request, an annual security report containing at least the following information with respect to the campus security policies and campus crime statistics of that institution:

   (A) A statement of current campus policies regarding procedures and facilities for students and others to report criminal actions or other emergencies occurring on campus and policies concerning the institution's response to such reports.

(B) A statement of current policies concerning security and access to campus facilities, including campus residences, and security considerations used in the maintenance of campus facilities.

(C) A statement of current policies concerning campus law enforcement, including—
  (i) the law enforcement authority of campus security personnel;
  (ii) the working relationship of campus security personnel with State and local law enforcement agencies, including whether the institution has agreements with such agencies, such as written memoranda of understanding, for the investigation of alleged criminal offenses; and
  (iii) policies which encourage accurate and prompt reporting of all crimes to the campus police and the appropriate law enforcement agencies.

(D) A description of the type and frequency of programs designed to inform students and employees about campus security procedures and practices and to encourage students and employees to be responsible for their own security and the security of others.

(E) A description of programs designed to inform students and employees about the prevention of crimes.

(F) Statistics concerning the occurrence on campus, in or on noncampus buildings or property, and on public property during the most recent calendar year, and during the 2 preceding calendar years for which data are available—
  (i) of the following criminal offenses reported to campus security authorities or local police agencies:
    (I) murder;
    (II) sex offenses, forcible or nonforcible;
    (III) robbery;
    (IV) aggravated assault;
    (V) burglary;
    (VI) motor vehicle theft;
    (VII) manslaughter;
    (VIII) arson; and

(IX) arrests or persons referred for campus disciplinary action for liquor law violations, drug-related violations, and weapons possession; and

(ii) of the crimes described in subclauses (I) through (VIII) of clause (i), of larceny-theft, simple assault, intimidation, and destruction, damage, or vandalism of property, and of other crimes involving bodily injury to any person, in which the victim is intentionally selected because of the actual or perceived race, gender, religion, sexual orientation, ethnicity, or disability of the victim that are reported to campus security authorities or local police agencies, which data shall be collected and reported according to category of prejudice.

(G) A statement of policy concerning the monitoring and recording through local police agencies of criminal activity at off-campus student organizations which are recognized by the institution and that are engaged in by students attending the institution, including those student organizations with off-campus housing facilities.

(H) A statement of policy regarding the possession, use, and sale of alcoholic beverages and enforcement of State underage drinking laws and a statement of policy regarding the possession, use, and sale of illegal drugs and enforcement of Federal and State drug laws and a description of any drug or alcohol abuse education programs as required under section 120 of this Act [20 USCS § 1011i].

(I) A statement advising the campus community where law enforcement agency information provided by a State under section 170101(j) of the Violent Crime Control and Law Enforcement Act of 1994 (42 U.S.C. 14071(j)), concerning registered sex offenders may be obtained, such as the law enforcement office of the institution, a local law enforcement agency with jurisdiction for the campus, or a computer network address.

(J) A statement of current campus policies regarding immediate emergency response and evacuation procedures, including the use of electronic and cellular communication (if appropriate), which policies shall include procedures to-

(i) immediately notify the campus community upon the confirmation of a significant emergency or dangerous situation involving an immediate threat to the health or safety of students or staff occurring on the campus, as defined in paragraph (6), unless issuing a notification will compromise efforts to contain the emergency;

(ii) publicize emergency response and evacuation procedures on an annual basis in a manner designed to reach students and staff; and

(iii) test emergency response and evacuation procedures on an annual basis.

(2) Nothing in this subsection shall be construed to authorize the Secretary to require particular policies, procedures, or practices by institutions of higher education with respect to campus crimes or campus security.

(3) Each institution participating in any program under this title shall make timely reports to the campus community on crimes considered to be a threat to other students and employees described in paragraph (1)(F) that are reported to campus security or local law police agencies. Such reports shall be provided to students and employees in a manner that is timely and that will aid in the prevention of similar occurrences.

(4) (A) Each institution participating in any program under this title that maintains a police or security department of any kind shall make, keep, and maintain a daily log, written in a form that can be easily understood, recording all crimes reported to such police or security department, including—

(i) the nature, date, time, and general location of each crime; and

(ii) the disposition of the complaint, if known.

(B) (i) All entries that are required pursuant to this paragraph shall, except where disclosure of such information is prohibited by law or such disclosure would jeopardize the confidentiality of the victim, be open to public inspection within two business days of the initial report being made to the department or a campus security authority.

(ii) If new information about an entry into a log becomes available to a police or security department, then the new information shall be recorded in the log not later than two business days after the information becomes available to the police or security department.

(iii) If there is clear and convincing evidence that the release of such information would jeopardize an ongoing criminal investigation or the safety of an individual, cause a suspect to flee or evade detection, or result in the destruction of evidence, such information may be withheld until that damage is no longer likely to occur from the release of such information

(5) On an annual basis, each institution participating in any program under this title shall submit to the Secretary a copy of the statistics required to be made available under paragraph (1)(F). The Secretary shall—

(A) review such statistics and report on campus crime statistics by September 1, 2000;

(B) make copies of the statistics submitted to the Secretary available to the public; and

(C) in coordination with representatives of institutions of higher education, identify exemplary campus security policies, procedures, and practices and disseminate information concerning those policies, procedures, and practices that have proven effective in the reduction of campus crime.

(6) (A) In this subsection:

(i) The term "campus" means—

(I) any building or property owned or controlled by an institution of higher education within the same reasonably contiguous geographic area of the institution and used by the institution in direct support of, or in a manner related to, the institution's educational purposes, including residence halls; and

(II) property within the same reasonably contiguous geographic area of the institution that is owned by the institution but controlled by another person, is used by students, and supports institutional purposes (such as a food or other retail vendor).

(ii) The term "noncampus building or property" means—

(I) any building or property owned or controlled by a student organization recognized by the institution; and

(II) any building or property (other than a branch campus) owned or controlled by an institution of higher education that is used in direct support of, or in relation to, the institution's educational purposes, is used by students, and is not within the same reasonably contiguous geographic area of the institution.

(iii) The term "public property" means all public property that is within the same reasonably contiguous geographic area of the institution, such as a sidewalk, a street, other thoroughfare, or parking facility, and is adjacent to a facility owned or controlled by the institution if the facility is used by the institution in direct support of, or in a manner related to the institution's educational purposes.

(B) In cases where branch campuses of an institution of higher education, schools within an institution of higher education, or administrative divisions within an institution are not within a reasonably contiguous geographic area, such entities shall be considered separate campuses for purposes of the reporting requirements of this section.

(7) The statistics described in paragraphs (1)(F) shall be compiled in accordance with the definitions used in the uniform crime reporting system of the Department of Justice, Federal Bureau of Investigation, and the modifications in such definitions as implemented pursuant to the Hate Crime Statistics Act [28 USCS § 534 note]. Such statistics shall not identify victims of crimes or persons accused of crimes.

(8) (A) Each institution of higher education participating in any program under this title shall develop and distribute as part of the report described in paragraph (1) a statement of policy regarding—

    (i) such institution's campus sexual assault programs, which shall be aimed at prevention of sex offenses; and

    (ii) the procedures followed once a sex offense has occurred.

  (B) The policy described in subparagraph shall address the following areas:

    (i) Education programs to promote the awareness of rape, acquaintance rape, and other sex offenses.

    (ii) Possible sanctions to be imposed following the final determination of an on-campus disciplinary procedure regarding rape, acquaintance rape, or other sex offenses, forcible or nonforcible.

    (iii) Procedures students should follow if a sex offense occurs, including who should be contacted, the importance of preserving evidence as may be necessary to the proof of criminal sexual assault, and to whom the alleged offense should be reported.

    (iv) Procedures for on-campus disciplinary action in cases of alleged sexual assault, which shall include a clear statement that—

        (I) the accuser and the accused are entitled to the same opportunities to have others present during a campus disciplinary proceeding; and

        (II) both the accuser and the accused shall be informed of the outcome of any campus disciplinary proceeding brought alleging a sexual assault.

    (v) Informing students of their options to notify proper law enforcement authorities, including on-campus and local police, and the option to be assisted by campus authorities in notifying such authorities, if the student so chooses.

(vi) Notification of students of existing counseling, mental health or student services for victims of sexual assault, both on campus and in the community.

(vii) Notification of students of options for, and available assistance in, changing academic and living situations after an alleged sexual assault incident, if so requested by the victim and if such changes are reasonably available.

(C) Nothing in this paragraph shall be construed to confer a private right of action upon any person to enforce the provisions of this paragraph.

(9) The Secretary shall provide technical assistance in complying with the provisions of this section to an institution of higher education who requests such assistance.

(10) Nothing in this section shall be construed to require the reporting or disclosure of privileged information.

(11) The Secretary shall report to the appropriate committees of Congress each institution of higher education that the Secretary determines is not in compliance with the reporting requirements of this subsection.

(12) For purposes of reporting the statistics with respect to crimes described in paragraph (1)(F), an institution of higher education shall distinguish, by means of separate categories, any criminal offenses that occur—

(A) on campus;

(B) in or on a noncampus building or property;

(C) on public property; and

(D) in dormitories or other residential facilities for students on campus.

(13) Upon a determination pursuant to section 487(c)(3)(B) [20 USCS § 1094 (c)(3)(B)] that an institution of higher education has substantially misrepresented the number, location, or nature of the crimes required to be reported under this subsection, the Secretary shall impose a civil penalty upon the institution in the same amount and pursuant to the same procedures as a civil penalty is imposed under section 487(c)(3)(B) [20 USCS § 1094(c)(3)(B)].

(14) (A) Nothing in this subsection may be construed to—

(i) create a cause of action against any institution of higher education or any employee of such an institution for any civil liability; or

(ii) establish any standard of care.

(B) Notwithstanding any other provision of law, evidence regarding compliance or noncompliance with this subsection shall not be admissible as evidence in any proceeding of any court, agency, board, or other entity, except with respect to an action to enforce this subsection.

(15) The Secretary shall annually report to the authorizing committees regarding compliance with this subsection by institutions of higher education, including an up-to-date report on the Secretary's monitoring of such compliance.

(16) The Secretary may seek the advice and counsel of the Attorney General concerning the development, and dissemination to institutions of higher education, of best practices information about campus safety and emergencies.

(17) Nothing in this subsection shall be construed to permit an institution, or an officer, employee, or agent of an institution, participating in any program under this title to retaliate, intimidate, threaten, coerce, or otherwise discriminate against any individual with respect to the implementation of any provision of this subsection.

(18) This subsection may be cited as the "Jeanne Clery Disclosure of Campus Security Policy and Campus Crime Statistics Act."

Source: Available at http://www.securityoncampus.org/index.php?option=com_content&view=article&id=318%3Ajeanne-clery-act-text&catid=64%3Acleryact&Itemid=60

Appendix 4: U.S. Supreme Court Cases Related to School and Campus Crime and Violence

Bethel v. Fraser, 478 U.S. 675 (1986):
Fraser was sanctioned for delivering a speech before the student body in which he used a series of sexual innuendoes. The Supreme Court upheld his punishment in determining that schools may regulate student speech during school-sponsored events.

Board of Education of Independent School District #92 of Pottawatomie County v. Earls. 536 U.S. 822 (2002):
The most recent case on school-based drug testing. The Court upheld the district's policy requiring all students who wished to participate in extracurricular activities to submit to a urinalysis.

Davis v. Monroe County Board of Education, 526 U.S. 629 (1999):
The Court ruled that schools can be held legally liable for not responding to peer-to-peer sexual harassment when they are aware it is occurring.

Doe v. Renfrow, 451 U.S. 1022 (1979):
An unannounced visit by drug-detecting canines resulted in the strip-search of a 13-year-old girl. The Court held that the strip search violated her Fourth Amendment right because the canine search was not reliable enough to make subsequent searches justified.

Gebser v. Lago Vista Independent School Dist., 524 U.S. 274 (1998):
School districts can be held liable under Title IX when there is deliberate indifference to teacher-on-student sexual harassment.

Goss v. Lopez, 419 U.S. 565 (1975)
In this pivotal case, the Court determined that students must receive due process prior to being suspended or expelled. At minimum, students must be notified of the charges and given an opportunity to respond.

Grutter v. Bollinger, 539 U.S. 306 (2003)
Barbara Grutter challenged the University of Michigan Law School's admissions policy, which she felt to be discriminatory. The Court held that diversity was a critical component of higher education and that institutions can lawfully include it as part of their admissions process.

Hazelwood v. Kuhlmeier, 484 U.S. 260 (1983)
Hazelwood East High School principal edited two articles out of the school newspaper, deeming them inappropriate. The Court held that administrators can limit students' free press when the outlet is a school-sponsored publication.

Morse v. Frederick, 551 U.S. 393 (2007)
Eighteen-year-old Joseph Frederick was suspended for displaying a banner reading "BONG HITS 4 JESUS during the 2002 Olympic Torch Relay. The Court held that Principal Deborah Morse's actions did not violate Frederick's constitutional rights, as educators can suppress student speech at school-sponsored events if it can be reasonably viewed as promoting illegal drug use.

New Jersey v. T.L.O., 469 U.S. 325 (1985)
The Court held that schools can search students based on reasonable suspicion, rather than having to obtain a search warrant. Searches must be justified at their inception and reasonable in scope.

Safford v. Redding, 557 U.S. (2009)
Savannah Redding was strip-searched by school officials based on information they had acquired from another student, who told officials Redding had ibuprofen pills she had not checked in at the school office. The search revealed no drugs. The court found this type of strip search to be in violation of Redding's Fourth Amendment right to privacy.

Rumsfeld v. Forum for Academic and Institutional Rights (FAIR), 547 U.S. 47 (2006)
The federal government can withhold funding from universities if those institutions refuse to allow military recruiters on campus. Several law schools had denied access to campus recruiters because they disapproved of the military's "Don't Ask, Don't Tell" policy.

Tinker v. Des Moines. 393 U.S. 503 (1969):
When three students wore black armbands to school to protest U.S. involvement in the Vietnam War, they were suspended for violating school policy. The Court sided with the students in holding that students have rights of expression within a public school.

U.S. v. Lopez, 514 U.S. 549 (1995):
A 12th-grade student was charged with violating the Gun-Free School Zones Act of 1990 when he carried a concealed handgun into his high school.

Vernonia School District 47J v. Acton, 515 U.S. 646 (1995):
The Court held that a school policy requiring all students engaged in extracurricular athletic programs to submit to random drug testing did not violate students' Fourth Amendment right to privacy.

Appendix 5: U.S. Supreme Court Decisions Relevant to School Crime and Violence

One of the most recent U.S. Supreme Court rulings related to school crime and violence addressed the constitutionality of school-based drug testing of students involved in extracurricular activities. In *Board of Education of Independent School District No. 92 of Pottawatamie County et al. v. Lindsay Earls et al.*, the Court ruled that drug testing of all students involved in extracurricular activities was constitutional.

Opinion of the Court

> NOTICE: This opinion is subject to formal revision before publication in the preliminary print of the United States Reports. Readers are requested to notify the Reporter of Decisions, Supreme Court of the United States, Washington, D C. 20543, of any typographical or other formal errors, in order that corrections may be made before the preliminary print goes to press.

SUPREME COURT OF THE UNITED STATES

No. 01-332

BOARD OF EDUCATION OF INDEPENDENT SCHOOL DISTRICT NO. 92 OF POTTAWATOMIE COUNTY, et al., PETITIONERS *v.* LINDSAY EARLS et al.

ON WRIT OF CERTIORARI TO THE UNITED STATES COURT OF APPEALS FOR THE TENTH CIRCUIT

[June 27, 2002]

Justice Thomas delivered the opinion of the Court.

The Student Activities Drug Testing Policy implemented by the Board of Education of Independent School District No. 92 of Pottawatomie County (School District) requires all students who participate in competitive extracurricular activities to submit to drug testing. Because this Policy reasonably serves the School District's important interest in detecting and preventing drug use among its students, we hold that it is constitutional.

I

The city of Tecumseh, Oklahoma, is a rural community located approximately 40 miles southeast of Oklahoma City. The School District administers all Tecumseh public schools. In the fall of 1998, the School District adopted the Student Activities Drug Testing Policy (Policy), which requires all middle and high school students to consent to drug testing in order to participate in any extracurricular activity. In practice, the Policy has been applied only to competitive extracurricular activities sanctioned by the Oklahoma Secondary Schools Activities Association, such as the Academic Team, Future Farmers of America, Future Homemakers of America, band, choir, pom pom, cheerleading, and athletics. Under the Policy, students are required to take a drug test before participating in an extracurricular activity, must submit to random drug testing while participating in that activity, and must agree to be tested at any time upon reasonable suspicion. The urinalysis tests are designed to detect only the use of illegal drugs, including amphetamines, marijuana, cocaine, opiates, and barbiturates, not medical conditions or the presence of authorized prescription medications.

At the time of their suit, both respondents attended Tecumseh High School. Respondent Lindsay Earls was a member of the show choir, the marching band, the Academic Team, and the National Honor Society. Respondent Daniel James sought to participate in the Academic Team.[1] Together with their parents, Earls and James brought a 42 U.S.C. § 1983 action against the School District, challenging the Policy both on its face and as applied to their participation in extracurricular activities.[2] They alleged that the Policy violates the Fourth Amendment as incorporated by the Fourteenth Amendment and requested injunctive and declarative relief. They also argued that the School District failed to identify a special need for testing students who participate in extracurricular activities, and that the "Drug Testing Policy neither addresses a proven problem nor promises to bring any benefit to students or the school." App. 9.

Applying the principles articulated in *Vernonia School Dist. 47J v. Acton,* 515 U.S. 646 (1995), in which we upheld the suspicionless drug testing of school athletes, the United States District Court for the Western District of Oklahoma rejected respondents' claim that the Policy was unconstitutional and granted summary judgment to the School District. The court noted that "special needs" exist in the public school context and that, although the School District did "not show a drug problem of epidemic proportions," there was a history of drug abuse starting in 1970 that presented "legitimate cause for concern." 115 F. Supp. 2d 1281, 1287 (2000). The District Court also held that the Policy was effective because "[i]t can scarcely be disputed that the drug problem among the student body is effectively addressed by making sure that the large number of students participating in competitive, extracurricular activities do not use drugs." *Id.*, at 1295.

The United States Court of Appeals for the Tenth Circuit reversed, holding that the Policy violated the Fourth Amendment. The Court of Appeals agreed with the District Court that the Policy must be evaluated in the "unique environment of the school setting," but reached a different conclusion as to the Policy's constitutionality. 242 F.3d 1264, 1270 (2001). Before imposing a suspicionless drug testing program, the Court of Appeals concluded that a school "must demonstrate that there is some identifiable drug abuse problem among a sufficient number of those subject to the testing, such that testing that group of students will actually redress its drug problem." *Id.*, at 1278. The Court of Appeals then held that because the School District failed to demonstrate such a problem existed among Tecumseh students participating in competitive extracurricular activities, the Policy was unconstitutional. We granted certiorari, 534 U.S. 1015 (2001), and now reverse.

II

The Fourth Amendment to the United States Constitution protects "[t]he right of the people to be secure in their persons, houses, papers, and effects, against unreasonable searches and seizures." Searches by public school officials, such as the collection of urine samples, implicate Fourth Amendment interests. See *Vernonia, supra,* at 652; cf. *New Jersey* v. *T. L. O.,* 469 U.S. 325, 334 (1985). We must therefore review the School District's Policy for "reasonableness," which is the touchstone of the constitutionality of a governmental search.

In the criminal context, reasonableness usually requires a showing of probable cause. See, *e.g.*, *Skinner* v. *Railway Labor Executives' Assn.*, 489 U.S. 602, 619 (1989). The probable-cause standard, however, "is peculiarly related to criminal investigations" and may be unsuited to determining the reasonableness of administrative searches where the "Government seeks to *prevent* the development of hazardous conditions." *Treasury Employees* v. *Von Raab,* 489 U.S. 656, 667–668 (1989) (internal quotation marks and citations omitted) (collecting cases). The Court has also held that a warrant and finding of probable cause are unnecessary in the public school context because such requirements " 'would unduly interfere with the maintenance of the swift and informal disciplinary procedures [that are] needed.' " *Vernonia, supra,* at 653 (quoting *T. L. O., supra,* at 340–341).

Given that the School District's Policy is not in any way related to the conduct of criminal investigations, see Part II—B, *infra,* respondents do not contend that the School District requires probable cause before testing students for drug use. Respondents instead argue that drug testing must be based at least on some level of individualized suspicion. See Brief for Respondents 12–14. It is true that we generally determine the reasonableness of a search by balancing the nature of the intrusion on the individual's privacy against the promotion of legitimate governmental interests. See *Delaware* v. *Prouse,* 440 U.S. 648, 654 (1979). But we have long held that "the Fourth Amendment imposes no irreducible requirement of [individualized] suspicion." *United States* v. *Martinez-Fuerte,* 428 U.S. 543, 561 (1976). "[I]n certain limited circumstances, the Government's need to discover such latent or hidden conditions, or to prevent their development, is sufficiently compelling to justify the intrusion on privacy entailed by conducting such searches without any measure of individualized suspicion." *Von Raab, supra,* at 668; see also *Skinner, supra,* at 624. Therefore, in the context of safety and administrative regulations, a search unsupported by probable cause may be reasonable "when 'special needs, beyond the normal need for law enforcement, make the warrant and probable-cause requirement impracticable.' " *Griffin* v. *Wisconsin,* 483 U.S. 868, 873 (1987) (quoting *T. L. O., supra,* at 351 (Blackmun, J., concurring in judgment)); see also *Vernonia, supra,* at 653; *Skinner, supra,* at 619.

Significantly, this Court has previously held that "special needs" inhere in the public school context. See *Vernonia, supra,* at 653;

T. L. O., supra, at 339–340. While schoolchildren do not shed their constitutional rights when they enter the schoolhouse, see *Tinker* v. *Des Moines Independent Community School Dist.,* 393 U.S. 503, 506 (1969), "Fourth Amendment rights . . . are different in public schools than elsewhere; the 'reasonableness' inquiry cannot disregard the schools' custodial and tutelary responsibility for children." *Vernonia, supra,* at 656. In particular, a finding of individualized suspicion may not be necessary when a school conducts drug testing.

In *Vernonia,* this Court held that the suspicionless drug testing of athletes was constitutional. The Court, however, did not simply authorize all school drug testing, but rather conducted a fact-specific balancing of the intrusion on the children's Fourth Amendment rights against the promotion of legitimate governmental interests. See 515 U.S., at 652–653. Applying the principles of *Vernonia* to the somewhat different facts of this case, we conclude that Tecumseh's Policy is also constitutional.

A

We first consider the nature of the privacy interest allegedly compromised by the drug testing. See *id.,* at 654. As in *Vernonia,* the context of the public school environment serves as the backdrop for the analysis of the privacy interest at stake and the reasonableness of the drug testing policy in general. See *ibid.* ("Central . . . is the fact that the subjects of the Policy are (1) children, who (2) have been committed to the temporary custody of the State as schoolmaster"); see also *id.,* at 665 ("The most significant element in this case is the first we discussed: that the Policy was undertaken in furtherance of the government's responsibilities, under a public school system, as guardian and tutor of children entrusted to its care"); *ibid.* ("[W]hen the government acts as guardian and tutor the relevant question is whether the search is one that a reasonable guardian and tutor might undertake").

A student's privacy interest is limited in a public school environment where the State is responsible for maintaining discipline, health, and safety. Schoolchildren are routinely required to submit to physical examinations and vaccinations against disease. See *id.,* at 656. Securing order in the school environment sometimes requires that students be subjected to greater controls than those appropriate for adults. See *T. L. O., supra,* at 350 (Powell, J., concurring) ("Without first establishing discipline and maintaining order, teachers cannot begin to educate their students. And apart from education, the school has the obligation to protect pupils from mistreatment by other children, and also to protect teachers themselves from violence by the few students whose conduct in recent years has prompted national concern").

Respondents argue that because children participating in nonathletic extracurricular activities are not subject to regular physicals and communal undress, they have a stronger expectation of privacy than the athletes tested in *Vernonia*. See Brief for Respondents 18–20. This distinction, however, was not essential to our decision in *Vernonia*, which depended primarily upon the school's custodial responsibility and authority.[3]

In any event, students who participate in competitive extracurricular activities voluntarily subject themselves to many of the same intrusions on their privacy as do athletes.[4] Some of these clubs and activities require occasional off-campus travel and communal undress. All of them have their own rules and requirements for participating students that do not apply to the student body as a whole. 115 F. Supp. 2d, at 1289–1290. For example, each of the competitive extracurricular activities governed by the Policy must abide by the rules of the Oklahoma Secondary Schools Activities Association, and a faculty sponsor monitors the students for compliance with the various rules dictated by the clubs and activities. See *id.*, at 1290. This regulation of extracurricular activities further diminishes the expectation of privacy among schoolchildren. Cf. *Vernonia*, *supra*, at 657 ("Somewhat like adults who choose to participate in a closely regulated industry, students who voluntarily participate in school athletics have reason to expect intrusions upon normal rights and privileges, including privacy" (internal quotation marks omitted)). We therefore conclude that the students affected by this Policy have a limited expectation of privacy.

B

Next, we consider the character of the intrusion imposed by the Policy. See *Vernonia*, *supra*, at 658. Urination is "an excretory function traditionally shielded by great privacy." *Skinner*, 489 U.S., at 626. But the "degree of intrusion" on one's privacy caused by collecting a urine sample "depends upon the manner in which production of the urine sample is monitored." *Vernonia*, *supra*, at 658.

Under the Policy, a faculty monitor waits outside the closed restroom stall for the student to produce a sample and must "listen for the normal sounds of urination in order to guard against tampered specimens and to insure an accurate chain of custody." App. 199. The monitor then pours the sample into two bottles that are sealed and placed into a mailing pouch along with a consent form signed by the student. This procedure is virtually identical to that reviewed in *Vernonia*, except that it additionally protects privacy by allowing male students to produce their samples behind a closed stall. Given that we considered the method of collection in *Vernonia* a "negligible" intrusion, 515 U.S., at 658, the method here is even less problematic.

In addition, the Policy clearly requires that the test results be kept in confidential files separate from a student's other educational records and released to school personnel only on a "need to know" basis. Respondents nonetheless contend that the intrusion on students' privacy is significant because the Policy fails to protect effectively against the disclosure of confidential information and, specifically, that the school "has been careless in protecting that information: for example, the Choir teacher looked at students' prescription drug lists and left them where other students could see them." Brief for Respondents 24. But the choir teacher is someone with a "need to know," because during off-campus trips she needs to know what medications are taken by her students. Even before the Policy was enacted the choir teacher had access to this information. See App. 132. In any event, there is no allegation that any other student did see such information. This one example of alleged carelessness hardly increases the character of the intrusion.

Moreover, the test results are not turned over to any law enforcement authority. Nor do the test results here lead to the imposition of discipline or have any academic consequences. Cf. *Vernonia, supra,* at 658, and n. 2. Rather, the only consequence of a failed drug test is to limit the student's privilege of participating in extracurricular activities. Indeed, a student may test positive for drugs twice and still be allowed to participate in extracurricular activities. After the first positive test, the school contacts the student's parent or guardian for a meeting. The student may continue to participate in the activity if within five days of the meeting the student shows proof of receiving drug counseling and submits to a second drug test in two weeks. For the second positive test, the student is suspended from participation in all extracurricular activities for 14 days, must complete four hours of substance abuse counseling, and must submit to monthly drug tests. Only after a third positive test will the student be suspended from participating in any extracurricular activity for the remainder of the school year, or 88 school days, whichever is longer. See App. 201-202.

Given the minimally intrusive nature of the sample collection and the limited uses to which the test results are put, we conclude that the invasion of students' privacy is not significant.

C

Finally, this Court must consider the nature and immediacy of the government's concerns and the efficacy of the Policy in meeting them. See *Vernonia*, 515 U.S., at 660. This Court has already articulated in detail the importance of the governmental concern in preventing drug use by schoolchildren. See *id.*, at 661–662. The drug abuse problem among our Nation's youth has hardly abated since *Vernonia* was decided in 1995. In fact, evidence suggests that it has only grown worse.[5] As in *Vernonia*, "the necessity for the State to act is magnified by the fact that this evil is being visited not just upon individuals at large, but upon children for whom it has undertaken a special responsibility of care and direction." *Id.,* at 662. The health and safety risks identified in *Vernonia* apply with equal force to Tecumseh's children. Indeed, the nationwide drug epidemic makes the war against drugs a pressing concern in every school.

Additionally, the School District in this case has presented specific evidence of drug use at Tecumseh schools. Teachers testified that they had seen students who appeared to be under the influence of drugs and that they had heard students speaking openly about using drugs. See, *e.g.*, App. 72 (deposition of Dean Rogers); *id.*, at 115 (deposition of Sheila Evans). A drug dog found marijuana cigarettes near the school parking lot. Police officers once found drugs or drug paraphernalia in a car driven by a Future Farmers of America member. And the school board president reported that people in the community were calling the board to discuss the "drug situation." See 115 F. Supp. 2d, at 1285–1286. We decline to second- guess the finding of the District Court that "[v]iewing the evidence as a whole, it cannot be reasonably disputed that the [School District] was faced with a 'drug problem' when it adopted the Policy." *Id.*, at 1287.

Respondents consider the proffered evidence insufficient and argue that there is no "real and immediate interest" to justify a policy of drug testing nonathletes. Brief for Respondents 32. We have recognized, however, that "[a] demonstrated problem of drug abuse ... [is] not in all cases necessary to the validity of a testing regime," but that some showing does "shore up an assertion of special need for a suspicionless general search program." *Chandler* v. *Miller,* 520 U.S. 305, 319 (1997). The School District has provided sufficient evidence to shore up the need for its drug testing program.

Furthermore, this Court has not required a particularized or pervasive drug problem before allowing the government to conduct suspicionless drug testing. For instance, in *Von Raab* the Court upheld the drug testing of customs officials on a purely preventive basis, without any documented history of drug use by such officials. See 489 U.S., at 673. In response to the lack of evidence relating to drug use, the Court noted generally that "drug abuse is one of the most serious problems confronting our society today," and that programs to prevent and detect drug use among customs officials could not be deemed unreasonable. *Id.*, at 674; cf. *Skinner*, 489 U.S., at 607, and n. 1 (noting nationwide studies that identified on-the-job alcohol and drug use by railroad employees). Likewise, the need to prevent and deter the substantial harm of childhood drug use provides the necessary immediacy for a school testing policy. Indeed, it would make little sense to require a school district to wait for a substantial portion of its students to begin using drugs before it was allowed to institute a drug testing program designed to deter drug use.

Given the nationwide epidemic of drug use, and the evidence of increased drug use in Tecumseh schools, it was entirely reasonable for the School District to enact this particular drug testing policy. We reject the Court of Appeals' novel test that "any district seeking to impose a random suspicionless drug testing policy as a condition to participation in a school activity must demonstrate that there is some identifiable drug abuse problem among a sufficient number of those subject to the testing, such that testing that group of students will actually redress its drug problem." 242 F.3d, at 1278. Among other problems, it would be difficult to administer such a test. As we cannot articulate a threshold level of drug use that would suffice to justify a drug testing program for schoolchildren, we refuse to fashion what would in effect be a constitutional quantum of drug use necessary to show a "drug problem."

Respondents also argue that the testing of nonathletes does not implicate any safety concerns, and that safety is a "crucial factor" in applying the special needs framework. Brief for Respondents 25–27. They contend that there must be "surpassing safety interests," *Skinner, supra,* at 634, or "extraordinary safety and national security hazards," *Von Raab, supra,* at 674, in order to override the usual protections of the Fourth Amendment. See Brief for Respondents 25–26. Respondents are correct that safety factors into the special needs analysis, but the safety interest furthered by drug testing is undoubtedly substantial for all children, athletes and nonathletes alike. We know all too well that drug use carries a variety of health risks for children, including death from overdose.

We also reject respondents' argument that drug testing must presumptively be based upon an individualized reasonable suspicion of wrongdoing because such a testing regime would be less intrusive. See *id.*, at 12–16. In this context, the Fourth Amendment does not require a finding of individualized suspicion, see *supra*, at 5, and we decline to impose such a requirement on schools attempting to prevent and detect drug use by students. Moreover, we question whether testing based on individualized suspicion in fact would be less intrusive. Such a regime would place an additional burden on public school teachers who are already tasked with the difficult job of maintaining order and discipline. A program of individualized suspicion might unfairly target members of unpopular groups. The fear of lawsuits resulting from such targeted searches may chill enforcement of the program, rendering it ineffective in combating drug use. See *Vernonia*, 515 U.S., at 663–664 (offering similar reasons for why "testing based on 'suspicion' of drug use would not be better, but worse"). In any case, this Court has repeatedly stated that reasonableness under the Fourth Amendment does not require employing the least intrusive means, because "[t]he logic of such elaborate less-restrictive-alternative arguments could raise insuperable barriers to the exercise of virtually all search-and-seizure powers." *Martinez and Fuerte,* 428 U.S., at 556–557, n. 12; see also *Skinner, supra,* at 624 ("[A] showing of individualized suspicion is not a constitutional floor, below which a search must be presumed unreasonable").

Finally, we find that testing students who participate in extracurricular activities is a reasonably effective means of addressing the School District's legitimate concerns in preventing, deterring, and detecting drug use. While in *Vernonia* there might have been a closer fit between the testing of athletes and the trial court's finding that the drug problem was "fueled by the 'role model' effect of athletes' drug use," such a finding was not essential to the holding. 515 U.S., at 663; cf. *id.,* at 684–685 (O'Connor, J., dissenting) (questioning the extent of the drug problem, especially as applied to athletes). *Vernonia* did not require the school to test the group of students most likely to use drugs, but rather considered the constitutionality of the program in the context of the public school's custodial responsibilities. Evaluating the Policy in this context, we conclude that the drug testing of Tecumseh students who participate in extracurricular activities effectively serves the School District's interest in protecting the safety and health of its students.

III

Within the limits of the Fourth Amendment, local school boards must assess the desirability of drug testing schoolchildren. In upholding the constitutionality of the Policy, we express no opinion as to its wisdom. Rather, we hold only that Tecumseh's Policy is a reasonable means of furthering the School District's important interest in preventing and deterring drug use among its schoolchildren. Accordingly, we reverse the judgment of the Court of Appeals.

It is so ordered.

Notes

1. The District Court noted that the School District's allegations concerning Daniel James called his standing to sue into question because his failing grades made him ineligible to participate in any interscholastic competition. See 115 F. Supp. 2d 1281, 1282, n. 1 (WD Okla. 2000). The court noted, however, that the dispute need not be resolved because Lindsay Earls had standing, and therefore the court was required to address the constitutionality of the drug testing policy. See *ibid.* Because we are likewise satisfied that Earls has standing, we need not address whether James also has standing.

2. The respondents did not challenge the Policy either as it applies to athletes or as it provides for drug testing upon reasonable, individualized suspicion. See App. 28.

3. Justice Ginsburg argues that *Vernonia School Dist. 47J* v. *Acton,* 515 U.S. 646 (1995), depended on the fact that the drug testing program applied only to student athletes. But even the passage cited by the dissent manifests the supplemental nature of this factor, as the Court in *Vernonia* stated that "[l]egitimate privacy expectations are *even less* with regard to student athletes." See *post,* at 5 (citing *Vernonia,* 515 U.S., at 657) (emphasis added). In upholding the drug testing program in *Vernonia,* we considered the school context "[c]entral" and "[t]he most significant element." 515 U.S., at 654, 665. This hefty weight on the side of the school's balance applies with similar force in this case even though we undertake a separate balancing with regard to this particular program.

4. Justice Ginsburg's observations with regard to extracurricular activities apply with equal force to athletics. See *post,* at 4 ("Participation in such [extracurricular] activities is a key component of school life, essential in reality for students applying to college, and, for all participants, a significant contributor to the breadth and quality of the educational experience").

5. For instance, the number of 12th graders using any illicit drug increased from 48.4 percent in 1995 to 53.9 percent in 2001. The number of 12th graders reporting they had used marijuana jumped from 41.7 percent to 49.0 percent during that same period. See Department of Health and Human Services, Monitoring the Future: National Results on Adolescent Drug Use, Overview of Key Findings (2001) (Table 1).

Recommended Films About School and Campus Crime and Violence

American Yearbook **(2004)**
Should bullying victims take revenge? This film grapples with the choices faced by victims of school bullying.

April Showers **(2009)**
Writer/director Andrew Robinson, a Columbine survivor, shows how students coped with the aftermath of Columbine and the loss of their friends.

Bang Bang, You're Dead **(2002)**
Students bully Trevor—that is, until Trevor calls in a phony bomb threat with a working bomb. After that, everyone except a group of outcasts is afraid of him, and Trevor takes the blame for anything that goes wrong at the school. One caring drama teacher is Trevor's only salvation.

Basketball Diaries **(1995)**
The film adaptation of about Jim Carroll's descent into drug addiction. Jim is a great basketball player, but little else in his life is great. It is only through drugs that he manages to escape the harsh reality of his life. The film depicts a dream sequence in which Jim (played by Leonardo DiCaprio) goes on a shooting rampage in his school.

Blackboard Jungle **(1955)**
This classic film, starring Sidney Poitier, shows an urban school rife with verbal and physical violence. It spawned numerous remakes.

Blue Chips **(1994)**
Blue Chips shows the cheating and NCAA rules violations that are far too common in college basketball. Coach Pete Bell (played by Nick Nolte) succumbs to the pressure to win and allows powerful athletic boosters to pay his

athletes. The film stars real and former NBA stars Shaquille O'Neal and Penny Hardaway.

Bowling for Columbine (2002)
This award-winning documentary by filmmaker Michael Moore addresses the culture of violence in the United States. It attempts to more deeply understand what motivated the Columbine shooters by looking at gun control, media, governmental violence, welfare policy, and many other factors. It includes interviews with the creators of *South Park,* Charlton Heston, and Marilyn Manson.

Bully (2001)
Not overtly about schools, *Bully* depicts what happens when a victim tires of being bullied and seeks revenge. He and a group of friends suffer the repercussions of their naïve actions.

Cry for Help (2009)
A PBS documentary examining teenage mental illness, suicide, and how to help. It can be viewed online at http://www.pbs.org/wnet/cryforhelp/

Dangerous Minds (1995)
This award-winning film documents the lives of urban youth and demonstrates how one teacher—in this case, an ex-Marine (played by Michelle Pfeiffer)—can help.

Dark Matter (2007)
Inspired by a 1991 school shooting, the film depicts the pressures of academia, in particular for Asian students.

Dead Poets Society (1989)
Set in an elite boarding school, the film depicts the tension students face to succeed and shows how one dedicated and creative teacher can help them explore their true passions.

Detention: The Siege at Johnson High (1997)
Starring Rick Schroeder, Freddy Prinze, Jr., Rodney Dangerfield, and Henry Winkler, this film largely depicts the school hostage situation perpetrated by Eric Houston at Lindhurst High School in 1992.

Duck! The Carbine High Massacre (2000)
One of the first films on this topic released after the Columbine massacre, this black comedy shows the problems with moral panics and conspiracy theories.

Elephant (2003)
This award-winning film from writer/director Gus Van Sant is based on the Columbine shootings. It documents the lead-up to a school massacre by seemingly "normal" students.

Freedom Writers (2007)
Starring Hilary Swank, this film tells the true story of a Long Beach, California, high school teacher who helps her at-risk students develop skills and empathy.

Hidden Rage (2008)
This film documents the traumatic effects of school bullying. The website www.hiddenrage.com provides resources for discussing school violence.

High School High (1996)
A satire that mixes parts of *Dangerous Minds* and *Stand and Deliver,* this film shows how a caring teacher can change a student's life.

Higher Learning (1995)
A diverse college campus grapples with racial tension, hate crimes, rape, and more. The film provides a highly dramatic depiction of how far awry things can go on a campus that is disconnected.

The Killer at Thurston High
This PBS *Frontline* episode tells the story of school shooter Kip Kinkel. The website http://www.pbs.org/wgbh/pages/frontline/shows/kinkel/ provides more information about the case and other school shooters.

Lean on Me (1989)
Morgan Freeman stars as Joe Clark, the principal of a dangerous, urban school in which test scores are so bad the school is close to being shut down. The film highlights the power of expectations.

Light It Up (1999)
Starring musician Usher and actress Rosario Dawson, *Light It Up* tells the story of a group of urban students who stand up for their right to be educated and treated fairly. After a school police officer mistreats one of them, the students take over the school and demand a quality education.

Mean Creek (2004)
A bullied teen and his friends lure the bully into a boat trip and seek revenge. The film shows what can happen when students believe revenge is the answer.

O (2001)
A modern-day retelling of Shakespeare's *Othello,* this film is set in a high school. "O," played by Mekhi Phifer, is the star of the team and the only African American student at the school. He is love with Desi (Julia Stiles), the dean's daughter. Jealous teammate Hugo (Josh Hartnett) is addicted to steroids and initiates a series of problems that explode into major atrocities.

One Eight Seven (1997)
Starring Samuel L. Jackson, this film shows how high school teachers deal with gang violence.

The Program (1993)
Starring James Caan, Omar Epps, and Halle Berry, this film offers a fictional yet realistic depiction of the pressure on college football teams. It includes cheating, recruiting violations, and more.

School Ties (1992)
A cast of young stars (Brendan Fraser, Matt Damon, Chris O'Donnell) show the problems with elite schools, including elitism, privilege, cheating, and anti-Semitism. When working-class newcomer David Greene takes over the quarterback position at an exclusive prep school, the animosity hits a boiling point.

Stand and Deliver (1988)
This film tells the true story of tough and demanding teacher Jaime Escalante, who shows urban high school students in a violence and gang-infested school that it is okay to succeed.

Teachers (1984)
A "day-in-the-life" film, *Teachers* depicts troubled students and shows how their teachers deal with them, both good and bad.

Tomorrow's Children (2001)
This documentary features the work of historian Riane Eisler. It shows how schools have been modeled on domination and hierarchy and the promise of a different model.

Tough Guise (1999)
This documentary by Media Education Foundation discusses how gender roles contribute to many forms of violent behavior today.

Varsity Blues **(1999)**
Shows how football in small-time football in Texas is king. The team is everything, and can get away with anything. Athletes drink illegally, use performance-enhancing drugs, and cheat.

Zero Day **(2003)**
This fictional depiction of the Columbine massacre shows the planning stages, including how the students acquired the weapons. It is acclaimed by journalist and author Dave Cullen as an especially realistic depiction.

Recommended Resources

Books

General

Balfour, S. (Ed.). (2005). *How Can School Violence Be Prevented?* Farmington Hills, MI: Greenhaven.

Bellini, J. (2001). *Child's Prey.* New York: Pinnacle.

Benbenishty, R., & Astor, R. (2005). *School Violence in Context: Culture, Neighborhood, Family, School, and Gender.* New York, NY: Oxford University Press.

Blanchard, K. (2003). *How to Talk to Your Kids About School Violence.* New York: Onomatopoeia.

Brezina, C. (2000). *Deadly School and Campus Violence.* New York: Rosen.

Casella, R. (2001). *At Zero Tolerance: Punishment, Prevention, and School Violence.* New York: Peter Lang.

Casella, R. (2001). *"Being Down": Challenging Violence in Urban Schools.* New York: Teachers College.

Chalmers, P. (2009). *Inside the Mind of a Teen Killer.* Nashville, TN: Thomas Nelson.

Cornell, D. (2006). *School Violence: Fears Versus Facts.* Mahwah, NJ: Lawrence Erlbaum & Associates.

DiGuilio, R. (2001). *Educate, Medicate, or Litigate? What Teachers, Parents, and Administrators Must Do About Student Behavior.* New York: Corwin Books.

Fearnley, F. (2004). *I Wrote on All Four Walls: Teens Speak Out on Violence.* Toronto: Annick.

Finley, L., & Finley, P. (2006). *The Sport Industry's War on Athletes.* Westport, CT: Praeger.

Fisher, B., & Sloan, J. (2007). *Campus Crime:Legal, Social, and Policy Perspectives.* Springfield, IL: Charles C. Thomas.

Flowers, R. (2009). *College Crime: A Statistical Study of Crime on College Campuses.* Jefferson, NC: McFarland.

Gerler, E. (2004). *Handbook of School Violence.* Binghamton, NY: Haworth.

Hunnicutt, S. (Ed.). (2006). *School Shootings.* Farmington Hills, MI: Greenhaven.

Kohn, A. (2005). *Shooters: Myths and Realities of America's Gun Cultures.* New York: Oxford University Press.

Langman, P. (2009). *Why Kids Kill: Inside the Minds of School Shooters.* New York, NY: Palgrave MacMillan.

Lawrence, R. (2006). *School Crime and Juvenile Justice*, 2nd ed. New York: Oxford.

Lieberman, J. (2006). *The Shooting Game: The Making of School Shooters.* Santa Ana, CA: Seven Locks Press.

Mortenson, G. (2007). *Three Cups of Tea: One Man's Mission to Promote Peace . . . One School at a Time.* New York: Penguin.

Mortenson, G. (2009). *Stones into Schools: Promoting Peace with Books, Not Bombs, in Afghanistan and Pakistan.* New York: Viking.

National Resource Council. (2002). *Deadly Lessons: Understanding Lethal School Violence.* Washington, DC: National Academies Press.

Newman, K., Fox, C., Roth, W., & Mehta, J. (2005). *Rampage: The Social Roots of School Shootings.* New York: Basic.

Orr, T. (2001). *Violence in Our Schools: Halls of Hope, Halls of Fear.* New York: Franklin Watts.

Paludi, M. (2008). *Understanding and Preventing Campus Violence.* Westport, CT: Praeger.

Sexton-Radek, K. (2005). *Violence in Schools: Issues, Consequences, and Expressions.* Westport, CT: Praeger.

Stevenson, L. (2003). *From the Inside Out: A Look into Teen Violence and Rebellion.* Bloomington, ID: Authorhouse.

Thomas, R. (2006). *Violence in America's Schools: Understanding, Prevention, and Responses.* Lanham, MD: Rowman & Littlefield.

Turk, W. (Ed.). (2004). *School Crime and Policing.* Upper Saddle River, NJ: Prentice Hall.

Webber, J. (2003). *Failure to Hold: The Politics of School Violence.* Lanham, MD: Rowman & Littlefield.

Weill, S. (2002). *We're Not Monsters: Teens Speak Out About Teens in Trouble.* New York: HarperTempest.

Bullying

Coloroso, B. (2003). *The Bully, the Bullied, and the Bystander: From Preschool to High School—How Parents and Teachers Can Help Break the Cycle of Violence.* New York: HarperCollins.

Fried, S. (2003). *Bullies, Targets, and Witnesses: Helping Children Break the Pain Chain.* New York: M. Evans.

Goodstein, A. (2007). *Totally Wired: What Teens Are Really Doing Online.* New York: St. Martin's Press.

Kelsey, C. (2007). *MySpace: Helping Your Teen Survive Online Adolescence.* New York: Marlowe.

Kowalski, R., Limber, S., & Agatston, P. (2007). *Cyber Bullying: Bullying in the Digital Age.* Malden, MA: Wiley-Blackwell.

Olweus, D. (2004). *Bullying at School: What We Know and What We Can Do.* Cambridge, MA: Blackwell.

Phillips, R., Linney, J., & Pack, C. (2008). *Safe School Ambassadors: Harnessing Student Power to Stop Bullying and Violence.* San Francisco, CA: Jossey-Bass.

Simmons, R. (2002). *Odd Girl Out: The Hidden Culture of Aggression in Girls.* New York: Harcourt.

Weisman, R. (2002). *Queen Bees and Wannabees: Helping Your Daughter Survive Cliques, Gossip, Boyfriends, and Other Realities of Adolescence.* New York: Three Rivers Press.

Willard, N. (2007). *Cyberbullying and Cyberthreats: Responding to the Challenge of Online Social Aggression.* Champaign, IL: Research Press.

Specific Cases

Agger, B. *There Is a Gunman on Campus: Tragedy and Terror at Virginia Tech.* Lanham, MD: Rowman & Littlefield.

Bellini, J. (2001). *Child's Prey.* New York: Pinnacle.

Bernstein, A. (2009). *Bath Massacre: America's First School Bombing.* Ann Arbor, MI: University of Michigan Press.

Brown, B., & Merritt, R. (2002). *No Easy Answers: The Truth Behind the Death at Columbine.* New York: Lantern.

Cullen, D. (2009). *Columbine.* New York, NY: Twelve.

Dolnik, A. (2007). *Negotiating the Impossible?: The Beslan Hostage Crisis.* London: Royal United Services Institute.

Eggington, J. (1991). *Day of fury: The Story of the Tragic Shootings That Forever Changed the Village of Winnetka.* New York: William Morrow.

Eglin, P., & Hester, S. (2003). *The Montreal Massacre: A Story of Membership Categorization Analysis.* Waterloo, ON: Wilfrid Laurier Press.

Gibson, G. (1999). *Gone Boy: A Walkabout.* New York: Anchor.

Giduck, J. (2006). *Terror at Beslan: A Russian Tragedy with Lessons for America's Schools.* Boulder, CO: Paladin Press.

Greenhill, J. (2006). *Someone Has to Die Tonight.* New York: Pinnacle.

Kaplan, J., Papajohn, G., & Zorn, E. (1991). *Murder of Innocence: The Tragic Life and Final Rampage of Laurie Dann, the Schoolhouse Killer.* New York: Warner Books.

Lansford, L. (2006). *Beslan: Shattered Innocence.* Charleston, SC: BookSurge,

Merritt, R., & Brown, B. (2002). *No Easy Answers: The Truth Behind Death at Columbine.* Herndon, VA: Lantern.

Phillips, T. (2007). *Beslan: The Tragedy of School Number 1.* London: Granta Books.

Roy, L. (2009). *No Right to Remain Silent: The Tragedy at Virginia Tech.* New York: Harmony.

Uschan, M. (2005). *The Beslan School Siege and Separatist Terrorism.* Strongsville, OH: Gareth Stevens.

Uttley, S. (2006). *Dunblane Unburried* London: Book Publishing World.

Hazing

DeSantis, C. (2007). *Inside Greek U: Fraternities, Sororities, and the Pursuit of Pleasure, Power, and Prestige.* Lexington, KY: University of Kentucky Press.

Guynn, K. L., & Aquila, F. D. (2005). *Hazing in High Schools: Causes and Consequences.* Bloomington, IN: Phi Delta Kappa Educational Foundation.

Johnson, J., & Holman, M. (Eds.). (2004). *Making the Team: The Inside World of Sport Initiations and Hazing.* Toronto: Canadian Scholar's Press.

Lipkins, S. (2006). *Preventing Hazing: How Parents, Teachers, and Coaches Can Stop the Violence, Harassment, and Humiliation.* San Francisco, CA: Jossey-Bass.

Nuwer, H. (2000). *High School Hazing: When Rites Become Wrongs.* London, UK: Franklin Watts.

Nuwer, H. (2002). *Wrongs of Passage: Fraternities, Sororities, Hazing, and Binge Drinking.* Bloomington, ID: Indiana University Press.

Nuwer, H. (Ed.). (2004). *The Hazing Reader.* Bloomington, ID: Indiana University Press.

Robbins, A. (2005). *Pledged: The Secret Life of Sororities.* New York, NY: Hyperion.

Civil Liberties

Dupre, A. (2009). *Speaking Up: The Unintended Costs of Free Speech in Schools.* Cambridge, MA: Harvard University Press.

Finley, L., & Finley, P. (2005). *Piss Off! How Drug Testing and Other Privacy Violations Are Alienating America's Youth.* Monroe, ME: Common Courage.

Gender

Brown, L. M. (2003). *Girlfighting: Betrayal and Rejection Among Girls*. New York: New York University Press.

Chesney-Lind, M. (2007). *Beyond Bad Girls: Gender, Violence, and Hype*. London: Routledge.

Ferguson, A. (2001). *Bad Boys: Public Schools in the Making of Black Masculinity*. Ann Arbor, MI: University of Michigan Press.

Garbarino, J. (2007). *See Jane Hit: Why Girls Are Growing More Violent and What We Can Do About It*. New York: Penguin.

Hinshaw, S. (2009). *The Triple Bind: Saving Our Teenage Girls from Today's Pressures*. New York: Random House.

Jones, N. (2009). *Between Good and Ghetto: African American Girls and Inner City Violence*. Piscataway, NJ: Rutgers University Press.

Katz, J. (2006). *The Macho Paradox: Why Some Men Hurt Women and How All Men Can Help*. Naperville, IL: Sourcebooks.

Kimmel, M. (2009). *Guyland: The Perilous World Where Boys Become Men*. New York: Parker.

Kindlon, D. (2007). *Alpha Girls: Understanding the New American Girl and How She Is Changing the World*. New York: Rodale.

Meyer, E. (2009). *Gender, Bullying, and Harassment: Strategies to End Sexism and Homophobia in Schools*. New York: Teachers College Press.

Prothrow-Stith, D., & Spivak, H. (2007). *Sugar and Spice and No Longer Nice: How We Can Stop Girls' Violence*. San Francisco, CA: Jossey-Bass.

Hate Crimes

Gerstenfeld, P. (2010). *Hate Crimes: Causes, Controls, and Controversies*. Thousand Oaks, CA: Sage.

Gerstenfeld, P., & Grant, D. (Eds.). (2002). *Crimes of Hate: Selected Readings*. Thousand Oaks, CA: Sage.

Levin, J., & McDevitt, J. (2002). *Hate Crimes Revisited: America's War on Those Who Are Different*. Boulder, CO: Westview.

Dating and Sexual Violence

Daigle, L. (2009). *Unsafe in the Ivory Tower*. Thousand Oaks, CA: Sage.

Miles, A. (2005). *Ending Violence in Teen Dating Relationships*. Minneapolis, MN: Augsburg Books.

Murray, J. (2007). *But He Never Hit Me*. Bloomington, ID: iUniverse.

Ottens, J., & Hotelling, K. (2000). *Sexual Violence on Campus: Policies, Programs, and Perspectives*. New York, NY: Springer.

Drugs

Mohamed, A., & Frtizvold, E. (2009). *Dorm Room Drug Dealers: Drugs and the Privileges of Race and Class.* Boulder, CO: Lynne Reinner.

Wilson, R., & Kolander, C. (2010). *Drug Abuse Prevention: A School and Community Partnership,* 3rd ed. Sudbury, MA: Jones and Bartlett.

Suicide, Eating Disorders, and Self-Harm

Bornstein, K., & Quin, S. (2006). *Hello Cruel World: 1010 Alternatives to Suicide for Teens, Freaks and Other Outlaws.* New York: Seven Stories Press.

Martin, C. (2007). *Perfect Girls, Starving Daughters: The Frightening New Normalcy of Hating Your Body.* Glencoe, IL: Free Press.

Mendelsohn, S. (2007). *It's Not About the Weight: Attacking Eating Disorders from the Inside Out.* Lincoln, NE: iUniverse.

Turner, V. (2002). *Secret Scars: Uncovering and Understanding the Addiction of Self-Injury.* Center City, MN: Hazelden.

Theories/Explanations

Fast, J. (2008). *Ceremonial Violence: A Psychological Explanation of School Shootings.* New York, NY: Overlook Press.

Garbarino, J. (2000). *Lost Boys: Why Our Sons Turn Violent and How We Can Save Them.* New York: Anchor.

Katch, J. (2001). *Under Dead Man's Skin: Discovering the Meaning of Children's Violent Play.* Boston: Beacon.

Kohn, A. (2005). *Shooters: Myths and Realities of America's Gun Culture.* New York: Oxford University Press.

Langman, P. (2009). *Why Kids Kill: Inside the Minds of School Shooters.* New York: Palgrave MacMillan.

Schier, H. (2008). *The Causes of School Violence.* Edina, MN: Abdo Publishing.

Responses

Aronson, E. (2000). *Nobody Left to Hate: Teaching Compassion After Columbine.* Orange, VA: W. H. Freeman.

Bodine, R., Crawford, D., & Schrumpf, F. (2003). *Creating the Peaceable School: A Comprehensive Program for Teaching Conflict Resolution.* Champaign, IL: Research PR Publisher.

Cohen, R. (2005). *Students Resolving Conflict.* New York: Good Year Books.

Cornell, D., & Sheras, P. (2006). *Guidelines for Responding to Student Threats of Violence.* New York: Sopris West.

Cremin, H. (2007). *Peer Mediation: Citizenship and Social Inclusion in Action.* Maidenhead, UK: Open University Press.

DiGuilio, R. (2000). *Educate, Medicate, or Litigate? What Teachers, Parents, and Administrators Must Do About Student Behavior.* New York: Corwin.

Eisler, R., & Miller, R. (Eds.). (2004). *Educating for a Culture of Peace.* Portsmouth, NH: Heinemann.

Fox, J., & Burstein, H. (2010). *Violence and Security on Campus: From Preschool to College.* Westport, CT: Praeger.

Harber, C. (2004). *Schooling as Violence: How Schools Harm Pupils and Societies.* New York: RoutledgeFalmer.

Hemphill, B., & LeBanc, B. (Eds.). (2010). *Enough Is Enough: A Student Affairs Perspective on Preparedness and Response to a Campus Shooting.* Sterling, VA: Stylus.

Hiber, M. (2008). *Should Juveniles Be Tried as Adults?* New York: Greenhaven.

Karp, D., & Allena, T. (2004). *Restorative Justice on the College Campus: Promoting Student Growth and Responsibility and Reawakening the Spirit of Campus Community.* Springfield, IL: Charles C. Thomas.

Lentz, M. (Ed.). (2009). *Campus Security for Public and Private Colleges and Universities.* Eagan, MN: Thomson West.

Lin, J., Brantmeier, E., & Bruhn, C. (2008). *Transforming Education for Peace.* Charlotte, NC: Information Age Publishing.

Nicoletti, J., Spencer-Thomas, S., & Bollinger, C. (2009). *Violence Goes to College: The Authoritative Guide to Prevention and Intervention.* Springfield, IL: Charles C. Thomas.

Schrage, J., & Giacomini, N. (Eds.). (2009). *Reframing Campus Conflict: Student Conduct Practice Through a Social Justice Lens.* Sterling, VA: Stylus.

Smith, P. K. (Ed.). (2003). *Violence in Schools: The Response in Europe.* London: RoutledgeFalmer.

Trump, K. (2000). Classroom *Killers? Hallway Hostages? How Schools Can Prevent and Manage School Crises.* New York: Corwin.

Media

Coleman, L. (2004). *The Copycat Effect: How the Media and Popular Culture Trigger the Mayhem in Tomorrow's Headlines.* New York: Simon & Schuster.

Jones, G. (2003). *Killing Monsters: Why Children Need Fantasy, Super Heroes, and Make-Believe Violence.* New York: Basic.

Potter, W. (2002). *The 11 Myths of Media Violence.* Thousand Oaks, CA: Sage.

Rafter, N. (2000). *Shots in the Mirror.* New York: Oxford University Press.

Ravitch, D., & Vilerette, J. (2003). *Kid Stuff: Marketing Sex and Violence to America's Children.* Baltimore, MD: Johns Hopkins University Press.

Strasburger, V. (2002). *Children, Adolescents and the Media.* Thousand Oaks, CA: Sage.

Websites

PBS *Frontline*: http://www.pbs.org/wgbh/pages/frontline/shows/kinkel/
  Informative video and resources on Kip Kinkel.
Stop Bullying Now! www.stopbullyingnow.hrsa.gov
  Information, resources, and links related to preventing and responding to bullying.
National Youth Violence Prevention Resource Center: http://www.safeyouth.org/scripts/topics/bullying.asp
  Information on a variety of types of school and campus violence.
Ophelia Project: http://www.opheliaproject.org/main/index.htm
  Resources and ideas for addressing girl-on-girl bullying and other issues relevant to girls.
National Center for Victims of Crime Dating Violence Resource Center: http://www.ncvc.org/ncvc/main.aspx?dbID=DB_DatingViolenceResourceCenter101
  Statistics, warning signs, and additional resources related to dating violence.
Stop Hazing: www.stophazing.org
  Statistics, stories, and resources about hazing at all levels.
Inside Hazing: http://www.insidehazing.com/
  Statistics, stories and resources about hazing at all levels.
Dating Violence: www.breakthecycle.org
  Information on warning signs and help available for victims of dating violence.
National Coalition Against Violent Athletes: www.ncava.org
  Focuses on identifying violent athletes at college and professional levels.
Mentors in Violence Prevention: http://www.sportinsociety.org/vpd/mvp.php
  Programs designed to help athletes and others as bystanders to crime and violence.
Security on Campus, Inc: www.securityoncampus.org
  Devoted to disseminating information and resources related to campus safety.
Center for the Prevention of School Violence: http://www.ncdjjdp.org/cpsv/
  Provides information, statistics, and links related to school violence.
Centers for Disease Control and Prevention, School Violence Resources: http://www.cdc.gov/violenceprevention/youthviolence/schoolviolence/index.html
  Resources for preventing and responding to school violence.
Brady Center for Prevent Gun Violence: www.bradycenter.org
  Devoted to informing the public and lobbying for greater control of handguns,
National Crime Prevention Council: www.ncpc.org
  Addresses the prevention of all forms of crime.
National School Safety Center: www.schoolsafety.us

Provides resources to schools on how to stay safe and how to respond to crises.
Safe and Drug-Free Schools Program, U.S. Department of Education: www.ed.gov/offices/OESE/SDFS
   Resources, statistics, and funding available.
Youth Crime Watch of America: www.ignitusworldwide.org
   Student-led groups help prevent crime.
American Academy of Pediatrics: www.aap.org
   Recommendations for safe and healthy children and youth.
American Civil Liberties Union: www.aclu.org
   Civil rights watchdog that is often involved in cases related to students' rights.
National Alliance for Safe Schools: www.safeschools.org
   Provides workshops and resources for educators and schools.
Oregon Social Learning Center: www.oslc.org
   Multidisciplinary center that promotes the scientific understanding of children's health and well-being.
Center for the Study and Prevention of Violence: www.colorado.edu/cspv
   Disseminates research and reports on school violence.
Prevention Institute: www.preventioninstitute.org
   Provides online workshops related to a number of topics.
Street Law: www.streetlaw.org
   Resource for materials on crime and violence, especially for classroom educators.
Violence Policy Center: www.vpc.org
   Performs research, investigation, analysis, and advocacy related to making the United States safer.
Students Against Violence Everywhere: www.save.org
   Student-led organization with multiple chapters.
Drug Free Schools: www.drugfreeschools.com
   Provides statistics and resources related to keeping schools drug free.
Monitoring the Future: www.monitoringthefuture.org
   Major survey of student drug use.
Center for Media Literacy: www.medialit.org
   Research and information related to critical analysis of media.
Stopping Corporal Punishment: www.stophitting.com
   Advocates the end of corporal punishment; provides statistics and reports.
School Violence Resource Center: www.svrc.net
   Information and resources related to all facets of school violence.
Bully Free: www.bullyfree.com
   Resources for ending bullying.
Free Vibe Facts About Drug Use: www.freevibe.com
   Provides fact sheets about a variety of drugs and their effects.
Peaceful Schools International: www.peacefulschoolsinternational.org

Provides support to schools across the globe that have declared their devotion to peace.

Consortium to Prevent School Violence: www.preventschoolviolence.org
  Fact sheets and resources on preventing school violence.

Center for Partnership Studies: www.partnershipway.org
  Sociological and historical information about creating partnership-based schools.

Stop Cyberbullying: www.stopcyberbullying.org
  Devoted to providing information about cyber bullying and its effects.

iSafe: www.isafe.org
  Provider of Internet safety education.

The Cool Spot: http://www.thecoolspot.gov/
  The young teen's place for info on alcohol and resisting peer pressure.

Amnesty International: www.amnesty.org
  Human rights watchdog group; provides information relevant to school violence, youth activism, and teaching human rights.

Hamilton Fish Institute: http://www.hamfish.org/
  Rigorous academic work devoted to safe and healthy children.

Canadian Safe School Network: http://www.canadiansafeschools.com/home.htm
  Information and resources regarding school violence in Canada.

Pennies for Peace: www.penniesforpeace.org
  Empowers young people to get involved so that all children have access to education.

Central Asia Institute: https://www.ikat.org/
  Builds schools in Afghanistan and Pakistan.

Save the Children: http://www.savethechildren.org/
  Helps build schools in many countries.

Free Child: www.freechild.org
  Provides tools and training to young people and adults so that youth can help effect social change.

Do Something: www.dosomething.org
  Information, project ideas, and grant money for young people seeking to make their world better.

Journals

African Journal of Criminology and Justice Studies
American Journal of Criminal Justice
Asia Pacific Journal of Police & Criminal Justice
Asian Journal of Criminology
British Journal of Criminology

Canadian Journal of Criminology and Criminal Justice
Contemporary Issues in Criminology & the Social Sciences
Contemporary Justice Review
Crime, Law, and Social Change
Criminal Justice: The International Journal of Policy and Practice
Criminal Justice Policy Review
Criminal Justice Review
Criminal Justice Studies: A Critical Journal of Crime, Law and Society
Criminology
Criminology and Public Policy
Critical Criminology
Critical Issues in Justice and Politics
Feminist Criminology
French Review of Criminology
Humanity and Society
International Criminal Justice Review
International Journal of Comparative and Applied Criminal Justice
International Journal of Comparative Criminology
International Journal of Criminal Justice Sciences
International Journal of Cyber Criminology
Journal of Contemporary Criminal Justice
Journal for Crime, Conflict and the Media
Journal of Crime and Justice
Journal of Criminal Justice Education
Journal of Criminal Justice and Popular Culture
Journal of Criminal Law and Criminology
Journal of Drug Issues
Journal of Educational Administration and Policy Studies
Journal of Ethnicity in Criminal Justice
Journal of Gang Research
Journal of Knowledge and Best Practices in Juvenile Justice & Psychology
Journal of Law and Conflict Resolution
Journal of Law and Social Challenges
Journal of Peace Education
Journal of Research in Crime and Delinquency
Journal of School Violence
Journal of Security Education
Journal of Social Criminology
Journal of Youth and Adolescence
Justice Policy Journal
Justice Quarterly

Justice Research and Policy
Justice System Journal
Juvenile Justice Journal
Security Journal
Social Problems
Solving Social Problems
Victims and Offenders
Violence Against Women
Violence and Victims
Women and Criminal Justice
Youth and Society

Index

*Page numbers for main entries are listed in **bold**.*

Abuse and crime and violence, **1–3**; children; 1–3; corporal punishment, 1–3, 112–13, 288–89, 384–85; domestic violence; 2, 140–41
Adams, John, 368
ADD/ADHD, **3–5**; psychoactive drugs; 4–5, 148, 150; school shooters; 5, 35–39
Adler, Freda, 208
Adult trials for juveniles, **5–7**; Abraham, Nathaniel, 5–6; Brazill, Nathaniel, 66–67; Brewer, Michael, case, 6, 492–93; concurrent jurisdiction, 6; juvenile waivers, 6; presumptive waivers, 6; statutory exclusion, 6; Treacy, Wayne, 6; Wemberly, Teah, 6
Adults and Children Together Against Violence, 340
Africa and school crime and violence, **7–11**
Agnew, Robert, 443–44
Akers, Ronald, 371
Al-Arian, Sami, 352–53
Alcohol and school crime and violence, **11–14**; binge drinking, 12–13; Canada, 82–83; property crimes, 369–70; responses, 378–80; social norms campaigns, 13, 157–60; suicide, 465–72; weapons, 12–13
Allaway, Charles, xxviii
Al-Nazari, Mohammad, xxxi
American Civil Liberties Union (ACLU), **14–15**; corporal punishment, 112; dress codes, 144; drug testing, 60, 499–501; freedom of speech, 14, 186–89, 490–92; hate crimes, 14–15; LGBTQ, 14; privacy, 352; strip searches, 14, 406–7; zero tolerance, 14, 543–45
American College Health Association (ACHA), 356
Amnesty International, **15–16**, 236
Anger management, **16–17**
Anomie, 442–43
Anonymous tip lines, **17–19**
Appalachian School of Law, 327–28
Arts-based programs, **19–21**; Branch Out, 21; *Elijah's Kite,* 21; Urban Improv, 21
Asia and school crime and violence, **22–24**
Asians, 22–24, 271–73, 275–76
Athletes, 24–35; bystanders, 34; Can I Kiss You?, 33; Coaching Boys Into Men, 34; college, 24–28; Columbine High School, 29; cultural spillover theory, 31; dating violence, 30; Duke lacrosse, 154–56; Glen Ridge, New Jersey, hazing, 29–30, 72, 225–31, 503, 512–13; high school, 32, 506–7; La Salle University, 263–64; Major League Baseball, 35; Mentors in Violence Prevention, 32, 33–34; modeling theory, 31; National Football League, 34–35; Northwestern High School, 324–25; Project Teamwork, 34; sexual assault, 26–27, 30, 33–34, 154–56, 263–64, 324–25, 455–56; violence prevention, 32–35
Athletes and crime and violence, college, **24–28**

Athletes and crime and violence, high school, **28–33**
Athletes and violence prevention, **33–35**
Auvinen, Pekka-Eric, xxxv, **35–39**

Barbaro, Anthony, xxvii
Bartley, Kenny, xxxiv
Basketball Diaries, 86, 296
Bath, Michigan, school bombing, **41–44**, 95
Baylor College basketball murder case, **44–46**
Beccaria, Cesare, 90
Becker, Howard, 261–62, 435
Bentham, Jeremy, 90
Berman, Alexa, 70
Beslan school hostage crisis, xxxiv, **46–49**
Bethel School District v. Fraser, 491, 643
Bias, Len, **50–51**
Big Brothers Big Sisters, **51–52**
Biological theories, **52–56**
Bishop, Amy, xxxvi, **56–59**, 368–69
Board of Ed. of Independent School District No. 92 of Pottawatomie Count v. Earls, **59–62**, 154, 419, 643, 647–57
Body type, 54
Booker, Quinshawn, xxxii
Bosse, Sebastian, xxxv, **62–63**, 259
Bowling for Columbine, **63–64**, 277–78, 335, 354
Boys and Girls Club of America, 35
Brady Handgun Violence Prevention Act, 216
Brazill, Nathaniel, xxxiii, **65–67**
Brewer, Michael, **67–69**
Brown, Asher, 70
Brown, Nathaniel, xxxvi
Bullycide, **69–71**; LGBTQ, 69–71, 430–34
Bullying, xxxvii, 9–10, 69–71, 72–80, 161, 386–89, 515–16, 553–59; bullycide, 69–71, 364–66, 430–34; Bully Police, 78–79; Canada, 82; cyberbullying, 72, 76–77, 118–23, 364–66, 484, 486–87; fiction, 180–84; girls, 75, 331–33, 364–66, 515–16; LGBTQ, xxxvii, 15–16, 69–71, 73, 75–76, 96, 252–54, 430–34; parents, 339–41; state rankings, 78–80; Stop Bullying Now, 460–61; teacher-perpetrated, 73, 479–82
Bullying, college, **72–74**, 409–11
Bullying, high school, **74–77**
Bullying laws, **78–80**, 553–59
Bush, Elizabeth, xxxiii
Bush, George W., 318–19
Buschbacher, Chris, xxxiii
Bystander interventions, 34

Cambridge Youth Study, 241
Campus Carry, 351
Campus Hate Crimes Right to Know Act, 551
Campus Sex Crimes Prevention Act, 356–57, 552
Campus Sexual Assault Bill of Rights, 356–57, 552
Canada and school crime and violence, **81–84**, 210–12, 266–71, 359–61
Capitalism, 104–108, 444–45
Carneal, Michael, xxxi, **84–87**, 280, 315
Center on Addiction and Substance Abuse (CASA), 146, 148
Centers for Disease Control and Prevention (CDC), 12–13, 20, **87–88**, 130, 265; bullying, 340; dating violence, 140–41; public health approach, 376–77
Central Asia Institute (CAI), **88–90**
Chambliss, William, 262, 461–62
Cheating, 231–33
Chivalry hypothesis, 208
Cho, Seung-Hui, xxxv, 279, 322, 362, 487, 507, 517–20
Choice theories, **90–93**
Chomsky, Noam, 105
Christian, John, xxviii
Classical school of criminology, 90–93
Clementi, Tyler, 70
Clery Act, **93–95**, 157, 176, 263, 356–59, 552, 635–42
Clinton, Bill, 142, 313, 335, 402–4
Cloward, Richard, and Ohlin, Lloyd, 443
Cohen, Albert, 443
Cohen, Lawrence, 92
Cohen, Stanley, 175–77
College campuses, 93–94, 165–69, 176–77, 179, 184–86, 222–24, 305–7, 321–23, 327–28, 343–45, 350–51, 356–59, 366–69, 378–80, 510–14, 517–20, 524–28, 633–35
Collins, Curtis, xxix

Columbine, 279
Columbine High School massacre, xxiii, 18, 29, **95–99**, 164–165, 179, 210–11, 279, 322, 390, 461–62
Cooley, Charles Horton, 261
Comer School Development Program, 349–50
Comprehensive Crime Control Act, **99–101**
Concealed carry laws, 216–17
Conflict resolution/peer mediation, **101–4**, 348, 391–93
Conflict theories, **104–8**
Control theories, **108–10**
Coon, Asa, xxxv, 2, **110–12**
Cordova, Victor, xxxii
Corporal punishment, 1, 7–11, 15–16, **112–13**, 288–89, 384–85, 450–51
Craft, Christopher, 363
Crime and violence in private secondary schools, **113–16**
Crime Stoppers, **116–18**
Critical theories, 445
Cullen, Dave, 279
Cultural transmission theory, 444
Cyber-offenses, 118–23; dating violence, 131; Facebook, 121, 439–41; MySpace, 121, 439–41; YouTube, 121
Cyber-offenses, college, **118–20**
Cyber-offenses, high school, **120–23**

Dann, Laurie, xxix, **125–28**, 280, 362
Dating violence, 30, 32, 128–33; DELTA project, 140–41; Expect Respect, 173–74; laws, 559–63; prevention, 132; technology, 131
Dating violence, college, **128–30**
Dating violence, high School, **130–33**
Davidson, Frederick, xxxi
Davis v. Monroe County Board of Education, **133–135**, 428, 643
Delinquent trajectories, 242
Democratic Front for the Liberation of Palestine attack on Ma'alot School, xxvii, **135–38**
Department of Homeland Security (DHS), 355
Detention: The Siege at Johnson High, 234
Deterrence, 92–93
Developmental tasks theory, 242
Dhein, Alaa Abu, xxxvi, **138–40**

Dickens, Charles, 180–81
Differential association theory, 208, 435
District of Columbia v. Heller, 218
Doe v. Renfrew, 643
Domestic violence, 2, 15, 140–41
Domestic Violence Prevention Enhancements and Leadership Through Alliances (DELTA) program, **140–41**
Donovan, John, 367
Doom, 96
Do Something, **141–42**, 539
Dress codes, **142–44**; gangs, 143–44
Drug Abuse Resistance Education (D.A.R.E.), **145–46**
Drug Enforcement Agency (DEA), 351
Drug offenses, college, **146–49**
Drug offenses, high school, **149–52**
Drug testing, 59–62, **152–154**, 419, 499–501
Drugs, 50–51; ADHD, 148, 150; Canada, 82–83; CASA, 146, 148; college, 146–49, 502; D.A.R.E., 145–54; high school, 149–52; marijuana, 146–47; prescription, 147–48, 150; South America, 448–52; testing, 152–54
Due process, 214–15
Dugdale, Richard, 52–54
Duke University lacrosse team sexual assault case, **154–56**
Duncan, Arne, xxxvii
Durkheim, Emile, 442

Eastwood, Bruco, xxxvi
Ecological systems theory, 371–72
Educational programs and training, 157–63
Educational programs and training, college **157–60**
Educational programs and training, high school, **160–63**
Elementary schools and crime and violence, **163–64**, 333–35, 380–83, 453–55, 458
Elephant, **164–65**
Elliott, Nicholas, xxix
Emergency response plans, **165–69**, 513
European Union and school crime and violence, 35–39, **169–73**, 219–21, 258–59, 401–2, 456–60
Expect Respect, **173–74**

Family Educational Rights and Privacy Act (FERPA), 356–57
Family Violence Prevention Fund, 34
Fear of school crime and violence, **175–77**
Federal Bureau of Investigation (FBI), **178–80**, 223
Federal Emergency Management Agency (FEMA), 167–68, 176
Federal Violent Crime Control and Law Enforcement Act of 1994, 381–82
Felson, Marcus, 92
Female perpetrators, 125–28, 331–33
Feminism, 266–71
Ferris, Nathan, xxviii
Fiction and school crime and violence, **180–84**, 296, 534–38
Films, 164–65, 296–301, 313–14, 659–63
Finland, xxxv, 35–39
Flores, Robert, xxxiii, **184–86**
Food and Drug Administration (FDA), 361–63
Frabricant, Dr. Valery, xxix
Franklin v. Gwinett County Public Schools, 428
Fraser, Matthew, 187
Freechild Project, 538–40
Free speech, 14, **186–89**, 490–92
Freire, Paulo, 538
Freud, Sigmund, 108, 207–08

Gadyrov, Farda, xxxvi
Gambling, **191–93**; athletes, 192–93; online poker, 192; prevention, 192
Gang Resistance Education and Training (G.R.E.A.T.), **193–95**
Gangs and school crime and violence, **195–99**, 450–51, 515; G.R.E.A.T., 193–95
Gay/straight alliance (GSA), 433–34
Gay, Lesbian and Straight Education Network (GLSEN), 69–71, 75–77, 433
Gebser v. Lago Vista Independent School District, 643
Gender and school crime and violence, college, **199–203**
Gender and school crime and violence, high school, **203–7**
Gender-related theories, **207–10**
General strain theory, 443–44
General theory of crime (GTC), 109–10
Genetics, 52–56

Germany, xxxiii, 62–63, 258–59, 456–60
Gibson, Greg, 273
Gill, Kimveer, xxxiv, **210–12**
Gillom, Edward, xxx
Giroux, Henry, 538
Glen Ridge, New Jersey, rape incident, **212–13**
Glueck, Sheldon and Eleanor, 241
Goffman, Erving, 437
Golden, Andrew, xxxii, 280
Gone Boy: A Walkabout, 273
Goring, Charles, 53–54
Goss v. Lopez, 187, **214–15**, 644
Gottfredson, Michael, 109–10
Gramsci, Antonio, 105–6
Grutter v. Bollinger, 644
Guns, 351–52; assault weapons, 381–82; college, 351–52; legislation, 215–18, 220, 259, 551, 563–631
Gun Control Act of 1968, 215
Gun control legislation, **215–18**, 220, 259, 551; Germany, 259, 459; Great Britain, 220

Hagan, John, 208
Hainstock, Eric, xxxiv
Halder, Biswanath, xxxiv
Halligan, Ryan, 70, 439
Hamilton, Thomas, xxxi, **219–21**
Hamilton Fish Institute, 17, **221–22**
Harclerode, Jack, 367
Harless, Jason, xxviii
Harris, Eric, xxxii, 63–64, 95–99, 164–65, 210–11, 262, 279, 315, 362, 507
Hate crimes, 14–15, 452–53, 513, 551
Hate crimes, college, **222–25**
Hate Crimes Statistics Act, 223
Hazelwood School District v. Kuhlmeier, 239, 491, 644
Hazing, 29–30, 225–31; alcohol, 226–27, 228
Hazing, college, **225–28**, 503, 512–13
Hazing, high school, **228–30**, 506–7
Hazing, laws, **230–31**
Heard, Robert, xxix
Hegemony, 105–6
Henkle v. Gregory, 429–30
Hirschi, Travis, 109–10, 208, 371
Hoffman, Jason, xxxiii
Honor codes, **231–33**

Hostile environment, 427–28
Hotspots, 93
Houston, Eric, xxix, **233–34**
Hughes, Richard, 181
Human rights, 8–10, 112, 234–35, 343–44
Human rights education, 16, **234–36**, 236–37, 343
Human Rights Education Associates, 235
Human Rights Watch (HRW), 8–10, 112, **236–37**

In loco parentis, **239–40**
Ingraham v. Wright, 112, 240
Integrated theories, **240–43**
IQ, 53, 54–56
It Gets Better Project, 71

Jackson, Lawanda, xxx
Jackson State massacre, xxvii
Jeremy, **245–46**
Johnson, Mitchell, xxxii, 280
Johnston, Jeffery, 70
Journals devoted to school crime and violence, **246**, 674–76
Juvenile court, 5–6, 66–67

Katz, Jack, 91–92
Katz, Jackson, 209
Kazmierczak, Steven, xxxv, 321–23, 363
Kearby, James, xxviii
Kehoe, Andrew, xxvii, 41–44
Kent State National Guard shootings, xxvii, **247–52**
Kimmel, Michael, 209
King, Lawrence, **252–54**
Kinkel, Kip, xxxii, 5, **255–58**, 280, 362
Klebold, Dylan, xxxii, 63–64, 95–99, 164–65, 210–11, 262, 279, 315, 507
Kohn, Alfie, 538
Kozol, Jonathan, 538
Kretschmer, Tim, xxxvi, **258–59**
Krueger, Paul, 368

Labeling theories, **261–62**, 435–37
Lasaga, Anonio, 367
La Salle University sex scandal and cover-up, **263–64**

Latin America and school crime and violence, **264–66**
Laub, John, and Sampson, Robert, 241
Law Enforcement Officers Safety Act, 217
Lawler, David, xxviii
Laws, 356–59; college, 356–59
Lazotte, Patrick, xxviii
Learning disabilities, 55–56
Ledeger, Keith, xxx
Legislation, 99–101, 216–17, 220, 223, 259, 318–30, 356–58, 378, 381–82, 402–4, 415, 459, 551–643
Lemert, Edwin, 261
Lépine, Marc, xxix, 209, **266–71**
LGBTQ youth, xxxvii, 14–16, 73, 75–76, 252–54, 404–5, 430–34, 480–81
Liberation hypothesis, 208
Lo, Wayne, xxix, **271–73**
Logan, Jessie, 70
Lombroso, Cesare, 53
Long, Tyler, 70, 364–65
Loukaitis, Barry, xxxi, **273–75**, 315
Lu, Gang, xxix, 273, **275–76**
Lucas, Billy, 70

Major League Baseball, 35
Manson, Marilyn, 63–64, **277–78**
Marijuana, 146–47
Martinez, Max, xxx
Marx, Karl, 104–8
McCoy, Jason, xxviii
McDowell, Leonard, xxx
McInerney, Brandon, xxxv
McLaughlin, Jason, xxxiv
Mead, George Herbert, 261
Media: Carneal, Michael, 86, 315, 507; Columbine High School massacre, 277–78, 315; fear, 175–77; Loukaitis, Barry, 315; moral panics, 175–177, 292–97; movies, 164–65, 296, 297–301, 313–14, 534–38, 534–38; news, 296–97; race, 383–85; Wurst, Andrew, 534–38
Mediation, xvii–xix
Meier, Megan, 70, 439
Mental illness and school crime and violence, **278–80**, 517–20, 522–23
Mentoring, 51–52, **280–83**
Merton, Robert, 442–43

Metal detectors, **283–85**, 482–83, 487
Michael Minger Act, 358
Middle East and school crime and violence, 88–89, 135–38, 139–40, **286–89**
Middle schools and crime and violence, **289–92**
Moffitt, Terrie, 242
Monitoring the Future survey, **291–92**
Moon, Joshua, 367
Mentors in Violence Prevention (MVP), 32, 33–34
Moore, Fredrick, 198
Moral panics, 175–77, 292
Moral panics and campus crime and violence, **292–94**
Moral panics and high school crime and violence, **294–97**
Morrison, Duane, xxxiv, 280, 363
Morse v. Frederick, 644
Mortenson, Greg, 88–89
Movies and school crime and violence, 164–65, 296, **297–301**, 313–14, 659–63
Murray, Thomas, 368
Music and school crime and violence, 210–11, 245–46, 277–78, **302–5**, 534–38
Music Television (MTV), 245, 265, 302–5
Muslims and school crime and violence, **305–7**, 390–91
MySpace, 14, 121

National Coalition Against Violent Athletes (NCAVA), 32
National Collegiate Athletic Association (NCAA), 24–28, 32, 44–45, 152–54, 155
National Crime Victimization Survey (NCVS), 114, 198
National Day of Remembrance and Action on Violence Against Women, 268–69
National Football League, 34–35; Youth Education Towns (YET), 34–35
National Household Survey on Drug Abuse, 12–13
National Institute Against Prejudice and Violence (NIAPV), 223
National School Safety Center, **309**
National Threat Assessment Center (NTAC), **310–11**
National Youth Survey, **312–13**

National Youth Violence Prevention Resource Center, **313–14**
Natural Born Killers, 245, **314–16**
Neblett, Rachel, 70
Neurology, 55
New Jersey v. T.L.O., 60, 153, 239, **316–18**, 419, 500–1, 644
Nicholas Nickleby, 180–81
Nielsen, Flemming, xxx
No Child Left Behind Act, **318–20**, 415, 551
Northeastern University Center for Sport in Society, 35
Northern Illinois University shooting, **321–23**
Northwestern High School sex scandal, **324–25**

Obama, Barack, xxxvii, 70, 320
Odighizuwa, Peter, xxxiii, **327–28**
Office of Juvenile Justice and Delinquency Prevention (OJJDP), 100, **329–31**
Olweus, Dan, 74
Ophelia Project, **331–33**
Osmanson, James, xxx
Owens, Dedrick, xxxii, **333–35**

Parens patriae, **337–39**
Parents and school crime and violence, **339–41**
Pathways to crime theory, 241–42
Peace and Justice Studies Association (PJSA), **341–42**
Peace education, 341–50
Peace education, college, **343–45**
Peace education, high school, **346–50**
Pearl Jam, 245–46
Peer mediation, 101–4, 391–93
Pennick, Jeffrey, xxxii
Pennies for Peace, 539
Pennington, Douglas, xxix, **350–51**
Petkovic, Dragoslav, xxxiii
Pitts, Marshawn, 384–85
Placencia, Mike, xxxiii
Police and surveillance, 351–56
Police and surveillance, college, **351–53**
Police and surveillance, high school, **354–56**
Policies and campus violence laws, **356–59**

Poulin, Robert, xxviii, **359–61**
Power-control theory, 208–9
Prejudice Institute, 224
Prescription drugs and school crime and violence, 280, **361–63**; serotonin norepinephrine reuptake inhibitors (SNRIs), 361–62; selective serotonin reuptake inhibitors (SSRIs), 361–62
Prince, Phoebe, xxxvi, 70, **364–66**
Printz v. United States, 216
Pritchard, Jason, xxxiii
Privacy rights, 152–54, 279–80, 283–85, 316–17, 353, 406–7, 419–21, 499–501
Private schools, 113–16
Professor-perpetrated crime and violence, 56–59, **366–69**
Project Teamwork, 34
Property crimes, 369–76
Property crimes, college, **369–73**
Property crimes, high school, **373–76**
Prothrow-Stith, Deborah, 208, 376–77
Public health approach, xix, **376–78**
Punitive responses, college, **378–80**
Purdy, Patrick, 280, 362, **380–82**

Quid pro quo, 427–28

Race and school crime and violence, **383–86**; African Americans, 384–85, 416–17; zero tolerance, 291, 384–85, 416–17, 543–45
Rage, 296
Ramos, Corey, xxxiii
Ramsey, Evan, xxxi, 2, **386–89**
Rape myths, 30
Reckless, Walter, 108–9
Reed, Karter, xxx
Religion and high school crime and violence, **389–91**; Amish, 395–98; Christians, 390; Muslims, 305–7, 390–91
Resiliency, xx
Resolving Conflict Creatively Program (RCCP), 348, **391–93**
Restorative justice, **393–95**
Risk and protective factors, 242–43
Robbins, Jillian, xxxi
Roberts, Charles, xxxv, **395–98**
Robinson, Robin, xxviii

Rodriguez, Andy, xxxvi
Roth, J. Reece, 366–67
Rouse, Jamie, xxxi
Routine activities theory, 92
Rumsfeld v. Forum for Academic and Institutional Rights (FAIR), 644
Rural school violence, **399–400**
Russia, xxxiv, 46–49

Saari, Matti, xxxv, 363, **401–2**
Safe and Drug-Free Schools and Communities Act (SDFSCA), 217, 378, **402–4**, 551, 563–631
Safe Schools/GLSEN, **404–5**
Safford Unified School District #1 v. Redding, **406–7**, 419–20, 644
Saints and the Roughnecks, 262, 461–62
Save the Children, **407–9**
Schmitt, Eric, xxx
School crime and school climate, 409–14
School crime and school climate, college, **409–11**
School crime and school climate, high school, **411–13**
School Crime Victimization Survey, **413–15**
School resource officers (SROs), 355
School-to-prison pipeline, 385, **415–18**, 543–45
Search and seizure, high school, 14, **418–21**
Security on Campus, Inc., 223, **421–22**
Seductions of crime theory, 91–92
Sexting, 22
Sexual assault crimes, college, **422–25**
Sexual assault crimes, high school, **425–27**
Sexual harassment, 9–10, 133–35, 199–207, 287–89, 367–68, 422–25, 425–27, **427–30**
Sexual orientation and school crime and violence, college, **430–32**
Sexual orientation and school crime and violence, high school, **432–34**
Sexual violence, 9–10, 15, 72, 95, 133–35, 154–56, 157–59, 199–207, 263, 287–89, 324–25, 367–68, 422–25, 425–27, 455–56, 633–35
Sheets, James, xxxiv
Sheldon, William, 54
Shrout, Clay, xxx
Siler, Jamar, xxxv

Simon, Rita, 208
Sincino, Tony, xxxi, 362
Situational crime prevention, 93
Skin-cutting, 506
Slobodian, Michael, xxviii
Smith, Todd, xxxii
Snow, Albert, 367
Social bond theory, 109–10, 208, 371
Social disorganization theory, 208
Social learning theories, 371, **434–38**
Social networking, 77, 118–23, **438–41**, 484–85, 486–87
Social structure theories, **441–46**
Solomon, T. J., xxxii, 5, 362, **446–48**
South America and school crime and violence, **448–52**
Southern Poverty Law Center (SPLC), 224, **452–53**
Spencer, Brenda, xxviii, 2, **453–55**
Spur Posse, **455–56**
Steinhäuser, Robert, xxxiii, 62, 259, **456–60**
Stop Bullying Now, 340, **460–61**
Strain theory, 442–43
Substance Abuse and Mental Health Services Administration (SAMHSA), 340
Suburban school violence, **461–65**
Suicide, 465–72; bullycide, 69–71, 364–66, 430–34
Suicide, college, **465–69**
Suicide, high school, **469–71**, 504–6
Supreme Court (U.S.), 59–62, 112, 133–35, 144, 153–54, 186–87, 214–15, 216, 218, 239, 240, 316–18, 406–7, 419, 428, 429–30, 491–92, 500–1, 538, 643–45, 647–57
Surveillance, 283–85, 351–56
Sutherland, Edwin, 208, 435
Systemic/structural violence, college, **472–75**
Systemic/structural violence, high school, **475–78**

Takuma, Mamoru, xxxiii
Tannenbaum, Franklin, 436
Tate, James, xxxiii
Teacher-perpetrated crime and violence, high school, **479–82**
Teaching Tolerance, 453

Technological responses, high school, **482–85**
Technology and campus crime and violence, **486–88**
Teen courts, **488–90**
Terrorism, 135–39; domestic, 352
Testosterone, 209
Theories: biological, 52–56; choice, 90–93; classical school, 90–93; conflict, 104–8; control, 108–10; cultural transmission, 444; delinquent trajectories, 242; deterrence, 92–93; developmental tasks, 242; ecological, 371–72; feminist, 207–10, 266–71; general theory of crime, 109–10; integrated, 240–43; labeling, 261–62, 435–37; learning, 208, 435; strain, 443–44
Timeline of significant events related to school crime and violence, xxvii–xxxvii
Tinker v. Des Moines School District, 144, 186–87, 239, 418, **490–92**, 538, 645
Title IX, 427–28
Todd, Joseph, xxxi
Tom Brown's Schooldays, 181
Treacy, Wayne, xxxvi, 6, **492–93**
Trickey, Seth, xxxii
Twin studies, 54–55

Uniform Crime Reports (UCR), 368, 374
United Kingdom, 219–21
United Nations Children's Fund (UNICEF), 265, 287–88, 450, **495–96**
United Nations Convention on the Rights of the Child, 16
U.S. Department of Education, **496–97**
U.S. Department of Justice, **497–98**
U.S. v. Lopez, 645
Universal Declaration of Human Rights (UDHR), 234–35
University of Central Arkansas, xxxv
Utilitarianism, 91

Varinecz, Trevor, xxxvi
Vernonia School District 47J v. Acton, 61, 153, 240, 419, **499–501**, 645
Victimless offenses, college, **501–4**
Victimless offenses, high school, **504–7**
Video cameras, 355, 483–84, 487

Video games, 96, 210–11, 321, 387, 401–2, **507–10**, 521–24
Vietnam War, 247–52
Violent nonsexual crimes, college, **510–14**
Violent nonsexual crimes, high school, **514–17**
Virginia Tech massacre, 179, 322, 487, 513, **517–19**

Weise, Jeff, xxxiv, 179, 279, 362, **521–24**
White, Joseph, xxix
White Ribbon Campaign, 268–69
Whitman, Charles, xxvii, xxxiii, 519, **524–28**
Williams, Christopher, xxxiv
Williams, Latina, xxxv
Williams, Steven, xxxiii
Wilson, James William Jr., xxix, 280, 362

Wimberly, Teah, xxxvi, **528–29**
Witsell, Hope, 70
Woodham, Luke, xxxi, **529–33**
Wurst, Andrew, xxxii, **534–36**

Young, Jock, 175
Youth activism, **537–39**
Youth Crime Watch of America (YCWA), **539–41**
Youth Gang Survey, 198
YouTube, 35–39
YouTube Killer, 35–39
Yuyuan, Xu, xxxvii

Zero-tolerance laws, 291, 416–17, **534–45**; ACLU, 14; Canada, 84, 163–64, 384–85, 543–45
Zinkhan, George, 368
Zinn, Howard, 538

About the Editor and Contributors

Editor

Laura L. Finley earned her PhD in sociology from Western Michigan University in 2002. She is currently Assistant Professor of Sociology and Criminology at Barry University. Dr. Finley is the author or co-author of eight books. She has also authored numerous book chapters and journal articles. In addition to her academic work, Dr. Finley is a community peace activist, with active involvement in local, national, and international groups. She regularly presents on topics related to peace and social justice and is a domestic and dating violence trainer. In addition, Dr. Finley is co-chair of the South Florida Diversity Alliance and is on the Board of Directors of No More Tears, a nonprofit organization that provides individualized assistance to victims of domestic violence and their children. Dr. Finley is also a member of the Board of Directors of Amnesty International USA and Floridians for Alternatives to the Death Penalty.

Contributors

Natasha Abdin is a student at Florida International University. She is actively involved with numerous community social justice activities.

Rebecca Ajo graduated in 2009 from Barry University in Miami with a degree in criminology. She is currently preparing for law school.

Megan Barnes is an undergraduate student at Barry University, pursuing a bachelor of science degree in sociology. She plans to attend medical school upon graduation and specialize in women's health.

Eric Bellone is an Assistant Professor of Legal Studies at Suffolk University. He is also a doctoral student in law, policy, and society at Northeastern University. His research focuses on specialized courts and the impact of technology on the legal process.

Tiffany Bergin is a PhD candidate in criminology at the University of Cambridge in the United Kingdom. She also obtained her MPhil in criminological research at Cambridge and received her BA with highest honors from the Woodrow Wilson School of Public and International Affairs at Princeton University.

Ben Brown is Associate Professor in the Department of Criminal Justice at the University of Texas–Brownsville. His work has been published in more than a dozen academic journals.

Dennis Bulen, PhD, is Associate Professor of Criminal Justice at Wright State University–Lake Campus.

Mary Christianakis, PhD, is an Assistant Professor of Education at Occidental College. She offers a course on U.S. Supreme Court cases related to education, as well as a course entitled "Prisons, Schools, and the Popular Media." She also teaches creative writing to incarcerated youth.

Justin Corfield teaches history and international relations at Geelong Grammar School in Australia. He has written extensively on topics connected with history and politics, and is the author or co-author of a number of books.

Patrice Delevante holds an MA in gender and cultural studies from Simmons College. Her work has appeared in *Ms. Magazine* and *Oxford Encyclopedia of Women in World History*.

Darius Echeverria, PhD, is Professor of History and of Latino and Hispanic Caribbean Studies at Rutgers University. His work focuses on Latino studies, comparative ethnic studies, U.S. political history, and Mexican American history.

Katie Ellis is the author of *Disabling Diversity*. She received a PhD in communications, disability, and media from Murdoch University in 2005 and has recently returned there to lecture in the School of Media Communication and Culture.

Curtis Fogel is a PhD candidate in the Department of Sociology at the University of Calgary in Canada. His primary research interests are in deviance in sport. His doctoral dissertation explores the legal issue of consent in relation to violence, hazing, and performance-enhancing drug use in Canadian football.

Tony Gaskew, PhD, is Assistant Professor of Criminal Justice and Coordinator of Criminal Forensic Studies at the University of Pittsburgh at Bradford.

Aviva Twersky Glasner is Assistant Professor of Criminal Justice at Bridgewater State University. She also coordinates internships for the program.

Arthur Holst, PhD, is Government Affairs Manager at the Philadelphia Water Department. He has previously contributed to other academic works, including the *Encyclopedia of Juvenile Violence.*

Jun Sung Hong is a doctoral student in the School of Social Work at the University of Illinois.

Hui Huang is a doctoral student in the School of Social Work at the University of Illinois.

Wendell Johnson is Social Science Librarian at Northern Illinois University.

Angelica Jones is a candidate for a juris doctorate at Stetson University College of Law. Her areas of interest include entertainment and international law.

Njoki-Wa-Kinyatti is an Associate Professor and Reference Librarian and Collection Development Coordinator of the Library at York College of The City University of New York. She specializes in gender discrimination in education and violence in Africa.

Carol Lenhart, PhD, received her bachelor's degree from State University of New York–Brockport, and earned her master's and doctorate degrees from the University of Delaware. She is currently Assistant Professor of Criminal Justice at Elmira College.

Karen Lindsey is a doctoral student in anthropology at American University. Her research interests include linguistics and the role of media in the social construction of history in the late modern era.

Len Lubitz is on hiatus from a PhD program at the City University of New York. He is currently working with a Lebanon-based nongovernmental organization dedicated to the cause of the missing and detainees who are neither free nor accounted for.

Joan Luxenburg received her EdD from Columbia University. She is currently Professor of Sociology, Criminal Justice, and Substance Abuse Studies at the University of Central Oklahoma.

Doreen Maller is a marriage and family therapist in private practice in Northern California as well as the Program Director of John F Kennedy University's Holistic Studies Master's in Counseling Psychology department.

Meghan McHaney is in the MSW program at the University of Illinois.

Claudia Megele is an author, researcher, and practitioner with extensive experience in both voluntary and statutory sectors. She has presented her research and papers in various national and international conferences. Ms. Megele is a founding director of A Sense of Self (http://asenseofself.org) and a board member in various organizations.

Elizabeth J. Meyer is Assistant Professor of Education at Concordia University in Canada. Her work focuses on homophobia, bullying, and harassment in schools.

Patit Paban Mishra is a professor in the Department of History at Sambalpur University in India. Mishra has authored more than 200 articles related to Asian history.

Richard Mora is a PhD candidate in sociology at Harvard University. He is currently Assistant Professor of Sociology at Occidental College.

Jonathan William Olson is a PhD student in the Department of Religion at Florida State University. His primary area of interest is in the intersection between religion and violence in American culture.

Andrea Quinlan is a PhD student in the Department of Sociology at York University. She is currently researching the legal handling of sexual assault in Canada.

Elizabeth Kelley Rhoades is an Associate Professor of Psychology at the University of Houston–Victoria, where she teaches courses in school psychology, human development, and biopsychology

Roger I. Roots, JD, PhD, is an assistant professor of criminal justice and behavioral science at the New York Institute of Technology (in Old Westbury, New York). His primary areas of research include corrections history and criminal procedure.

Nick Sciullo, JD, is an independent scholar whose publication and conference speaking revolves around issues of law, race/class/gender, and critical theory.

Jeffrey Shantz, PhD, teaches human rights and community advocacy at Kwantlen Polytechnic University in Vancouver, British Columbia. He is also a union and antipoverty organizer.

Scott Sheidlower is Assistant Professor and Head of Information Literacy at York College at the City University of New York.

Kamesha Spates, PhD, is an Assistant Professor of Sociology at Colorado State University–Pueblo. Her research interests include race relations, criminology, mental health, and qualitative methodologies.

Christopher J. Stapel is a PhD candidate in sociology at the University of Kentucky. His research focuses on the intersection of rural sociology, sociology of education, and sociology of sexualities. He is a former public high school mathematics teacher.

James Steinberg, PhD, is Associate Professor of Sociology at Wright State University–Lake Campus.

Sharon Thiel graduated from Florida Atlantic University with a master's degree in sociology. She currently works as a volunteer coordinator at a nonprofit organization.

Ebony Thomas is in the MSW program at the University of Illinois.

Sandra Gall Urban is Instructor/Head of Cataloging and Acting Head of Reference Services at York College of the City University of New York.

Sheena Vega graduated from Florida Atlantic University in 2008 with a degree in English literature. She recently finished teaching English in a program in Santiago, Chile.

Annika Vorhes is currently attending Wright State University–Lake Campus, where she is studying human behavior. She plans to pursue a degree in clinical psychology.

Gerald Walton is an Assistant Professor in the Faculty of Education at Lakehead University in Thunder Bay, Ontario. His research focuses on analyzing bullying as a social phenomenon rather than as mere bad behavior.

Stan C. Weeber is Associate Professor of Sociology and Criminal Justice at McNeese State University. His interests in sociology include sociological theory, political sociology, social movements, and the sociology of violence. He is the author of 13 books and numerous journal articles.

Robert Worley is Assistant Professor of Criminal Justice at Texas A&M University–Central Texas. Among his other work, he has previously contributed to the *Encyclopedia of Juvenile Violence*.